Henry Eyster Jacobs

The Lutheran Movement in England

During the Reigns of Henry VIII and Edward VI

Henry Eyster Jacobs

The Lutheran Movement in England
During the Reigns of Henry VIII and Edward VI

ISBN/EAN: 9783337126902

Printed in Europe, USA, Canada, Australia, Japan

Cover: Foto ©ninafisch / pixelio.de

More available books at **www.hansebooks.com**

A STUDY IN COMPARATIVE SYMBOLICS.

THE

Lutheran Movement in England

DURING THE REIGNS OF

HENRY VIII. AND EDWARD VI.,

AND

Its Literary Monuments.

BY

HENRY EYSTER JACOBS, D. D.,

Norton Professor of Systematic Theology in the Theological Seminary of the Evangelical Lutheran Church in Philadelphia; Translator and Editor of the " Book of Concord," Schmid's " Doctrinal Theology of the Ev. Lutheran Church," etc. etc.

PHILADELPHIA:
G. W. FREDERICK,
1890.

Copyrighted, 1890, by G. W. Frederick.

PREFACE.

INVESTIGATIONS into the history of the English translations of the Augsburg Confession, made several years ago, in co-operation with the late Rev. B. M. Schmucker, D. D., led the writer into a much wider field than he had originally intended to enter. Notes taken, in the beginning, for his own information, soon accumulated to such extent, that he embodied their results in a series of articles, that appeared in *The Lutheran* in 1887. During the preparation of the articles, every available source of information was laid under contribution for additional facts. The number of articles grew beyond expectation. Requests having been made from various quarters, that they should be published in a more permanent form, this volume is the result. The material here given has only in part appeared before. Much has been rewritten, while several of the earlier chapters, and nearly all of the latter part of the book, are entirely new.

It will speak for itself. Its facts, supported by the documentary evidence, will suggest their own lessons. It has not been written chiefly in a polemical interest. Its great end is to promote a thorough understanding of the historical relation of the Lutheran Church to the various English-speaking communions of this country, whose course has been influenced by the history of the Church in England during the Sixteenth Century.

With so much material on the subject, readily accessible, it is surprising that a book filling this place, has not appeared before. English writers, however, as a rule, have felt little interest in acknowledging their dependence on the German Reformation; a few, like Archbishop Laurence and Archdeacon Hardwick, forming brilliant exceptions. German writers have generally assumed that the English could be relied upon for the facts of their own history, and, therefore, have not exercised their characteristic caution, or their customary practice of being saisfied with nothing short of the first sources. Although the correspondence of Luther and Melanchthon, and that rich storehouse of documentary evidence, Seckendorf's *Historia Lutheranismi* abound in most valuable information on the subject, but little attention has hitherto been given to what, with a little industry, could have been drawn from their pages.

The time has come, however, for a more careful and thorough examination of these facts. In this country, the Lutheran Church has become a communion of over a million communicants, and not less than four or five millions of a population. The English language has again become the medium for the Lutheran faith. As the various nationalities which its adherents represent, merge in the one American nationality, so their various languages, sooner or later, are laid aside for the common language of the country. Even before this process is complete, the one medium through which those worshipping in different languages can confer with and know one another, must necessarily be the English. The problem of the hour for the Lutheran Church in America, is, how to unite these various elements in the historical faith of the Lutheran Church as embodied in her historical Confessions, and with the worship prescribed in her historical Liturgies and

Church Orders. As in the earlier efforts of Cranmer, Fox, Barnes, Coverdale, Rogers, Taverner and others in the Sixteenth Century in England, so here, the English language is again employed to furnish the mould in which Lutheran Theology is to be recast. In this work, the historical connection is again preserved. The good foundation then laid is not to be ignored. We gladly resume the undertaking, at the stage in which it was left by our predecessors in the same field, and, with humble recognition of their admirable success, take it up simply where it was left incomplete by the intervention of the Calvinistic reaction, during the second period of the reign of Edward VI, as examined in these pages. But in doing so, it becomes necessary to explain our relations to the Church of England, and to carefully discriminate between what is common territory, and what is peculiar to each Church. It is a matter, not of regret, but of rejoicing, that the Church of England, and her daughter in America, have jealously preserved, and heartily commended by constant usage so much of the common heritage, not only antedating the Reformation and extending even far back beyond the corruptions of the Middle Ages, but also of what they have directly drawn from the Lutheran Reformers. It must not, however, be forgotten that the political complications, as well as other elements that entered, rendered the work of the Lutheran Church in reforming the old Church Service incomplete in many parts of Germany, and that even among those who have been faithful Lutherans in their Confessional position, there may be found those who are ready to indiscriminately censure what is common property, as though it were alien to the Lutheran Church.

Nor must the aggressive attitude of the Churches of the Anglican family be overlooked. The challenge to all other bodies of Christians to establish their historical position, has been bravely made, and, with a determination, that shows that it will not be satisfied with skilful evasions of the question. It will certainly be of service, in giving this subject the serious consideration which it justly demands, to take into the account all the historical factors accessible. The effort to require all movements at union to rest upon a clear, distinct and unequivocal historical basis is certainly in the right direction. It is to be hoped, however, that this principle will be consistently maintained. No progress can be made, nor any permanent results gained, by laying emphasis upon one class of facts, and resolutely closing the eyes to another; urging the examination of History at one point, and begging to be excused from looking into it at another. We sincerely hope that this book may inspire among our Lutheran people a true respect for much that is valuable and scholarly, and admirable in the results of the faith of the Reformation that have abounded in the English Church and her daughters in all periods since; and, that, on the other hand, it may introduce some readers from these communions to the rich stores of gospel truth, with which their fathers were familiar, and which have most powerfully influenced their entire career since.

The question of the revision of Creeds and Confessions, is now attracting wide-spread attention. This is a critical age, persistently demanding all professions to be put to a rigid test. Much light will be found upon the subject, by a careful reading of the accounts of the discussions between the English and the Lutheran theologians, in their several Conferences. There is scarcely an item which enters into a discriminating view of the subject that was not there anticipated. There were many hints given then by the Wittenberg theologians which are just as applicable to the present situation and movements, in the Presbyterian and Lutheran, as well as the Episcopal Church.

At the risk of violating somewhat the unity of the subject, an Excursus on "The Typical Lutheran Chief Service," has been introduced. While treating of the relation of the English Service to the Lutheran Orders, there seemed to be a call for giving some attention to a Service, for whose explanation even Lutherans are entirely d pendent upon material not found in the English language.

Beyond the acknowledgment of the generous aid rendered the writer, above all, by the late Dr. B. M. Schmucker, mention should be made of others to whose kindness he is much indebted. Among them, he wishes especially to name Rev. Karl Wolters, Pastor of St. Peter's Church, Hamburg, Germany, who has taken much interest in making researches for this book in the Archives at Hamburg. We only regret that information he communicated concerning the visit of John Æpinus, afterwards Superintendent at Hamburg, to England, and his conferences with Henry VIII, on ecclesiastical matters, before the sending of the English Commission to Wittenberg, whose history is given in Chapter IV, came after that chapter had already been set up. We refer to it for the information of those who may make this volume the starting-point for further investigations. Rev. J. A. Seiss, D.D., LL. D., kindly furnished his copy of Cranmer's Catechism, with notes showing the results of his comparisons with the Latin edition. Rev. Prof. W. J. Mann, D. D., LL. D., especially interested himself in gathering information concerning Ernest Sarcerius, the Nassau theologian. Rev. Prof. A. Spaeth, D. D., has freely given aid on Hymnological and Liturgical questions.

Pencil notes of the late Rev. Prof. C. P. Krauth, D. D., LL. D., on the margin of books, now in the Library of the Theological Seminary at Mt. Airy, Philadelphia, indicate that he had progressed far in similar investigations, and have repeatedly given us the clue to much valuable information.

In addition to the many friends in the Lutheran Church who have assured us of their interest in these studies, we wish especially to recognize the courtesy of Rev. Prof. George P. Fisher, D. D., LL. D., of Yale University, for urging that they should be embodied in a volume, as well as for his kind reference to what we had previously published on the Anglican Catechisms, in an address delivered in the Autumn of 1888, at Harvard University.

Trusting that the facts here given will contribute towards the clearer understanding of the causes of difference among the various American churches, and, thus, in God's own time, if possible, towards their ultimate adjustment, we offer this volume to the calm and unprejudiced consideration of thoughtful readers.

HENRY E. JACOBS.

Theological Seminary of the Evangelical Lutheran Church at Philadelphia (Mt. Airy), July 9th, 1890.

CONTENTS.

CHAPTER I.
The Beginnings of the English Reformation, . . 1

CHAPTER II.
Tyndale's Dependence on Luther, . . . 14

CHAPTER III.
The Political Complications, ... 39

CHAPTER IV.
The English Commission to Wittenberg, . . 55

CHAPTER V.
Progress of the War for the Faith in England, . 74

CHAPTER VI.
The Ten Articles of 1536, ... 88

CHAPTER VII.
The Bishops' Book of 1537, ... 104

CHAPTER VIII.
The English Bibles of 1535 and 1537, . . . 115

CHAPTER IX.
The Lutheran Commission to England of 1538, . 127

CHAPTER X.
More Lutheran Literature, ... 140

CHAPTER XI.
Fruitless Negotiations of 1539, ... 148

CHAPTER XII.
A Literary Forgery, ... 159

CHAPTER XIII.
Luther's "St. Robert," 179

CHAPTER XIV.
Closing Events of Henry's Reign, . . . 190

CHAPTER XV.
New Difficulties in the Reign of Edward VI., . 198

CHAPTER XVI.
Conflict of Theological Parties in England during the Reign of Edward VI., ... 206

CHAPTER XVII.
Lutheran Sources of the Book of Common Prayer, . 218

CHAPTER XVIII.
The Litany of the English Church, . . . 230

CHAPTER XIX.
The Communion Service of the English Church, . 241

CHAPTER XX.
The Morning and Evening Services of the English Church, ... 245

CHAPTER XXI.

The Order of Baptism in the English Church, . . 253

CHAPTER XXII.

The Orders for Confirmation, Marriage, Visitation of the Sick, Burial, ... 265

CHAPTER XXIII.

The Second Prayer Book of Edward VI., . . . 275

CHAPTER XXIV.

An Excursus on the Typical Lutheran Chief Service, 283

CHAPTER XXV.

The Anglican Catechisms, ... 314

CHAPTER XXVI.

The Homilies of 1547, ... 333

CHAPTER XXVII.

The Thirty-Nine Articles, ... 339

CHAPTER XXVIII.

The Subsequent History, ... 343

CHAPTER XXIX.

Bibliographical, ... 350

THE
LUTHERAN MOVEMENT IN ENGLAND

DURING THE

REIGNS OF HENRY VIII. AND EDWARD VI., AND ITS LITERARY MONUMENTS.

CHAPTER I.

THE BEGINNINGS OF THE ENGLISH REFORMATION.

Not independent of the movement in Germany. Not due to the controversy concerning the divorce of Henry VIII. Preparatory influences in the XIV Century. Thomas of Bradwardin. Wiclif. The Lollards. Dean Colet. Erasmus and the New Learning. Greeks and Trojans. Froude on the immediate effect of Luther's Theses. The war against Lutheran Books. Warham's Correspondence. Henry VIII vs. Luther. Bishop Fisher's Sermon. The Young "Lutherans" of Cambridge. Bilney. Latimer's Inaugural address against Melanchthon. His Conversion. The House called "Germany." Stafford, Barnes, Coverdale, etc. The Lutheran Colony transferred to Cardinal College, Oxford. Clark, Cox, Frith, etc. Persecution, Espionage. The Humiliation of Barnes. Wolsey's Last Message. The Index Prohibitorum of 1529.

TWO VERY superficial theories concerning the English Reformation are current. One affirms that it was a movement originating almost entirely within the English Church, and culminating in the assertion of its independence of the Church of Rome by the casting off of the yoke whereby for centuries it had been unjustly oppressed, but having little to do with contemporaneous movements in Germany. The other regards its religious character purely accidental, and ascribes it altogether to the quarrel of the King of England with the Pope, overlooking the fact, that the relation of Henry VIII to it was a hinderance rather than an advantage, that it began against his will, and received its greatest injury when he became its champion. A careful review of the facts, shows first, that the evangelical leaven had been working in England for many years, and, secondly, that this latent power at length emerged into vigorous action and became a widely-extended and deep movement, as it received support from the fearless testimony proclaimed at Wittenberg, and diffused among the scholars of England by the instrumentality of the press.

In the Fourteenth Century, already, the way for the Reformation had been prepared. Thomas of Bradwardin (*Doctor profundus*), Professor in Merton College, Oxford, and afterwards Archbishop of Canterbury (b. 1290, d. 1349) was the earnest representative of Augustinianism, who complained that "almost the whole world had fallen into the errors of Pelagianism," and started the career of his more eminent pupil John Wiclif. Wiclif spent the greater part of his life at Oxford, where in 1363, he became Professor of Divinity. The sole authority of the Holy Scriptures in matters of faith, the rejection of prayers to saints, of purgatory, of transubstantiation, of the necessity of private confession, the conception of the Church on its inner instead of its outward side, marked a new era, even though his teaching on justification and the most closely allied doctrines, was not as clear. But still wider influence was exerted by his translation of the Bible, industriously circulated in short sections throughout all England by followers so numerous, that one writer says, that every other person met on the road could be so reckoned. The Lollards, as those whose interest had been aroused by Wiclif, were called, after a continental sect, spread far and wide the seed of the future harvest. The Universities of Oxford in England and of St. Andrews in Scotland, became centers of the movement, which, although externally suppressed by bloody persecution, still lived beneath the surface. Although men were consigned to the stake for such utterances, yet in 1506 we find Dean Colet of St. Paul's, London, an Oxford alumnus (d. 1519) expounding the Scriptures thrice a week in the scientific form of divinity lectures. As late as 1521, the bishop of London arrested nearly five hundred Lollards, who probably had no connection with the movement then beginning in Germany.

To this influence was added that of "the New Learning," of which Erasmus was the advocate at Cambridge. It is sometimes forgotten that while this great scholar belonged to Holland, his student life was passed in part at the two distinguished English universities. He was the intimate friend of Colet, and, returning to England in 1510, was, for four years from 1511, Lady Margaret Professor of Divinity and Lecturer in Greek in Queen's College, Cambridge. The stimulus which his attention to the original of the New Testament gave his pupils, may be traced in the many eminent names of reformers hereafter to be noted among them. Great teachers often inculcate premises, whose conclusions are so far-reaching that, instead of drawing them for themselves, they leave this work to their pupils. Erasmus never broke with Rome; but his teaching led many to that act, for which he himself was too feeble, or, rather prepared them for the influence emanating from Wittenberg. The years of his Cambridge Professorship were not as serene as this great lover of peace desired. The publication of his Greek New Testament invalidated the authority of the Vulgate, and aroused the apprehensions of those who were attached to the old order of things. The war of words between "Greeks," and "Trojans" or "Obscurantists," as the champions of the new studies and their opponents were respectively called, waxed fiercer and fiercer, and was of just such character as would excite the enthusiasm of students at that season of life when they are most apt to become intense partisans. When, therefore, they heard from him such statements as the following: "The Holy Scriptures, translated into all languages should be read not only by the Scotch and Irish, but even by Turks and Saracens. The husbandman should sing them as he holds the handle of his plough; the weaver repeat them as he plies his shuttle; and the wearied traveler, halting on his journey, refresh himself under some shady tree by these goodly narratives,"[1] what wonder that aspirations were excited for a better order, wherein every Englishman might read the Word of God for himself, and that young hearts already resolved, that if God would spare them, this should be accomplished?

Luther's act of October 31st, 1517, was not altogether unexpected. Who was to break the silence and first utter the protest, or in what form or place, it was to be given, no one, indeed, could divine. But many eyes were looking for the crisis, in which the oppressed conscience would speak with a power that could not be restrained. As Mr. Froude says: "The thing which all were longing for was done, and in two years from that day, there was scarcely perhaps a village from the Irish channel to the Danube, in which the name of Luther was not familiar as a word of hope and promise."[2] "As early as 1520, Polydore Vergil mentions the importation into England of a great number of 'Lutheran books.'"[3] To such an extent were Luther's writings diffused, and with such effect, that in March 1521, Archbishop Warham wrote to Cardinal Wolsey concerning the condition of affairs at the University of Oxford, in a letter which Sir William Ellis, formerly librarian of the British Museum, has published:[4]

"I am enformyd that diverse of that Universitie be infectyd with the *heresyes of Luther* and others of that sorte, havyng theym a grete nombre of books of the saide perverse doctryne. . . It is a sorrowful thing to see how gredyly inconstaunt men, and specyally inexpert youthe, falleth to newe doctrynes be they never so pestilent. . . Pytie it were that through the lewdnes of on or two cankerd members, . . the hole Universitie shuld run infamy of soo haynouse a cryme, the heryng whereof shuld be right delectable and plesant to open *Lutheranes* beyond the see. . . If all the hole nombyr of yong scolers suspectyd in this cause (which

---

[1] *Paraclesis ad lect. pium*, Vaughan's *Revolutions in English History*. I: 101.
[2] *History of England*, II: 40.
[3] Hardwick's *History of the Reformation*, p. 182.
[4] *Original Letters*, First Series, I: 239 sqq.

as the Universitie writeth to me be marvelouse sory and repentaunt that ever they had any such books or redde or herde any of Luther's opynyon) shulde be callyd up to London, yt shuld engendre grete obloquy and sclandre to the Universite, bothe behyther the see and beyonde . . the said Universite hathe desyred me to move. Your Grace, to be so good and gracyouse unto theym, to gyve in commission to some sadd father which was brought up in the Univeristie of Oxford to syt ther, and examyne, not the hedds, but the novicyes which be not yet yet thoroughly cankered in the said errors. . . Item, the said Universite hath desieryd me to move your good Grace to ncte out, besyde *werks of Luther* condemyd alredy, the names all other suche writers, *Luther's adherents and fautors.*" The request for such inquisition was in accordance with a proclamation which Warham had succeeded in inducing Wolsey to publish, entitled "A commission to warn all persons, both ecclesiastical and secular, under penalty of excommunication and of being dealt with as heretics, that, within the time assigned [fifteen days], they bring and deliver into the hands of the bishop or his deputy, *all writings ana books of Martin Luther, the heretic.*"[5] The proclamation was accompanied by the rehearsal of forty-two alleged errors of Luther, quoted from the Papal bull of excommunication, some of which are the greatest perversions of what he taught, while others, even as stated by enemies, can condemn only those who deem them reprehensible, as *e. g :* "32. In every good work, the just man sinneth." "33. A good work done best, is a venial sin." "34. To burn heretics is contrary to the will of the Spirit."[6] The fact that this demand to surrender the writings of Luther was to be read in every church at the time of mass, shows the progress which they had made throughout the Kingdom. The day before this proclamation, Fisher, bishop of Rochester, had preached in St. Paul's "Again ye pernicious doctryn of

---

[5] The decree is given in full in Strype's *Memorials of the Reformation*, V : 332; Gerdesius, *Hist. Ref.*, IV : 112.

[6] Strype's *Memorials*, I : 57–61.

Martin Luther."[7] A week later, the King himself sent a most urgent letter to Lewis, Duke of Bavaria, insisting upon employing extreme measures against Luther.[8] Nor must it be forgotten that the famous book by which he earned the title of "Defender of the Faith," but suffered for it from Luther's pen far more than he gained, belonged also to the same year, 1521. Two years later, Bishop Fisher followed his sermon by a treatise against Luther,[9] and Henry wrote a long letter to the princes of Saxony. Its temper may be learned from the following: "I am compelled to admonish and exhort you that you give your attention at as early a date as possible to repressing *that execrable sect of Luther*, without the execution of any one, if it can be done, or, with blood, if it cannot be otherwise accomplished."[10] In 1524, when Hugh Latimer, at that time, like Saul of Tarsus, a bitter zealot against the cause for which he afterwards laid down his life, availed himself of his inaugural address as B. D. at Cambridge, to make a sweeping attack upon the friends of the revived Gospel, he chose as his theme: "Philip Melanchthon and his opinions."[11]

But nothing could check the progress of the truth. It swept all obstacles before it. The young scholars of Cambridge could not be suppressed. Chief among them was Thomas Bilney. The story of his conversion, narrated by himself in a letter written from prison in 1528, has been summarized as follows: "In Trinity College, Cambridge, there was a young man, engaged in the study of canon law, remarkable for his seriousness, his modesty and his conscientiousness. His priest was to his soul, what his physician was to his body. He often took his place, pale and anxious, at the feet of his confessor. But the prescriptions given did not reach his case. Masses, vigils, indulgences and free contributions in money, all were tried, but the patient only seemed to grow worse. At times the thought would arise 'Am I in

---

[7] Hardwick, 179.   [8] Gerdesius, IV: 117.
[9] Hardwick, 179.   [10] Letter in Gerdesius, IV: 125.
[11] Cooper's *Athenæ Cantabrigienses*, I: 130.

the right path? May not the priest be in error, or be a self-seeker in all that he does?' But the suspicion was instantly rejected as a suggestion from the enemy. One day the troubled scholar heard two friends talking of a new book. The book was the Greek Testament by Erasmus, with an elegant Latin translation. The scholar was pleased with the sound of the Latin, and would fain have taken up the volume, and have examined it. But he knew that the authorities of the University had condemned all such books, and especially that book as tending to nothing but heresy. He abstained; but his desire to look into the volume grew stronger. He stole into the house in Cambridge, where the book was secretly sold. Having obtained a copy, he returned to his room, to read it, and the first text that arrested his attention, was: 'This is a faithful saying and worthy of all acceptation,' etc. This was to the spirit-worn student as the voice of an oracle. He pondered it and derived from it what the priestly impositions to which he had so long submitted, had failed to give him, peace of conscience and enlargement of heart. Henceforth he sits at the feet of his Lord, and of his inspired messengers."[13] "A perusal of Erasmus' N. T. and the *works of Luther*," says the historian of his University,[14] "taught him other views of religion, and he embraced the tenets of the reformers, except the denial of transubstantiation. He labored earnestly to promulgate his views, and amongst those whom he converted were John Nicholas, *alias* Lambert, Thomas Arthur, Robert Barnes, prior of the Augustinians, and Hugh Latimer. Bilney and Latimer visited and consoled the sick and needy, and the unhappy inmates in the town and country prisons."

Latimer's conversion also illustrates the connection with the Lutheran Reformation, since it was his famous attack upon Melanchthon above mentioned, that prompted Bilney to hasten to the study of the young preacher, and beg him "for God's sake

---

[12] Foxe's *Acts and Monuments*, II: 217; Gerdesius, IV: 129.
[13] Vaughan's *Revolutions in English History*, I: 104.
[14] Cooper's *Ath. Cantab.*, I: 42.

to hear his confession," with the result that "from that time forward he began to smell the Word of God, and forsook the school-doctors and such fooleries."

Gradually the circle of such men enlarged. "There," viz. at Cambridge, said a Bampton lecturer some few years ago,[15] "even so early as 1528, had been seen a little society of religious men who (like the Wesleys two hundred years later at Oxford) encouraged each other in reading the Scriptures, in mutual confession and similar prescribed acts of personal piety. They visited the prisoners at jails; they preached anew the vital spiritual truths—formerly enshrined, but now obscured by the ritual and ceremonies of their Church, and were in short engaged in reviving religion in England under its ancient forms. The names of twenty-seven of these men have been preserved to us; and just as the early Methodists obtained the honors of ridicule and social persecution, so the house where these *first English Lutherans* met, was called '*Germany*'" Fuller particulars are furnished by Strype in his "Life of Archbishop Parker."[16] "Parker's lot was to fall into the University in those days, when learning and religion began to dawn there; when divers godly men resorted together for conference sake; who also oftentimes flocked together in open sight, both in the schools, and at the sermons in St. Mary's and at St. Augustine's, where Dr. Barnes was prior, and at other disputations. Of which sort were several; and of these colleges, especially, viz. King's College, Queen's College, St. John's, Peter House, Pembroke Hall, Gonwell Hall and Benet College. Their meetings to confer and discourse together for edification and Christian knowledge, were chiefly at an house called 'The White Horse,' which was, therefore, afterwards named '*Germany*' by their enemies. This house was chosen because they of King's College, Queen's College and St. John's might come in with the more privacy at the back door."

---

[15] Curteis, "*Dissent in its relation to the Church of England*," p. 56.
[16] P. 12.

This company of twenty-seven included first of all Bilney. Next among them is named George Stafford of Pembroke Hall, from 1523. He had introduced an innovation by lecturing on the Holy Scriptures, instead of the "Sentences." In his visitations to the sick, he became infected with the plague, and died in 1529. "There was one of Clement Hostel, called Sir Henry, the conjurer, on account of his skill in the black art. Falling sick of the plague, Mr. Stafford visited him, argued on his wicked life and practices, brought him to repentance, and caused all his conjuring books to be burned before his face; but Mr. Stafford caught the infection, and died thereof between 19th of June and 17th November 1529." [17]

A third, Thomas Arthur, was intimidated to take an oath, "abjuring Luther's opinions," from which he does not seem to have recovered, as did several of his comrades. Of Robert Barnes and Hugh Latimer we shall hear much in what follows. Miles Coverdale was to acquire distinction as a translator of the Bible and of Luther's hymns. Paynell or Parnell was to be active in later years as a diplomat. Heynes, in 1528 was President of Queen's College, and afterwards Vice-Chancellor of the University. He baptized Edward VI., was on an embassy to France in 1525, and was employed on various important commissions connected with the reform of the English Church. Thixtell in 1529 was a member of commissions concerning the divorce, and in 1530 was a censor of publications. Distinguished as a debater, he continued to the end a warm friend of the Reformation. The son of the Lord Mayor of London was in the band, viz. Thomas Allen, who comforted Bilney in his hour of martyrdom. Turner was destined to be the most versatile of them all in his scholarship, a clergyman, physician, member of parliament, botanist, ornithologist, mineralogist, critic of N. T. text, translator and prolific author of both religious and scientific books.

There also were Nicholas Ridley, the future martyr bishop, Edward Crome already a doctor of divinity, who had years of

[17] Cooper's *Ath. Cantab.*, p. 39.

imprisonment before him, Rudolph Bradford, who, after exile for circulating the New Testament, was to return and aid in preparing "The Institution of a Christian Man," Shaxton and Skip, future apostates, and Sygar Nicholson, who was treated with much cruelty for having in his house the works of Luther.[18]

Of this band of twenty-seven, Skip, Ridley and Heynes were associated with Cranmer in the preparation of the liturgy of Edward VI.

But this group did not comprise all "the first English Lutherans" of Cambridge From Cambridge, a colony of select scholars had been sent to Oxford as the nucleus of Cardinal College, founded by Wolsey. We learn from the notes in Ellis:[19] "*Lutheranism* increased daily in the University of Oxford, and chiefly in Cardinal College, by certain of the Cantabrigians that then remained. The chiefest Lutheran at this time was John Clark, one of the junior canons, to whose private lectures and disputations in public, divers graduates and scholars of colleges resorted. So great a respect had they for his doctrine and exemplary course of life, that they would often recur to him for resolution of doubts. They had also their private meetings. wherein they conferred about the promotion of their religion. They prayed together and read certain books containing the *principles of Luther*. . . . Notwithstanding many eminent men did dispute and preach in the University against it, yet the *Lutherans proceeded*, and took all private occasions to promote their doctrine."

Shortly afterwards the Archbishop of London wrote to Wolsey: "With respect to the most accursed works of Luther, I have received through the doctor mentioned certain pamphlets which I will both most diligently read and note ; and, that I may do this the more carefully, I will betake myself as soon as possible to Oxford, where I will endeavor carefully to examine some codices of John Wiclif." [20]

[18] Cooper's *Ath. Cantab.*, 1: 51.
[19] *Original Letters*, Third Series, II: 71.
[20] Ellis, *Original Letters*, Third Series, I: 246.

Among this group of Lutheran students, transferred from Cambridge to Oxford, was Richard Cox, afterwards tutor to Edward VI., Chancellor of the University, one of the compilers of the "Book of Common Prayer," Bishop of Norwich, and whose exile under Mary was distinguished for his controversy with John Knox at Frankfort, and his triumph over Puritanism. Another was the martyr, John Frith, associated with Tyndale in the translation of the Bible, who afterwards accepted either the Zwinglian or Calvinistic view of the Lord's Supper. Richard Taverner, the translator of the Bible and of the Augsburg Confession, was a third. Among the others were Clark, before mentioned, Sumner, Betts, Harmann, Frier, Akars, Godman, Lawney, Dominick and Drumm. The entire party was arrested and imprisoned. Some were exiled. Taverner escaped by his skill as a musician. Clark "died in August 1528, of a distemper occasioned by the stench of the prison in which he was confined. In his last moments he was refused the communion, not perhaps as a special act of cruelty, but because the laws of the Church would not permit the holy thing to be profaned by the touch of a heretic. When he was told it would not be suffered, he said '*Crede et manducasti.*' " Sumner died from the same cause.

At Cambridge, as well as at Oxford, strict measures were taken to suppress Lutheranism. Unfortunately, not all its adherents manifested the greatest prudence. Bilney and Latimer, though subject to the closest surveillance deserve credit for their course, marked by sound judgment and discretion. The bishop of Ely endeavored to throw the latter off of his guard, by entering unexpectedly, with a retinue of dignitaries, the chapel at Cambridge where he was preaching. With complete mastery of the situation, the preacher adroitly changed his text, and spoke eloquently concerning the duty of bishops to follow Christ as their great model. Dr. Robert Barnes was of another temperament. Vehement, impulsive, direct, he could scarcely be restrained from at once assailing publicly all that he felt to be wrong. In December 1525, he precipitated a crisis which ended in his deep humiliation, by inveighing with most direct personalities against the bishops. The truth seems to be that he took Luther's sermon on the Epistle for the Fourth Sunday in Advent (1521), and reproduced it, with some changes, for his Cambridge audience. "He so postilled the whole epistle," says Foxe, "following the Scripture and *Luther's postil*, that for that sermon he was immediately accused of heresy."[21] Whatever may have been the excellences of "St. Robert," as Luther called Barnes after his death, he certainly did not know how to observe times and seasons. The Church of England of 1525 was not prepared for what suited admirably an audience in Wittenberg in 1521. A martyr's courage failed him at this time, although fourteen years later, he joyfully maintained his fidelity to the Gospel at the stake. The ceremony of his recantation, February 11th, 1526, was made as humiliating as possible. After a sermon preached in St. Paul's, London, by Bishop Fisher, in the presence of thirty-six bishops, abbots and priors "*Against Luther* and Dr. Barnes," he knelt and asked forgiveness which was granted with the penance attached of walking thrice around a blazing pile of large basketsful of Lutheran books. Bilney and Arthur also were unequal to the trial, into which Barnes' indiscreet ardor had brought them. Latimer bore himself with such shrewdness that, instead of punishment, he received the Cardinal's license to preach anywhere in England.

The last message of Cardinal Wolsey to his sovereign, sent from his death-bed, was to "have a vigilant eye on the new sect, the Lutherans, that it do not increase through your negligence in such sort as you be at length compelled to put harness on your back to subdue them."

An "Index of Prohibited Books" of 1529 gives the names of the works which had been so diligently circulated by the young scholars of these two universities and their friends. It has the title "*Libri sectæ sive factionis Lutherianæ importati ad civi-*

---

[21] *Acts and Monuments; History of* (Presbyterian Board of Publication, Phila.,) p. 78.

tatem London." After four books of Wiclif, it reads:

"Dr. Martin Luther 'Concerning Good Works.' Letter of Luther to Pope Leo X. Tessaradecas Consolatoria of Martin Luther. Tract of Luther 'Concerning Christian Liberty.' Sermons of Dr. Martin Luther. Exposition of the Epistles of St. Peter by Martin Luther. Reply of Martin Luther to Bartholemew Catharinus. 'Of the Works of God' by Martin Cellarius. Deuteronomy, from the Hebrew, with annotations of Martin Luther. Luther's Catechism in Latin by J. Lonicerus. The Prophet Jonah, explained by Martin Luther. Commentary of Martin Luther on the Epistle of Paul to the Galatians. Selections from the letters of Martin Luther, full of piety and learning, with the interpretation of several psalms, Narrations of Postils of Martin Luther upon the lessons from the Gospels, etc. Sixteen Conclusions of the reverend father, Martin Luther, concerning Faith and Ceremonies. Most Wholesome Declaration of the same concerning Faith and Works. Most Learned Explanation of Ceremonies. Fifty Conclusions by the same for timid consciences. Luther's Explanation of his thirteenth proposition 'Concerning the Power of the Pope.' Oration of Didymus Faventinus on behalf of Martin Luther. New narrations of Martin Luther on the prophet Jonah. Judgment of Martin Luther, 'Concerning Monastic Vows.' Enchiridion of the Godly Prayers of Martin Luther. Several brief sermons of Martin Luther on the Virgin, the Mother of God."

Then follow works of Œcolampadius, Billicanus, Zwingli, Bugenhagen, Bucer, Regius, Melanchthon, Agricola, Brentz, Lambert, Wessel, Gochius and Carlstadt.[23]

Who, after reading this list would venture to maintain that the reformatory movement in England was independent of that in Germany? It shows very clearly that the theologians of England were keeping abreast of the entire development of theological literature on the Continent.

[23] This list is found in Gerdesius, IV: 139 sqq.; Foxe, *"Acts and Monuments."*

CHAPTER II.

TYNDALE'S DEPENDENCE ON LUTHER.

Tyndale's Birth and Education. Relation to Colet and Erasmus. **Early Work.** A significant Prophecy. Life in London. Repulsed by the Lord Bishop. Humphrey Monmouth and his Troubles. Tyndale at Hamburg. Was Tyndale at Wittenberg? Insufficient arguments of Anderson and Walter. The English Genesis of 1530 published by Luther's publisher, Hans Luft. Where was Marlboro? The flight from Cologne. Two editions of New Testament, instead of one. Proclamations of Tunstal and Warham. Fifteen thousand English testaments sent from Germany to England. Arrest and execution. Tyndale's translation and that of Luther. Testimony of Hallam, Westcott and Mombert. Tyndale and Luther in parallel columns. His prefaces from Luther. His glosses from Luther. His treatise "The Wicked Mammon," from Luther. "The Obedience of a Christian Man," Anne Boleyn's devotional manual. His "Exposition of the Sermon on the Mount," from Luther. Was Tyndale a Lutheran? Arguments of Dr. Eadie in the negative; of V. E. Löscher, in the affirmative.

AMONG the scholars of Oxford and Cambridge, there is one who had left the Universities years before the events just narrated, but whose influence from abroad was a very important factor in advancing the movement. His work is so prominent and far-reaching, and, except in his preparation as a student, so isolated from the rest, until through his translation of the New Testament and his various evangelical treatises, he acted upon his countrymen, that it justly requires separate treatment. William Tyndale was a quiet and retired scholar, who wrought diligently in his study with a fixed end in view from which he never swerved, and which required his withdrawal from the intimate associations, and the wider spheres of discussion in which others felt called upon to promote the same cause. He, therefore, was content to stand during his life-time almost alone, in order to effect the Reformation of his country, and to reach future generations through the English Bible, which, even in its present form, is properly speaking his Bible, revised.

Born probably about 1484, on the boundary of Wales, he was "brought up," says Foxe, "from a child at the University of Oxford, where he, by long continuance, grew and increased as well in the knowledge of tongues and other liberal arts, as specially in the knowledge of the Scriptures, to which his mind was singularly addicted; insomuch that he, lying there in Magdalen Hall, read privily to certain students and fellows of Magdalen College some parcel of divinity, instructing them in the knowledge and truth of the scriptures, whose manners also and conversation, being correspondent to the same, were such that all they that knew him, reputed and esteemed him, to be a man of most virtuous disposition, and of life unspotted. Thus he, in the University of Oxford, increasing more and more in learning, and proceeding in degrees of the schools, spying his time, removed from thence to the University of Cambridge, where after he had likewise made his abode a certain space, being now further ripened in the knowledge of God's Word, leaving that university also, he resorted to one master Welsh, a Knight of Gloucestershire; and was there school-master to his children, and in very good favor with his master." At Oxford, he undoubtedly came under the influence of Dean Colet. His removal to Cambridge "was probably for the purpose of profiting by Erasmus' lectures, who taught Greek there from 1509 till the beginning of 1519; whereas there was no regular Greek lectureship founded in Oxford till about 1517."[1] At the house of Sir John Welsh or Walsh, whither he went about 1519, he soon became involved in controversies with the priests, translated against them Erasmus' "Enchiridion Militis" and destroyed their influence with the family, from which they previously had derived large con-

---

[1] Walter's *Life of Tyndale*, prefixed to "*Doctrinal Treatises*" (Parker Society,) p. XV.

tributions. He was a zealous preacher at Bristol, and was summoned to answer before the chancellor, but while treated "as though I had been a dog," escaped punishment. Shortly after this it was, that in a discussion with a learned, but bitter advocate of the Papacy he made the often quoted remark that he defied the Pope and all his laws, and, further added, that if God spared him life, "ere many years he would cause a boy that driveth the plough to know more of the scriptures than he did." His position becoming more and more uncomfortable, and being involved in constant disputes, he saw that the evangelical cause was relatively helpless until the Bible could be read by the laity in their own language. In his "Preface to the Pentateuch," he says: "I perceived how that it was impossible to establish the lay-people in any truth, except the scripture were plainly laid before their eyes in their mother-tongue, that they might see the process, order and meaning of the text. For else whatever truth is taught them, these enemies of all truth quench it again, partly with apparent reasons of sophistry, founded without ground of scripture; and partly, in juggling with the text, expounding it in such sense as is impossible to gather of the text, if thou see the process, order and meaning thereof." With this end in view, he resigned his place, and, about 1523, went to London, where, relying upon an extravagant idea of the interest of the Bishop of London, Tonstall, in such work, he hoped to receive a home in his house and encouragement. He carried with him, as an evidence of his scholarship, a translation, which he had made, of one of the orations of Isocrates. But the English Bible was not to be translated in an episcopal palace. He found no home or encouragement where he had expected it. The Lord, however, raised up for him a faithful friend in a wealthy merchant, Humphrey Monmouth, who had heard him preach in St. Dunstan's church, and provided for him at his own house. Years afterwards Monmouth was imprisoned for this act of kindness. In his testimony in his defence, he throws some light upon Tyndale's habits: "He studied most part of the day and of the night at his book; and he would eat but sodden meat, by his good will, nor drink but small single beer. I never saw him wear linen about him. . . . When I heard my Lord of London preach at Paul's Cross, that Sir William Tyndale had translated the New Testament in English, and was naughtily translated, that was the first time that ever I suspected or knew any evil by him."

Tyndale soon found it necessary, in order to prosecute his work successfully, to repair to Germany. Accordingly about May 1524 he left London for Hamburg. In April 1525, he is known to have been in Hamburg. Had he been there the entire time, or had he been elsewhere in the meantime? Concerning this, there has been a diversity of opinion. There has been a widely diffused tradition that he repaired at once from Hamburg to Wittenberg. All of Tyndale's contemporaries who have written concerning his movements, so affirm. In the articles against Monmouth in 1528, he is charged with aiding "Sir William Hutchin, otherwise called Tyndale," who "went into Almayne [Germany] to Luther, there to study and learn his sect." Sir Thomas More in his "Dialogue" declares that "at the time of his translation of the New Testament, Tyndale was with Luther at Wittenberg, and the confederacy between him and Luther was well known." Cochlaeus speaks of Tyndale and Roy as "two English apostates who had been sometime at Wittenberg." Foxe in his "Acts and Monuments" says: "On his first departing out of the realm, Tyndale took his journey into the further parts of Germany, as into Saxony, where he had conference with Luther and other learned men in those quarters."

Some writers of the present century, especially Anderson in his "Annals of the English Bible," and Walter in his "Life of Tyndale," prefixed to the Parker Society edition of his works, question his visit to Wittenberg, but as Demaus[2] shows upon the basis of too wide an application of a denial by Tyndale to the charge of More. Tyndale denies that he was confederate with Luther. He does not deny that he was at Wittenberg. "The

---

[2] *William Tyndale, A Biography.* 94 sqq.

truth is," says Demaus,³ "that the whole of this theory of Tyndale's movements, constructed, as we have seen, in direct opposition to all contemporary authority, has sprung from a narrow and ill-grounded fear, that Tyndale's reputation would be injured by the admission of his having been at Wittenberg with Luther. The admirers of our great English translator have been justly indignant at the ignorant misrepresentations which have sometimes treated him as a mere echo and parasite of his German contemporary, and in their zeal to maintain their hero's originality, they have discarded ancient authority, and have denied that the two Reformers ever met. The motive for such a defence may be praiseworthy, but its wisdom is questionable. To maintain, in defiance of all contemporary evidence, that Tyndale remained for a year in a bustling commercial town where there were no printers, where he would be disturbed by bitter quarrels, and deprived of all opportunities of consulting books, or conferring with friends that might have aided him in the work, this is surely a strange method of vindicating Tyndale; this is an attempt to defend his originality, at the cost of his good sense." Mr. Anderson's theories about Tyndale's residence in Hamburg, his ignorance of German, his never having met Luther, are theories adopted in the face of all ancient testimony.⁴

Prof. Walter's argument that Tyndale's stay at Hamburg was for the purpose of learning Hebrew from the numerous Jews there, and that proof of this can be shown from the fact that whereas Hebrew at that time was not taught in any English University, Tyndale's progress becomes soon manifest from the insight into the peculiarities of that language shown by some remarks in his "Mammon," is not conclusive. The passage would effectually prove this, if that book were original with Tyndale; but since it is only a translation from Luther, as will hereafter appear, the progress in Hebrew asserted, cannot be shown.

Dr. Eadie,⁵ while trying to show that Tyndale was no Luth-

---

³ Ib. p. 96.
⁴ Ib. p. 495.

eran, after weighing the evidence, concludes: "Arguments against the visit to Wittemberg are of no great moment."

Mr. George Offer, in the "Memoir of Tyndale," prefixed to a reprint of his New Testament of 1526, published by the Bagsters says: "It was at Wyttemburg, that with intense application and labor, Tyndale completed his translation of thew New Testament."

Dr. Mombert[6] says: "In the absence of positive historical data it is impossible to make a reliable positive statement. It is probable that Tyndale did meet Luther; it is clear that he used Luther's version, as I expect to prove. . . . The preponderance of evidence points immediately to Tyndale's visit to Wittemberg." The same writer has also conclusively proved that the statement hitherto current that Tyndale's translation of Genesis of 1530 was printed by Hans Luft at Marburg is incorrect, the librarian of the University of Marburg having made a special examination into the matter in 1881, with the result that he found that Hans Luft never had a printing-office at Marburg, and that the album of the University has no entry of the names of Tyndale and Frith. Hans Luft, being the famous Bible printer at Wittenberg, the name "Marlborow in the lande of Hesse," given as his place of printing, is in all probability a pseudonym to conceal the actual place, just as he himself assumed the pseudonym of Hutchyns, to thwart the designs of his vigilant enemies. Wittenberg, therefore, a second time becomes connected with Tyndale's work, and our English Bible.[7]

But we have anticipated somewhat the chronological order. After returning from Wittenberg to Hamburg in 1525, and having his translation of the New Testament finished, Tyndale went to Cologne for the purpose of having it printed. Here he was discovered by Cochlaeus an enemy of the Reformation, who promptly reported what he had learned. The story is interest-

---

[5] *History of English Bible*, I: 127.
[6] *A Handbook of the English Versions*, 82 sqq.
[7] Ib., pp. 107-115.

ing: "Cochlaeus, intending to print a work of his own, had gone to Cologne, where some of the compositors he was about to employ, in an unguarded moment, intimated that they were engaged in preparing a work for two Englishmen[8] lately arrived from Wyttemberg, which would soon make England Lutheran. By plying them with drink, he discovered that there were in the press three thousand copies of the Lutheran New Testament translated into English. By his efforts, the Senate prohibited the work from proceeding any further. It had reached the signature K in 4to. Upon which the two Englishmen, carrying away with them the sheets already finished, fled up the Rhine to Worms, in hope that, as the inhabitants were generally Lutheran, they might find some printer to bring their undertaking to completion.."[9]

This attempt to suppress the publication resulted in two simultaneous editions, instead of one. Peter Schoeffer of Worms printed an octavo edition, while, at the same time, the quarto edition was completed and bound. The opponents of the Reformation, being on the watch for the quarto editions, it was generally intercepted on its way to England; but the octavo edition, not being suspected, made its way for a time without interference. There was no little strategy in such procedure. No less than six thousand copies were printed in these two editions which appeared early in 1526. Even before this, December 2d, 1525, Dr. Edward Lee writing from Bordeaux,[10] warned Henry VIII. of what was coming:

"Please it your Hyghnesse, moreover, to understand that I am certainlie enformed, as I passed in this contree that an Englishman, your subject, at the sollicitation and instance of Luther, with whome he is, hathe translated the Newe Testament into English, and within fewe dayes entendeth to arrive with the same emprinted in England, I neede not to advertise your Grace

---

[8] William Roye was Tyndale's amanuensis.
[9] Ellis *Original Letters* Third Series, II: 88.
[10] Ellis, Or. Letters, II: 71 sqq.

what infection and daunger maye ensue heerbie, if it be not withstonded. This is the next way to fulfill your Realme with Lutherians. For all Luther's perverse opinions bee grownded opon bar words of Scriptur, not well taken ne ondrestonded. All our forfadres, governors of the churche of England, hathe with all diligence forbed and eschued publication of Englishe bibles, as apperethe in constitutitions provinciall of the Churche of England, . . . Hidretoo, blessed be God, your Realme is save from infection of Luther's sect, as for so mutche that althoug anye peradvertur bee secretlie blotted within, yet for fear of your royall Majestie, wiche hathe drawen his swerd in God's cause, they dar not openlie avow."

It is interesting to note that only two months before this (Sept. 1st, 1525), Luther apologizing to Henry VIII for his attack upon his book, does so by excusing the King on the ground that it was not really written by Henry, but by Sophists who abused his title, especially as De Wette thinks, by the writer of the above letter, Edward Lee, whom he ironically calls "Cardinal of York," and terms "that monster and public odium of God and men." [11] May there not be in this at least some indication of indignation aroused by information given him, through Tyndale? This becomes the more probable when we read in the same letter that Luther has been moved to write, because he was informed that Henry "was beginning to favor the gospel and to be not a little weary of such a set of worthless fellows." He prays that the Lord may continue the work which he has begun, so that with a full spirit, he may favor and obey the Gospel."

In spite of all efforts to suppress them, the copies of the New Testament made their way through England. Who the translator was, no one then knew. Some Lutherans or other, of course; but that was all. Henry, in his reply to Luther's letter, said that Luther "fell into device with one or two lewd fellows, born in this our realm, for the translating of the New Testament into English." Tonstal, Bishop of London, issued his prohibi-

---

[11] De Wette's *Luther's Briefen*, III: 24.

tion, October 24th, 1526, in which he said: "We, having understanding by the reports of divers credible persons, and also by the evident appearance of the matter, that many children of iniquity, maintainers of Luther's sect, blinded through extreme wickedness, wandering from the way of truth and the catholic faith, craftily have translated the New Testament into our English tongue." [12] This was followed by a similar proclamation by Archbishop Warham on November 3d. Efforts were made to arrest their importation by destroying them as they passed through Antwerp in the Netherlands. But the very proposal, on the request of the English government, to have them made illegal there, brought to light the fact that in January 1527, an enterprising Antwerp printer was at work on a reprint for the English market; and the burgesses of that city declined to interfere with what would cripple any industry of their citizens. Then Tonstal devised another expedient. At great cost, he employed agents to buy up all copies as they appeared. This did not diminish the number of copies, as the press continued to send them forth; but proved of great advantage to Tyndale by giving him the means of life, while translating the Old and revising the New Testament. The older and less correct copies were also thus speedily withdrawn from the market, to give place to revised editions. By 1530, no less than six editions of the New Testament appeared, numbering 15,000 copies. Nevertheless "so fierce and systematic was the persecution, that there remains of the first, one fragment only, which was found about thirty years ago attached to the fragment of another tract; of the second, one copy, wanting the title-page, and another very imperfect; and of the others, two or three copies, which are not, however, satisfactorily identified." [13] In 1530, his translation of the Pentateuch appeared, and, in the following year, that of the prophet Jonah. Other books of the Old Testament were translated but not published. He was steadily

---

[12] Foxe's *Acts and Monuments*, IV: 666.
[13] Westcott's *History of the English Bible*, p. 45.

at work upon the unfinished portions during his imprisonment. He was also the author of a number of Doctrinal and Expository treatises, "A Pathway into Holy Scripture," "The Wicked Mammon," "The Obedience of a Christian Man," "Exposition of First John," "Exposition of the V, VI and VII chapters of Matthew."

His end is well-known. For years living in various places, and under an assumed name, he was diligently sought for by the agents of Henry VIII. When the Reformation had progressed in England, and the rupture with the Papacy seemed complete, he supposed it safe to abandon secrecy, and publicly lived and labored at Antwerp. Here he was soon apprehended (May 23d or 24th, 1535,) by the emissaries of the English prelates and after an imprisonment of over a year at the castle of Vilvorden, was strangled and burned, October 6th, 1536. Henry VIII has enough sins for which to answer. We cannot hold him responsible for this murder, upon the amount of evidence now to be furnished.[14] Persevering as had been Henry's endeavor in former years to apprehend him, time had brought its changes. The guilt must ultimately fall upon the Emperor, Charles V, and those from England, who instigated him to the act.

We come now to the relation between the literary work of Tyndale, and that of Luther. On the one hand, Tyndale's ability as an independent translator has been denied, as by Hallam, who traces his translation entirely to the Vulgate and Luther; on the other hand, his indebtedness to Luther has been ignored. Canon Westcott, the eminent New Testament critic, while endeavoring to prove the utmost independence of Luther, says that it is impossible to read a single chapter without noting that the Greek text was directly used, and at the same time tracing the influence of Luther, together with that of the Vulgate and of Erasmus' Latin version.[15] Dr. Mombert

---

[14] Demaus' *Life of Tyndale*, p. 424.
[15] *History of English Bible*, p. 174.

makes a comparison of Luther's German and Tyndale on Deuteronomy 6: 6–9, as follows:[16]

6. Und diese Worte, die ich dir heute gebiete, sollst du zu Herzen nehmen.	6. Let these words which I command thee this day stick fast in thine heart.
7. Und sollst sie deinen Kindern schärfen, und davon reden, wenn du in deinem Hause sitzest, oder auf dem Wege gehest, wenn du dich niederlegest, oder aufstehest.	7. And whet them on thy children, and talk of them as thou sittest in thine house, and as thy walkest by the way, and when thou liest down, and when thou risest up.
8. Und sollst sie binden zum Zeichen auf deine Hand, und sollen dir ein Denkmal vor deinen Augen seyn.	8. And bind them for a token to thine hand, and let them be a remembrance between thine eyes.
9. Und sollst sie über deines Hauses Pforten schreiben und an die Thore.	9. And write them on the posts and gates of thine house.

"There was nothing," says this writer, "in the English language he could have used *e g.*, for the rendering of the Hebrew *Shinnaen* by the English '*Whet,*' which conveys an idea contained neither in the Greek of the Septuagint, nor the Latin of the Vulgate, but it had been employed by Luther. Had he been a servile imitator of Luther, he would have rendered, after the example of the dreadful translators of the period: 'And whet them in or into thy children;' but he knew that that would have violated the English idiom, and, therefore, he rendered 'whet on,' and he understood the Piel force of the root *Shanan*. . . . Again in verse 8, Luther translates the Hebrew *Letotaphoth beyn eynecha:* 'Denkmaal vor deinen *Augen*.' It is evident that he deliberately gave preference to Luther's admirable free rendering, as much superior to the vague Greek, and still vaguer Latin of the literal Hebrew 'bands or fillets'; but knew Hebrew enough to perceive that 'remembrance *between* thine eyes' conformed at once to the Hebrew and English idioms. These two examples, I think, will suffice to convince and prove to scholars, that Tyndale used Luther and understood Hebrew."

"To any scholar," says the biographer of Tyndale, Rev. R. Demaus, "who sits down to collate with care the versions of the English and German translators, two facts speedily become

---

[16] *Handbook to English Version*, p. 115.

plain and indisputable, viz., that Tyndale had Luther's work before him, and constantly consulted and occasionally adopted it; and that he never implicitly follows Luther, but translates from the original with the freedom of a man who had a perfect confidence in his own scholarship." [17]

Instances, however, may be cited, where his independence is not as great as is sometimes claimed for him. For instance, Luke 22: 20, where Tyndale's "blood which shall for you be shed," is not English in its order of words, but is that of Luther's German; while he obtains the future by misunderstanding *vergossen wird*, especially when compared with the Vulgate *fundetur*. Here he clearly has abandoned the Greek in order to follow Luther. [18]

The indebtedness of Tyndale to Luther in other respects than as a translator of the Bible, is very great. "The extent," says Canon Westcott, "to which Tyndale silently incorporated free or verbal translations of passages from Luther's works into his own, has escaped the notice of his editors. To define it accurately would be a work of very great labor, but the result, as showing the points of contact and divergence in the opinions of the two great reformers, would be a most instructive passage in the doctrinal history of the time." [19]

We give the following examples:

I. PROLOGUES PREPARED INTRODUCING TRANSLATIONS.

1. *To the New Testament*

Luther (*1522*.)	Tyndale (*1526*.)
Gleichwie das Alte Testament ist ein Buch, darinnen Gottes Gesetz und Gebot, daneben die Geschichte beide dere, die dieselbigen gehalten und nicht gehalten haben, geschrieben sind; also ist das Neue Testament ein Buch, darinnen das Evangelium und Gottes Verheissung, daneben auch	The Old Testament is a book, wherein is written the law of God, and the deeds of them which fulfil them, and of them also which fulfil them not. The New Testament is a book, wherein are contained the promises of God; and the deeds of them which

---

[17] *William Tyndale*. A biography, p. 237.
[18] Other examples may be found in "*A Revised English Bible, the want of the Church*," by John R. Beard, D. D., London, 1857.
[19] *History of English Bible*, p. 192.

Geschichte beide dere, die daran gläuben und nicht gläuben, geschrieben sind. Denn Evangelium ist ein griechisch Wort und heisst auf Deutsch gute Botschaft, gute Mähre, gute neue Zeitung, gut Geschrei, davon man singet, saget und fröhlich ist: als da David den grossen Goliath uberwand, kam ein gut Geschrei und tröstliche neue Zeitung unter das jüdische Volk, dass ihr gräulicher Feind erschlagen, und sie erlöset, zu Freude und Friede gestellet wären, davon sie sungen, und sprungen und fröhlich waren.

believe them, or believe them not. Evangelion (that we call Gospel) is a Greek word, and signifieth good, merry, glad and joyful tidings, that maketh a mans heart glad, and maketh him sing, dance, and leap for joy; as when David had killed Goliath, the giant, came glad tidings unto the Jews, that their fearful and cruel enemy was slain, and they delivered out of all danger; for gladness whereof, they sung, danced and were joyful.

2. To Epistle to the Romans.

Luther (1522.)

Diese Epistel ist das rechte Hauptstücke des Neuen Testaments, und das allerlauterste Evangelium, welche wohl würdig und werth ist, dass sie ein Christenmensch nicht allein von Wort zu Wort auswendig wisse, sondern täglich damit umgehe, als mit täglichem Brod der Seelen. Denn sie nimmer kann zu viel und zu wohl gelesen, oder betrachten werden, und je mehr sie gehandelt wird, je köstlicher sie wird und bass schmecket.

Darumb ich auch meinem Dienst dazu thun will, und durch diese Vorrede einen Eingang dazu bereiten, so viel mir Gott verleihen hat, damit sie deste bass von Jedermann verstanden werde. Denn sie bisher mit Glossen und mancherlei Geschwätz ubel verfinstert ist, die doch an ihr selbs ein helles Licht ist, fast genugsam, die ganze Schrift zu erleuchten.

Tyndale (1526.)

Forasmuch as this Epistle is the principal and most excellent part of the New Testament, and most pure Evangelion, that is to say, glad tidings and that we call gospel, and also is a light and a way unto the whole scripture; I think it meet that every Christian man not only know it, by note and without the book, but also exercise himself therein evermore continually, as with the daily bread of the soul. No man verily can read it too oft, or study it too well; for the more it is studied, the easier it is; the more it is chewed, the pleasanter it is; and the more grandly it is searched, the preciouser things are found in it, so great treasure of spiritual things lieth hid therein. I will therefore bestow my labour and diligence, through this little preface or prologue, to prepare a way in thereunto, so far forth as God shall give me grace, that it may be the better understood of every man; for it hath been hitherto evil darkened with glosses and wonderful dreams of sophisters, that no man could spy out the intent and meaning of it; which, nevertheless, of itself is a bright light, and sufficient to give light unto all Scripture.

3 To Second Corinthians.

Luther (*1522*.)

In der ersten Epistel hat S. Paulus die Korinther hart gestrafet in vielen Stücken, und scharfen Wein in die Wunden gegossen, und sie erschreket; nu aber ein Apostel soll ein tröstlicher Prediger sein, die erschrocken und blöden Gewissen aufzurichten, mehr denn zu schrecken: darumb lobet er sie nun wiederumb in dieser Epistel, und geusset auch Ole in die Wunden, und thut sich wunderfreundlich zu ihnen, und heisset den Sünder mit Liebe wieder aufzunehmen.

Im 1. und 2. Cap. zeiget er seine Liebe gegen sie, wie er alles geredt, gethan und gelitten habe zu ihrem Nutz und Heil, dass sie ja sich alles Besten zu ihm versehen sollen.

Darnach preiset er das evangelische Ampt, welchs das höheste und tröstlichste Werk ist, zu Nutz und Heil der Gewissen, und zeiget wie dasselbige edler sei, denn das Gesetzes Ampt, und wie dasselbige verfolget wird, und doch zunimpt an den Gläubigen, und eine Hoffnung machet durchs Kreuz der ewigen Herrlichkeit. Aber mit dem allen rühret er die falschen Apostel, welche das Gesetz wider das Evangelium treibet, und eitel äusserliche Heiligkeit (das ist, Heuchelei) lehreten, und liessen die inwendige Schande des Unglaubens stehen.

Tyndale (*1526*.)

As in the first epistle he rebuketh the Corinthians sharply, so in this he comforteth them, and praiseth them, and commandeth him that was excommunicated to be received lovingly into the congregation again.

And in the first and second chapters, he showeth his love to themward, how that all that he spake, did, or suffered was for their sakes, and for their salvation.

Then in the third, fourth and fifth, he praiseth the office of preaching the Gospel, above the preaching of the Law; and showeth that the Gospel groweth through persecution, and through the cross, which maketh a man sure of eternal life.

And here and there, he toucheth the false prophets, which studied to turn the faith of the people from Christ, unto the works of the Law.

4 To Galatians.

Luther (*1522*.)

Die Galater waren durch S. Paulum, zu dem rechten Christenglauben, und ins Evangelium von dem Gesetz gebracht. Aber nach seiner Abschied kamen die falschen Apostel, die der rechten Apostel Jünger warden, und wandten die Galater wieder umb, dass sie gläubten, sie müssten durch des Gesetzes Werk selig werden, und thäten Sünde, wo sie nicht des Gesetzes Werk hielten.

Tyndale (*1526*.)

After Paul had converted the Galatians, and coupled them to Christ, to trust in him only for the remission of sins, and hope of grace and salvation, and was departed, there came false Apostles unto them, and that, in the name of Peter, James and John, whom they called the high Apostles, and preached circumcision and the keeping of the Law, to be saved by.

5 To Ephesians.

Luther (*1522*.)

In dieser Epistel, lehret S. Paulus aufs erst, was das Evangelium sei, wie es allein von Gott in Ewigkeit versehen, und durch Christum verdienet und ausgegangen ist, dass alle, die daran gläuben, gerecht, frumm, lebendig, selig und vom Gesetz, Sünde und Tod frei werden. Das thut er durch die drei ersten Kapitel.

Tyndale (*1526*)

In this Epistle, namely in the first three chapters, Paul showeth that the Gospel and grace thereof, was foreseen and predestinate of God from before the beginning and deserved through Christ, and now at the last sent forth, that all men should believe therein; thereby to be justified, made righteous, living and happy; and to be delivered from under the damnation of the law, and captivity of ceremonies.

6. To Philippians

Luther (*1522*.)

In dieser Epistel, lobet und ermahnet S. Paulus die Philipper, dass sie bleiben und fortfahren sollen im rechten Glauben, und zunehmen in der Liebe. Dieweil aber den Glauben allezeit Schaden thun die falschen Aposteln und Werklehrer, warnet er sie für denselbigen, und zeiget ihnen an mancherlei Prediger, etliche gute, etliche böse, auch sich selbs und seine Jünger, Timotheum und Epaphroditus; das thut er im 1, 2 Kap.

Tyndale (*1526*.)

Paul praiseth the Philippians, and exhorteth them to stand fast in the true faith and to increase in love. And because that false prophets study always to impugn and destroy the true faith, he warneth them of such work-learners, or teachers of works, and praiseth Epaphroditus; and all this doth he in the first and second chapters.

Similar examples might be given from the prologues to Colossians, 1 Thessalonians, 2 Thessalonians, 1 Timothy, 2 Timothy, Titus, Philemon, 1 Peter, 2 Peter, the Three Epistles of St. John, and to a less degree, 1 Corinthians. The long prologue to Hebrews keeps in view what Luther's brief prologue suggests, and argues against a statement of Luther. Even where his prologues do not reproduce similar prologues of Luther, no one who knows the latter will fail to see that Tyndale presents in another form what Luther has elsewhere taught. We cite, as an example, Tyndale's treated of the allegorical interpretation of Scripture in the prologue to Leviticus, for every statement of which a corresponding passage of Luther could be given. Peculiar expressions, too, incline one greatly to most thoroughly search Luther's works for them, as e. g. " The Holy Ghost is no dumb God, nor a God that goeth a mumming." So, as Canon Westcott[20] has remarked, "Tyndale at the close of his prologue to St. Matthew, which is an extensive essay, reproduces, in a modified form, Luther's famous judgment on the relative worth of the apostolic books in his Preface to the New Testament."

Luther (*1522*.)	Tyndale (*1526*.)
Summa, S. Johannis Evangel. und seine erste Epistel, S. Paulus Epistel, sonderlich die zu den Römern, Galatern, Ephesern, und S. Peters erste Epistle, das sind die Bücher, die dir Christum zeigen, und alles lehren, das dir zu wissen noth und selig ist.	And thereto Paul's Epistles, with the Gospel of John, and his first epistle, and the first epistle of St. Peter, are most pure Gospel and most plainly and richly describe the glory of the grace of Christ.

The Appendix on "Repentance is only a reproduction of Luther's well-known discussion of metanoia, with special reference to the defects of the Latin translation '*ago poenitentiam*.'"

II. THE GLOSSES.

"The marginal notes, those 'pestilent glosses,' against which the indignation of the clergy was especially excited, have been to a large extent translated by Tyndale from those of Luther. Not that Tyndale translated like a servile imitator, whose intellect was too barren to be capable of originality; everywhere he uses his own judgment; sometimes he curtails Luther's notes; sometimes he omits them; often he inserts notes of his own, and these of various kinds, explanatory and doctrinal. Some of the longest of these marginal glosses, as well as some of those which most emphatically propound the doctrine of justification by faith, are original to Tyndale; in other cases the words of Luther have been expanded, and have formed not so much the source of Tyndale's notes as the nucleus out of which it has grown. Of the whole number of *ninety* marginal glosses which occur in the fragment of Tyndale's quarto that has come down to us, *fifty-two* have been more or less literally taken from Luther, and *thirty-eight* are original."[21]

[20] *History of English Bible*, p. 198.
[21] Demaus, *William Tyndale. A Biography*.

We give two illustrations:

Luther.	Tyndale.
Matth. 5: 13. (Das Salz). Wenn die Lehrer aufhören Gottes Wort zu lehren, müssen sie von Menschengesetzen überfallen und zutreten werden.	(Salt). When the preachers cease to preach God's Word, then must they need be oppressed and trod under foot with man's traditions.
Luther.	*Tyndale.*
Rom. 5: 14: Wie Adam uns mit frembder Sünde, ohn unser Schuld, verderbet hat; also hat uns Christus mit frembder Gnade ohn unser Verdienst selig gemacht.	Adam's disobedience damned us all ere we ourselves wrought evil; and Christ's obedience saveth us all ere we ourselves work any good.

III. THE WICKED MAMMON.

This is a treatise written by Tyndale at Worms, and published under his own name, May 8th, 1527. Its real theme is "Justification by Faith." A number of scriptural texts, urged by the Papists against this doctrine, are examined and explained in an evangelical manner. The first, and the one accorded most prominent treatment is "The Parable of the Unjust Steward." From beginning to end it has Luther's spirit and style.

A large portion of it is from Luther's Sermon on the Ninth Sunday after Trinity. We select from pages that might be here inserted, only the passage on the meaning of unrighteous Mammon, which Prof. Walter triumphantly adduces as an indication of Tyndale's profound Hebrew attainments. [22]

Luther (1522.)	*Tyndale (1527.)*
Auf erste: Mammon ist Hebraisch, und heisst so viel als Reichthumb oder zeitlich Gut, nämlich das, dess jemand ubrig hat zu seinem stande, und damit er dem andern wohl kann nütz sein ohne Schaden. Denn Hamon auf Hebraisch heisst Menge, oder grosser Hauf und viel; daraus wird denn *Mahamon* oder *Mammon*, das ist, die Menge des Gutes oder Reichthumbs.	First, *mammon* is an Hebrew word, and signifieth riches or temporal goods; and, namely, all superfluity, and all that is above necessity, and that which is required to our necessary uses; wherewith a man may help another, without undoing or hurting himself; for *hamon* in the Hebrew speech, signifies a multitude or abundance, or many; and there hence cometh *mahamon* or *mammon*, abundance or plenteousness of goods or riches.

[22] Tyndale's *Doctrinal Treatises* (Parker Society), Note on p. 68.

Aufs ander heisst es unrecht Mammon, nicht dass es mit unrecht oder Wucher erworben sei; denn von unrechtem Gut, kann man kein gut Werk thunn, sondern soll es wiedergeben, wie Jesaias (61, 8) hat gesagt.	Secondarily, it is called "unrighteous mammon," not because it is got unrighteously, or with usury; for of unrighteous gotten goods, can no man do good works, but ought to restore them home again: as it is said, Esay. LXI.

The entire book is one of the most devout, earnest, and evangelical in the English language; and should be reprinted as a most solid Lutheran devotional work for the people. On every page passages of great force and beauty abound, where we feel Luther back of them, even when unable to trace them to his works, *e. g.:*

"Prayer is a mourning, a longing, and a desire of the spirit to God-ward, for that which she lacketh; as a sick man mourneth and sorroweth in his heart, longing for health. Faith ever prayeth. For after that by faith we are reconciled to God, and have received mercy and forgiveness of God, the spirit longeth and thirsteth for strength to do the will of God, and that God may be honored, his name be hallowed, and his pleasure and will fulfilled. The spirit waiteth and watcheth on the will of God, and ever hath her own fragility and weakness before her eyes; and when she seeth temptation and peril draw nigh, she turneth to God, and to the testament that God hath made to all that believe and trust in Christ's blood."

"God looketh *with what heart* thou workest, and not *what* thou workest." "If thou compare deed to deed, there is difference betwixt washing of dishes, and preaching of the word of God; but as touching to please God, none at all; for neither that, nor this pleaseth, but as far forth as God hath chosen a man, hath put his Spirit in him, and purified his heart by faith and trust in Christ."

"Faith, the mother of all good works, justifieth us before we can bring forth any good work: as the husband marrieth his wife before he can have any lawful children by her."

"Deeds are the fruits of love; and love is the fruit of faith. Love and also the deeds are great or small, according to the proportion of faith. Where faith is mighty and strong, there is love fervent, and faith plenteous: where faith is weak, there love is cold, and the deeds few and seldom, as flowers and blossoms in winter."

The following is an echo of the famous passage in Luther's Preface to Romans (*O es ist ein lebendig, schäftig, thätig, mächtig Ding!*):

"Faith is mighty in operation, full of virtue, and ever working; which also reneweth a man, and begetteth him afresh, changeth him and turneth him altogether into a new nature and conversation; so that a man feeleth his heart altogether altered and changed, and far otherwise disposed than before, and hath power to love that which before he could not but hate, and delighteth in that which before he abhorred; and hateth that which before he could not but love."

IV. *The Obedience of a Christian Man*.

In this treatise, published in 1528, we have been unable to find any translations from Luther, although it is probable that they are to be found. The topics treated are those on which Luther was constantly writing and speaking. It treats, *first*, of the obedience which all subjects (children, wives, civil subjects) should yield, with an Appendix on "The Pope's False Power;" *secondly*, of the duties of rulers (fathers, husbands, masters, landlords, kings and judges), with an appendix on Antichrist; thirdly, the subjects of Penance, Confession, Contrition, Satisfaction, Absolution, Confirmation, Anointing, Miracles and Worshippings of Saints, Prayer, The Four Senses of the Scripture.

In 1529 Anne Boleyn had a copy of this book which she loaned to one of her attendants. It passed from the attendant into the hands of her suitor, and he was detected with it. The book was seized and came into the possession of Cardinal Wolsey, from whom the king, on the intercession of the owner, obtained it. When he had read it, he expressed his great satisfaction. Henry was especially delighted with the manner, in which it enjoined the duty of obedience to rulers. "This book," said he, " is for me and all kings to read." "And in a little time," adds Strype, "the King, by the help of this virtuous lady, by the means aforesaid, had his eyes opened to the truth, to search the truth, to advance God's religion and glory, to abhor the pope's doctrine." Alas! that it was only the interest of the stony-ground hearer.[23]

We cannot forbear giving a few paragraphs of the Preface as indicative of the spirit which animates the book:

"Mark this: If God send thee to the sea, and promise to go with thee, and to bring thee safe to land, he will raise up a tempest against thee, to prove whether thou wilt abide by his word; and that thou mayest feel thy faith, and perceive his goodness. For if it were always fair weather, and thou never brought into such jeopardy, whence his mercy only delivered thee, thy faith would be a presumption, and thou wouldest be ever unthankful to God and merciless unto thy neighbor.

If God promises riches, the way thereto is poverty. Whom he loves, him he chastens; whom he exalts, he casts down; he brings no man to heaven, except he send him to hell first; when he builds, he casts all down first; he is no patcher, he cannot build on another's foundation; he will not work until all be past remedy, that men may see how his hand, his power, his mercy, his goodness and truth, have wrought altogether.

Joseph saw the sun and moon and the eleven stars worshipping him. Nevertheless ere that came to pass, God laid him where he could see neither sun nor moon, neither any star of the sky, and that for years; and also undeservedly: to nurture him, to humble, to make him meek, and to teach him God's ways, and to make him apt and meet for the place and honor, against he came to it, that he might perceive and feel that it came of God, and that he might be strong in the Spirit, to minister it in a godly manner.

He promised the children of Israel a land with rivers of milk and honey, but brought them for the space of forty years into a

---

[23] Strype's *Memorials*, I: 177.

land, where not only rivers of milk and honey were not, but where so much as a drop of water was not.

He promised Daniel a kingdom, and immediately stirred up King Saul against him to persecute him; to hunt him as men do hares with greyhounds, and to ferret him out of every hole, and that for the space of many years. This was to tame him, to make him meek; to kill his lusts; to make him feel other men's diseases; to make him merciful; to make him understand that he was made a king to minister and serve his brethren, and that he should not think that his subjects were made to minister unto his lusts.

Tribulation is our right baptism. We that are baptised in the name of Christ, saith Paul, are baptised to die with him."

V. *Exposition of the Sermon on the Mount.*

In November 1530, during Bugenhagen's absence from Wittenberg, Luther occupied his pulpit, in which he preached a series of sermons on "The Sermon on the Mount." These were published in German in 1532, and in Latin in 1533. In 1532, Tyndale's Exposition appeared. George Joye, whose attempt to pirate Tyndale's translation of the New Testament occasioned an exciting controversy, in Tyndale's life-time asserted that "Luther made it, Tyndale only but translating and powdering it here and there with his own fantasies." This charge, however, is at once seen to be unjust, if we compare the two. The "Exposition" is Tyndale's. The use made of Luther is perfectly legitimate. But it is equally clear that either notes of Luther's discourses, or the printed volume were before Tyndale, and freely used. There are not many passages, where the correspondence is as close as the following:[24]

Luther (*1532*.)	Tyndale (*1532*.)
Gerechtigkeit muss an diesem Ort nicht heissen die christliche Hauptgerechtigkeit, dadurch die Person frumm und angenehm wird fur Gott.	Righteousness in this place is not taken for the principal righteousness of a Christian man, through which the person is good and accepted be-

[24] *Luther's Works*, Erl. Ed., XLIII: 41.

Denn .. diese acht Stuck nicht Anders sind, denn eine Lehre von den Früchten und guten Werken eines Christen, vor welchen der Glaube zuvor muss da sein, als der Baum und Häuptstuck, oder Summa seiner Gerechtigkeit und seligkeit, ohn alle Werk und Verdienst, daraus solche Stuck alle wachsen und folgen mussen.	fore God. For these eight points are but doctrines of the fruits and works of a Christian man, before which the faith must be there, to make righteous without all deserving of works, and as a tree out of which all such fruits and works must spring.

WAS TYNDALE A LUTHERAN?

Dr. Eadie, the eminent commentator of the United Presbyterian Church of Scotland, urges that it is a great wrong to term him such.[25] "It was a mistake of no common magnitude," he says, "to associate the name and work of Tyndale with the name and work of Luther. The mistake, however, can be easily explained, as it was common at the time to call all men Lutherans who showed any leaning towards reformation. The great Reformer had so stamped an image of himself upon the Teutonic movement, that similar tendencies in other lands, were vaguely named after him. Sir Thomas More, King Henry, Lee and Cochlaeus regarded Tyndale as a promoter of Lutheranism, and his testament was loosely spoken of as a translation of Luther's German version. The title page of Sir Thomas More's Dialogue reads: 'Touching the pestilent sect of Luther and Tyndale.' But it is against all evidence to call Tyndale Lutheran, or to aver that his purpose was to promote Lutheranism in his own country. He was no sectarian, was never allied to Luther as colleague or instrument, and nothing was farther from his thoughts than to found a sect and identify his own name with it."

The conception of "Lutheran," here presented by Dr. Eadie, is that of one who went forth from the Church of Rome "to found a sect." Then, Luther himself was not a Lutheran; nor were any of his co-laborers Lutheran. A Protestant theologian who traces its beginnings to a movement in Germany to found a new sect, certainly has a strange view of the Reformation. The name 'Lutheran,' a term of reproach, against which Luther pro-

---

[25] *History of English Bible*, I: 122 sqq.

tested loud and long, became the current name for that pure Scriptural doctrine which Luther asserted and maintained in opposition to the corruptions of the Papacy. Even up to the diet of Augsburg, the hope had not altogether become extinct that the Roman Church would yet return to this doctrine. The Lutheran movement had nothing to do with a separate organization, until the act of its enemies, in casting out those who professed this doctrine as heretics, separated the enemies themselves, from the confessors of the faith of the Gospel.

An appeal is made by Dr. Eadie to a "Protestation," by Tyndale in his revised New Testament of 1534. All, however, that it shows, is, that it is worthy to be placed alongside of similar numerous protestations of Luther. Tyndale says: "I take God which alone seeth the heart to record to my conscience, beseeching Him that my part be not in the blood of Christ, if I wrote, of all that I have written, throughout all my books, aught of an evil purpose of envy, or malice to any man, or to stir up any false doctrine or opinion, in the Church of Christ; or to be author of any sect; or to draw disciples after me; or that I be esteemed or had in price above the least child that is born; save only of pity and compassion I had, on the blindness of my brethren, and to bring them into the knowledge of Christ; and to make every one of them, if it were possible, as perfect as an angel of heaven; and to weed out all that is not planted of our Heavenly Father, and to bring down all that lifted itself against the knowledge of the salvation that is in the blood of Christ."

But this is only an echo of what Luther wrote in 1522: "I beg of you, keep silent about my name; and call yourselves not Lutherans, but Christians. What is Luther? The doctrine is not mine. I have been crucified for no one. St. Paul (1 Cor. 4: 5) will not allow Christians to be called Pauline or Petrine, but only Christians. How have I come to it, that the children of Christ should be called by my miserable name? Not so, dear friend, blot out party names, and be called Christians from him whose doctrine we have." [26] But this was explained the very

---

[26] Erl. Ed. 22: 55.

same year. "True it is that you should not say: 'I am Lutheran, or Popish;' for he has not died for any of you, neither is he your Master, but Christ only, and you should confess Christ. But if you hold that Luther's doctrine is evangelical and the Pope's unevangelical, you must not entirely reject Luther; otherwise, with him, you reject his doctrine which you have learned to know as Christ's doctrine. You must say: 'Whether Luther be rascal or saint, matters not; but his doctrine is not his, but Christ's himself.' You see that the tyrants are trying not merely to destroy Luther, but to exterminate his doctrine; and because of the doctrine, they feel for you and ask you whether you be Lutheran. Here truly you must not waver, but must freely confess Christ, whether he have been preached by Luther, Claus or George. The person, you may let go; but the doctrine, you must confess." [27]

The question, then, is simply as to whether the doctrine of Tyndale was the same as that of Luther. Concerning this, Valentine Ernst Löscher says: "He who has received his knowledge from Luther's writings, and of whom one has no report that he has taught in any article otherwise than Luther, may justly be accounted Evangelical Lutheran, even though he have not lived in full connection with a Lutheran congregation, or we do not have from him a confession concerning every article in controversy." [28] Löscher's information concerning Tyndale, however, is defective. In all the treatises we have noted, his apprehension of the doctrine of justification by faith in all its relations, and of the distinction between Law and Gospel, drawn from Luther, is so clear and full, as to leave little to be desired further. In the "Obedience of a Christian Man," the doctrine of the Sacraments is not treated with the same clearness, and a weakening is already manifest. Luther's statements concerning baptism appear, however, in the foreground: "The washing without the word helpeth not; but through the word it purifieth and cleans-

[27] Ib. 28: 316.
[28] Ausführliche *Historia Motuum*, p. 89.

eth." The influence of his friend John Frith, who had embraced the Zwinglian doctrine made Tyndale hesitate between the two sides. But he plead with Frith to desist from controversy: "Of the presence of Christ's body in the Sacrament, meddle as little as you can, that there appear no division among us. Barnes will be hot against you. The Saxons are sore on the affirmative; whether constant or obstinate, I commit it to God. . . . I would have the right use preached, and the presence to be an indifferent thing. . . . To believe that the body of Christ is everywhere, though it cannot be proved, hurts no man, that worships him nowhere save in the faith of his Gospel." This was written in 1532, two years before his death. The next year, Frith's imprisonment in England induced him to write a defence of his friend's views. Still later he wrote the very mild and moderate treatise called "A Brief Declaration of the Sacraments." It directly argues against the Lutheran doctrine. Frith's influence had gradually overcome that which Luther had so completely held over this retired scholar, while the very extent of his former indebtedness to Luther, and the exaggeration of this debt by enemies, rendered him more apt to find some point on which to assert his independence. But one need only compare Tyndale's writings with Zwingli's, to find how relatively thorough a Lutheran, the former always remained. It was impossible for him to carry out to their consequences what was involved in his later doctrine of the Lord's Supper.

CHAPTER III.

THE POLITICAL COMPLICATIONS.

Henry VIII, a retarding factor. The Divorce Question. Relations to Charles V and Francis I. Wolsey's Antipathy to Catherine. The Pope's embarrassment. Wolsey's Overthrow. The Rise of Cranmer. His Connection with the Cambridge Lutherans, and with the Boleyns. Ambassador to Germany. At Nürnberg. The Reformation, Reformers and *Literati* of Nürnberg. Cranmer finds a wife at Nürnberg. His description of the Order of Worship in one of the Nürnberg churches. The Brandenburg-Nürnberg Order of 1533. Opinions of Theologians and Universities on the Divorce. Melanchthon's Diplomacy. Luther, the Advocate of Catherine. The Smalcald League, and its Confessional Basis. Francis I and the French Lutherans. Melanchthon and Margaret of Navarre. Henry's efforts to enter the League.

THE Evangelical leaven, thus working at the English universities, and carried forth thence, to return to those centers with increased power, was far more influential, than either the indignation deeply felt at the exemption from secular jurisdiction claimed by the Romish clergy, which found expression especially in the protests of Henry Standish, or the resentment of the King at the Pope's refusal to grant him a divorce. The latter factor seems at first sight to overshadow all else, and to have been the actual determining cause which effected the break with Rome. No one can deny that the movement was thereby accelerated. But the interference of the government on the Protestant side, before this had sufficiently matured by a true inward growth, was in the end a misfortune rather than a benefit. If Henry had remained the champion of Rome ten years longer, the independent development of English Protestantism would have been retarded, and been tempered by the fires of persecution until it might have been ready for a complete rejection of hierarchical claims and tendencies. As things were, the external rupture occurring before the inner separation was complete, it had to meet a crisis prematurely, and has ever since suffered from the confusion and compromise between diametrically opposing elements within the same communion, which resulted.

The zeal of Henry VIII on the Pope's side, when Luther's hammer startled a sleeping world, is well known. His controversy with Luther in 1521, instigated probably by Cardinal Wolsey, and entered into by the King in order to exhibit his acquaintance with scholastic theology, obtained as its reward the Papal title of *Defensor fidei*, but with it such a severe handling from the miner's son that it is doubtful whether he felt himself repaid. Only a few years elapse, before we find him in negotiation with the Wittenberg Reformers, in order to support himself against the Pope.

The political side of the question is so important as to demand somewhat extended consideration. Henry VIII, had ascended the throne of England in 1509, being at that time eighteen years old. Seven years before, his elder brother Arthur, had died after a marriage of four months with Catherine of Aragon, daughter of Ferdinand and Isabella of Spain. Political motives doubtless conspired with those of the sordid avarice generally alleged, viz., the retention of the dowry, to influence Henry VII, to marry her to his second son. But as marriage with a brother's wife was clearly forbidden by the canonical law, a dispensation of the Pope was asked, and readily granted in 1503. In 1505 already, when sixteen years old, Henry VIII, had entered protest in these words; "That whereas he, being under age was married to the princess Katherine, yet now coming to be of age, he did not confirm that marriage, but retracted and annulled it, and would not proceed in it, but intended in full form of law to void it and break it off."[1] After his accession, he had the case learnedly argued before him on both sides. The

---

[1] Burnet's *History of the Reformation*, I: 22.

desirability of a close alliance with Spain, and the attractive character of Catherine, for the time silenced all scruples; and the marriage was publicly celebrated June 3d, 1509. Two sons born of this marriage died shortly after birth. Only Mary, afterwards Queen, survived infancy.

It was the great ambition of Henry to control the politics of Europe. His great rival, who in large measure gained the position to which Henry aspired, was the Emperor Charles V. In Charles' opinion, Francis I of France was a more formidable antagonist. Both rulers, therefore, competed for Henry's favor. Charles repeatedly made promises which were never fulfilled. Cardinal Wolsey was twice assured that he would succeed to the Papacy at the very next vacancy; and twice, Charles saw to it that the promise was broken. In 1522, Charles promised to marry his cousin, the princess Mary; but five years later, not being inclined to wait for a bride who was only ten years old, excused himself upon the ground that she was the child of an unlawful marriage.

It was not, then, a mere fancy for Anne Boleyn which suggested the thought of divorce. The same desire to secure an undisputed succession (for so far England had never been ruled by a queen) which led Napoleon to his wrong against Josephine, undoubtedly had much force, augmented, as it was, by the superstitious inferences which he drew from the death of his sons, as a divine judgment because of the supposed unlawful marriage, and by the dogmatic statements of his favorite schoolman, Thomas Aquinas. We have no doubt that he read every sentence of the chapters in the supplement to the *Summa Summarum*, treating "Of the Impediments to Marriage," and that his eye lingered on the conclusion of Art. VI. Quest. LV.: "Preceding affinity not only hinders marriage that is to be contracted but also destroys that which has been already contracted;" and that he weighed carefully the arguments of Art. IX., which insist that the same rule must be applied to affinity as to consanguinity, and that in both cases, the continuance of the marriage, when the original wrong has been discovered, is a mortal sin. Not necessarily a tender conscience, but a regard for that consistency, in which, as the sworn defender of Roman orthodoxy he prided himself, contributed much to the result, and led him even to doubt the Pope's authority to give any dispensation.

But there was a power behind the throne. Wolsey's coarse and licentious character, and his arrogant and arbitrary proceedings were in the highest degree offensive to the pure minded queen ; and a personal antagonism between them was the result. Besides she was not without considerable political influence, the Privy Council being summoned before her at times for the discussion of pending questions. She was a Spaniard; and her sympathies were against France. It was Wolsey's policy, at this period, to make the separation from the Emperor the widest, and, if possible, to form an alliance with France. "If a definitive rupture was to take place between England and the Burgundo-Spanish power, Henry's marriage with Catherine must be dissolved, and room thus made for a French princess. Wolsey formed the plan of marrying his King in Catherine's stead, with the sister or even the daughter of Francis I. When he was in France in 1527, he said to the Regent, the King's mother, that within a year she would live to see two things, the most complete separation of his sovereign from Spain, and his indissoluble union with France." [2]

Such being the case, it was not wonderful that Wolsey's influence with his subordinates, determined the opinion of all the bishops in England, the bishop of Rochester (Fisher) alone excepted, in favor of the divorce. The queen, however, refused to recognize any authority capable of deciding the question, below that of the Pope. Clement VII was reluctant to interfere on either side, and advised Henry to act on his own responsibility; but, at length, after an ineffectual attempt, through his legate, Cardinal Campeggi, to induce Catherine to yield her claims, was compelled to decide against the King, partly in order to

---

[2] Ranke's *England*, I: 122.

maintain the sanctity of papal dispensations, and partly because of the overpowering influence of the Emperor, who in 1527 had humbled his spiritual father, captured Rome and held him prisoner for months. Charles was unyielding in his opposition to the divorce, not only because of their political rivalry, but also because Queen Catherine was his aunt, and, however inconsistent with his own repudiation of Princess Mary in 1522, he regarded Henry's course as an indignity to his family. As the Pope was thus subservient to the Emperor, Henry took matters into his own hands in a sense far different from that to which he had been previously advised by the former. Wolsey fell, horrified that, instead of a French princess, Anne Boleyn was in view, and Thomas Crumwell rose (1530). Archbishop Warham died; and Cranmer was summoned from Germany to succeed, with much reluctance, to the see of Canterbury.

As this brings before us the most prominent figure in the English Reformation, it is fitting that some account of Cranmer should be here given. He was born of an ancient family in Nottingham, July 2d, 1489. His boyhood was largely devoted to the sports and exercises of the English gentry, to which his father belonged. After his father's death, he was sent, at the age of fourteen, to Cambridge, where, until he was twenty-two, his attention was given almost exclusively to the subtilties of scholasticism. After 1511, he fell under the influence of Erasmus. "He gave himself to the reading of Faber, Erasmus, and good Latin authors, four or five years together, unto the time *that Luther began to write.* And then, considering what great controversy was in matters of religion, not only in trifles, but in the chiefest articles of our salvation, be bent himself to try out the truth therein. And forasmuch as he perceived he could not judge indifferently in such weighty matters, without the knowledge of the Holy Scriptures; therefore, before he was infected with any man's opinions or errors, he applied his whole study three years therein. After this, he gave his mind to good writers, both new and old; not rashly running over them; for he was a slow reader, but a diligent marker of whatsoever he read, seldom reading without pen in hand. And whatsoever made either for the one part, or the other, of things in controversy, he wrote it out, if it were short, or at least noted the author, and the place, that he might find it, and write it out at leisure; which was a great help to him in debating of matters ever after. This kind of study, he used till he was made doctor of divinity: which was about the thirty-fourth year of his age. and about the year 1523."[3]

Before this, by marrying, he had lost his fellowship in Jesus' College, and became lecturer in another of the colleges of Cambridge; but his wife dying, he had soon been restored to his old fellowship. He had been selected among the band of scholars (Clark, Cox, Taverner, etc.,) to be transferred to Cardinal Wolsey's new College at Oxford, but declined. He became lecturer on divinity in Jesus' College, and examiner of candidates for theological degrees; and his examination laid special stress upon the candidates' proficiency in Holy Scripture. At this time, Henry called upon the theologians of the Universities for their opinions concerning his divorce. Cranmer was found to be one of the few who from the beginning favored it. The King at once demanded his services, and had him assigned a home at Durham with Sir Thomas Boleyn, father of the future queen, while he wrote a book in the cause of Henry. Boleyn was also an earnest student of the Word of God, as Strype[4] quotes from Erasmus, who, in a letter to Sir Thomas, says: "I do the more congratulate your happiness, when I observe the sacred scriptures to be so dear to a man, as you are, of power, one of the laity and a courtier." Cranmer's home in her father's house, had much to do with Anne Boleyn's future connection with the cause of the Reformation. After this, he had to personally appear and argue the matter in both universities. We next find him engaged in answering a book of Cardinal Pole's against the divorce. Then,

[3] Strype's *Memorials of Archbishop Cranmer*, I: 3.
[4] Ib. p. 8.

in 1530, he was sent on the same mission to France, Italy and Germany. At Rome he remained for several months, but with no success. He soon appears as ambassador from England to Germany.

The Emperor being a long time during the year 1532 at Ratisbon (Regensburg), in attendance on the Diet, Cranmer was with him there, and made visits to the city of Nürnberg, fifty-three miles distant, to confer with the Elector of Saxony, where, of course, he became a deeply interested spectator of all the changes which the Reformation had wrought in that city since its introduction in 1524. At Nürnberg, he found the place of which Luther had written, that it "shines throughout all Germany, like the sun amidst moon and stars," and which Melanchthon had called " *Lumen, oculum, decus et ornamentum praecipuum Germaniae* " Longfellow has sung of it:

Quaint old town of toil and traffic, quaint old town of art and song,
Memories haunt thy pointed gables, like the rooks that round them throng:
Memories of the Middle Ages, when the emperors, rough and bold,
Had their dwelling in thy castle, time-defying, centuries old.

In the church of sainted Sebald, sleeps enshrined his holy dust,
And, in bronze, the Twelve Apostles guard from age to age their trust.

In the church of sainted Lawrence, stands a pix of sculpture rare,
Like the foamy sheaf of fountains, rising through the painted air.

Here when Art was still religion, with a simple, reverent heart,
Lived and labored Albrecht Dürer, the Evangelist of Art;

Emigravit is the inscription on the tombstone where he lies;
Dead he is not—but departed—for the artist never dies.

Here was the Gymnasium that boasted of Melanchthon, as its founder, and at whose dedication, he had delivered the address. Here Staupitz had preached years before, and Luther had visited on his way to Augsburg in 1518. It had been the home of the humanist Perkheimer, who, on account of his friendship for Luther, had been named in the Pope's bull against the reformer. Here Albrecht Dürer the great painter had died in 1528. Among those whom Cranmer doubtless met, was the jurist, Lazarus Spengler, who had been a deputy from Nürnberg to the Diet of Augsburg in 1530. He was the author of the hymn *Durch Adam's Fall ist ganz verderbt*, and had shared Perkheimer's honor of being included in the bull against Luther. Another celebrity of Nürnberg then living, was Hans Sachs.

" Not thy Councils, not thy Kaisers, win for thee the world's regard;
But thy painter, Albrecht Dürer, and Hans Sachs, thy cobbler-bard."

Among the theologians, were Camerarius, the intimate friend, correspondent and biographer of Melanchthon, who was Professor in the Gymnasium, and also had been a deputy to Augsburg; Wenceslaus Link, preacher of St. Sebald's church, and the intimate friend of the Wittenberg reformers; and Andrew Osiander, preacher in St. Lorenz church, who had participated both in the Marburg Colloquy and in the conferences of the theologians at the Diet of Augsburg, with John Brentz, sharing the part of Melanchthon's chief counselor. With Osiander, Cranmer soon became especially intimate. He persuaded him to write in favor of Henry's divorce, and Cranmer, in turn, urged the preparation for publication, of Osiander's "Harmony of the Gospels." Then Osiander's niece captivated the heart of the English ambassador, so that the future Archbishop of Canterbury took to himself a Lutheran wife. The intimacy thus begun, was continued for years. The correspondence was frequent and extended. Long afterwards (1540) Cranmer wrote to Osiander that he was always reproached for whatever faults could be charged upon the German reformers, and "that he was fain to make the best answers he could, either out of their books or out of his own invention."[5]

Cranmer's first visit to Nürnberg was before March 14th, and even then, he closely observed and criticized the Order of Service in use. We learn this from an interesting letter of Sir Thomas Eliot: "Touching Nurenberg, it is the moste propre towne and best ordered publike weale that ever I beheld. . . . Although I had a chaplayn, yet could I not be suffred to have

[5] Strype, *Mem. of Cranmer*, I: 180.

him sing Mass, but was constrayned to here there Mass, which is but one in a churche, and that is celebrate in forme folowing: The Preeste in vestments, after oure manner, singith everi thing in Latine, as we use, omitting suffrages. The Epistel he readeth in Latin. In the meane time, the sub-Deacon goeth into the pulpite and readeth to the people the Epistle in their vulgare; after thei peruse other things as our prestes doo. Than the Preeste redith softly the Gospell in Latine. In the meane space the Deacon goeth into the pulpite, and readith aloude the Gospell in the Almaigne tung. *Mr. Cranmere sayith* it was shewid to him that in the Epistles and Gospels, thei kept not the ordre that we doo, but doo peruse every daye one chapitre of the New Testament. After, the preste and the quere do sing the *Credo* as we doo; the secretes and preface they omitt, and the priest singith, with a high voyce, the wordes of the consecration; and after the Levation, the Deacon torneth to the people, telling to them in Almaigne tunge a longe process how thei shold prepare theim selfes to the communion of the flesh and blode of Christ; and than may every man come that listith, without going to any confession. But I, lest I sholde be partaker of their communyon, departid than, and the Ambassador of Fraunce, which caused all the people in the churche to wonder at us as though we had been gretter heretikes than thei. One thing liked me well (to shew your Grace freely my hart.) All the preestes hadd wyves; and thei were the fayrist women of the towne." [6]

The service, thus described was to be replaced the next year by the Brandenburg-Nürnberg *Kirchenordnung*, in course of preparation that very summer, during which the Würtemberg reformer, John Brentz, spent six weeks in joint labor with Osiander, in the very house where Cranmer met his bride. He heard there the Exhortation to the Communion composed by Wolfgang Volprecht († 1528) who in 1524, had administered the Holy Communion for the first time in both forms, to three thousand persons. This "Exhortation" is familiar to us, from its use in a

---

[6] Ellis, *Original Letters*, III, vol. II: p. 189.

somewhat condensed form in the "Church Book" and "Common Order of Service."

Cranmer having gained the confidence of Osiander was probably admitted into the full knowledge of the grievances from which Osiander was then complaining. Notoriously arbitrary and head-strong, he at first had regarded it his right to prepare a liturgy without any aid or assistance; and the interference of Spengler, in an attempt to secure the co-operation of others, was indignantly resented, until Osiander was at length obliged to yield, and Brentz was called in to mediate. Nor is it improbable that Cranmer learned much of the details of the work in contemplation or even in progress. He certainly knew of the great desire of the Lutheran theologians to unite upon one Common Order of Service, and thus remove the reproach that in our Church, there was nothing but disorder.[7] Cranmer's presence in Nürnberg, therefore, was destined to bear rich fruit in England in years to come.

As Bucer in 1536 dedicated to Cranmer his "Metaphrasis et Enarratio" on the Epistle to the Romans, in a flattering letter, it is probable that about the same time as that of the events above mentioned, they also had met.

But to return to the question of the divorce. The negotiations in which Cranmer was engaged met with varied results. Oxford, after three months controversy, decided just as the King wished. Cambridge, with much difficulty, was induced to follow, the Lutheran element there having been, in Burnet's opinion, a most serious obstacle. Richard Crook was sent to Italy to make researches, examine Greek manuscripts, copy everything in the Fathers relating to degrees of marriage and obtain the opinions of learned Jews. Money was freely used, and bought precisely such opinions as suited Henry. Franciscans, Dominicans, Servites, Conventuals, the University of Padua, the divines of Bononia and Ferrara, the faculty of the Canon Law at Paris, that at the Sorbonne, that of Law at Angiers, of Divinity of Bourges,

---

[7] *Acta Hist. Eccles.* XLIX: 718.

and the whole University of Toulouse, coincided with wonderful harmony. Among the Reformed, Oecolampadius favored, but Bucer opposed the king; Zwingli advised that the marriage be dissolved, yet with the legitimization of the issue born in it. Calvin also declared the marriage void, and advised that the queen be put away. Fortified by these opinions, Cranmer, who, during his stay in Germany, had not succeeded in gaining for his side any Lutheran opinions, except that of Osiander, after holding an ecclesiastical court for the trial of the case, pronounced the marriage null and void (May 23d, 1533). In the succeeding year, 1534, the Papal authority was completely abolished by the necessary legislation, "The Act of Supremacy," investing the King with the supreme headship on earth of the Church of England; while in 1535, Crumwell was made vicegerent for the King in all ecclesiastical matters, outranking even the Archbishop of Canterbury.

The Wittenberg theologians had not been neglected in the request for opinions concerning the divorce. In August and September, 1531, Dr, Robert Barnes, whose open advocacy of Lutheranism already in 1526 has been noticed, appears at Wittenberg on a commission from the king. Melanchthon's opinion of Aug. 23d, shows the general character of this great scholar as an ecclesiastical diplomatist, in seeking a most unfortunate compromise between two antagonistic positions. First he attempts to demonstrate that the prohibition of marriage with the wife of a deceased brother given in Leviticus, belongs to the Ceremonial Law, and is no longer binding. If it were binding, he argues that the other provision compelling a brother to marry his brother's widow, if the first marriage be without children, must also be enforced. Regarding the marriage, therefore, as entirely lawful, he urges that a divorce would be sinful, on the ground that the divine law is immutable in its prohibition of divorce *extra casum adulterii*. The queen must always have the place of a lawful wife; and Mary be regarded a legitimate daughter. But if the succession is to be guarded, he has another remedy to propose. "This can be done without any peril to the conscience or reputation of any one, by *polygamy* (! ! !). Although I would not concede polygamy as a common matter, yet in this emergency, on account of its great advantage to the kingdom, possibly on account of the conscience of the king, I say that it would be safest for the king to marry a second, without repudiating his first wife. . . . Abraham, David and other holy men had many wives," etc.[8] In our admiration of the rare gifts of Melanchthon, and the eminent service which he rendered the cause of Christ, we ought not to close our eyes to the mistakes into which he was often betrayed whenever he entered the field of politics, and allowed considerations of temporary expediency to prevail. Luther's judgment of two weeks later shows how deeply he was exercised by the wrong proposed. "If the adversaries carry the king with them, let *our men* try with all their might at least to keep the queen from in any way consenting to the divorce. Let her rather die than become an accomplice to such a crime in God's sight, and let her most firmly believe that she is the true and legitimate Queen of England, made so by God himself. If they cannot save the king (which may God avert), let them at least save the soul of the queen, so that if the divorce cannot be prevented she may bear this great evil as her cross, but in no way approve or consent to it. Since I can do nothing else, my prayer is directed to God that Christ may hinder this divorce and make void the counsels of Ahithopel in persuading it, and that the queen may have firm faith and constant assurance that she is and will be Queen of England, even though the gates of the world and of hell may oppose."[9] As to the succession, Luther suggests what Henry may have recalled years afterwards, when he asks as to what assurance the king has that the child of any other marriage would be a son.[10] While there is one clause in his opinion of eleven pages, declaring that even polygamy

---

[8] Mel. *Opera*, C. R. II: 520-537.
[9] De Wette's *Luther's Briefen*, IV: 306.
[10] Ib. p. 296.

would be preferable to a divorce, there is no more evidence of such an expedient being seriously proposed by Luther as it was by Melanchthon, than that he advised suicide when he declared that the queen should die rather than become an accomplice to a crime. We are at once impressed by the candor of Luther, when contrasted with the course of the Pope. The latter sought to evade the difficulty by persuading the queen to surrender her claims; the former urges that the queen especially must be urged not to yield an hair's-breadth. To him it is a question neither of ecclesiastical nor civil policy, but one of fidelity in his testimony to the truth involved. There is another judgment given by the entire body of Wittenberg theologians, found in Burnet's History, Vol. II: Doc. No. 35, and in Melanchthon's Works, C. R. II: 523, which shows such a divergence in the character of the arguments adduced, so that though the conclusion is the same, some of the premises have been entirely changed, that the difference would be inexplicable, if we had not the clue given in Seckendorf,[11] that in the archives at Weimar, the original is dated 1536, a suggestion which is confirmed by the fact that it is not the single legate of 1531, but the three legates of 1535 and 1536, who are there mentioned.

These answers, however, did not repel the king of England from seeking further aid at Wittenberg when he needed it. Although the Pope had been defied, Henry dreaded far more the wrath of the Emperor, and sought for such Continental alliances as might strengthen his position. The Smalcald League had been formed, March 29th, 1531, between the Lutheran confederates, the Elector of Saxony, the Dukes Philip Ernst and Franz of Brunswick-Lüneburg, the Landgrave Philip of Hesse, Prince Wolfgang of Anhalt, Counts Gebhardt and Albrecht of Mansfeld, and the cities of Strassburg, Ulm, Constance, Reutlingen, Memmingen, Lindau, Biberach, Issni, Lübeck, Magdeburg and Bremen. On July 23d, 1532, the league concluded with the Emperor the Religious Peace of Nürnberg, guaranteeing, until

[11] III: 212.

the convening of a General Council, peace to all the Confederates by name, upon the stipulation that "they make no further and other innovation beyond the *Confession*, Assent [12] and *Apology* presented at Augsburg, and that which agrees therewith, according to a lawful, Christian and just sense, and that they introduce no ceremonies adverse to, or which do not agree with the *Augsburg Confession and the Apology*." [13]

These terms by no means satisfied the Landgrave, and a number of the theologians, as Urbanus Riegius, Erhard Schnepf, Antony Corvinus, etc., who were averse to the acceptance of any pledge of peace which did not secure protection also for all who should hereafter accept the Confessional basis, Riegius maintaining that the peace proposed was worse than war. [14] But Luther urged the more moderate course, and succeeded in having it adopted. [15]

The League thus formed became a very important factor in the politics of Europe. It was to the interest of both Francis I. of France, and Henry VIII., to have its sympathy and co-operation in their plans against the Emperor, or, at least, to prevent its members from giving the Emperor their support. Francis, in order to break the confederacy between the Pope and the Emperor, had in October, 1533, formed a compact with the former at Marseilles, according to which his son, Henry, married Catherine de Medici, the niece of the Pope. But his plans failed by the death of Clement VII. in the succeeding October. Foiled thus in his efforts to use the Papal power against the Emperor, he next turned to the Lutheran princes. In February, 1535, he wrote to them a long letter, among other things apologizing for the persecution of the French Lutherans, by the assurance that no German within his realm has suffered. [16] Then follows some

---

[12] "This term added because of those who after the diet of 1530, had assented to the Confession." *Seckendorf*, III : 24.

[13] Ib. pp. 24, 25.

[14] Ib. p. 22.

[15] Ib.; De Wette's *Luther's Briefen*, IV : 369, 373, 380.

[16] For letter, see C. R. II : 828.

correspondence between Melanchthon and Cardinal Bellay, resulting in an invitation to the former to visit France in order to effect an agreement in doctrine with the French theologians. Even prior to these negotiations, in the preceding August, Melanchthon, possibly at the suggestion of Margaret of Navarre, sister of Francis, and favorably disposed to the Lutheran cause, had transmitted an outline of doctrine according to which he proposed to reconcile the differences. But as cruelties towards Protestants in France were not abated, and the princes deemed the pledges even of the Emperor more trustworthy than any that could be offered by the king, Melanchthon's desire to accept the invitation was denied by the Elector. At the meeting of the Smalcald League in December, Cardinal Bellay is present with new propositions,[17] only to hear his schemes, intended purely for political expediency, answered by the admirable Confession that "the League had been established among them for no other reasons than for the pure Word of God, and for preserving and propagating the sound doctrine of faith." Bent on war, however, Francis at last found an ally in the Turks; and hostilities began in 1536.

These difficulties of the Emperor were propitious to Henry, and he hastened to make the best of them. If he could only be admitted into the Smalcald League, and be made its chief, he imagined that he would soon humble both Pope and Emperor, and that Francis also might be made pay a severe penalty for not having espoused his cause. For the League had begun to show an aggressive spirit. The Emperor's brother, Ferdinand, had been compelled by the Landgrave to surrender the royal power of Würtemberg, and to restore it to Duke Ulrich, who in 1534, introduced the Reformation. The League itself was just about extending its provisions to the limits for which Riegius and his associates had so urgently plead to no effect in 1532. The purpose was being formed which at last was regularly adopted in December, 1535, in the enactment "that all be received into the

---

[17] C. R. II: 1009 sqq.

League who have applied for admission, or shall hereafter apply, provided that they purely, freely and openly confess God and his Gospel, love peace, and live as becomes honorable and upright men." [18]

[18] *Seckendorf*, III: 100.

CHAPTER IV.

THE ENGLISH COMMISSION TO WITTENBERG.

Preliminary Negotiations. Melanchthon's letter to Henry VIII. Renewed Negotiations, and Correspondence. Melanchthon invited to England. The Augsburg Confession as a Basis of Union. The Third Series of Negotiations. Sketches of Fox and Heath. The Oration of Fox. The The Thirteen Articles of 1535. Henry entangled in his own toils. The Discussions at Wittenberg. Diplomacy vs. Faith. The Augsburg Confession under Debate. The Ambassadors won. The *Repetitio.* Chief difficulty, with the articles on "Abuses." Henry demands an Amendment. The Convention at Frankfort. The Proposed Embassy to England.

WE have thus far noticed how the truly evangelical element connected with the English Reformation was working at those great centers of religious thought and life, the two great English universities, notwithstanding all the opposition which the power of the government could interpose, until finally political motives caused Henry's break with the Pope, and induced him to try to turn to his own service, and to control and lead the very movement against which he had been previously·arrayed. Unchanged in principle, and guided solely by secular considerations, he sought to be the head of Protestantism, not only in his own land, but on the Continent, and to direct its course in a channel far different from that which it first took, when, with irrepressible force, the yearning of the heart for the assurance of forgiveness of sins burst through the bonds which had been interposed between the sin-burdened soul and its God.

In accordance with this plan of Henry to become master of the Lutheran Smalcald League, Dr. Robert Barnes, was on March 11th, 1535, once more in Wittenberg. Melanchthon writes on that date to his friend Camerarius, and inserts several Greek sentences to the effect that "a stranger has come to us, sent from Britain, treating only of the second marriage of the king; but, as he says, the king has no concern for the affairs of the Church," and then he adds in Latin: "There is this advantage about it, that no cruelty is now exercised against those of the purer doctrine."[1] Two days later Melanchthon, at the suggestion of Dr. Barnes, wrote Henry a letter[2] whose terms of extravagant praise of the king recall the sagacious diplomat rather than the sober and discriminating theologian. "Your Royal Majesty ought justly to be loved by all good men on account of your eminent moderation and justice." His reign is praised as "the golden age" of Britain. Then after having completely fulfilled in many words of flattery, the rule of the great Latin writer on Oratory, first to make the hearer well-disposed, he introduces the suggestion, to which Archbishop Laurence in his Bampton Lectures on The Thirty-nine Articles,[3] ascribes the origin of the formularies of faith which were promulgated during the reign of Henry. "I have no doubt," he writes, "that the controversies concerning religion would be mitigated if your Royal Majesty were to use your authority both to bend other kings to moderation and to deliberate with learned men concerning the kind of doctrine. For it is in no way a doubtful matter that some abuses which are not to be dissembled, have insinuated themselves into the church, and that kings are not taking pains to *have a simple and sure form of doctrine issued*"; and then he adds that "care ought to be taken that cruelty be not inflicted upon good men." In August, Melanchthon dedicates to Henry the edition of his *Loci* of 1535, not as a patron, but as a censor, whom in the most courtly language he asks to study and criticise the book. The

---

[1] C. R. II: 851.
[2] C. R. II: 861–864.
[3] "Nor is it too much to suppose, that the formularies of faith, which were promulgated in the reign of Henry, originated in the advice of Melanchthon, as contained in a letter to that Prince, dated March 3, [13] 1535." *Archbishop Laurence's Lectures*, Fourth Edition, Oxford, 1853, p. 200.

whole document is a most earnest plea for attention above all things to reformation in doctrine. "It is manifest," he writes, "that some chief articles of Christian doctrine have lain for a long time enveloped in densest darkness. When the works of some learned and good men began to be produced from this, at once unusual severity, unworthy of the lenity which should characterize the Church, began to be exercised. Not only are good and learned men put to death, and abuses confirmed, but zeal for Christian doctrine is altogether extinguished."—"Good and wise princes should seek for suitable remedies. Why is it that they are under any obligations to preserve the Church for posterity? This Church will indeed be rent asunder in infinite ways, unless some plan be adopted for the *propagation to posterity, of a godly and sure form of doctrine.*" "I have thought it of the highest importance to present this document to you, the most learned of all kings, that from it, rather than from the calumnies of others, your Majesty may form a judgment concerning me, and the entire kind of doctrine, with which I am employed."[4] Diplomatic as the methods of Melanchthon are, yet back of them we find the earnest effort to win the king and his kingdom over to the truth of the Gospel. His heart is set upon the propagation of the pure doctrine of God's Word, and not upon any scheme of ecclesiastical polity, or any other external relations. The book was entrusted to Alexander Alesius, a Scotchman, to carry, together with a letter to Cranmer, to England.

About the middle of September, while the plague was raging at Wittenberg, Dr. Barnes returned with a three-fold proposition:

1. Would an embassy or ambassador be received, who would be sent for the purpose of conferring calmly with Dr. Luther and the others doctors concerning certain articles?

2. Would Melanchthon be allowed to visit England, in order to confer with the King?

3. The King would not be averse to connection with the Smal-

[4] C. R. II: 921 sqq.

cald League, provided a place were accorded him proportioned to his rank, and the articles of faith which the League was pledged to defend, were transmitted to him.

Even Luther becomes sanguine as to the result, and unites with Jonas, Cruciger and Bugenhagen in a most urgent petition that the Elector give Dr Barnes an audience. "Who knows," they write, "what God will work? His wisdom is higher, and his will better than ours." [5]

The Elector's answer to Dr. Barnes, of September 21st, is important:

1. The doctors of the University shall be directed to meet the proposed legate, attentively hear him, and confer with him in the spirit of love.

2. The question concerning Melanchthon's leave of absence must be deferred until after the return of the other professors to Wittenberg.

3. The terms of the admission of the King of England into the League cannot be decided by the Elector, since he can act only for himself; and has no authority to speak for his colleagues. But one thing is sure. If the King and the Elector are to be members of the League at the same time, the former must be prepared to cordially accept and subscribe the Augsburg Confession. "We will never reject the correct and pure doctrine of the Gospel, useful to the Church, which both our Most Illustrious Fathers and we, with the other allies, confessed at the Diet of Augsburg before the Most Invincible Emperor, our Most Clement Lord, and the other princes and the States of the Roman Empire." [6]

On leaving, Dr. Barnes took with him a letter written for the Elector by Melanchthon, September 26th, professing much affection for the king, not only because of the unbroken friendship between the rulers of Saxony and the Kings of England, but chiefly "since we have learned that your Serene Highness is

---

[5] De Wette's *Luther's Briefen*, IV: 633.
[6] C. R. II: 942.

possessed of a great desire *to reform the doctrine of religion.* For this is a care especially worthy the highest kings; nor can they who govern states, render God any service more grateful. Nor can it be dissembled that many faults have for many generations insinuated themselves into the Church, through the negligence and cupidity of the Roman pontiffs, and that these have need to be corrected. If your Serene Majesty, therefore, will devote his zeal *to reforming the doctrine* and correcting ecclesiastical abuses, he will in the first place make a most pleasing sacrifice to God, and, in the second, will deserve well from the whole Church, and all posterity."[7]

A few days later (October 1st), Henry, using his new title of "Supreme Head on Earth of the English Church," acknowledges Melanchthon's courtesy in the dedication of his *Loci*, by a brief note, assuring him of the gratification it had afforded, complimenting the author's learning, but affording no trace of any serious attention paid to the treatment of doctrine.[8] The letter was accompanied by a present of two hundred crowns, and the promise that Crumwell would communicate with him further. Burnet regards Melanchthon's invitation to England at this time, simply as a plan which Henry had adopted to counteract the effect upon Melanchthon and the Elector, of the similar invitation which had been received from the French king.

The King of England had thus far been made to plainly understand that, while the Lutheran princes and theologians were kindly disposed to the English people, and deeply interested in their welfare, questions of faith and the reformation in doctrine overshadowed all others, and no union could be even for a moment entertained that had not as its basis the unreserved acceptance of the Confessional basis laid at Augsburg. This will still further appear in what is to follow.

Early in November 1535, there were further conferences with Barnes and other English legates.[9] Melanchthon, who so often

[7] Ib. 944.
[8] Ib. 948.
[9] C. R. II: 967 sqq.

was called into service to prepare State papers in which religious questions were involved, wrote for the Elector on November 17th, a letter which accepted the professed earnestness of the king, in regard to a religious reform as though it were serious, and informed him that so far as he and his associates were concerned their purpose is: "In this cause, nothing else but that the glory of Christ may be proclaimed, and godly and sound doctrine, harmonizing with the Holy Scriptures be restored to the whole world. . . . Let not the King of England have the least doubt but that the confederated princes and states are of such a mind, that since, by God's blessing, they have learned to know the truth of the gospel, so also they will use all care and diligence, throughout all life in defending this holy and godly doctrine, and, by God's help, will never depart from the truth which they have learned. It is, indeed, very agreeable for the princes and confederated states to learn that the King also desires to aid the pure doctrine; and they pray that he may continue in this opinion." Then, after stating how necessary harmony among the members of the League on this subject, is, he continues: "Nor do those embraced in this confederation have among them any dissent in doctrine or opinions with respect to faith, and they hope by God's aid to persevere and be harmonious in that doctrine which they confessed at the Diet of Augsburg before the Emperor and the entire Roman Empire."

They close by expressing their great gratification that the King of England is of such a mind as to desire to agree with them in the matter of Evangelical religion and doctrine, being ready to declare, on every possible occasion his favor in, and zeal for, this most holy cause, as becomes a King of Christian and evangelical doctrine, and to afford with the greatest diligence every means for advancing the cause of the Gospel."

Two more influential English commissioners now appeared upon the scene, representing more directly Henry than did Dr. Barnes in whom the King had thus far used an agent, already committed to Lutheranism, and serviceable chiefly because it was supposed that he would most likely be heard by the Reformers. Among the English clergy of that period, the names of Edward Fox and Nicholas Heath, are of the very first rank.

Fox was unquestionably one of the most brilliant men of his day. A graduate of Eton and Cambridge, his very first sermon had so captivated the King that he at once became his chaplain. He had been the King's Almoner, as well as Secretary of State. His gifts shone especially in the pulpit, where "his exposition was so thorough and clear, that the inference might be drawn that all his time was occupied with Biblical studies; his division was so analytical, as to give the impression that his attention had been devoted chiefly to Logic; while his development was as rich in thought, as though he had laid all the fathers and schoolmen under contribution." [10]

Cooper, in his *Athenae Cantabrigienses*, says, that he was called "the wonder of the University and darling of the court," that "he had a vast capacity for business and was an able and suitable negotiator," and that his skill as a diplomatist expressed itself in several proverbs that have become current phrases with posterity, as "The surest way to peace is a constant preparedness for war;" "Two things support a government; Gold to reward its friends, and iron to keep down its enemies;" "Time and I, will challenge any in the world," etc. He had been sent by Wolsey to Rome in 1518 to negotiate with the Pope concerning the proposed divorce. He had been the prominent member of an embassy to France. He was largely instrumental in discovering Cranmer, and starting the series of events by which the latter became Primate of the English Church. He had fought the battle of Cambridge where after a long resistance, the nullity of the first marriage was affirmed. Although greatly distrusted by the Elector and Melanchthon, this visit to Germany seems to have decided his theological position, as after his return to England, he becomes the leading representative of Lutheran opinion

---

[10] H. L. Benthem's *Neu-eröffneter Engeländischer Kirch und Schulen-Staat*, p. 889 sqq.

in the negotiations that follow, and in the preparation of Henry's first formulary; even though he be open to the charge of inconsistency. Unfortunately his career was but a brief one, as he died in 1538.

The third of the envoys especially fascinated Melanchthon, who in his private letters cannot speak in sufficiently high terms of his scholarship and character. Nicholas Heath, (born about 1501), educated at Oxford and Cambridge, had been chaplain to Wolsey, and at the time when sent to Germany, was Heury VIII's own chaplain. After some wavering, in 1548 he identified himself with the Roman Catholic side; in 1555 became Archbishop of York, and afterwards Lord High Chancellor of England. It was Heath who, under the reign of Mary, was to issue the writ for the execution of Cranmer. No less than two hundred and seventeen persons were to be put to death for Evangelical convictions when he would hold the seal. The executor of Queen Mary, he was made a member of the Privy Council at the beginning of the reign of Elizabeth; but was soon committed to the tower and excommunicated. After his release he lived in retirement until his death in 1579.

Such were the ambassadors with whom the Lutheran theologians were to treat. At first Luther and Melanchthon were directed to meet them at Jena, but Wittenberg was finally designated as the place of conference. Meanwhile, however, the convention of the League was held at Smalcald. The English commission was present, and on the 24th of December, Fox, as their spokesman, delivered an oration. Notes of it were taken by Spalatin. He claimed that he and his associates were present, not on behalf of a human cause, but for the sake of the Word of God and truth. He showed with what incredible zeal and love in religious matters, their sovereign had been actuated, and how anxious he was to co-operate with the other princes in propagating the pure knowledge of God. The King, he says, does not heed the slanders which have been published concerning the members of the League, but esteems them as evangelical men, who would neither design, nor commit anything unworthy of themselves as confessors the Gospel. The King acknowledges the abuses in the Church of England, and is endeavoring to reform them. The cause and work of English Christians is the same as that of their brethren in Germany. They should aim at perfect harmony, and, as its basis, should endeavor to come to an understanding touching matters of Christian doctrine. Concert of action should also be determined, if possible, concerning the proposed Council. Peace and harmony of Christian doctrine constitute, however, the very first thing, which, above all others, is to be settled."[11] Certainly a most admirable speech!

On the next day, Christmas, Melanchthon prepared a paper for the Princes which, after being amended, was adopted, and subscribed both by the Elector and Landgrave, and the English ambassadors, as "The Thirteen Articles of 1535."

As the translation, given in Strype's Memorials of the Reformation,[12] is defective, we translate anew from the Corpus Reformatorum:[13]

"I. That the Most Serene King promote the Gospel of Christ, and the pure doctrine of faith according to the mode in which the Princes and confederated States confessed it *in the diet of Augsburg, and defended it according to the published Apology*, unless perhaps some things meanwhile justly seem to require change or correction from the Word of God by the common consent of the Most Serene King, and the princes themselves.

II. Also, That the Most Serene King, together with the Princes and States confederated, *defend and maintain the doctrine of the gospel mentioned*, and ceremonies harmonizing with the gospel in a future general council.

III. That neither the Most Serene King, without the express consent of the confederated princes and states mentioned, nor the confederated princes and states mentioned, without the ex-

---

[11] Ib. pp. 1028 sqq.
[12] Ib. V: pp. 559 sqq.
[13] II: pp. 1032 sqq.

press consent of the Most Serene King mentioned, consent or assent to any call for a general council, which the Pope of Rome, present or future, or any one else, whatever be the pretence of authority, now makes or shall make, nor agree to any place of a future Council, or to the Council itself, but that all these things be conducted and done with the advice and consent of the King and princes, provided, nevertheless, that if certainly, and by just arguments and reasons, it appear that such a Christian, free and general council have been called, as the confederates demand in their answer to Peter Paulus Vergerius, the ambassador of the Pope of Rome, such council is not to be refused.

IV. Also, if it should happen that, without the consent of the Most Serene King and the confederated states, concerning the place of the council, or the calling of the council, and yet, the Pope of Rome and the other princes, joined with him in this matter should determine to proceed to the convening of the council or rather caucus (*conciliabuli*), and that, too, in a place upon which the aforesaid Most Serene King, princes and states have not agreed, that then, and in that case, the aforesaid Most Serene King, as well as the aforesaid Most Illustrious Princes and States confederate shall first strive with all their power, that such calling be hindered and brought to nought, and reach no result.

V. Secondly that they will make public and formal protests, and, likewise, cause them to be made by their clergy, by which they will both prove the purity of their faith, and that they dissent altogether from such convocation, nor, if such council actually follow, will they be bound by the decrees or constitutions of that council, nor, in the future, will they, in any way, obey the same.

VI. Besides, that they never will obey or permit their subjects to obey any decrees, mandates or sentences, bulls, letters or briefs, from any council thus convoked and held, or which proceed in the name of the Bishop of Rome himself or any other power, but that they will account and declare all such writings, decrees, bulls and briefs null and void, and, to remove all scandal, will cause such to be thus declared to the people by their bishops and preachers.

VII. Also, that as the Most Serene King is, by the grace of God, *united, both in Christian doctrine and in its confession* with the confederated princes and states, so also is he deemed worthy, on honorable conditions, to be associated with their league in such manner that his Most Serene Majesty obtain the name and place of Defender and Protector of said league.

VIII. Also, that neither the aforesaid Most Serene King, nor the aforesaid Most Illustrious Princes or States confederated, ever will recognize, maintain or defend that the primacy or monarch be held to-day or ever hereafter *de jure divino*. Nor will they ever agree or concede that it is expedient for the Christian State that the bishop of Rome be over all the rest, or hereafter exercise, in any way, any jurisdiction whatever in the realms or dominions of the aforesaid Kings and Princes.

IX. Also, if it should so happen, that war or any other contention, whether on account of religion, or even without such cause, for any other cause or matter whatsoever, should be excited or carried on by any prince, state or people, against the aforesaid Most Serene King, his realms, dominions or subjects, or, also, against the aforesaid Most Illustrious Princes or States confederated, that neither of the parties mentioned bring aid, or supplies against the other party, nor by advice or favor, directly or indirectly, publicly or privately, assist prince or people, thus invading and waging war.

X. Also that the Most Serene King see fit, for the defence of the league and of the cause of religion, to contribute and deposit with these most illustrious princes, sureties being afforded, as is added below, the sum of 100,000 crowns; the half of which money, it shall be lawful for the confederates to use, whenever there shall be need, for the purpose of defence. The other half, the confederates shall take of such money, as they themselves have contributed and deposited to that sum.

XI. That if there be need of a longer defence because of the continuation of war, or the invasion of enemies, in such event, since princes and confederates are under obligation not only for a further contribution of money, but also for mutual defence with their bodies and all their resources and property, the Most Serene King would not refuse, in urgent necessity, to contribute even more, viz. a second 100,000 crowns. This money, nevertheless, the confederates may use to the amount of one half, with their own. And should it so happen, that the war should end earlier, then what is left should be faithfully kept, and be mentioned to the Most Serene King at the conclusion of the confederation.

XII. That if the King would have it so done, the Princes promise that they will pledge with sufficient sureties, not only that they will not convert such money to another use than for the defence of the league and the cause of religion together with their own money, which they contribute in such confederation, but also that they will faithfully pay and restore to the same Serene Majesty, whatever sum either, be not needed, or that remains after the defence, in case it shall not have been devoted to that use.

XIV. Also, since the Most Revered Legates of the Most Serene King are to remain for a time in Germany, and are to confer with men learned in sacred literature on certain articles, the princes ask that they would as soon as possible inquire and learn the mind and opinion of the Most Serene King, concerning the conditions presented in the League, and, that when they have been informed thereon, they would signify it to us, the Elector of Saxony, and the Landgrave of Hesse. When this is done, the Princes will immediately send legates in their own name and that of the confederated States, to the Most Serene King, and among them one of eminent learning, not only to diligently confer with His Most Serene Royal Majesty on the articles of Christian doctrine, and to deliberate faithfully concerning changing, establishing and ordaining other ceremonies in the Church, but also to agree and conclude with His Most Serene Majesty concerning all the articles whereof we have spoken."

                                  Edward Herefordens,
                                  Nicolaus Heyth,
                                  Antonius Barns,
John Frederick, Elector.   Philip, L. of Hesse." [14]

The English King was certainly placed in an embarassing position, as men who dissemble, so often are. His ambassadors' word had been received in good faith, that he was anxious chiefly about a reform of doctrine, and wished the aid of Lutheran theologians; and accordingly, measures to which his representatives feel themselves constrained to assent, were taken to aid him in the important work. Yet a letter of Crumwell at this time, preserved in Burnet,[15] declares: "The King, knowing himself to be the learnedest prince in Europe, thought it became not him to submit to them, but them to submit to him." The matter however, has assumed the shape that Fox and Heath, with Barnes, are to spend several months in theological conferences at Wittenberg, studying the Augsburg Confession and Apology, under the instructions of Melanchthon, and that then if they can accept such basis, some competent Lutheran doctor is to go to England to help them to complete the work. So scheme was met by scheme, the children of light being for once as wise as the children of this generation; for the English historian is perfectly justified in his inference, that the coolness of the Elector came from the impression, that "the King had only a political design in all this negotiation, intending to bring them into a dependence on himself, without any sincere intentions with relation to religion."[16] However, this may be, the course of our princes and theologians in this matter was perfectly clear and consistent. It was solely on questions of religion that they had been forced into a seeming opposition to the Emperor. On these and these

---

[14] C. R. II: 1032 sqq. "XIII" is not found in the document.
[15] *Burnet's History*, II: 698.
[16] Ib. p. 699.

only, they were ready to stand or fall. They were unwilling to be embarassed by any alliances that were based on any other grounds. Every convert to these principles, even though the Pope himself, they were ready to welcome to the League; every one, who sought the friendship of the League from other motives, whether he were the King of France, or the King of England, might as well understand from the beginning that he could not enter. These religious principles on which their League was founded, they had clearly defined already at Augsburg. Every applicant, therefore, was simply asked to read the platform there presented in the Confession and Apology; and his future relation to the League must be decided by his willingness or unwillingness to subscribe what was there set forth. Nor must any opportunity of winning over to the truth those who had come to them from what were probably other reasons than a regard to God's honor, be neglected. They would accept these ambassadors on their professions, however much they distrusted them, and devote on the part of the theologians, months of time and labor, and on the part of the Elector, the expense of the entertainment of royal commissioners in a style becoming their rank, even though he found it a heavy burden.

After the adjournment of the Smalcald League, the English ambassadors accordingly repaired to Wittenberg. The beginning of the conference there was delayed until the close of January, partially because of the absence of Melanchthon on a tour of investigation and counsel concerning the Anabaptists. Antonius Musa wrote from Jena on the day after Melanchthon's departure for Wittenberg that "he is to discuss at Wittenberg the subject of 'Private Mass.' For the King of England has sent a bishop with several learned men to present their argument, and to endeavor to show that Private Mass ought to be retained. The King of England *has become a Lutheran to this extent*, viz., that since the Pope would not approve his divorce, he has forbidden all men in his realm at the peril of their lives to regard the Pope as Supreme Head of the church, but commanded them to regard himself instead. All other papistical affairs, monasteries, masses, indulgences, prayers for the dead, etc., they not only retain in England, but even obstinately defend. On this account, ambassadors have been sent to fortify and defend masses in a public disputation at Wittenberg." [17] Even after Melanchthon's return however, on January 15th, there was a reluctance of the ambassadors to proceed to serious work. On January 21st, they assured Melanchthon that they were ready to begin the discussion " of each article of doctrine in order," [18] yet it is not for weeks that they are disposed to treat on any other subject than the legitimacy of the king's divorce. "They are excessively fond of quibbling," Melanchthon writes. Luther's letters show how greatly he was annoyed by their course. First, he speaks playfully of the great importance that must be attached to the opinion of himself and his associates, in that while eleven universities have already given their decisions, it seems that all the world will be lost, "unless we poor beggars, the Wittenberg theologians, be heard." [19] He is determined, however, not to recede from his former opinion that the first marriage was legitimate, but "in other respects I will show myself not unfriendly towards them, in order that they may not think that we Germans are stone or wood." Melanchthon testifies at first that "Luther lovingly embraces them, and is even delighted by their courtesy." But he becomes vexed that in three days they do not finish the entire matter, stating that in four weeks he had completed much more important business than that which occupies them twelve years; [20] and is indignant at the expense occasioned the elector by their entertainment. [21] Melanchthon grew weary of waiting for the discussion on matters of doctrine, and after two weeks at Wittenberg returns to Jena to continue his conflict with the Anabaptists. He

[17] C. R. III: 12.
[18] Ib. p. 26.
[19] De Wette's, *Luther's Briefen*, IV: 663, 668.
[20] C. R III: 26.
[21] De Wette's *Luther's Briefen*, IV: 671.

wrote to his friends that nothing at all has been under consideration but the divorce.[22] Heath followed Melanchthon to Jena. The latter was much gratified by the visit; and on February 10th, returned to Wittenberg. The whole plan of the English ambassadors was probably arranged for the purpose of gaining time, so as to receive instructions from England. They must have soon perceived that any attempt to have the Lutheran theologians justify the divorce was useless. We can scarcely conceive that they could have had in thought a bargain by which, if the divorce were endorsed by the Lutherans, every confessional requirement would then be at once met by the Anglicans, and the Augsburg Confession and Apology be received for the English Church. It would be a more charitable interpretation to regard the ambassadors as sympathizing more or less with the reform in doctrine, and hoping to win over their sovereign to the faith which they recognize as truth, by obtaining from the Wittenberg theologians a concession which would have been sure to have greatly gratified him. Had the divorce been endorsed, it is probable that the English Church would have been pledged to the Augsburg Confession and the Apology!

However this may have been, the critical examination of the Augsburg Confession article by article, and the earnest discussion of the points of divergence began at length shortly after Melanchthon's second return, and continued throughout the entire month of March. Strype is altogether in error, when he states: "The ambassadors returned home in January, excepting Fox, who, it seems, stayed behind,"[23] as both Melanchthon's and Luther's letters of that period will at once show. Melanchthon again and again speaks of his discussions with them, and especially names Heath; and at the very close of the month (March 30th,) writes: *Sic me Angli exercent, vix ut respirare liceat.*[24]

On the 28th, of that month, Luther sent to the Elector a translation of the articles on which they had been able to agree,[24]

---

[22] Ib.
[23] *Memorials*, I: 367.
[24] C. R. III: 53.

and stated that the English ambassadors before proceeding further, had referred the last four articles to the king, since if any serious modification of them were required, further conference was useless. Two days later, Melanchthon wrote that "the contention between them had not been light, but, nevertheless, there was an agreement concerning most things."[25] Seckendorf[26] gives more ample details: "They made an examination of all the articles of the Augsburg Confession, and the opinions of Luther and his colleagues seem to have been given on all things . . . There is extant a Repetition and Exegesis of the Augsburg Confession, elaborated by the Wittenbergers, and received and carried home by the Anglican legates. . . . In addition to the Repetition[27] of the Augsburg Confession, the Wittenberg theologians elaborated the most troublesome articles into special dissertations." Among other stipulations upon which they agreed was not only the denial of the power of the Pope by divine law, but also the promise that neither side would under any consideration maintain any pre eminence of the bishop of Rome over other bishops, as useful or expedient.[28] Although Fox affirmed that there had been an abrogation in England of godless pontifical abuses and especially of indulgences, Melanchthon in one of the dissertations referred to, expressed his astonishment that in the English decree no reformation of the abuses of the Mass was proposed. For on reading Henry's decree, the Wittenberg theologians saw at a glance that only the less important had been touched upon, while the chief abuses had all been retained.[29] Melanchthon writes on the margin the very significant Greek words *ouden hygies*, "nothing sound."

[25] Ib. p. 683.
[26] I p. 111. sq.
[28] Ib. p. 112.
[27] Of this "Repetitio," however, we can find no trace, the document ordinarily known as the "Rep. Aug. Conf.," being the Saxon Confession of 1551. See Feuerlin, p. 250. Strype regards it confined to the doctrine of the Lord's Supper.
[29] *Seckendorf*, III: 112.

During these discussions, Henry's answer to the "Articles of 1535" was received, and his legates communicated its purport,[30] stating among other things that harmony was unattainable, unless "something first, *in your Confession and Apology be modified* by private conferences and friendly discussions between his and your learned men," and that his Majesty asks that "a man of eminent learning be sent to him, to confer diligently on the articles of Christian doctrine, and changing, establishing and ordaining other ceremonies in the Church."

April 24th, the Protestant princes met at Frankfort, and early in the month, the English ambassadors made preparations for attendance there. Because of his distrust of the bishop of Hereford, whom he evidently thinks well named Fox, the elector refuses a farewell audience.[31] He writes however, April 22d,[32] that if the King would propagate in his kingdom "the pure doctrine of the Christian religion according to the *Confession and Apology*," and adopt ceremonies in accordance with the pure doctrine of the Gospel, he would use every effort that the king should receive the title of "Defender of the Evangelical Faith." But that "if the King hesitated about admitting into his kingdom *the pure doctrine of the Gospel according to the Confession and Apology*," according to the articles recently drawn up at Wittenberg; the Elector could not imagine what use it would be, either for the King or his allies to make a league or exchange ambassadors. In a letter to Henry of the same date, he assures him of his good will and begs him to undertake the thorough reformation of the English Church. Seckendorf[33] states that the Elector endeavored besides to have an embassy appointed to visit England, composed of George, Prince of Anhalt, Melanchthon and Vice-chancellor Francis Burkhard. The Landgrave proposed sending the theologians Bucer and Schnepf or Brentz, and the civilians, Count Solm and Jacob Sturm. There was some discus-

---

[30] C. R. III: 49.
[31] *Seckendorf*, III: 111.
[32] C. R. III: 62.
[33] III: 113.

sion among the princes as to the terms to be proposed by this embassy, but they were finally reduced, first to the acceptance of the Augsburg Confession, unless amended from the Word of God, and, secondly, its defence in the coming Council; and, if the King did not approve of the articles, to treat concerning mutual assistance. But as most of the princes and cities were averse to any union with the King of England, the attempt was vain; while new events in England suddenly made a very material change in the situation.

CHAPTER V.

PROGRESS OF THE WAR FOR THE FAITH IN ENGLAND.

Conjectures as to the cause of Anne Boleyn's fall. Her sympathy with tne Reformation. Cranmer's Grief. Melanchthon's Indignation. Melanchthon warned by Barnes not to visit England. Antagonistic Elements in the English Church. Taverner's English Augsburg Confession and Apology. Convocation of Canterbury. Sensation caused by Latimer's Sermon. The Sides drawn. The Sixty-Seven Points. The Debates. Alexander Alesius, and his Speech. Foxe's Tribute to German Lutheranism.

It is not improbable that the fate of Anne Boleyn was sealed by Henry's failure to gain for his second marriage the endorsement of the Wittenberg faculty. We have already noted how closely connected she was with Cranmer, the months which he had spent in her father's house, and the effect of his visit. We have also seen that she was a diligent reader of Evangelical books, surreptitiously introduced from the Continent, as the discovery of her copy of Tyndale's "Obedience of a Christian Man," and its influence upon Henry, prove. She had generously maintained a number of scholars at the Universities; and all of them, among whom was Heath, were during her life-time earnest champions of the Reformation. One of these scholars was especially active in circulating the works of Luther and Melanchthon. Strype gives a letter in which she intercedes for a merchant in trouble for circulating the New Testament: "Anne the queen, trusty and well-beloved, we greet you well. And whereas you be credibly enformed, that the bearer hereof, Rychard Herman, merchant and citizen of Antwerp, in Brabant, was, in the time of the late Lord Cardinal, put and expelled from his freedom and fellowship of, and in the English House there, for nothing else, as he affirmeth, but only for that, that he did both with his goods and policy, to his great hurt and hindrance in this world, help to the setting forth of the New Testament in English; we therefore desire, and instantly pray you with all speed and favor convenient, ye woll cause this good and honest merchant, being my lord's true, faithful and loving subject, to be restored to his pristin freedom, liberty and fellowship aforesaid."[1]

"The Romanists reckoned her (and that truly enough) a great instrument in putting the King forward to what he had done in reforming religion. Pole, in a letter to the King, written within two months after her death, takes leave to call her the King's domestic evil, which God, as he said, had rid him of; and that she was thought to be the cause of all his evils."[2]

With such evidence, it is not difficult to see how Cranmer could say: "I never had better opinion in woman than I had in her. . . . Next unto your grace, I was most bound unto her of all creatures living. . . . I loved her not a little for the love I judged her to bear towards God and his Gospel."[3]

Although her writings have no very high authority, it is, nevertheless, interesting to notice that Miss Benger in her "Memoirs of Anne Boleyn," also suggests the failure of the Wittenberg negotiations as one of the causes of the Queen's downfall. "Drs. Fox and Hethe were sent to Germany, on a mission to the Lutheran divines, with whom many conferences took place, of which the conclusion was little satisfactory to the pride or prejudices of Henry, since even Anne's popularity could not entice them to acknowledge the legality of his divorce, and neither arguments nor promises atoned for his rejection of the Confession of Augsburg. It is, however, more than probable, these difficulties might have been obviated in a subsequent negotiation, but for the influence of Gardiner, who was, at the same

[1] *Memorials of Reformation*, I: 446.
[2] Ib. p. 456.
[3] Jenkyn's *Cranmer*, I: 164.

time, employed on an embassy to France, which afforded him facilities for counteracting the united efforts of Hethe and Melanchthon, and rendering the whole plan abortive. The unprosperous issue of the negotiation, was a severe disappointment to Anne."[4]

The death of Queen Catherine, January 6th, 1536, had introduced a new situation. As his marriage to Anne Boleyn was regarded illegal, not only by the Pope, but also by the Lutherans, the opportunity was now offered, if he could in some way rid himself of her, to contract a matrimonial alliance which would be undisputed by all. Both Pope and Emperor might thus be reconciled, and an unquestioned succession be still obtained. Besides, the King's dignity had been offended by a just reproof from his queen; and his superstitions had been quickened, as in the former marriage, by the birth of only princesses. These various motives combined to induce him to find some ground, if possible, for a capital charge. The Queen, who, unconscious of the processes already begun against her, had sat by his side at the tournament at Greenwich, May 1st, dies eighteen days later on the scaffold. It was a severe blow to Cranmer. "Do you know what is to happen to-day?" the Primate asked Melanchthon's pupil, Alexander Alesius, who was tarrying with him. "No," said Alesius; "since the Queen's imprisonment, I have not left my room." "She who has been the Queen of England on earth," said Cranmer, his eyes raised to heaven, and his face wet with tears, "will this day be a Queen in heaven." The Wittenberg theologians, notwithstanding their position concerning the divorce, were so greatly shocked that they felt for the time as though all further negotiations with Henry must end. Melanchthon writes to Camerarius, June 9th: "I am altogether freed from anxiety about a journey to England. Since such tragic calamities have occurred there, a great change of plans has followed. The late Queen, accused rather than convicted of adultery, has suffered the extreme penalty. How astonishing the

[4] Jenkyn's *Cranmer*, pp. 286 sq.

charges, how they declare to all men God's wrath, into what calamities at this time do even the most powerful fall from the highest eminence! When I think of these things, I maintain that all our troubles and dangers should be borne with the greater patience."[5] And in a letter to Agricola: "How horribly does this calamity disgrace the king! Such is the evil which the divorce has brought him!"[6] To Justus Jonas also he writes that Dr. Barnes has written to him not to undertake the voyage to Britain.[7]

On the same day on which Melanchthon wrote these letters, the Convocation met in England, at which the first Confession of the English Church was framed. This is a matter of such importance, that it will aid us to glance first at the course of ecclesiastical affairs in England, since the Act of Supremacy. Every record of those days bears the marks of confusion. "The Old" and "the New Learning," both had their warm adherents. There were those urgent for a thorough reform of religion, prominent among whom were both Cranmer and Crumwell. There were others to whom it seemed as though even the Wittenberg Reformers had not proceeded far enough. Without any fixed formulary by which to guide them, they passed by various gradations to Zwinglianism and even Anabaptism, although numbering among their adherents no names of influence. The zeal of Latimer, however, even then seems to be beginning to carry him beyond the moderation of the Lutheran Reformation. Emissaries of the Pope were at hand, ready to excite the people against any innovations which might be proposed. Still others vigorously defended the Supremacy of the King, and assailed the Pope, while opposing to the very death any change of doctrine. Their ideal of the English Church was simply the Mediæval Church minus the Pope. Their zeal for Roman orthodoxy was made a sufficient answer to the reproach of disloyalty from the successor of

---

Corpus Reformatorum III: 89 sq.
[6] Ib.
[7] Ib. p. 90 sq.

St. Peter. The Evangelical element had favored the divorce simply because in it they found an irreparable breach with the Papacy. These various elements had necessarily to come into conflict. Martyrs had fallen, like Sir Thomas More and Bishop Fisher, because they were faithful to the Pope; and John Fryth, soon to be followed by Francis Lambert, because of ultra-Protestantism.

BISHOP GARDINER.

As in all periods of confusion, there were leaders that successively rose and fell, now gained their point, and then had to submit to defeat; and, as their fortunes had vicissitudes, so also the policy of the government veered now to the one side, and then to the other. The negotiations and deliberations that are now to occur cannot be appreciated without some estimate of the character and influence of Stephen Gardiner. Three young men had grown up together and been trained for their future work in the household of Cardinal Wolsey, viz., Thomas More, Thomas Crumwell and Stephen Gardiner. The latter had proved an apt pupil of his great master, and become a veritable second Wolsey, only of greater acuteness and more obstinate will. The Cardinal was proud to call him "*mei dimidium*," "half of my very self." Henry though distrusting him soon learned to use him. The young secretary was busy plotting with foreign cardinals for Wolsey's elevation to the Papacy, and at the same time carrying on a correspondence for the king on other matters, which was carefully concealed from the Cardinal's knowledge. With Fox, he had been active in effecting the divorce; with Fox, he had plead Henry's cause before the Pope in 1528; with Fox, he had brought Cranmer to the front, in order by his learning to support the king; with Fox, he had shared in the honors of the victory of Cambridge. But he never forgave Cranmer for having been preferred to him as Archbishop of Canterbury. As Bishop of Winchester, as Secretary of State, as Ambassador to France, as Lord Chancellor, he henceforth had but one purpose, and that was to prevent any change within the English Church beyond what had already been effected by the transfer of the Supreme Headship to the King. "He deemed the work of reformation complete," says Archdeacon Hardwick, "when the encroachments of the foreign pontiff had been successfully resisted."[8] No life was so precious but that it must be sacrificed rather than be allowed to influence any inner change. Shakespeare did not err when he put into his mouth the words:

> "It will ne'er be well,
> Till Cranmer, Crumwell, her two hands and she [9]
> Sleep in their graves."

"He was vindictive, ruthless, treacherous," says Froude, "of clear eye, and hard heart."[10] Such a discriminating jurist as Lord Campbell in his "Lives of the Lord Chancellors,"[11] characterizes him thus: "Of original genius, of powerful intellect, of independent mind, at the same time, unfortunately, of narrow prejudices." "He was always a determined enemy of the general Lutheran doctrines; but for a while he made his creed so far coincide with his interests, as to believe that the Anglican Church, rigidly maintaining all its ancient doctrines, might be severed from the spiritual dominion of the Pope." It was only "for a while;" as on the accession of Mary, he had no difficulty whatever in utterly ignoring all that he had written concerning Henry's true suppremacy, and in not only returning to servile obedience to the Pope, but also in wielding his power as "a man of many wiles," to suppress all other authority. A true Papist at heart through the whole period, and the type of a large class who still boast of the independence of the English Church, and pride themselves in having nothing in common with Protestantism! To such persons, the Lutheran Reformation is still a great offence, and all traces of connection with it must be thoroughly eradicated!

Gardiner had not been inactive while Fox and his associates

---

[8] Hardwick "*On the Articles*," p. 48.
[9] Anne Boleyn.
[10] *History of England*, VI: 370.
[11] II: p. 61, 63.

were conferring with the theologians at Wittenberg, but from France, where he was watching the course of Francis, and where he had heard of the proposition of a union on the basis of the Augsburg Confession and the Apology, "unless some things be changed by common consent," he urges Henry, not to entertain such proposition, as "the granting of this article would bind the King to the sense of the Church of Germany, and this would be under an obligation, not to make use of the permissions of revelation." [12]

The great significance of Gardiner, however, becomes prominent in the series of deliberations we are about considering.

THE ENGLISH AUGSBURG CONFESSION.

Cranmer and Crumwell knew well the character of the conflict before them, and made preparations accordingly. We have no record of the precise circumstances which determined the publication in 1536, of Taverner's translation of the Augsburg Confession and Apology, recently brought to the attention of the Church by the scholarly researches of the late Dr. B. M. Schmucker. But when in addition to the constant references to these confessions in the negotiations between the English and the German theologians, and the peremptory ultimatum of the Elector on the withdrawal of the English ambassadors, that only on such basis could any agreement in the future be hoped for, we read the speech of Bishop Fox, in the convention hereafter to be noticed, in which he glows with enthusiasm over what the German theologians are doing, and trace the influence of especially the Apology on the English Ten Articles of 1536, there seems little doubt that it appeared prior to the Convocation. Its publication afterwards would not have been opportune, nor likely to have met the approval of the government, in view of the many Romish errors still endorsed with emphasis in the same Janus-faced "Articles," which nevertheless the Apology most severely arraigns and refutes. But, that it was not only for the deliberations of theologians and princes, that this book was published, its very

---

[12] Collier's *Ecc. History of Great Britain*, II: 323.

preface shows. Richard Taverner, who even as a youth at Oxford, had been persecuted for his sympathy with evangelical doctrine, had in view a still greater range of influence, and hoped by the use of the name of Crumwell to enlist the interest of a wide circle of English readers. "To the end," he says, "that *the people, for whose sakes this book was commanded to be translated,* may the more greedily devour the same," etc. As this translation of the Augsburg Confession has so recently been reprinted and republished (Philadelphia, 1888), further comment upon it here is needless.

THE CONVOCATION AT CANTERBURY.

We come now to the formulation of the first Confession of the English Church, in the Southern Convocation which began its sessions in St. Paul's, London, June 9th, 1536.[13] On that day, Hugh Latimer, Bishop of Worcester, by the appointment of Cranmer preached the opening sermon. Latimer, as a youth at Cambridge, had distinguished himself by his zeal against Lutheranism, and had taken as the theme for his inaugural discourse, when in 1524 he received the degree of B. D., an "Examination of the Theological Opinions of Melanchthon," in which the *Praeceptor Germaniae* was severely criticised. Recognized on this occasion by Bilney as a frank, able and earnest novice, whose chief error was his ignorance of the subject which he handled ; a private interview soon put him on the track, which brought him to the lasting esteem of Protestantism, as an eccentric, but godly, fearless, and eloquent champion of the faith which he once assailed. Latimer did nothing by halves. His opening sermon, which seems to have continued through two sessions, was a most scathing denunciation of the great body of his audience for their indifference to a thorough purging of the Church of England, from Pontifical abuses, and while admirable as exhibiting the progress which the great preacher had made, was not calculated to prepare the minds of his hearers for a calm and impar-

---

[13] *History of England*, III : 57.

tial consideration of the great questions before them.

"The mass," says Froude, "had been sung. The roll of the organ had died away. It was the time for the sermon, and Hugh Latimer, Bishop of Worcester, rose into the pulpit. Nine-tenths of all those eyes which were then fixed on him, would have glistened with delight, could they have looked instead upon his burning." His text was "The Unjust Steward." A few of his sentences which fully justify Ranke's remark, that "Latimer opened the war in a fierce sermon," may serve as a sample: "What have ye done these seven years or more? What one thing that the people of England hath been the better of an hair? Ye have oft sat in consultation, but what one thing is put forth, whereby Christ is more glorified or else Christ made more holy? Then, after enumerating abuses: "Lift up your heads, brethren; and see what things are to be reformed in the Church of England. Is it so hard for you to see the many abuses in the clergy, the many in the laity; abuses in the court of arches, abuses in the consistorial courts of bishops; in holidays, in images and pictures, and relics, and pilgrimages; in religious rites, in masses, etc."[14]

"The sermon," continues Froude,[15] "has reached us, but the audience,—the five hundred fierce, vindictive men, who suffered under the preachers' irony—what they thought of it; with what feelings on that summer day the heated crowd scattered out of the cathedral, dispersing to their dinners among the taverns in Fleet Street and Cheapside, all this is gone, gone without a sound. . . . Not often perhaps has an assembly collected where there was such heat of passion, such malignity of hatred."

Crumwell took the precaution of himself presiding over the House of Bishops, as vicegerent of the King. Though two Archbishops were present, they were obliged to yield to a layman; and when his duties in parliament required his absence, he sent another layman, Dr. William Peter, to temporarily fill his place.

---

[14] Demaus' *Latimer*, pp. 224-8.
[15] *History*, III: 61.

The two sides were clearly drawn. There seems to be no difference in the classification that has made:

PROTESTANTS, FOR THE REFORMATION: Thomas Cranmer, Archbishop of Canterbury; Thomas Goodrich, Bishop of Ely; Nicholas Shaxton, Bishop of Sarum; Hugh Latimer, Bishop of Worcester; Edward Fox, Bishop of Hereford; John Hilssey, Bishop of Rochester; William Barlow, Bishop of St. David's.

HIERARCHISTS, AGAINST THE REFORMATION: Edward Lee, Archbishop of York; John Stokesley, Bishop of London; Cuthbert Tunstall, Bishop of Durham; Stephen Gardiner, Bishop of Winchester; Robert Sherborne, Bishop of Chichester; Richard Nyx, Bishop of Norwich; John Kite, Bishop of Carlisle.

THE SIXTY-SEVEN POINTS.

While the Upper House, of the Convocation was thus about equally divided, in the Lower House, the hierarchists were largely in the majority. On June 23d, the Lower House accordingly sends the bishops a catalogue of erroneous doctrines, which were publicly preached in the realm, and ironically declares, that they are "worthy special reformation." They comprise sixty-seven items, which are compared by old Thomas Fuller[16] to "Jeremy's basket of figs; those that are good, exceeding good, those that are bad, exceeding bad, Jer. 24: 3." It is a strange mixture of truly evangelical statements, with exaggerations and fanatical extravagances, of which some are perversions that are clearly traceable, and others can be explained by the well-known law concerning the relation between extremes. Wherever taught they were the penalty necessarily to be expected where the attempt is made to suppress the true conservatism of evangelical teaching. We have found many of the specifications presenting statements either directly given in the Augsburg Confession and Apology, or else such as have been twisted by sinister interpretation.

The first charge that the sacrament of the altar is not to be esteemed, is only a perversion of what those confessions teach

---

[16] *Church History of Britain*, II: 74.

concerning the Romish Mass. The second concerning Extreme Unction correctly states what is taught in the Apology. The third, that priests have no more authority than laity to administer the Lord's Supper is a perversion of what may be found in the Apology, Article XXII. The fourth, concerning Confirmation is probably suggested by the Apology's treatment of the subject. The sixth, concerning Anti-Christ and the withholding of the cup is correct (Apology, pp. 280, 244). The seventh is the substance of Art. XXIV in both Confession and Apology. The eighth is especially interesting in its connection. "It is preached and taught that the church which is commonly taken for the church is the old synagogue."

Now compare the Apology, page 164: 14: "What difference will there be between the people of the Law and the Church, if the Church be an outward polity?" The paragraph continues: "And that the church is the congregation of good men only." With this, compare the Augsburg Confession in Taverner's translation: "The church is a congregation of holy persons." The ninth item, concerning the Litany, is only a misrepresentation of what is taught in Art. XXI concerning the Invocation of Saints. The tenth, "that man hath no free will" at once suggests Article XVIII. The eleventh seems at first sight to be an Anabaptistic or Lollard extravagance: "That God never gave grace nor knowledge of Holy Scripture to any great estate or rich man;" yet it is easily explained by what the confessions, in treating of the Freedom of the Will, declare concerning the impotence of those in the highest station, especially the learned of this world without the illuminating work of the Holy Spirit, to attain a knowledge of divine things; the standard of these critics, with respect to eminent position, being that of wealth, instead of learning. In the twelfth, "that all religions and professions are clean contrary to Christ's religion" we find a distortion and misapplication of Art. XXVII "On Monastic Vows." The history of the controversies concerning the Lutheran confessions in this country will supply many examples of perversions and misinterpretations no less forced and absurd. Were it necessary we might in the same way continue the examination of the entire list, and though we could not trace all, yet we could find the majority either incorrectly stating or misinterpreting what is taught in the Confession and Apology. This catalogue of alleged errors begins with the sacraments, and first, devotes to them seven paragraphs, that had doubtless been the first, and we may even say, the main, subjects of heated and prolonged debate in the Upper House; and nearly two weeks of the session had passed before this paper from the Lower House appears.

DEBATES AMONG THE BISHOPS.

"O! what tugging was there betwixt those opposite sides,"[17] writes one in the next century. Three speeches on the Protestant side are especially noticeable. One is that of Cranmer, in which he urges the consideration of "the weighty controversies," which he defines as not concerned about "ceremonies or light things," but such questions as the following: "The difference between the Law and the Gospel, how to receive the forgiveness of sins, the manner to comfort doubtful and wavering consciences, the true use of the sacraments, justification by faith, and not by any *ex opere operato* virtue of the sacraments, what are truly good works, whether human traditions be binding, whether confirmation, ordination, etc., should be called sacraments."[18] If he had intended to urge the adoption of the Apology how could he have introduced the subject better, or have presented with more correctness an outline of the scope of its matchless discussions?

Another speech was that of a Lutheran scholar, whom Melanchthon had sent from Wittenberg to Crumwell in August, 1535, as the bearer of the presentation copy of his *Loci* to the king, with the endorsement that "he was a man of such learning, honor and energy that he could carry no recommendation

[17] Ib. p. 75.
[18] See extract in *Hardwick's Articles*, pp. 52 sq.

higher than his own virtue." Alexander Alesius (Allan), born in Edinburgh, and Canon of St. Andrew's had left his country because of his faith in 1532, studied at Wittenberg, was the confidential friend of Melanchthon, and after 1540 until his death in 1565, Professor in the University of Leipzig. Crumwell introduced him before the bishops to argue the question of the number of the sacraments, which he did with great vigor and learning, but his presence provoked the bishops, so that Cranmer, on the ground that his life was imperilled, prevailed on him not to return the day after he had begun his argument. Alesius himself narrates the occurrence in a document, part of which is published in Ellis' Original Records.[19] The date 1537 there given, has led some to infer that he narrates the circumstances of another conference; but the error is, as most writers maintain, most probably in the year stated. His argument began:

"Right honorable and noble lord, and you most reverend fathers and prelates of the church, although I come unprepared unto this disputation, yet trusting in the aid of Christ, which promiseth to give mouth and wisdom unto us, when we be required of our faith, I will utter my sentence and judgment of this disputation. And I think that my lord archbishop hath given you a profitable exhortation that ye should first agree of the signification of a sacrament: Whether ye will call a sacrament a ceremony institute of Christ in the Gospel to signify a special or a singular virtue of the Gospel, or whether ye mean that every ceremony generally which may be a token or signification of an holy thing, to be a sacrament. For after the latter signification I will not stick to grant that there be seven sacraments and more too, if ye will."[20] When Alesius was proceeding to prove this "not only from Scripture, but by the old doctors and by the school writers also," Bishop Fox interrupted him: "Brother Alexander, contend not much about the mind and sayings of the doctors and school writers, for ye know that they in many

[19] Vol. III: 196 sqq.
[20] Compare with this argument, *Apology*, p. 215.

places do differ among themselves, and that they are contrary to themselves in almost every article. And there is no hope of any concord if we must lean to their judgment in matters of controversy."

The speech of Fox, Bishop of Hereford, who only three months before had been conferring with Luther and Melanchthon at Wittenberg, shows how he had been influenced by what he had seen and heard:

"Think not that we can by any sophistical subtleties steal out of the world again the light which every one doth see. Christ hath so lightened the world at this time that the light of the Gospel hath put to flight all misty darkness, and it will shortly have the higher hand of all clouds, though we resist in vain never so much. The lay people do know the Holy Scripture better than many of us. And the Germans have made the text of the Bible so plain and easy by the Hebrew and the Greek tongue that now many things may be better understood without any glosses at all than by all the commentaries of the Doctors. And moreover they have so opened their controversies by their writings that women and children may wonder at the blindness and falsehood that hath been hitherto. There is nothing so feeble and weak, so that it be true, but it shall find place and be able to stand against all falsehood. Truth is the daughter of time, and time is the mother of truth: and whatsoever is besieged of truth cannot long continue; and upon whose side truth doth stand, that ought not to be thought transitory as that it will ever fall. All things consist not in painted eloquence and strength of authority; for the truth is of so great power that it could neither be resisted with words, nor be overcome with any strength, but after she hath hidden herself long, at last she putteth up her head and appeareth."

It is also worthy of note that Alesius in the account above referred to, reports also: "The right noble Lord Crumwell did defend the pure doctrine of the Gospel hard."

CHAPTER VI.

THE TEN ARTICLES OF 1536.

Thomas Fuller's Comparison. Archbishop Laurence's Discovery. The Articles of Melanchthonian Origin. The Evidence in Parallel Columns. Romish Leaven. Explanation of Inconsistencies. Estimates of Foxe (1559), Fuller (1662), Strype (1694), Laurence (1804), Lingard (1819), Tracts for the Times (1836), Lathbury (1842), Hardwick (1852), Ranke (1859), Blunt (1868), Schaff (1877), Geikie (1879), Perry (1879), Jennings (1882), Franklin (1886). Canon Dixon's criticism examined.

THE result of the Convocation of 1536 was the subscription and publication of the first English Confession: "Articles devised by the Kinges Highest Majestie to stablyshe Christen Quietnes and Unitie amonge us, and to avoyde contentious opinions."[1] It is certainly a strange medley, combining the evangelical and Romish doctrines in such strange proportions and with such startling contradictions, as to vividly recall the Roman poet's figure: "If a painter would put a horse's neck to a human head, and attach feathers to the members," etc. Thomas Fuller, writing a little more than a hundred years afterwards says:[2] "As when two stout and sturdy travelers meet together and both desire the way, yet neither are willing to fight for it in their passage, they so shove and shoulder one another, that dividing the way betwixt them both, yet neither get the same; so those two opposite parties were fain at last in a drawn battle to part the prize between them, neither of them being

---

[1] They may be found in the Appendix to *Burnet's History;* in *Hardwick's Articles;* in *Strype's Memorials;* in *Fuller's Church History;* and in *Collier's Church History.*

[2] *Church History,* II: 75.

conquering or conquered; but a *medley-religion* as an expedient being made up betwixt them both, to salve the credits of both." We defer making an estimate of this unique document, until we have first examined its contents. The Melanchthonian origin of much that it contains was asserted by Archbishop Laurence in 1804, because of several sentences which he believed had been from Melanchthon's *Loci*. Every writer has peculiar phrases, and every teacher fixed definitions which are necessarily repeated in various connections. We propose to show that the Apology formed the ground-work for the articles. The Augsburg Confession was also used; as well as certain Articles[3] which in February, 1536, Melanchthon prepared against the Anabaptists. One of the papers which Melanchthon himself wrote during the March conferences, (possibly the *Repetitio* of 1536, which the commission carried with them to England) may have embodied all these elements; or one of the evangelical English theologians as Bishop Fox, may have prepared a document thoroughly Lutheran in its character. This was then amended, and interpolated by Romanizing qualifications, and supplemented by Romanizing articles, possibly by the King's own hand, possibly by that of hierarchical theologians who were scarcely their monarch's equal, or possibly by Cranmer's policy of surrendering much to gain what he regarded more for the cause which he represented, until it is no wonder that its relation to the Apology has not been suspected by English writers. We submit the evidence that has convinced us.

The "Ten Articles" are divided into two sections, the first treating of doctrines, and the second of ceremonies. The First Article, on "The principal articles concerning our faith" defines the relation of the English Church to the three œcumenical creeds, and is possibly in the main from the pen of Melanchthon, although we have not been able to trace it more definitely. It greatly resembles the Introduction to the First Part of the *Confessio Saxonica* of 1551, and both may have a common origin.

[3] *Corpus Reformatorum* III: 29 s q.

The next three articles treat of the Sacraments, as this was the first subject of discussion in the Convocation. The very fact that the number of sacraments is here determined as three, first led us to suspect the fact that the Apology was used in its preparation, it being well-known that this is the number fixed in the Apology. The Sacrament of Baptism is treated at considerable length, principally in order to prove the validity of Infant Baptism. That one-seventh of the space devoted to doctrine should be occupied with the recapitulation of arguments on a subject concerning which there was no difference between the two sides, and no false charge made in the list of sixty-seven points, embracing as one would think, every conceivable item of misrepresentation, will scarcely admit of any other explanation, than that of the controversies with Anabaptists in Germany, with which Melanchthon was occupied during the presence of the English embassy in Wittenberg. Although Hardwick says of the Anabaptists: [4] "Traces of them occur in England as early as 1536," yet they could not have had such importance as to have demanded such conspicuous treatment at this time. Here we find Melanchthon's "Adversus Anabaptistas" used.

ADV. ANABAPTISTAS.[5]

"Outside of the Christian Church, there is no salvation; therefore children must be incorporated into the Christian Church. But if children are to be members of the Christian Church, they must be cleansed by the Holy Ghost and baptism. Therefore Christ says: "No man can enter the Kingdom of Heaven except he be born again of water and the Holy Ghost.'"

"It is certain that the grace of Christ, remission of sins and salvation, promised in the gospel, belong also to children."

TEN ARTICLES.

"The sacrament of baptism was instituted and ordained in the New Testament by our Saviour Jesus Christ, as a thing necessary for the attainment of everlasting life according to the saying of Christ: 'No man can enter the Kingdom of Heaven except he be born of water and the Holy Ghost.'"

"It is offered unto all men, as well as infants as such as have the use of reason, that by baptism they shall have remission of sins, and the grace and favor of God."

[4] *History of Reformation*, p. 197.
[5] *Corpus Reformatorum* 3: 33 sq.

The traces of the Apology become then more apparent.

APOLOGY (173: 51.)	TEN ARTICLES.
Latin: "The promise of salvation pertaineth also to little children." German: "The promises of grace and of the Holy Ghost belong not alone to the old, but to children."	"The promise of grace and of everlasting life pertaineth not only unto such as have the use of reason, but also to infants, innocents and children."

Next the Augsburg Confession is called into service.

AUGSBURG CONFESSION (ART. II.)	TEN ARTICLES.
[Original Sin] "is truly sin, condemning and bringing eternal death now also upon all that are not born again by baptism and the Holy Spirit."	"Infants must needs be christened because they be born in original sin, which sin must needs be remitted; which cannot be done but by the sacrament of baptism, whereby they receive the Holy Ghost."

Passing to Article III, "The Sacrament of Penance," which with certain qualifications the Apology allows as a sacrament, although with a different conception of *Poenitentia*, which is no longer Penance, but Repentance, the resemblance is, if anything, more striking.

AUGSBURG CONF., (ART. XII: 1.)	TEN ARTICLES.
"Such as have fallen after baptism may find remission of sins at what time they are converted."	"Such men which after baptism fall again into sin ... whensoever they convert themselves ... shall without doubt attain remission of sins."
APOLOGY, (181: 28.)	
"We have ascribed to repentance these two parts viz., Contrition and faith. If any one desire to add a third, viz., fruits worthy of repentance, i. e., a change of the entire life and character for the better, we will not make any opposition." [Cf. Melanchthon's *Examen Ordinandorum* (1556): "How many parts of repentance are there? There are three: Contrition, Faith and Obedience."]*	"The sacrament of perfect penance which Christ requireth, consisteth of three parts, that is to say, contrition, confession and amendment of the former life, and a new obedient reconciliation unto the laws and will of God, which be called in Scripture, the worthy fruits of penance."

The hand of the Romanizing emendator is apparent in the above substitution of "Confession" for "Faith." As a com-

---

* Although the *Examen* is twenty years later, we cite it to show that the formula is Melanchthonian.

promise, he introduces "Faith" as an element of "Contrition." The "Contrition" of the Ten Articles, therefore, is the "Repentance" of the Confession and Apology.

AUGSBURG CONF., (XII: 3-5.)

"Repentance consisteth properly of these two parts: One is contrition, or terrors stricken into the conscience through the acknowledgment of sin; the other is faith, which is conceived by the gospel, or absolution, and doth believe that for Christ's sake sins be forgiven."

TEN ARTICLES.

"Contrition consisteth in two special parts, which must always be conjoined together, and cannot be dissevered; that is to say, the penitent and contrite man must first acknowledge the filthiness and abomination of his own sin . . .; the second part, that is to wit, a certain faith, trust and confidence of the mercy and goodness of God, whereby the penitent must conceive certain hope and faith that God will forgive him his sins and repute him justified, and of the number of elect, not for the worthiness of any merit or work done by the penitent, but for the only merits of the blood and passion of our Saviour Jesus Christ,"

APOLOGY, (181: 29.)

"Contrition is the true terror of conscience which feels that God is angry with sin."
"And this contrition occurs when sins are censured from the Word of God. . . When this is taught, it is the doctrine of the Law."

"Feeling and perceiving in his conscience that God is angry with him for the same."
"Unto which knowledge he is brought by hearing and considering of the Will of God declared in His laws."

APOLOGY, (183: 42.)

"This faith is nourished through the declarations of the gospel, and the use of the sacraments; for these are the signs of the New Testament."

TEN ARTICLES.

"This certain faith is gotten and also confirmed and made more strong by the applying of Christ's words and promises of His grace and favor, contained in His gospel, and the sacraments instituted by Him in the New Testament."

APOLOGY, (196: 2.)

"We also retain confession, especially on account of the absolution, which is the Word of God, that, by divine authority, the Power of the Keys proclaims concerning individuals" 183: 39: "The Power of the Keys administers and presents the gospel through absolution."

"To attain this certain faith, the second part of penance is necessary, i. e., confession to a priest." [Here again in "priest," the hand of the emendator is seen.] "For the absolution given by the priest was instituted of Christ to apply the promises of God's grace and favor to the penitent."

AUGSBURG CONF., (XXV: 3.)
"Men are taught that they should not lightly regard absolution, inasmuch as it is God's voice, and pronounced by God's command."

"They ought to believe that the words of absolution pronounced by the priest be spoken by authority given to him by Christ in his gospel."

APOLOGY, (183: 40.)
"The voice of the one absolving must be believed not otherwise than we would believe a voice from heaven." Cf. Aug. Conf. xxv. 4: "God requires faith, that we believe that absolution is a voice sounding from heaven."

"That they ought and must give no less faith and credence to the same words of absolution . . . than unto the very words of God Himself if he should speak unto us out of heaven."

There is a very skillful combination of two arguments which by changing the emphasis, and removing the passages from their connection, somewhat changes the meaning of our Lutheran Confessions:

APOLOGY, (204: 43.)
"Besides the death of Christ is a satisfaction not only for guilt, but also for eternal death."

(212: 77.)
"We have already frequently testified, that repentance ought to produce good fruits, and what good fruits are the ten commandments teach, viz., prayer, thanksgiving, the confession of the gospel . . . to give to the needy," etc.

TEN ARTICLES.
"Although Christ and his death be the sufficient oblation, sacrifice, satisfaction and recompence, for which God the Father forgiveth and remitteth to all sinners not only their sin, but also eternal pain due for the same; yet all men truly penitent, contrite and confessed, must needs also bring forth the fruits of penitence, that is to say, prayer, fastings, alms, deeds," etc.

The argument of the Apology concerning the rewards granted the obedience of believers, not as rewards of merit, but as the promised free gifts of God's love, is also dexterously turned, to a Romish interpretation.

APOLOGY, (133: 147.)
"Even we concede that the punishments by which we be chastised, are mitigated by our prayers and good works, and finally by our entire repentance, 1 Cor. 11: 31, Jer. 15: 19, Zech. 1: 3."

TEN ARTICLES.
"By penance, and such good works of the same, we shall not only obtain everlasting life, but also we shall deserve remission or mitigation of these present pains and afflictions in this world, 1 Cor. 11: 31, Zech. 1: 3."

Article IV. "Of the Sacrament of the Altar," is very Melanchthonian in its style, but seems at first sight to vary from the Lutheran doctrine by maintaining that, "under the form and figure of bread and wine the very selfsame body and blood of our Saviour Jesus Christ is verily, substantially, and really contained and comprehended." Thus stated, it may be regarded as teaching impanation. Yet the deviation from the phraseology which Melanchthon was in the habit of using at that time, before it was liable to be misinterpreted, is comparitively slight. Thus the Schwabach Articles of Luther and Melanchthon, and their associates, of October 10th–15th, 1529, forming the groundwork of the first part of the Augsburg Confession read (Art. X): "There is truly present *in* the bread and wine the body and blood of Christ."[6] Melanchthon's opinion concerning the Sacramentarians of August 1st, 1530, reads: "We teach that Christ's body is truly and really present with the bread, or *in* the bread," although with the limitation : "We reject the opinion of those who say that the body is contained in the bread like wine in a goblet." "We deny that the body is locally present in the bread."[7] The "contained and comprehended" are possibly an interpolation and the article in its original form, is possibly also from Melanchthon. It does not teach transubstantiation as some have inferred.

In Article V, " Of Justification," Archbishop Laurence found the sentence by which he connected the Articles with Melanchthon's *Loci*.

MELANCHTHON'S LOCI

" Justification signifieth remission of sins and the reconciliation or acceptation of a person unto eternal life." (C. R. xxi ; 412.)

APOLOGY, (109 : 37.)

" Since justification is reconciliation for Christ's sake, we are justified by faith, because it is very certain that by faith alone the remission of sins is received." Id. 114: 61: " We are justified before God by faith alone, because by faith alone we receive remission of sins and reconciliation."

TEN ARTICLES.

" Justification signifieth remission of sins, and our acceptation or reconciliation into the grace and favor of God."

[6] *Book of Concord*, (Jacobs), II : 72.
[7] Ib. p. 242, sq.

Even the passage in the Apology which seems to confound Justification with Renovation, and which finds its explanation in the fact that like the terms Regeneration, Sacrament, etc., the Protestant definition had not as yet attained its fixed form as determined in the Formula of Concord, is here employed:

APOLOGY, (96: 78.)	TEN ARTICLES.
"The making of a righteous man out of an unrighteous."	"Our perfect renovation in Christ."

The correspondence in the definition of good works is especially marked:

APOLOGY, (85: 8.)	TEN ARTICLES.
"The Decalogue requires not only outward civil works, but also other things placed far above reason, viz., to truly fear God, to truly love God, to truly call upon God, to be truly convinced, that God hears."	"God necessarily requireth of us to do good works commanded by Him; and that, not only outward and civil works, but also the inward spiritual motions and graces of the Holy Ghost; that is to say, to dread and fear God, to love God, to have firm confidence and trust in God, to invocate and call upon God."

These citations could be readily multiplied; but what have been given are sufficient to establish the fact that the evangelical statements of the articles were taken not only largely from the Apology, but also from the Augsburg Confession, and other writings of Melanchthon. "It has been denied," says Canon Dixon in his recent "History of the Church of England,"[8] "that there was any Lutheranism in the First English Confession, and certainly it must not be forgotten that this time the doctrines of Germany were heresy in England. But with all that is known of Henry's negotiations with German princes, it seems impossible to explain away the plain evidence which Laurence has brought to prove that the reformed doctrine infused into the Confession came from Germany." And yet Archbishop Laurence's inference was based upon the evidence of but one or two sentences! Mr. Froude's plea for Henry VIII, on the supposition that the deep theological reasoning, employed in the book, (which without sufficient evidence he thinks prepared by the King's own hand)

[8] Vol. I: p. 418.

is a complete refutation of the generally received opinion of his guilt in the execution of one wife, and the marriage of another only three weeks before,[9] of course falls to the ground, when the parts of the Articles worthy of especial admiration are found to be the rich fruit of Melanchthon's labors. So far as the articles vary from the Apology, and the other Melanchthonian documents, they certainly do not exhibit any distinguished merit. Ranke approaches very closely the true solution of the origin of the Ten Articles when he says that the first five have their origin " in the Augsburg Confession or in commentaries on it." [10]

THE ROMISH LEAVEN.

While the main treatment in "The Ten Articles" has been shown to be from Melanchthon, yet a little Romish leaven, leavens the whole lump. Much that is conceded to the Lutheran position is neutralized by other statements to which no evangelical Christian could knowingly subscribe. Scripture is to be received "only as the holy approved doctors of the Church do entreat and defend the same." Repentance is still "doing penance." Faith can be attained in no other way than through Confession and Absolution. The relation of faith to justification is altogether misinterpreted. It is placed in the same category with prayers, fastings, works of charity, as co-ordinate means of apprehending the merits of Christ. While the very language of the Apology is so freely appropriated, the main point of the most elaborate chapter in that matchless document is directly antagonized, when, "perfect charity" with "perfect faith," is made a condition of justification. Prayers to the saints

---

[9] "The King, then three weeks married to Jane Seymour, in the first enjoyment, as some historians require us to believe, of a guilty pleasure purchased by an infamous murder, drew up with his own hand, a body of articles, interesting as throwing light upon his state of mind, and of deeper moment as the first authoritative statement of doctrine in the Anglican Church." Froude's *History of England*, (London edition), III : 67.

[10] *History of England*, I: 157. Cardwell, Hare, Jennings and other Anglican writers concede the connection of the Articles with the Augsburg Confession, but know nothing of its closer dependence on the Apology.

and Purgatory are strenuously maintained. The retention of images in the churches, and the long list of ceremonies approved, are less objectionable features, as their defence is accompanied with injunctions that the people shall be taught "they have no power to remit sins, but only to stir and lift up our minds to God," and the "kneeling to, and censing" of images is forbidden.

ESTIMATES.

The evangelical theologians of the type of Cranmer, Fox, and Latimer, doubtless thought that so great an advance had been made in the acceptance of the principles of the Augsburg Confession, that the Romanizing elements interpolated could be allowed to stand and could even be subscribed, as liable, in the presence of the fuller light of the truth, to gradually die out. Of course such an agreement was doomed the very moment it was signed. Opposing systems cannot he reconciled by compromise. What is truth is truth, and must disengage itself from all compromises with error. Yet we must not regard the English Lutheran theologians of that period mere temporizers. Men do not become great reformers all at once ; nor do they understand the full force of concessions they may be inclined to make in the interest of peace and external harmony. In the beginning, contradictory opinions may be held by the same person, in his unconsciousness that they are contradictory. Luther's Ninety-five Theses are as full of contradictions as the "Ten Articles," and, therefore, could never have had any permanence as a Church Confession. The two elements which they contained had to come into conflict, in which the one was to be conquered and expelled by the other. It has been said that when a man is found half way up hill, it makes all the difference, in judging him, if we find from which direction he has come ; and on the same principle we are not disposed to harshly condemn those who unconsciously surrendered the cardinal doctrines of the Reformation, while, at the same time, confessing so much that is precious. The Interim of 1548 has sometimes been compared with these articles, as both being unfortunate compromises. But the Interim was favored by men who had had the full light of Evangelical truth, and had done praiseworthy service in its diffusion; it was a retrogression by which expelled Papacy was again to be gradually introduced where the gospel had been established; while "The Ten Articles," with all their objectionable features give royal endorsement to doctrines heretofore known as heresies, and secure their introduction in churches where previously they had never been heard. Luther appreciated the real conditions involved when a few months before, after the negotiations at Wittenberg had ended, he wrote concerning affairs in England: "It is indeed true, that we ought to have patience even though everything in doctrine be not realized all at once, (as this has not occurred even among us.)" [11]

Nevertheless we cannot but admire the consistency of Gardiner on the other side, in withholding his signature, however strongly we may suspect that his course was only a stroke of policy. It is well to note some of the various estimates placed upon these articles. We must bear in mind in so doing, that from a Lutheran standpoint some of the principles maintained, must necessarily be seen in a far different light than from a Reformed standpoint. There are some features which the latter might judge as Romanizing, that we do not concede as such, however we may agreee in a joint condemnation of the articles on other subjects.

JOHN FOXE, (1559): "Wherein although there were many and great imperfections, and untruths not to be permitted in any true reformed church, yet notwithstanding, the king and his council, to bear with the weaklings which were newly weaned from their mother's milk of Rome, thought it might serve somewhat for the time." [12]

---

[11] Letter of April 20th, to Vice Chancellor Burkhard, *De Wette's Briefen*, IV: 688.

[12] *Acts and Monuments*.

THOMAS FULLER (1662): "Some zealots of our age will condemn the Laodicean temper of the Protestant bishops. Such men see the faults of the Reformers, but not the difficulties of the Reformation. These Protestant bishops were at this time to encounter with the Popish clergy, equal in number, not inferior in learning, but far greater in power and dependencies. Besides the generality of the people of the land, being nestled in ignorance and superstition, could not on a sudden endure the extremity of absolute Reformation. Should our eyes be instantly posted out of midnight into noonday, certainly we should be blinded with the suddenness and excellency of the lustre. Nature therefore hath wisely provided the twilight as a bridge, by degrees to pass us from darkness to light." [13]

STRYPE, (1604): "We find, indeed, many Popish errors mixed with evangelical truths; which must either be attributed to the defectiveness of our prelate's knowledge as yet in true religion, or being the principles and opinions of the king, or both. Let not any be offended herewith, but let him rather take notice what a great deal of gospel doctrine came to light, and not only so, but was owned and propounded by authority to be believed and practiced. The sun of truth was now but rising and breaking through the mists of that idolatry, superstition and ignorance, that had so long prevailed in this nation and the rest of the world, and was not yet advanced to its meridian brightness." [14]

ARCHBISHOP LAURENCE, (1804), "Certain articles of religion were drawn up and edited in the king's name, which were evidently of a Lutheran tendency." [15]

LINGARD, (Roman Catholic, 1819–25): "Throughout the work Henry's attachment to the ancient faith is most manifest; and the only concession which he makes to the men of the new learning, is the order for the removal of abuses, with perhaps the omission of a few controverted subjects." [46]

---

[13] *Church History*, II: 76.
[14] *Memorials of Archbishop Cranmer*, I: 90.
[51] *Bampton Lectures*, p. 201.
[16] *History of England*, VI: 272.

TRACTS FOR THE TIMES, (1836):—"It is now universally admitted as an axiom in ecclesiastical and political matters, that sudden and violent changes must be injurious; and though our own revolution of opinion and practice was happily slower and more carefully considered than those of our neighbors, yet it was too much influenced by secular interest, sudden external events and the will of individuals, to carry with it any vouchers for the perfection and entireness of the religious system thence emerging. The proceedings for instance of 1536 remind us at once of the dangers to which the church was exposed, and of its providential deliverance from the worst part of them; the articles then framed, being according to Burnet, in several places corrected by the king's own hand." [17]

LATHBURY, (1842): "Though much error was retained, yet these articles were calculated to advance the Reformation, for they embody many sentiments at variance with the received doctrines of the Romish Church. That Cranmer was concerned in the preparation of these articles, there is good reason to believe." [18]

HARDWICK, (1852): "They are the work of a transition period, of men who had not learned to contemplate the truth in all the fulness of its harmonies and contrasts, and who consequently did not shrink from acquiescing in accommodations and concessions which to their riper understanding might have seemed a betrayal of a sacred trust. . . . They were treading upon ground with which few of them were as yet familiar, and we need not wonder if they sometimes stumbled or even wholly lost their way. An example of this want of firmness may be traced in the conduct of Bishop Latimer. Although one of the sermons which he preached at the assembling of the Convocation is distinguished by a resolute assault upon the received doctrine of purgatory, he ultimately put his hand to the statement, enjoining men to 'pray for the souls of the departed in the

---

[17] Tract 71, vol. III: 25.
[18] *History of the Convocation of the Church of England*, p. 126.

masses and exequies, and to give alms to other to pray for them, whereby they may be relieved and holpen of their pain.' " [19]

RANKE, (1859): "The first five are taken from the Confession of Augsburg or from commentaries on it; as to these the Bishop of Hereford [Fox], agreed with the theologians of Wittenberg. In the following articles, the veneration, even the invocation, and no small part of the existing ceremonies is allowed—though in terms which with all their moderation, cannot disguise the rejection of them in principle. Despite these limitations the document contains a clear adoption of the principles of religious reform as they were carried out in Germany." [20]

BLUNT, (1868): "It will be observed, that the clergy were now feeling their way to a sound theological basis for the reformation of doctrine. . . . Both sides gave way in some particulars, for the sake of coming to a common standing ground." [21]

SCHAFF, (1877): "They are essentially Romish, with the Pope left out in the cold. They cannot even be called a compromise between the advocates of the 'old learning' headed by Gardiner, and of the 'new learning' headed by Cranmer." [22]

GEIKIE, (1879): "Like all compromises the Ten Articles pleased neither side." [23]

PERRY, (1879): "The Ten Articles were the declaration as to how far the English Church was prepared to go with the Augsburg Confession." [24]

JENNINGS, (1882): "In the preparation of the Ten Articles the king was helped probably by Cranmer and Fox. Policy or higher motives infused into this formulary, a spirit of concession, so that while it was a compliment to the Protestants, it enforced

---

[19] *History of Articles*, p. 57.
[20] *History of England*, I: 157.
[21] *Reformation in the Church of England*, I: 443.
[22] *Creeds of Christendom*, I: 611.
[23] *English Reformation*, p. 286.
[24] *History of the Church of England*, p. 147.

on the conservative party at home nothing which they would deem objectionable."[25]

FRANKLIN, (in Church Cyclopædia, 1886): "The hands of both Gardiner and Cranmer appear in them with not a little of the dash of Henry VIII."

We defer, to the last, the words of Canon Dixon, whose "History of the Church of England" in three large octavos, has been received with high favor within that communion and its affiliated branches:

"From the beginning to the end, the English Confessions, (of which these articles were the first) have borne the impression of a settled intention which was such as caused them to be different from the curious, definite and longsome particularity of the Continent. They had the design of preserving the unity of the English Church. This was the characteristic of the nation, and exhibited an undeviating determination which has survived the violence of every age. . . . Though he enslaved and robbed the Church of which he was the Supreme Head, he had no thought of destroying her."[26]

This is a candid acknowledgment; and it is worth while not only to seriously test the assertion here made, that it is the aim of the whole series of English Confession to avoid such "definite particularity" as characterizes the Lutheran Confessions, but also, if the statement be true, to note the price that is paid, for readiness to accept even error, or to subscribe in the same document to contradictory and mutually exclusive doctrines, in order thereby to escape from the calamity of "destroying" the Church. There is also another matter worthy of some thought, viz., as to how if a communion be the Church, its clear and definite confession of the truth can destroy it, when to the truth of the Church's confession the promise is attached, that "the gates of hell shall not prevail against it?" Can any association that is in such peril be the Church?

[25] *Ecclesia Anglicana*, p. 182.
[26] *History of the Church of England*, I: 411.

There is besides another important lesson here suggested, and that is the fatality attending all efforts to modify and adjust to peculiar relations of time and place the unalterable principles set forth in the Augsburg Confession and Apology.

CHAPTER VII.

THE BISHOPS' BOOK OF 1537.

Failure of the Ten Articles. Cranmer and Luther's Catechism. The Commission to prepare another Document. Cranmer and Fox vs. Stokesley. Indebtedness of the "Book" to Luther's Catechisms, the Augsburg Confession, the Apology, and Luther's explanation of the *Ave Maria*. Other Sources. The King's Amendments, and Cranmer's Answer.

THE Articles of 1536, like all compromises, inspired no enthusiasm. They were too Lutheran for the hierarchists; they were too Romish for the Lutherans. They were too ambiguous for those whose consciences demanded the clearest and most definite answers to the questions which, by the agency of the Holy Spirit, most profoundly move the heart. They were too meagre, even where they were clearest. They were too theological for popular use. The evangelical leaven was doubtless spreading among the people; a model of plain instruction to be furnished pastors was much needed. There can be no doubt, that Cranmer, during his stay in Germany in 1531 and 1532, and especially while tarrying with Osiander at Nürnberg, learned to know well Luther's Catechisms and their vast influence; and the result shows that they gave an important suggestion concerning a new Confession.

Early in 1537, we find, therefore, a commission assembled at Cranmer's residence, composed mostly of bishops, engaged in the preparation of a book to be promulgated by authority, for the purpose of meeting these various wants. Gardiner and Stokesley were the leading hierarchists. Cranmer and Fox, again headed the Lutheranizing element, while Latimer also was

(104)

present with his practical and impetuous mind vexed at the labor spent in the discussion of speculative points of theology, which to him had little interest, and longing to escape from the turmoil by once more becoming rector of Kingston, instead of Bishop of Worcester. At certain stages of the work, especially that pertaining to the sacraments, questions were submitted by the Archbishop to which each member of the commission gave his answers in writing, which, when gathered, were used in the final formulation of the document. It was completed early in the summer, and its publication was superintended by Bishop Fox. Although generally known as "The Bishops' Book," its proper title is that of "Institution of a Christian Man." Erasmus, had published a book with this very same title in 1518. Tyndale's book of 1528 was "The Obedience of a Christian Man." Cranmer is universally conceded to have contributed by far the most part to it, while Fox also must have much of the credit for the contents, as he was their chief advocate in the commission. Although still retaining some Romish elements, it was a great triumph for the Lutheran side, especially as all opposition was for the first time silenced, and even Gardiner added his signature. "By this work, the Reformation was placed on the loftiest ground which it was ever destined to reach during the reign of Henry."[1] "It is altogether an illustrious monument of the achievements of Cranmer and his colleagues against the intrigues and opposition of a party, formidable at once for their zeal, number and power."[2]

The very list of contents makes us suspect its origin. They are: "1. The Apostles' Creed. 2. The Sacraments. 3. The Ten Commandments. 4. The Lord's Prayer. 5. The Ave Maria. 6. Justification. 7. Purgatory." This is the framework of an exposition which in ordinary type would form a large volume. If some of its contents seem strange, it is well to remember that among Luther's earlier catechetical works is his

---

[1] Le Bas' *Cranmer*, p. 155.
[2] Wordworth's *Ecclesiastical Biography*, III: 317.

"Betbüchlein" of 1522, containing: 1. The Ten Commandments. 2. The Apostles' Creed. 3. The Lord's Prayer. 4. *The Ave Maria;* and that Melanchthon's "Handbüchlein" of 1523 contains, 1. The Lord's Prayer, 2. The *Ave Maria,* 3. The Apostles' Creed, etc. Our readers should remember that the angelic salutation in Luke certainly admits of an evangelical explanation, and, as such, is not to be lightly esteemed.

Into this scheme, the material of the Ten Articles wherever possible is introduced, occasionally with slight changes, but generally with verbal exactness. The exposition is to a great extent changed into the form of a personal confession, prayer, etc., after the model of Luther's Small Catechism. What Löhe says of Luther's Catechism: "It is a fact which no one denies, that no other catechism in the world can be *made a prayer* of but this," must be modified if parts of the Bishops' Book are examamined, which are after all nothing but paraphrases of Luther's Catechism, of exquisite beauty, and which should be cherished as of imperishable worth. Froude, writing entirely from a literary standpoint, pronounces it[3] "in point of language beyond all question the most beautiful composition that had as yet appeared in the English language."

For those well acquainted with the Small Catechism, we need only quote some extracts from this second confession of the Church of England.

"I believe also and confess, that among his other creatures he did create and make me, and did give unto me this my soul, my life, my body, with all the members that I have, great and small, and all the wit, reason, knowledge and understanding that I have; and finally all other outward substance, possessions and things that I have or can have in this world." This is not exactly Luther's Small Catechism, though the same in substance. But its correspondence with Luther's Large Catechism is still closer, which reads (p. 440). "I believe that I am a creature of God, that is, that he has given and constantly preserves to me

[3] *History of England,* III: 229.

my body, soul and life, members great and small, all my senses, reason and understanding, food and drink, shelter and support, wife and child, domestics, house and possessions, etc."

The Bishops' Book continues :

"And I believe also and profess that he is my very God, my Lord, and my Father, and that I am his servant and his own son, by adoption and grace, and the right inheritor of his kingdom, and that it proceedeth and cometh of his mere goodness only, without all my desert, that I am in this life preserved and kept from dangers and perils, and that I am sustained, nourished, fed, clothed, and that I have health, tranquility, rest, peace, or any other thing necessary for this corporal life. I acknowledge and confess that he suffereth and causeth the sun, the moon, the stars, the day, the night. the air, the fire, the water, the fowls, the fishes, the beasts and all the fruits of the earth, to serve me for my profit and my necessity."

With the latter sentence compare again Luther's Large Catechism :

"He causeth all creatures to serve for the necessities and uses of life—sun, moon and stars in the firmament, day and night, air, fire, water, earth and whatever it bears and produces, bird and fish, beasts, grain and all kinds of produce."

The exposition of the Second Article of the Creed is of such extraordinary beauty and force, and so happily expands the most precious section of our Catechism, as to justify a long extract.

"And I believe also and profess that Jesus Christ is not only Jesus, and Lord to all men that believe in him, but also that he is my Jesus, my God, my Lord. For whereas of my nature I was born in sin, and in the indignation and displeasure of God, and was the very child of wrath, condemned to everlasting death, subject and thrall to the power of the devil, and sin, having all the principal parts or portions of my soul, as my reason and understanding, and my freewill, and all the other portions of my soul and body, not only so destituted and deprived of the gifts of God, wherewith they were first endowed, but also so blinded, corrupted and poisoned with error, ignorance and carnal concupiscence, that neither my said powers could exercise the natural function and office, for the which they were ordained by God at the first creation, nor I by them could do or think anything which might be acceptable to God, but was utterly dead to God and all godly things, and utterly unable and insufficient of mine own self to observe the least part of God's commandments, and utterly inclined and ready to run headlong into all kinds of sin and mischief; I believe, I say, that I being in this case, Jesus Christ, by suffering most painful and shameful death upon the cross, and by shedding of his most precious blood, and by that glorious victory which he had, when he descending into hell, and there overcoming both the devil and death, rose again the third day from death to life, and ascended into heaven, hath now pacified his Father's indignation towards me, and hath reconciled me again into his favor, and that he hath loosed and delivered me from the tyranny of death, of the devil, and of sin, and hath made me so free from them, that they shall not finally hurt or annoy me. . . . So that now I may boldly say and believe, as indeed I do perfectly believe, that by his passion, his death, his blood, and his conquering of death, of sin, and of the devil, by his resurrection and ascension, he hath made a sufficient expiation or propitiation towards God, that is to say, a sufficient satisfaction and recompense, as well as for my original sin, as also for all the actual sins[4] that ever I have committed, and that I am so clearly rid from all the guilt of my said offences, and from the everlasting pain due for the same, that neither sin, nor death, nor hell shall be able or have any power, to hurt me or to let me, but that after this transistory life I shall ascend into heaven, there to reign with my Saviour Christ perpetually in glory and felicity."

We find also the following amplification of one of the articles in the Third Part of the Creed:

"I believe that in this catholic church, I, and all the lively

---

[4] See *Augsburg Confession*, Art. III: 3.

and quick members of the same, shall continually and from time to time, so long as we shall live here on earth, obtain remission and forgiveness of all our sins as well original as actual,[5] by the merits of Christ's blood and passion, and by the virtue and efficacy of Christ's sacraments, instituted by him for that purpose, so oft as we shall worthily receive the same."

We add yet the explanation of the First Commandment, which the reader will do well to compare with that of Luther in the Large Catechism:

" To have God is not to have him as we have other outward things, as clothes upon our back, or treasure in our chests; nor also to name him with our mouth, or to worship him with kneeling or other such gestures; but to have him our God is to conceive him in our hearts, to cleave fast and surely unto·him with heart, and to put all our trust and confidence in him, to set all our thought and care upon him, and to hang wholly on him, taking him to be infinitely good and merciful unto us."

THE BISHOPS' BOOK, AND THE OTHER LUTHERAN CONFESSIONS.

We find in the Bishops' Book traces, not only of Luther's Catechisms, but also of the other Lutheran Confessions which were then extant. Not only does it incorporate within itself " The Ten Articles," which are based upon the Apology and the Augsburg Confession, but other passages are directly taken from the same sources.

AUGSBURG CONFESSION, (Art. V.)	BISHOPS' BOOK.
" For the obtaining of this faith, the ministry of teaching this gospel, and administering the sacraments was instituted. For by the Word and Sacraments, as by instruments, the Holy Spirit is given who worketh faith."	" To the attaining of which faith, it is also to be noted, that Christ hath instituted and ordained in the world but only two means and instruments, whereof the one is the ministration of his word, and the other is the administration of his sacraments instituted by him; so that it is not possible to attain this faith, but by one, or both of these two means. '

[5] See *Augsburg Confession*, Art. III : 3.

APOLOGY (*Latin* Eng. Trans. p. 163.)

"It says *Catholic church*, in order that we may not understand the church to be an outward government of certain nations, but rather men scattered throughout the whole world, who agree concerning the gospel and have the same Christ, the same Holy Ghost, and the same sacraments."

APOLOGY (*German*, Mueller, p. 153.)

"That no one may think that the church is like any other outward polity, bound to to this or that land, kingdom or rank, as the Pope of Rome wants to say; but that it abides certainly true, that that body and those men are the true church, who here and there in the world from the rising of the sun to its setting, truly believe in Christ, who have one Gospel, one Christ, one Baptism and Sacrament, and are ruled by one Holy Ghost."

"I believe that, this Holy Church is catholic, that is to say, that it cannot be coarcted or restrained within the limits or bonds of any one town, city, province, region, or country; but that it is dispersed and spread universally throughout all the whole world. Insomuch that in what part soever of the world—be it in Africa, Asia, or Europe, there may be found any number of people, of what sort, state or condition soever they be, which do believe in one God the Father, Creator of all things, and in one Lord Jesu Christ, his Son, and in one Holy Ghost, and do also profess and have all one faith, one hope and one charity, according as it is prescribed in holy scripture, and do all consent in the true interpretation of the same scripture, and in the right use of the sacraments of Christ."

It will be noticed that the English paraphrase follows the German almost as closely, as the German translation follows the text of the original Latin.

The explanation of the *Ave Maria* shows traces of a sermon of Luther of 1523.[6]

LUTHER.

Du siehestu dass hierinne Kein Gebet, sondern eitel Lob und Ehre begriffen ist. Gleichiwie in den ersten Worten des Vater Unsers auch Kein Gebet ist, sondern Lob und Ehre Gottes, dass er unser Vater und im Himmel sei.

BISHOPS' BOOK.

This *Ave Maria* is not properly a prayer, as the Paternoster is Nevertheless the church hath used to adjoin it to the end of the Paternoster, as an hymn, laud and praise, partly of our Lord and Saviour Jesus Christ, for our redemption, and partly of the blessed virgin for her humble consent.

Even the Smalcald Articles which had been subscribed only on February 22d, 1537, in their completed form being but four months earlier than the English Confession may have been utilized. For the resemblance between not only the historical portions of Melanchthon's Appendix "On the Power and Primacy

[6] Erlangen Ed. xv: 318.

of the Pope," but also Luther's treatment in Part II. Art. IV., and the argument against the Papacy in the formula before us, is very marked. The Augsburg Confession, the Apology and the Smalcald Articles all seem to have been laid under contribution in the preparation of the chapter on " The Sacrament of Orders," although a hierarchical doctrine pervades it not found in the Lutheran formularies.[7] We know that on March 5th, Melanchthon's paper on the reasons why " the princes, estates and cities of the Empire, professing the pure and catholic doctrine of the Gospel, declined to attend the Council at Mantua," was signed, that it was at once published, and copies sent to the Kings of England and France,[8] that it was "immediately translated into English,"[9] and published. The translator was Miles Coverdale, distinguished as a translator of the Bible. Such was the importance which the evangelical element of the English Church then attached to everything which emanated from the Wittenberg Faculty. Even though Melanchthon's *De Recusatione Concilii*" were not officially transmitted until November 14th, as seems probable from a letter in the *Corpus Reformatorum*, the argument for proving the dependence of the English theologians is in no way invalidated.

Nor would time be lost, if space permitted, in a careful examination of the source in Lutheran authorities of much of the teaching of this book, even where no special formulary has been closely followed. Sometimes it has been regarded as receding from " The Ten Articles," since while the former, following

---

[7] The argument is summarized by Hardwick (*History of the Christian Church during the Reformation*) : " They contended that the fabric of the Papal monarchy was altogether human ; that its growth was traceable partly to the favor and indulgence of the Roman emperors, and partly to ambitious artifices of the popes themselves ; that just as men originally made and sanctioned it, so might they, if occasion should arise, withdraw from it their confidence, and thus reoccupy the ground on which all Christians must have stood anterior to the Middle Ages."

[8] Corpus Reformatorum III : 314.

[9] *Hardwick's Articles*, p. 31.

the Apology, gives only three sacraments, the Bishops' Book allows the full number of seven claimed by the Romanists. But the Rev. Henry Jenkyns who has edited the works of Archbishop Cranmer, found a manuscript in the Chapter House at Westminster showing that this supposition is erroneous. In connection with the Ten Articles a declaration had been made and signed by the evangelical theologians, conceding the name of sacrament to the four other ordinances, but with limitations which the advocates of the Old Learning were unwilling to publish. In the Bishops' Book, what is essentially this declaration comes to light. Its argument is mainly that of the Apology, which is directed entirely to the importance of making a distinction between rites instituted by God's command, in which, through a visible element, the promise of the gratuitous forgiveness of sins is sealed, and all others. If this distinction be conceded, Melanchthon maintains that it does not make much difference what is called a sacrament, and suggests that even prayer and almsgiving and afflictions might be called sacraments, provided the distinction between them, and what he regarded then as three sacraments, be kept unimpaired. So the Bishops' Book declares: "There is a difference between them and the other three sacraments. First. These three be instituted of Christ. Secondly. They be commanded by Christ to be ministered and received in their outward visible signs. Thirdly. They have annexed and enjoined unto their said visible signs, such spiritual graces whereby our sins be remitted and forgiven, and we be perfectly renewed, regenerated, purified, justified, so oft as we worthily and duly receive the same."

THE KING'S AMENDMENTS.

Without attempting an examination and enumeration of Romanizing elements still retained, which are principally those of "The Ten Articles," though to a considerable extent less, there is yet one item of interest connected with its history, that is worthy of notice. There is in the Bodleian Library a copy of "The Institution," or Bishops' Book, with marginal criticisms in the handwriting of Henry VIII., and in the Library of Corpus Christi College at Cambridge, the annotations of Cranmer upon these proposed corrections of his sovereign, are to be found. Henry's notes indicate no little critical ability, but, at the same time, his real want of thorough understanding or appreciation of the doctrine of the Gospel as there set forth. It is his main purpose to introduce limitations and qualifications, whereby the universality of the divine provisions and promises may be modified, so as to include, if possible, the conditions of the application. Cranmer shows that he has been a sufficiently faithful pupil of the Reformers, to be able with clearness and decision to declare to his monarch the real points of discrimination that should be made. For instance, in the explanation of the First Article of the Creed, where the Bishops' Book, says: "He is my very God, my Lord, my Father, and that I am his servant and his own son," Henry proposes to add "as long as I persevere in his precepts and laws." To this Cranmer would not hear. The declaration, he maintains, is that of "the very pure Christian faith and hope which every good Christian man ought to profess." It belongs to the sphere, he says, of special faith, and not to that of general faith, which even devils have. The voice of true faith claims God as its own, without the interposition of any such condition; although of course when this condition is not present, the pure faith thus confessed is "only in the mouth," and not in the heart. He maintains that every man should examine himself as to whether he actually have "the right faith and sure trust of God's favor;" but, this done, "it shall not be necessary to interline or insert in many places, where we protest our pure Christian faith, these words or sentences, that be newly added, namely, 'I being willing to follow God's precepts,' 'I rejecting in my will and heart the Devil and his works,' 'I willing to return to God,' 'If I continue not in sin,' 'If I continue a Christian life.'" When the Second Article is reached "that Jesus is my Lord," the king again wants this limited by the clause, "I being Christian, and in will to follow his precepts;" and when it says "I am restored to the light and knowledge of God," he proposes the insertion of "Rejecting, in my will and heart, the Devil and his works," both of which receive a similar answer. There are other corrections of the king, showing more decidedly his essentially Romanistic position, as, for example, where he qualifies the statement, which to Cranmer is so important, that Christ's sufferings were a satisfaction for original as well as for all actual sins, by a clause limiting the actual sins for which atonement was made, to those alone which were committed "before my reconciliation." Unfortunately, Cranmer's answer shows at this point a weakening, since while opposing the insertion of the qualifying clause, he, at the same time, concedes that the propitiation of Christ cannot be extended to sins committed after reconciliation.

CHAPTER VIII.

THE ENGLISH BIBLES OF 1535 AND 1537.

Petition of the Convocation of 1534. Miles Coverdale. His Bible of 1535 from "the Douche and Latyn." His dependence on the Zürich Translation. Relation of the Zürich Translation to Luther. Relation to Tyndale. Influence on the Authorized Version. His Exposition of Ps. XXII., a literal Translation from Luther. His Hymns, from Lutheran Sources. Illustrated by a number of Examples. Herford's Table of Coverdale's Hymns, and their German Originals. His Theory of their Origin. Matthew's Bible of 1537. John Rogers. His Residence in Wittenberg. A Lutheran Pastor. The first Martyr under Mary. Why he used a Pseudonym? Probably printed at Wittenberg.

WE leave for awhile the diplomatic side of the history of the English Reformation, and turn to the less public sphere, in which the quiet work of scholars from the privacy of their studies, was making itself felt.

It was one of Cranmer's first efforts to secure a complete translation of the Bible into English, and to authorize and promote its circulation among the people. But, in accord with the well-known unwillingness of men to recede from a false position, unless under some expedient whereby to give the appearance of consistency to their action, the Convocation, in petitioning the king, December 10th, 1534, that the Bible should be translated by some learned men, also asked that a demand should be made for all books of suspected doctrine, and that, within three months, they should be surrendered.[1] This was followed by the publication, October 4th, 1535 of *The Bible: that is, the holy*

---
[1] Strype's *Memorials of Cranmer*, p. 50.

Scripture of the Old and New Testament, faithfully translated out of Douche and Latyn into Englishe. MDXXXV. The translator was Miles Coverdale, afterwards bishop of Exeter. Coverdale, born about 1488, was one of the band of Cambridge students, whom we have seen meeting for prayer and the study of the Bible and Luther's works, in the house called "Germany." He had entered the monastery of the Augustinians at Cambridge, and there had come under the influence of its prior, Dr. Robert Barnes, so active afterwards at Wittenberg, to whom he ever remained a most faithful friend. When Dr. Barnes was arrested in 1526, Coverdale had voluntarily accompanied him, and helped to support him under the trial; and when, after his martyrdom in 1540, his Confesssion at the stake was maliciously assailed by John Standish, Coverdale again came nobly forward, and published a book in vindication of his deceased friend. He had early formed the acquaintance of Crumwell, and enjoyed his confidence, as is shown by letters which have been preserved, and are published in his collected works. When Tyndale's New Testament was published, Coverdale appears among those most prominent in its circulation. For some years, before the first publication of the Bible, the precise residence of Coverdale is not known. Foxe, who knew him well, states that he was for a time with Tyndale at Hamburg, and had assisted the latter in the translation of the Pentateuch. This statement, generally discredited by modern writers, is accepted by Westcott. The work on his own translation undoubtedly occupied his time for years. When the Convocation of December 1534 had, accordingly, passed the resolution above given, Crumwell probably informed him that the time had come for its publication. The title-page gives no information as to the place where it was printed and published. Those who have made a special study of the typography of bibles of that period, have no hesitancy in saying that it came from the press of Froschover of Zürich, the publisher of the Zürich Bible.[2] Notwithstanding the fact that the title-page ex-

---

[2] The comparison may be made in the library of the Lutheran Theological Seminary at Mt. Airy, Philadelphia.

pressly states the dependence of the translation upon the German and Latin versions, recent writers have undertaken to deny it. Not only the title-page, but the " Prologue to the Translation " is against this theory. "To help me herein," says Coverdale, " I have had sundry translations, not only in Latin, but also of the Dutch interpreters, whom, because of their singular gifts and special diligence in the Bible, I have been the more glad to follow for the most part."

In the light of such words by Coverdale himself, Canon Westcott is undoubtedly not unjust when he says: " His critics have been importunately eager to exalt his scholarship at the cost of his honesty. If the title-page, said one who had not seen it, runs so, 'it contains a very great misrepresentation.' To another, the notice appears to be a piece of advertising tact. Expediency, a third supposes, led Coverdale to underrate his labors. And yet it may be readily shown that the words are simply and literally true."[3] Ginsburg, followed by Westcott, Mombert, and others, has shown the great dependence of Coverdale upon the Zürich translation of the Bible. This is mainly Luther's translation of the other books, with a translation of the prophets by Leo Judae, Zwingli, Pellicanus and others. It appeared at intervals 1524–9, while Luther's Bible was not complete until 1534, the translation of the prophets not having been finished until 1532. Coverdale, therefore, followed the Zürich edition, largely in order to have the benefit of that in which it anticipated Luther. The direct, as well as the indirect influence of Luther, may be traced. Tyndale was also laid under contribution. While some knowledge of the Hebrew and Greek original is not denied, he followed closely preceding translators rather than ventured to use his own judgment.[4]

[3] *History of the English Bible*, p. 213.
[4] " His Old Testament is not taken at all from the original Hebrew, either professedly or in fact, but is only a secondary translation, based chiefly on the Swiss-German, or Zürich Bible." Eadie, I: 285. " In every instance, where he forsakes Tyndale, he is led by Luther and the Zürich Bible," Ib. p. 294.

"Though he is not original, yet he was endowed with an instinct of discrimination which is scarcely less precious than originality, and a delicacy of ear which is no mean qualification for a popular translator." [5] "No little of that indefinable quality that gives popular charm to our English Bible, and has endeared it to so many generations, is owing to Coverdale. The semitones in the music of the style are his gift. What we mean will be apparent to any one who compares the Authorized Version, especially in the Old Testament, with the exacter translations of many of the books which have been made by scholars and critics. Tyndale gives us the first great outline distinctly and wonderfully etched, but Coverdale added those minuter touches which soften and harmonize it. The characteristic features are Tyndale's in all their boldness of form and expression, the more delicate lines and shadings are the contribution of his successor, both in his own version, and in the 'Great Bible.'" [6]

Two years afterwards, in 1537, two editions of a reprint of Coverdale's Bible of 1535, were published in London.

The same year, Coverdale published "A very excellent and swete exposition upon the two and twentye Psalme of David, called in latyn: *Dominus regit me, et nihil*. Translated out of hye Almayne in to Englyshe by Myles Coverdale, 1537." This is a very literal translation of Luther's *Der 23st Psalm auf einen Abend über Tisch nach dem Gratias ausgelegt*, 1536." This exposition was very likely delivered during the stay of the English ambassadors at Wittenberg. As Dr. Barnes, Coverdale's friend, was a frequent table guest of Luther, he was possibly at the table (*über Tisch*) where this explanation was given.

A still more important work must have been occupying him at this time, if not already finished. His "Goostly Psalmes and Spirituale Songs, drawn out of the holy Scripture" is without date. But as it is on the list of books prohibited by Henry VIII in 1539, its publication is necessarily prior to that date. It is

---

[5] Westcott, pp. 216, sq.
[6] Eadie, *The English Bible*, I: 302.

especially interesting as furnishing the beginning for English Hymnody. They are nearly all readily traceable to Lutheran sources. We are sure that a liberal selection from them will be appreciated. Of Luther's *Komm Heiliger Geist Herre Gott* there are three translations. If the readily accessible rendering by Miss Winkworth be consulted by the English reader, he will note how nearly one of the translations of the Sixteenth, anticipated that of the Nineteenth Century:

> Come, holy Spirite, most blessed Lorde,
> Fulfil our hartes nowe with thy grace;
> And make our myndes of one accorde,
> Kyndle them with love in every place.
> O Lorde, thou forgevest our trespace,
> And callest the folke of every countre
> To the ryght fayth and truste of thy grace,
> That they may geve thankes and synge to thee,
>   Alleluya, Alleluya.
>
> O holy lyght, moste principall,
> The worde of lyfe shewe unto us;
> And cause us to knowe God over all
> For our owne Father most gracious.
> Lord, kepe us from lernyng venymous,
> That we may folowe no masters but Christe.
> He is the veritie, his word sayth thus;
> Cause us to set in hym our truste.
>   Alleluya, Alleluya.
>
> O holy fyre, and conforth moste swete,
> Fyll our hertes with fayth and boldnesse,
> To abide by the in colde and hete,
> Content to suffre for ryghteousnesse;
> O Lord, geve strength to our weaknesse,
> And send us helpe every houre;
> That we may overcome all wyckednesse,
> And brynge this olde Adam under thy power.
>   Alleluya, Alleluya.

Luther's summary in verse of the Ten Commandments, is another of Coverdale's translations.

Mensch, willt du leben seliglich,	Man, wylt thou live vertuously,
Und bei Gott bleiben ewiglich :	And with God reign eternally,
Sollt du halten die zehn Gebot,	Man, must thou keep these commandments ten,
Die uns gebeut unser Gott.	
Kyrieleis.	That God commanded to all men.
	Kirielyson.

Nun freut euch lieben christen gmein appears in the following form. There is no abbreviation by Coverdale. We select several stanzas.

> Be glad now, all ye Christen men,
> And let us rejoyce unfaynedly.
> The kindnesse cannot be written with penne,
> That we have receaved of God's mercy;
> Whose love towards us hath never ende
> He hath done for us as a frende ;
> Now let us thanke him hartely.
>
> I was a prysoner of the devell ;
> With death, was I also utterly lost;
> My synnes drove me day'ly to hell ;
> Therein was I borne ; this may I bost.
> I was also in them once ryfe ;
> There was no virtue in my lyfe,
> To take my pleasure I spared no cost.
>
> Than God eternall had pitie on me,
> To ryd me fro my wyckednesse.
> He thought of his plenteous great mercy,
> And wolde not leave me comfortlesse.
> He turned to me his fatherly herte,
> And wolde I shoulde with hym have parte
> Of all his costly ryches.
>
> He spake to his deare beloved Sonne,
> The time is now to have mercye ;
> Thou must be man's redempcyon,
> And lowse hym from captivite.
> Thou must hym helpe from trouble of synne ;
> From paynfull death thou must hym wynne,
> That he may lyve eternally.

Luther s paraphrase of *media vitæ* is closely followed.

Mitten wir in Leben sind	In the myddest of our lyvynge,
Mit dem Tod umfangen;	Deathe compaseth us rounde about :
Wen such wir, der Hülfe thu,	Who shulde us now sucour brynge,
Dass wir Gnad erlangen?	By whose grace we maye come out?
Das bist du, Herr, alleine.	Even, thou, Lorde Jesu, alone :
Uns reuet unser Missethat,	It doth oure hartes sore greve truly,
Die dich, Herr, erzürnet hat.	That we have offended the.
Heiliger Herre Gott,	O Lord God, most holy,
Heiliger starker Gott,	O Lord God, most myghtie,
Heiliger, barmhertziger Heiland,	O holy and merciful Savior,
Du ewiger Gott,	Thou most worthy God eternall,
Lass uns nicht versinken	Suffre us not at our laste houre
In des bittern Todes Noth.	For any death from the to fall.
Kyrieleyson.	Kyrieleyson.

ON THE BIRTH OF CHRIST.

Gelobet seist du, Jesu Christ,	Now blessed be thou, Christ Jesu;
Dass du Mensch geboren bist	Thou art man borne, this is true :
Von einer Jungfrau, das ist wahr,	The angels made a merry noise,
Des freuet sich der Engel Schaar.	Yet we have more cause to rejoyse.
Kyrieleis.	Kyrielyson.
Des ewigen Vaters einig Kind,	The blessed son of God onely,
Jetzt man in der Krippen findt,	In a crybbe full poore dyd lye :
In unser armes Fleisch und Blut,	With oure poore flesh and our poore bloude,
Verkleidet sich das ewig Gut.	Was clothed that everlasting good.
Kyrieleis.	Kyrielyson.

ON THE RESURRECTION.

Christ lag in Todesbanden,	Chrift dyed and suffred great payne,
Für unser Sünd gegeben,	For our synnes and wickednesse;
Der ist wieder erstanden,	But he is now risen agayne,
Und hat uns bracht das Leben :	To make us full of gladnesse.
Dess wir sollen fröhlich sein,	Let us all rejoyse therfore,
Gott loben und dankbar sein,	And geve him thanks for evermore,
Und singen Halleluja.	Synginge to him, Alleluya.
Halleluja.	Alleluya.
Es war ein wunderlich krieg,	It was a marvelous great thynge,
Da Tod und Leben rungen,	To se how death with death dyd fyght ;
Das Leben behielt den Sieg,	For the one death gat the wynnynge,
Es hat den Tod verschlungen.	And the other death lost his myght.
Die Schrift hat verkündet das,	Holy Scripture speaketh of it,
Wie ein Tod den andern frass,	How one death another wolde byte :
Ein Spott aus dem Tod ist worden,	The death of Christ hath wonne by ryght.
Halleluja.	Alleluya,

'NUNC DIMITTIS.

Mit Fried und Freud, ich fahr dahin,	With peace and with joyfull gladnesse,
In Gottes Wille.	And with a mery harte,
Getrost ist mir mein Herz und Sinn,	Accerdynge to thy swete promesse,
Sanft und stille.	Lorde, let me now departe:
Wie Gott mir verheissen hat;	Now geve me leave, that I may dye;
Der Tod ist mein Schlaf worden.	For I would be present with the.

In *Ein feste Burg*, the meter is adopted, but Coverdale follows the Forty-Sixth Psalm more closely than he does Luther.

> Oure God is a defence and towre,
> A good armoure and good weapen;
> He hath been ever oure helpe and sucoure,
> In all the troubles that we have ben in.
> Therefore wyl we never drede,
> For any wonderous dede
> By water or by lande,
> In hilles or the see side:
> Oure God hath them al in his hand.

Of other Psalms paraphrased by Luther, there are translations of the Twelfth (*Ach Gott von Himmel sieh darein*) the Fourteenth (*Es spricht der Unweisen Mund wohl,*) Sixty-seventh, One hundred and twenty-fourth, One hundred and twenty-eighth, and One hundred and thirtieth.

"UNTO THE TRENTIE."

Gott der Vater wohn uns bei,	God the Father, dwell us by,
Und lass uns nicht verderben,	And let us never do amysse;
Mach uns aller Sünden frei,	Geve us grace with wyll to dye,
Und helf uns selig sterben.	And make us redy to thy blysse.
Für dem Teufel uns bewahr,	From the devel's myght and powre,
Halt uns bei festem Glauben,	Kepe us in fayth every houre;
Und auf dich lass uns bauen,	And ever let us buylde on the,
Aus Herzengrund vertrauen.	With hole herte trustynge stedfastly.

Another Lutheran hymn-writer from whom Coverdale drew was Paul Speratus, from whom two hymns were taken (*Es ist das Heil uns Kommen*, "Kirchenbuch," No. 270, and *In Gott gelaub ich*, Wackernagel, *Kirchen-Lied*, III: 33.)

Lawrence Spengler, whose acquaintance Cranmer must have

formed while at Nürnberg, is represented by his principal hymn, afterwards quoted in the Formula of Concord "*Durch Adams Fall ist ganz verderbt* (Kirchenbuch, No. 271). Hans Sachs also furnishes a hymn (*Wach auf in Gottes Name*, Wackernagel III: 58). Justus Jonas' paraphrase of Psalm 124, found in *Kirchenbuch*, No 171, is also followed. Agricola appears in *Ich ruf zu dir, Herr Jesu Christ* (Kirchenbuch No. 415), and Decius in *Allein Gott in der Höh sei Ehr.*

One of the most interesting translations is that of a Reformation hymn, of uncertain authorship, but composed before the Diet of Augsburg, *O Herre Gott, Dein göttlich Wort* (*Kirchenbuch*, No. 191.)

> O hevenly Lorde, thy godly worde
> Hath longe bene kepte alwaye from us:
> But thorow thy grace now in oure dayes,
> Thou hast shewed the so plenteous.
>
> That very well we can now tell,
> What thy apostles have written al;
> And now we see thy worde openly
> Hath geven anthyechrist a great fall.
>
> It is so cleare, as we may heare,
> No man by ryght can it deny,
> That many a yeare thy people deare
> Have been begyled perlously
>
> With men spirituall, as we them call,
> But not of thy Spirite truly;
> For more carnall are none at al,
> Than many of these spirites be.
>
> They have bene ever sworne altogether,
> Theyr owne lawes for to kepe alwaye;
> But mercyfull Lorde, of thy swete worde
> There durst no man begynn to saye.
>
> They durst them call great heritikes al,
> That did confess it stedfastly;
> For they charged, it shuld be hyd,
> And not spoken of openly.

> O mercyfull God, where was thy rod,
> In punyshynge soch great tyranny?
> Why slept thou then, knowynge these men
> Resist openly the veritie?

For such a hymn semi-papal England was not yet prepared, as the martyrs of 1540, and the six Articles were yet to show. That a volume containing such an arraignment of much that still existed, under authority in England, and with which the king sympathized, should have been prescribed, is only what could have been expected.

To recapitulate: Of Coverdale's forty-one hymns, twenty-two are from Luther, two from Speratus, one each from Spengler, Sachs, Agricola, Justus Jonas, Decius, and Greiser, four are well-known Lutheran hymns of uncertain origin, and seven we have not been able to identify, although their entire structure and spirit plainly show where they belong.[7]

When, then, the Church of England, and her various daughters, cling so tenderly to the Psalter in the "Book of Common Prayer," and prefer its animated and rythmical expressions to the acknowledged more accurate translation of the Authorized Version, the secret of the charm is found in the influence which the treasures of the first period of Lutheran hymnology had upon the style of him who came to the work of translating the Psalter, with the notes of so many of the masterpieces of Luther and his associates ringing in his ears, and filling his heart with a glow of devout feeling. Coverdale's forty-one hymns were probably the growth of years. None of the originals which he translated is

---

[7] Reference may be made to the interesting tables, tracing the origin of Coverdale's entire list by Prof. Mitchell in *The Academy* for June 28, 1884; and in Herford's *Literary Relations of Germany and England in the XVI. Century* (Cambridge 1886) pp. 17 sqq. The summary of the latter is: From the Latin 6; from Luther, 18; Creutziger, 1; Speratus, 2; Hegenwalt, 1; Agricola 1; Moebanius, 1; Sachs, 1; Spengler, 1; Dachstein, 1; Greiser, 1; Decius, 2; Anonymous, 5.

later than 1531.[8] The translations of the hymns and the translation of the Bible may have proceeded cotemporaneously, the former having afforded a relief from the severer work of the latter.

We are not through with Coverdale, but must interrupt the narrative at this point, to consider another edition of the English Bible, and its translator, rapidly following that which has just been noticed. John Rogers, born about 1500, was another Alumnus of Cambridge; but does not seem to have been influenced by the Protestant movement until, after being rector for two years of "Trinity the Less," in London, while chaplain to the merchant adventurers in Antwerp, he became intimate with Tyndale. The latter having been martyred October 6th, 1536, Rogers the succeeding year married Adriana Pratt or de Weyden, and *moved to Wittenberg*. All authorities agree in this, and state that he so thoroughly mastered the German, that he became superintendent or pastor of a church at Wittenberg, "to which he ministered for many years with great ability and success." We can find no trace of such pastorate among German authorities. It may have been a church near Wittenberg which he served. Salig[9] states that he was ordained at Wittenberg; which necessarily implies a pastoral care. On his trial,[10] he explained and defended the order of service used in Wittenberg. Previously he had translated and published in English "Melanchthon on the Interim," in connection with a defence of Melanchthon's course, then severely criticized. All these facts show the substantial truth of the cotemporaneous account. He remained in Wittenberg or its neighborhood from 1537 to 1547

---

[8] " Of the Lutheran hymnology of 1524-31, Coverdale's ' *Goostly Songs* ' is a fair selection. . . Almost devoid of lyric faculty, his verse limps laboriously after the stirring measures of Luther. . . He has not the good translator's sensitiveness and elasticity of style. Yet his very sincerity and simplicity often do the work of refined taste."—*Herford*, pp. 11, 15.

[9] II: 491.

[10] *British Reformers*, (Philada.), p. 9; Salig, II: 491.

or '48. Returning on the accession of Edward VI., in whose reign he enjoyed great influence, he was the first of the martyrs under Mary, having been burned at Smithfield, February 4th, 1555. The story of his farewell to his wife and eleven children when on the way to martyrdom, is well known to readers of English history. His son, Daniel, was afterwards educated in part at Wittenberg, some affirm at Melanchthon's cost, and became a distinguished diplomat under Queen Elizabeth.

Rogers fell heir to the manuscripts which Tyndale left at his death. It is well known how diligently employed he was during his imprisonment in completing his translation from the Hebrew of the Old Testament. As St. Paul sent from the Roman dungeon, for his books and parchments, so also Tyndale had asked: "I wish permission to have a candle in the evening. . . But above all I entreat . . that he may kindly permit me to have my Hebrew Bible, Hebrew grammar and Hebrew dictionary, that I may spend my time with that study." Rogers, therefore, took the printed New Testament and Pentateuch of Tyndale, added to them Tyndale's manuscript translation from Joshua to the end of 2 Chronicles, and completed the Bible by adopting Coverdale's version in what was lacking. Foxe says: "He added prefaces and notes out of Luther." Thomas Matthewe was given as the name of the translator, possibly because he hesitated to claim as his own what was only a compilation, or because the publishing of Tyndale's name would have prevented its endorsement and circulation in England. Some assume that Thomas Matthewe was the name of the person who, in the beginning, assumed the financial responsibility. Before the printing was complete, the English printers, Grafton and Whitchurch, became its proprietors. It was printed in 1537. Dr. Mombert [11] argues that the printer was Hans Luft, and the place of printing Wittenberg, whither Rogers moved that year. Thus the first authorized version, of the English Bible, like its two predecessors, was prepared and published under Lutheran influences and auspices.

[11] *Handbook of English Versions*, p. 176.

CHAPTER IX.

THE LUTHERAN COMMISSION TO ENGLAND OF 1538.

An ominous Silence. Anxiety of Melanchthon. His letter to Henry VIII. His Criticism of the Ten Articles. Henry seeks Renewal of Negotiations. Christopher Mount at Brunswick. Arrangements for Conference of 1538. The Lutheran Commissioners. Sketch of Myconius. Luther's letter to Fox. Death of Fox. Its Effect on the Lutheran Movement. Reception of the Commission. The Augsburg Confession Discussed. Agreement on the Doctrinal Articles. Conflict on "Abuses." An Agreement Imminent. Henry's Schemes to end the Conference. The Commission withdraws. Their admonition. Handsome Presents for Inhospitable Entertainment. Results. XIII Articles of 1538. Relation to Augsburg Confession shown in parallel columns.

WHILE the English Bible was thus working like leaven among the English people, the diplomatic side of the Reformation was also progressing. In chapter VI. we have traced the formulation of "The Ten Articles" of 1536, and shown their relation to the Augsburg Confession and the Apology. It becomes an interesting subject of inquiry to note how the movement in England, in which they originated was regarded by the leaders of the Reformation in Germany. In reading their correspondence, we find that for a long time, they were almost entirely cut off from direct communication with England. Gardiner's plots to defeat the adoption of the Augsburg Confession and Apology comprehended also the prevention of any communication between the English party of reform and those upon whose labors and judgment they were so dependent. We have previously referred to the fact that after his return to England, Dr. Barnes, noting the change that had occurred, wrote to Melanchthon (June,

1536),[1] not to think of making the visit to England, for which the king had been so importunate. July 31st, of the same year, Alesius, desiring to send a copy of "The Ten Articles" to Melanchthon, could accomplish his purpose only by transmitting it to Aepinus, from 1529 pastor, and from 1532 the Lutheran Superintendent at Hamburg, who was on most intimate terms with Crumwell, and asking him to have it sent from Hamburg to Wittenberg.[2] Certainly it was not the most considerate treatment of the accomplished author from whose pen a great portion of "The Ten Articles" was derived, that he could receive a copy in no other way than through such a surreptitious channel. But, to be sure, it was the king's own book, and "the learnedest prince in Christendom," could do with it as he saw best! Yet before the Articles could reach Melanchthon, the Elector of Saxony grew very indignant at the long silence. Bishop Fox was regarded by some of the princes and theologians as having most shamefully falsified, since his promises were unfulfilled. We shall see later that in this impression, Luther did not share. July 12th, 1536, the Elector thought of sending some one to England to find out what was the matter, or of requesting Aepinus to intercede with those in authority there.[3] Six weeks more passed, and on September 1st, Melanchthon wrote a letter for the Elector to Henry, in which he said, among other things:

"We do not doubt that your Royal Highness has learned from the Bishop of Hereford what was our will and that of our confederates at the conference at Frankfort, as well as our disposition towards your Royal Highness. We are under the impression, too, that the letters which were sent, June 5th, from Naumburg have been delivered to your Royal Highness. We expect a reply from your Royal Highness, or at least we hope that the Bishop of Hereford will write, as we asked in the letter from

[1] *Corpus Reformatorum*, III: 89.
[2] Ib. 104.
[3] Seckendorf, III: 113.

Naumburg, informing us what was the will of your Royal Highness, when he had read *the articles concerning doctrine on which the legates and the Wittenberg theologians had agreed."*

At last on November 28th, Melanchthon had received "The Ten Articles," and wrote to Veit Dietrich: "We have the Anglican Articles complete, which I will have described by Cruciger; they have been put together with the greatest confusion. There are, it is true, still intervals taken from my affairs. But I will write of them at another time."[4] Three days later, he wrote to the same correspondent: "We hear that in England everything is full of seditions. I wonder that you have not indicated with what countenance Dr. Osiander has regarded the picture of his prophecy."

THE COMMISSION OF 1538.

Henry at last responded, January 2d, 1538, in a very conciliatory strain. He praised the course of his German brethren concerning the proposed Council, thought that every Christian man must admire it, and hoped that by future conferences, with the Divine assistance, they may come to an agreement, and that the pure doctrine of Christ which cannot lie hidden long may be displayed to the salvation of all.[5] At the close of the next month, he sent Christopher Mount to the meeting of the League at Brunswick with the assurance that he would use every effort for the promotion and establishment of the pure religion, and stating that it was now the time to send the promised embassy.[5] It was accordingly determined to accept the proposition, and the embassy was constituted by the appointment of Francis Burkhard, Vice Chancellor of Saxony, George a Boyneburg, LL. D., a Hessian nobleman, and Frederick Myconius, Superintendent of Gotha—a statesman, a jurist and a theologian. The very constitution of the commission showed that it was not antici-

---

[4] The translator is compelled here to be an interpreter: "De meis rebus adhuc quidem sunt induciae." Ib. p. 192.

[5] Seckendorf, III: 180.

pated to admit of any compromises. Melanchthon was evidently kept at home intentionally. Myconius (1491-1546) who supplied his place, is described as a man of deep spirituality, a former monk, whose experience in his search for the assurance of the forgiveness of sins in many respects resembled that of Luther, small of stature, and for years a victim of consumption, of scholarly habits, wonderful energy, distinguished executive ability, and marked eminence as a public speaker, with Melanchthon's calm and unruffled disposition, love of peace and habits of introspection, tinged with well-tempered sentiment, but without Melanchthon's fondness for diplomacy,—a man deeply beloved by both Luther and Melanchthon, who, when the circumstances demanded it, on more than one occasion, showed that he could be a true Boanerges, as well as the St. John of the Lutheran Reformation. However such a representative might win the love of all with whom he dealt, he could be implicitly relied upon not to yield an hair's breadth, as in his inner experience he had fought over every point involved in the controversy, and knew that life or death hung upon them all. What better representative could be selected to encounter the disguised Romanism, than he who, as a youth, still in the toils of the Papacy, had stood before Tetzel begging an indulgence upon the ground that to the poor it must be given gratuitously, and, when offered the price by some of Tetzel's attendants, refusing it with the words: "No, I purchase no forgiveness. I must have it gratuitously," and charging the indulgence vender to his face: " You will have to give an answer before God, if for the sake of a couple of pennies, you regard the salvation of my soul of no account."

LUTHER ON BISHOP FOX.

Already on March 11th, the instructions of the commission were prepared. May 12th, Luther wrote a letter to Bishop Fox commending its members to its kind reception. Alas the accomplished prelate had died four days before! With his death, Lutheranism in England received a blow from which it never recovered. If that same hand, whose chief work, one would think, should have been, to transmit the holiest office to those who were to be the ambassadors of the Gospel of peace and love, but which so often touched the key at whose signal, the friends of a purified church, fell beneath the blows of the executioner, had administered poison to one whose power and influence were too great to admit of his removal by ordinary methods, he could not have accomplished his plans more effectually. Without the vacillation of Cranmer, every movement which the Bishop of Hereford had made, showed a steady progress towards the ideal position. He had greater depth of character, wider range of experience, and more facility and readiness as an ecclesiastical diplomat, than the archbishop. Besides he had always access to the king—a privilege which Cranmer enjoyed only on rare occasions. The letter of Luther shows in what esteem the Reformer held him, and fully counteracts the suspicions felt by Melanchthon, who, we must acknowledge, was readily deceived in his estimate of men. Nor do Luther's letters deal in empty compliments. Whatever he writes he means. Here is his letter:

"Grace and peace in Christ our Lord. As these men, our friends and the legates of the princes, are about making a journey to your Most Serene King, I could not refrain from giving them a letter to you, dreading especially lest I might incur the charge of being an ungrateful and forgetful man. For since, in addition to the most agreeable intimacy which we enjoyed here, you also did me a very great favor, and profited me by your advice against my enemy, the stone; it is impossible for me to forget you. Often has our conversation been concerning you, especially since affairs have been taking such turns in your kingdom, that either you have been unable to send us letters, or when sent they were possibly intercepted. By such suppositions we comforted our anxiety. For we were hesitating and dreading, lest possibly this persistent silence might be a sign of some sadder calamity against the progress of the Gospel. There were some who imagined that your King, circumvented at some time by skilful Romanists would return again into favor with the Pope. We here prayed, and amid hope and fear besought that Satan be beaten under your feet. Neither are we informed what is being done, among you, with respect to the Gospel, or how. But we hope on the return of these legates to hear a good report concerning your Anglican Church with respect to what is verily the Gospel. How the State and Church are in Germany, you will learn fully and thoroughly from our representatives. The Lord Jesus Christ increase in you and in us both grace and his gifts to the glory of God the Father. Amen. My Katie reverently salutes you. In Christ, farewell. Your most devoted,

"MARTIN LUTHER."[6]

THE EMBASSY IN ENGLAND.

The ambassadors received a very cordial reception. They were honored with the embrace of the king, who expressed his great regret at the absence of Melanchthon, but candidly stated that there were some points in the articles of the Protestants which he did not approve, and that he thought that they ought to make the platform sufficiently broad that the French also might be included. The ambassadors, however, were duly warned by the friends of the Evangelical cause that he was greatly influenced by bishops opposed to the Gospel, and that they should not place much dependence upon his flattery.[7] This they soon found to be only too true.

Three bishops and four doctors of divinity, with Cranmer, as president of the commission, were appointed to represent the English side, while Dr. Barnes was assigned by the king a place in the conference on the Lutheran side! There is perfect agreement concerning the facts of the Conference. "The two parties went together through the Augustan Confession."[8] "The course of the discussion was regulated by the plan pursued in the

---

[6] De Wette's *Luther's Briefen*, V: 110 sq.
[7] Seckendorf, III: 180.
[8] Dixon's *History of the Church of England*, Vol. II: p. 3.

Augsburg Confession." "The king appointed certain bishops and doctors, to enter into conference and debate with them, of each of the heads of Christian doctrine contained in the Augustine Confession, and of divers abuses brought into the church."[9] They were not long in coming to an agreement on the Doctrinal Articles, but after these were finished, a disagreement arose, the Lutherans insisting that the consideration of the Confession must be finished, and the articles on Abuses also included, while the bishops were just as urgent that the seven sacraments must form the next subject of consideration. Back of the bishops was the king; but the Lutherans had the satisfaction of having on their side Cranmer, who wrote with no little feeling to Crumwell concerning the course of his associates. The fact could not be concealed that it was the intention of the King by this procedure to break up the conference, which threatened to go too far. It actually began to look as though, if the discussions were to continue, the whole Augsburg Confession would be approved. Melanchthon wrote to Brenz on the basis of the reports received at Wittenberg: "There is hope that the Anglican churches will be reformed, and the doctrine and godly rights restored."[10] Nevertheless it would have been a serious matter from a political standpoint to have dismissed the representatives of the Smalcald League too abruptly. So Henry announced that he himself would undertake to answer the Lutheran argument on Abuses. Cranmer also describes the entertainment furnished the Lutheran ambassadors as being such as would lead them to desire a summons homeward at the earliest moment. "As concernyng the Oratours of Germanye, I am advertised, that thei are very evill lodged where thei be: For besides the Multitude of Ratts, daily and nyghtly runnyng in their chambers, which is no small Disquietnes; the Kechyn standeth directly against their Parlar, where they dayly Dine and Supp; and by reason thereof, the

[9] Hardwick's *History of Articles*, p. 70.
[10] *Corpus Reformatorum*, III: 587.

House savoreth so yll, that it offendeth all Men that come into it." [11]

The king was trifling; and the ambassadors were quick enough to perceive it. "He wants," writes Myconius, "nothing else than to sit as Antichrist in the temple of God, and that King Harry be Pope. The precious treasures, the rich income of the Church—these are Harry's Gospel." [12] The Bishop of Hereford is no longer at hand to plead for the evangelical faith with his hardened monarch. Political considerations have again interfered. Francis and Charles V. have concluded a peace. Charles V. has sent a proposition to the afflicted widower on the throne of England, that his fourth wife should be the Emperor's niece. Henry interprets this as an indication that his power is actually feared by the Emperor, and that he can now cope with the Pope without bothering himself with the terms of church fellowship which these obstinate and narrow-minded Lutherans want to impose.

The ambassadors understood the situation and prepared to retire. Myconius felt his strength failing, and feared that if he tarried much longer in the fogs of London, his struggle for life would soon end. He wrote to Cranmer September 10th. "Although for the sake of advancing Christ's glory I am ready also to suffer all things; yet since, in the articles and summary of Christian doctrine, we have advanced so far as to agree now concerning the chief; and since, as to what is left touching abuses, we have explained the opinion of our princes, doctors, churches and of ourselves both verbally and in writing, and the doctors now know our judgment, they will be able also in our absence to weigh them, and to determine what they see to be pleasing to the divine will and useful to the church of God." [13] Nor is the official letter which they left in England without great

[11] Burnet, *Record Book* III: xlviii.
[12] Piper's "*Die Zeugen der Wahrheit*," Vol. III: p. 445.
[13] *Strype's Memorials*, VI: 139.

interest. We quote from the summary of it which the king had prepared:

"After they had related what was given them in commandment, and that they had conferred of the articles of the Christian religion for two months with some bishops and doctors of divinity, appointed them by the King's Majesty; they doubt not that a firm and perpetual concord betwixt their princes and the king's majesty, and their bishops, divines and subjects would follow in the doctrine of the gospel, to the praise of God, and the ruin of the Roman Anti-Christ. And because they cannot stay for the rest of the disputation concerning abuses, before they depart they think it their duty to declare their sentence of some articles of abuses; which, after their departure, the king's majesty may take care that his bishops and divines confer together of. They say, the purity of doctrine cannot be conserved, unless those abuses be taken away, that fight with the Word of God, and have produced and maintained the tyranny and idolatry of the Roman Anti-Christ."

Yet when the time for the departure of the commission came, the king was profuse in compliments. Writing to the Elector he styled them his "most blameless friends, who have presented arguments so eminent in sound learning, wisdom, uncommon candor, and supreme devotion to Christian godliness, that their intercourse has been in the highest degree charming and agreeable to us, and we entertain the well-assured hope that, with God's assistance, fruit and success will follow the counsels that have been begun." The Saxon Vice-Chancellor took with him, as a memorial of his sumptuous entertainment, three horses and a carriage presented by the king. When, a few weeks later, their owner exhibited them at Smalcald, the ludicrousness of the whole procedure was such, that Luther could not refrain from some amusing remarks, which may be found in his Table-Talk.[14]

The subject, however, has its serious as well as its humorous

[14] Erlangen Ed. *Luther's Works*, Vol. 62, p. 453.

side. As Seckendorf remarks: "The just judgment of God against the horrible vices of the king ought to be recognized."[15]

"The failure of these negotiations with the German princes was one of the heaviest blows sustained by the English Reformation during the reign of Henry VIII. It both removed the salutary restraint hitherto imposed on the King's caprices by an unwillingness to break with those who were embarked in the same cause, and it also enlisted his personal feelings on the side of the tenets he had so zealously pledged himself to defend."[16]

THE THIRTEEN ARTICLES OF 1538.

If the question, then, be asked, why is not the Church of England a Lutheran Church? the true answer is, Because a wicked ruler interfered within a sphere that did not belong to him, and abruptly terminated the measures of the true representatives of the Church, which clearly indicated a readiness to accept the Lutheran Confessions.[17]

This is shown further by the Articles of 1538, evidently drawn up at the Conference, and preserved with other documents pertaining to it, which were discovered about 1830 by Dr. Jenkyns among the manuscripts of Cranmer. They have no weight except as historical evidence of the facts which we are tracing, having failed of their purpose, and, not having received any formal sanction. They were filed away, to serve an important purpose afterwards in the preparation of the Articles of 1552, through which they continue to live in the Thirty-Nine Articles. The subjects of the articles are I. Of the Unity of God and the Trinity of Persons. II. Of Original Sin. III. Of the Two Natures of Christ. IV. Of Justification. V. Of the Church. VI. Of Baptism. VII. Of the Eucharist. VIII. Of Repen-

---

[15] Vol. III : p. 180.

[16] Jenkyn's Cranmer, I : xxv.

[17] "It is an unjust scandal of our adversaries, and a gross error in ourselves, to compute the nativity of our religion from Henry the Eighth ; who, though he rejected the Pope, refused not the faith of Rome."—Sir Thomas Browne's *Religio Medici*, § 5.

tance. IX. Of the Use of the Sacraments. X. Of the Ministers of the Church. XI. Of Ecclesiastical Rites. XII. Of Civil Affairs. XIII. Of the Resurrection of Bodies, and the Final Judgment.

The reader may judge for himself how closely the Augsburg Confession is followed:

AUGSBURG CONFESSION, (1530). Art. I.	ARTICLES (1538.) Art. I.
The churches with common consent among us, do teach that the decree of the Nicene Synod concerning the unity of the divine essence and of the three persons is true, and without any doubt to be believed: to wit., that there is one divine essence, which is called and is God, eternal, without body, indivisible, of infinite power, wisdom, goodness; the Creator and Preserver of all things visible and invisible; and that yet there be three persons of the same essence and power, who are also co-eternal, the Father, the Son, and the Holy Ghost.	We judge that the decree of the Nicene Synod concerning the unity of the divine essence and the three persons is true, and without any doubt to be believed: to wit., that there is one divine essence, which both is called and is God, eternal, without body, indivisible, of infinite power, wisdom, goodness; the Creator and Preserver of all things visible and invisible; and that yet there be three persons of the same essence and power, and co-eternal, the Father, the Son, and the Holy Ghost.
And they use the name person in that signification which the ecclesiastical writers have used it in this cause, to signify, not a part or quality in another, but that which properly subsisteth.	And we use the name person in that signification which the ecclesiastical writers have used in this case to signify not a part or quality in another, but that which properly subsisteth.
They condemn all heresies which have sprung up against this article, as the Manichees, who set down two principles, good and evil; in the same manner, the Valentinians, Arians, Eunomians, Mahometans and all such like.	We condemn all heresies which have sprung up against this article, as the Manichees who set down two principles, a good and an evil; also the Valentinians, Arians, Eunomians, Mahometans and all such like.
They condemn also the Samosatenes, old and new; who when they earnestly contend that there is but one person, do craftily and wickedly trifle after the manner of Rhetoricians about the Word and the Holy Ghost, that they are not distinct persons, but that the Word signifieth a vocal word, and the Spirit a motion created in things.	We condemn also the Samosatanes old and new, who when they earnestly contend that there is but one person, do craftily and wickedly trifle after the manner of Rhetoricians about the Word and the Holy Ghost, that there are not distinct persons, but that the Word signifieth a vocal word, and the Spirit a motion created in things.

Art. II.	Art. II.
Also they teach that after Adam's fall, all men begotten after the common course of nature, are born with sin; that is, without the fear of God, without trust in him, and with fleshly appetite; and that this disease or original fault is truly sin, condemning and bringing eternal death now also upon all that are not born again by baptism and the Holy Spirit.	All men begotten after the common course of nature are born with original sin; that is with an absence of the original righteousness that ought to be in them,[18] on which account they are children of wrath, and fail in knowledge of God, fear of God, trust towards God, etc. And they have fleshly appetite conflicting with the law of God; and this disease or fault of origin is truly sin, condemning and bringing eternal death now also upon those who are not born again by baptism and the Holy Spirit.
They condemn the Pelagians and others, who deny this original fault to be sin indeed; and who, so as to lesson the glory of the merit and benefits of Christ, argue that a man may, by the strength of his own reason, be justified before God.	We condemn the Pelagians and others, who deny the fault of origin to be sin; and who, so as to lessen the glory of the merit and benefits of Christ argue that man can satisfy God's law by his own natural strength without the Holy Spirit, and by the good works of reason be pronounced righteous before God.

Article III. corresponds to Article III. of Augsburg Confession except in the second word, where we find "*docemus*," instead of "*docent*." Art. IV. "Of Justification" is much longer than the corresponding Article of the Augsburg Confession, which it includes but amplifies. The definition of the "Ten Articles" is introduced, but so modified by qualifying clauses as to bring it into nearer accord with the Confession. Objections to the Lutheran doctrine are also met by the formulation of the statement that the faith described is not inoperative knowledge, or simply a knowledge of the articles of faith, etc. It closes with a verbal reproduction of Art. V. of the Augsburg Confession. Art. V. discusses at length the definition of the Church in harmony with the Lutheran Confession, drawing material both from the Augsburg Confession and the Apology.

[18] This variation from the Aug. Conf. is derived from the Apology (78: 15): "The ancient definition, understood aright, expresses the same thing when it says: 'Original sin is the absence of original righteousness.'"

Art. VI. includes Art. IX. of the Augsburg Confession, and Art. I. of "The Ten Articles" of 1536, concerning Infant Baptism, taken as we have seen from Melanchthon's "*Adversus Anabaptistas,*" and adds a statement concerning Adult Baptism. Art. VII. teaches the Lutheran doctrine of the Lord's Supper in the terms agreed upon at Wittenberg in 1536. The only article of the "Repetitio" there framed of which we have any knowledge is quoted by Seckendorf:

REPETITIO (1536).	ARTICLES (1538).
"We constantly believe and teach that in the sacrament of the Body and Blood of the Lord, Christ's body and blood are truly, substantially and really present under the forms of bread and wine, and that under the same forms, they are truly and corporeally tendered and distributed to all those who receive the sacrament."	"Of the Eucharist we constantly believe and teach that in the sacrament of the Body and Blood of the Lord, Christ's body and blood are truly, substantially and really present under the forms of bread and wine, and that under the same forms, they are truly and really tendered and distributed to those who receive the sacrament, whether good or bad."

Of the remaining Articles, IX., X. and the first paragraph of XI. are substantially derived from the Augsburg Confession, though expanding the doctrine, guarding it from misconceptions and answering objections. Articles VIII. "Of Repentance,". XII., "Of Civil Affairs," and XIII. "Of the Resurrection," are treated at much greater length, but also bear clear marks of the source whence they come.

CHAPTER X.

MORE ENGLISH LUTHERAN LITERATURE.

The First English Systematic Theology. Taverner's Sarcerius. Its Significance and Purpose. Connection between Myconius and Sarcerius. Sarcerius and the Reformation of Nassau. Count William of Nassau. Sarcerius as an Organizer. His Examinations. His Skill as a Teacher. Relation to William of Orange. Henry VIII's delight with the Book of Sarcerius. Letter of Sarcerius to Henry. The Wittenberg Faculty on Henry's Study of Sarcerius. Coverdale's Revision of Matthewe's Bible (the Great or Crumwell's Bible); of the Great Bible (Cranmer's). Taverner's Revision of Matthewe's Bible.

WHILE these negotiations were pending, (August 12th, 1538) the first English work on Systematic Theology appeared in a translation of "The Common Places" of Erasmus Sarcerius. Even the German language could not boast of a Lutheran system of theology as early as this, which appeared, first in Latin, and then, so soon afterwards, in English. The dedication to Henry VIII, by the translator, Richard Taverner, states that it was translated by order of Crumwell. " Now of late he hath impelled me to translate into English this book of Erasmus Sarcerius, a treasure inestimable unto Christian men." "Whatsoever this book is, like as by the impulsion and commandment of my said old master, my Lord privy seal, I have translated it into our vulgar tongue; so his Lordship hath willed me to offer and dedicate the same unto your most noble and redoubted Majesty." It is also stated that this treatise of Sarcerius was preferred to the " Common Places" of Melanchthon, in making the selection of the work to be translated, because "only in this they differ, that Melanchthon directeth his style to the understanding only of the learned persons well exercised in Scriptures. This tempereth his pen also to the capacity of young students of scripture, and such as have not had much exercise in the same."

We see, therefore, in this book, another provision made for the thorough reformation of the Church of England. It was hoped that entire harmony would be reached in the confessional basis adopted; that, not only the doctrinal articles of the Augsburg Confession, but also those on abuses, would be received; and that, then, since, in other Lutheran countries, the Church Orders contained a summary of doctrine, according to which the pastors were to conform their preaching, such a provision would be made in this translation of Sarcerius. Myconius, the theologian of the embassy, possibly had recommended this course to Cranmer or Crumwell. At the birth-place of Sarcerius, Annaberg in Saxony, Myconius had not only been educated, but had lived for years as a Franciscan monk. Although Sarcerius was ten years younger, they had both attended the same Latin school; and though scarcely cotemporary in school, the son of one of the most wealthy and influential citizens of the place could not have been unknown to the young monk even in the days of his subjection to the Papacy. Since both were now active in the same cause, the local attachments were not without their influence.

Just at that time, Sarcerius was engaged, at the call of Count William, father of the great William of Orange, Stadtholder of Holland, in re-organizing the church in Nassau upon an evangelical basis. He had been prepared for this work by studying at Wittenberg, under Luther and Melanchthon and by extensive experience as a teacher. He had left Wittenberg in 1530, and, from 1530–36, had been Subrector of a Gymnasium at Lübeck established, in 1530, by Bugenhagen, with the exception of several brief intervals during which he taught at Rostock, and at Gratz. Called as teacher to Nassau in 1536, when, in 1538, the time had come for a more thorough reformation of that country, he was appointed Superintendent and at once set vigorously to work.

The story of the preparatory efforts at reformation in Nassau is exceedingly interesting. Count William and his family had always been on intimate terms with Charles V.; and personal considerations were, therefore, an obstacle to his acceptance of the purified Gospel. But Tetzel's sale of indulgences in his realm had excited his opposition. He had heard Luther's defence at Worms with admiration; and, on returning home, had sent to the Elector Frederick for Luther's writings, which Frederick transmitted with the message: "By God's help, I will make, through these, a good Christian of you." Again at the Diet of Augsburg, he was impressed by the arguments of the reformers; but was so much under the influence of the Emperor, of whose retinue his brother was a member, that, after the diet, he accepted a commission to Wittenberg, for the purpose, if possible, of winning the young elector from the Lutheran cause. But his visit to Wittenberg, instead of changing the elector, brought Count William to a decision; and he returned in full sympathy with the reformers. Two evangelical preachers, Heilmann of Van Crombach, and Leonhard Mogner, were appointed by him to important positions, the former, as his chaplain, at Dillenburg, and the latter at Siegen, and entrusted with the work of preparing a new "Church Order," which appeared in 1531, and abolished the grosser Papistical abuses. Entering the Smalcald League in 1534, at Dillenburg and Siegen the Brandenburg-Nürnberg Order was introduced. Sarcerius' call as a teacher was to prepare for the more radical changes to be effected in 1538. His first work was to thoroughly instruct the pastors. He was still the accomplished teacher, who regarded it his first work to drill his new pupils, the clergy of Nassau, in fundamental definitions. Both at the Synods which he held, and in his visitations, the pastors were thoroughly examined, and were expected to show their familiarity with the definitions which their Superintendent had carefully wrought out and published for their use. We read in his report to Count William how he examined the pastors "Concerning God; the Trinity in general; the Father;

the Son; the Holy Ghost; the holy angels; the Wicked Angels; the Creation of man and his Fall; the promise to the Church; the Law, and its species; the Gospel and its revelation; Faith; Justification and Life Everlasting; Good Works; the Cross; the Sacraments; Prayer; the Magistracy and Ministers;" and, then, examined the people, to learn what their pastors had taught them on these topics. This was certainly far more thorough than even the excellent plan elsewhere pursued of attaching to the "Church Order" adopted, a simple outline of doctrine for the guidance of pastors. Besides as Gerdesius remarks,[1] the philosophical training of Sarcerius rendered him especially happy in his doctrinal statements. It was, therefore, one of these books prepared by Sarcerius for his clergy, that Taverner translated.

From the reprint of Taverner's translation, published in 1577, when William of Orange was in the midst of his conflict with the Duke of Alva, the placid but determined features of this skilful teacher and organizer stand forth in an excellent engraving, which we find also precisely reproduced in the second volume of Gerdes' Miscellanies. Underneath the engraving are the Latin lines connecting the work of Sarcerius in the reformation of Nassau, with the work of the son of his patron in the Netherlands.

> Quam claram facis, haec eadem NASSAVIA clarum
> Te facit; et Scriptis nobile nomen habes;
> Romanum oppugnas; MAGNUS GUILIELMUS at ille
> Hispanum, Factis nobile nomen habens.

"Nassau, which thou dost make renowned, this maketh thee renowned. By thy writings, thou hast a noble name; thou attackest the Roman; but the GREAT WILLIAM, by his deeds, having a noble name, is attacking the Spaniards."

This means simply that the work begun by Sarcerius was not understood in its full significance, until the great struggle in the Netherlands occurred. William of Orange, until his fifteenth year, was trained under the influences determined by Sar-

[1] *Miscellanea Groningina*, II: 606.

cerius; his temporary Romanism was due to the attractions of the Imperial Court, and the confidence of Charles V., when, as a youth, he became his page; but his sound Lutheran early education at length gained the victory over the error in which he was bound. Nevertheless, not being a theologian, the form of Protestantism of which he was the champion in that terrific struggle, was that of Calvinism.

King Henry was at first greatly delighted with this book of Sarcerius. In March 1539, in a conference at Frankfort to be hereafter mentioned, his ambassadors met Sarcerius, and referring to the translation of his book, induced him to write a letter, to be carried by them to England. It is as follows:

"Grace and peace from our Lord Jesus Christ. Most Serene King: When a few days ago, by command of the illustrious prince, William of Nassau, my most clement lord, I came to Frankfort, I found that at the abode of Philip Melanchthon, the ambassadors of your Serenity, men of high repute both in doctrine and in integrity of life; who, since, among other things, they heard my name, asked whether I were that Erasmus Sarcerius, who had published 'a method' upon the chief articles of Scripture, I replied that I was he. Then they at once began to tell me, that, by the command of your Serenity, my method had been translated into the English language; and that I am now speaking English. Then they added that if I would please write to your Serenity, they would see to it that my letter would be delivered. Although disinclined to follow their advice, since I measured myself by my own rule, i. e., considering my inexperience and amount of learning inadequate to satisfy your Serenity, since you are endowed with talent unexcelled in acuteness and depth both of knowledge and judgment, yet when I heard of the kindness of your Serenity towards all zealous for, and lovers of the pure religi n, I began to write in my unlearned style, commending myself humbly to your Serenity. If I see that my writings please you, I will see that you shortly receive my 'Common Places, methodically arranged' somewhat enlarged, more topics being added, and also terms for vices, of which Scripture makes mention. Since also in the realm of your Serenity, the true religion is now being planted, to the glory of God and the benefit of men, I will send also Postils upon the Gospels for the Lord's Days and the Festivals; as well as upon the Epistles for the Lord's Days and Festivals, dedicated to your Serenity. The Lord keep your royal Majesty safe and secure, to the glory of the Gospel and the peace of the church. Frankfort, March 10th, 1539. ERASMUS SARCERIUS."

A few months later, (October 22d, 1539), the Wittenberg Faculty, in a paper to be hereafter more fully described, declared that Henry, with respect to "The Six Articles," was acting against his conscience, because "he himself has had a little book of Sarcerius translated and printed in his own language, which he has used as a prayer-book, wherein the matter is briefly presented."[2]

Steadily also the work of Bible revision and Bible circulation advanced. With Matthews' or Rogers' version, the English Bible was at last complete, but very unequal in the merits of its several parts, and requiring early revision. With remarkable self-abnegation, Coverdale undertook this work. That he had already prepared a translation, whose defects he thus acknowledged, was with him no consideration. He was content to make Matthews' Bible the basis. Paris was determined upon as the place of publication, and thither he went, with his publisher Grafton, in May 1538. Obtaining a royal license from the French King, the work of printing continued until December 17th, when, by the interference of the French ecclesiastics it was prohibited, editor and publisher compelled to flee, and the sheets confiscated. Sold, however, for waste paper, instead of being burned, the most of them were saved; and the printing was completed in April 1539, the book being called from its size, (15 x 9 inches) the "GREAT BIBLE," or Crumwell's Bible, as it owed its origin to the "Lord Privy Seal," Copies were

[2] *Corpus Reformatorum*, III: 796; De Wette's *Luther's Briefen*, V: 213.

placed in every church where parishioners could always have access to them, and where the people would congregate in large numbers, as successive readers would take their turn in reading aloud from the Word of Life. Almost everyone who could command the means sought a copy for himself. "Even little boys flocked among the rest to hear portions of the Holy Scripture read."[3]

In making this revision, Coverdale omitted the polemical notes and prefaces of Rogers, doubtless in order to make the edition less offensive to those inclined to the old order. This is the edition from which the Psalter of "The Book of Common Prayer," was taken.

Again, revising the "Great Bible" of 1539, in 1540 (April, July and November) and in 1541 (November and and December), Coverdale gave the public what is known as Cranmer's Bible, making many changes in his previous work, and in some instances reverting to his older renderings. Dr. Eadie[4] has reached the conclusion that though it was a double revision of Matthew's of 1537, the Great Bible is not only inferior as a translation, but has interspersed through it a great variety of paraphrastic and supplementary clauses from the Vulgate, some being preserved in the Bishops."

The two editions which are known as Tonstal and Heath's, are not revisions as they profess to be, but only Cranmer's Bible with a deceiving title-page. The Romish power was in temporary sway, but the king and the people still demanded the Bible; hence these representatives of the hierarchical party, unable to prevent the demands, adopted this futile expedient.

Prior, however, to this, and almost cotemporaneous with the first appearance of the "Great Bible," the revision of Matthews' Bible by Richard Taverner, the learned translator of the Augsburg Confession and Sarcerius' "Common Places," was published. Taverner was a very accomplished Greek scholar, and

[3] Strype's *Memorials of Cranmer*, I: 142:
[4] *The English Bible*, I: 383.

a number of his changes have been incorporated into our Authorized Version. His accuracy in the rendering of the Greek article has been especially noted. For this work, he was imprisoned after the death of his friend, Crumwell.

But we must not anticipate events too far. The political negotiations of 1539 have been already passed over.

CHAPTER XI.

FRUITLESS NEGOTIATIONS OF 1539.

Pharaoh again seeks Moses. Conferences at Frankfort. Another Commission asked for. Lutherans decline to send Theologians. An Embassy of Civilians. Melanchthon's Hopes. His long letters to Henry. Gardiner in the Ascendant. Henry's Answer to the Articles "On Abuses" —"the Bloody Statute of the Six Articles." Luther's Indignation. Shall Melanchthon go to England? Negotiations concerning Anne of Cleves. Firmness of the Elector of Saxony. Opinion of the Wittenberg Faculty. Their Opinion adverse to further Negotiations. Melanchthon's Minute Review of "the Six Articles." An Eloquent Appeal.

THE English King soon apprehended that he could not afford to be as independent as he imagined, when he broke up the conference of 1538, after the doctrinal articles of the Augsburg Confession had been received. Pharaoh again seeks Moses. A cloud was rising on the continent, which seemed to portend that, unless prompt measures be taken, the lightning of the Vatican might yet strike England. Henry became uneasy, lest the Lutheran princes and the Emperor might reach an agreement, in the conferences held at Frankfort-on-the-Main from February to April 1539, and that he would be left alone to oppose Charles. A formidable array of Lutheran theologians were present at Frankfort; among them Melanchthon, Spalatin, Myconius, Aepinus, Blaurer, Osiander and Sarcerius. Christopher Mount and Thomas Paynel were sent to represent the English cause. They protested against any action on the part of the Lutheran princes without a previous consultation with Henry. Again the proposition was made that a commission of theologians be sent to England. To this, the princes answer that it would be useless, since there could be no change from what had been already decided in the conferences of 1536 at Wittenberg with Fox, Heath and Barnes;[1] and give a summary of the Scriptural arguments against abuses, to aid the King in coming to a correct decision. Until the force of these be conceded, no provision is to be made for negotiations on theological points. Two civilians, however were appointed to confer personally with Henry, explain the situation, and arrange the preliminaries for a military alliance in case they were attacked by the same enemy. Vice Chancellor Burkhard and Ludwig a Baumbach were designated for such service and proceeded to England. Melanchthon once more is hopeful. It seems to him as though his scheme, "that an agreement with respect to godly doctrine be established among all those churches which condemn the tyranny and godlessness of the Bishop of Rome,"[2] had another fair opportunity for consideration. Henry had spoken to the commission of 1538 in such exalted terms of Melanchthon, that the latter now treats the English monarch to two long letters (March 25th, April 1st),[3] full of those compliments in which the king delighted, and which the classical pen of Melanchthon could so gracefully give. He praises Henry's heroic virtues, and compares him to Achilles. Melanchthon, alas, was using carnal weapons, instead of those which are mighty through God for the pulling down of strongholds. Yet, however ill-chosen the weapons, there is no questioning the ultimate purpose of his letters. He is urgent that the subject of abuses be at once considered. "Your Highness has already successfully begun to remove certain superstitions. I ask, therefore, that the reform of the other abuses be undertaken."[4] Nor is he content with addressing Henry. He not only recalls his delightful intercourse with Heath three years before and writes to him, but also sends a long communication

---

[1] *Seckendorf* III: 224; *Strype's Memorials*, VI: 156.
[2] *Corpus Reformatorum* III: p. 672.
[3] Ib. pp. 671, 682.
[4] Ib. p. 673.

to Cranmer, which while very severe in its complaints of the English bishops, bears testimony to the fidelity of Cranmer, Crumwell and Latimer. Melanchthon could not have foreseen how useless all these efforts would be. Since the death of Fox, the influence of Gardiner outweighs that of Cranmer. Two days' conference in Crumwell's residence, May 16th and 18th, showed that no agreement was possible.

THE SIX ARTICLES OF 1539.

The hierarchial element was rapidly maturing its boldest measures, which were to bring with them persecution and martyrdom for some of the more prominent champions of the evangelical faith. The project of enforcing uniformity in religion became a a matter of deliberation in Parliament. The laymen in the House of Lords relinquished the floor to the bishops. Cranmer, Latimer and Shaxton, supported feebly by Heath, held for days a drawn battle with the other side, led by Gardiner and Tunstall, when the king himself entered the arena, and spoke with such decision, that Shaxton alone remained firm. Strype infers that in this discussion, Cranmer was greatly aided by a little treatise of Urban Regius.[5] The bill of the Six Articles enforced belief (1) in transubstantiation; (2) in non-necessity of communion in both kinds; (3) in the sinfulness of marriage after entering the priesthood; (4) in the absolute obligation of vows of chastity; (5) in the efficacy of private masses; (6) in compulsory auricular confession. Disbelief of the first article had attached to it the penalty of death at the stake; while the rejection of the other articles had a gradation of penalties attached, with death as the extreme. It has often been termed "the bloody statute of the Six Articles," or "the whipe with sixe strings."

Such was Henry's answer to the articles of the Augsburg Confession, "On Abuses." "It would be difficult," says Charles Knight,[6] "to understand how such a statute could have passed,

[5] Strype's *Cranmer*, I: 166.
[6] *History of England*, (Amer. ed.) p. 276.

if the great body of the people had been inclined to a higher species of reformation than consisted in the destructive principle which assailed the externals of the Church. Cranmer was too yielding, and Crumwell too politic, to oppose the party which carried the statute backed by the irresistible force of the king's will. The subservient courtiers, who had become improprietors, and provided half-starved monks to do the service of the altar at the cheapest rate, were wholly indifferent to the principles through which the continental reformers were daily waxing in strength." Cranmer sends away his wife to avoid the penalties of the statute. Latimer resigns his bishopric. Alesius flees to Wittenberg. Dr. Barnes, who had been sent as an ambassador by the king to Hamburg, does not venture for awhile to return.

LUTHER'S OPINION.

July 12th was fixed as the date at which the statute should begin to be enforced. Two days before, Luther thanks God "that he has freed our Church from the vexatious King of England, who with the greatest diligence desired and sought alliance with us, and was not received; undoubtedly because God for some special purpose hindered it, for he has always been inconstant and vacillating. I am glad that we are free from the blasphemer. He wants to be Head of the Church in England without any means sanctioned by Christ, who will give the title to no bishop, however pious or godly he may be, to say nothing of any king or prince. The devil is driving this king, so that he vexes and martyrs Christ. I am mortified and pained that Master Philip M. has dedicated the most beautiful prefaces and introductions to the most rascally fellows."[7] About the same time, we find also this estimate: "He is still the same King Harry whom I portrayed in my first book. He will indeed find his judge. His plan never pleased me, in that *he wants to kill the Pope's body but to keep his soul, i. e. his false doctrine.*"[8] "The

[7] Erlangen Ed. *Luther's Works*, LXI: 365.
[8] Ib. p. 304.

King of England is an enemy to the Pope's person; but not of his nature and doctrine: he kills only the body, but lets the soul live."[9]

A FAITHFUL PRINCE.

But Luther's rejoicing that he and his colleagues are at last done with Henry forever, is not of long duration. Crumwell was defeated, but his influence with the king was not altogether lost, and even during that summer the preliminary negotiations looking towards the marriage with Ann of Cleves, the Elector's sister-in-law, were begun. The Landgrave of Hesse was anxious for a favorable consideration of the propositions made through Christopher Mount; but the Elector wished to hear nothing more. Bucer interposed, writing a long letter from Strasburg, describing the extremities to which the friends of the Gospel in England were put, and begging that Melanchthon may be sent as a special ambassador to use his influence in a personal interview with Henry, in order to cause a cessation of the persecution. How can we help but admire the candor of the Magnanimous Christian prince in his answer? He has a clear conscience, he says, that for four or five years he has spared himself no effort which might aid the cause of religion in England. He had, at a great expense, supported the Bishop of Hereford at Wittenberg for three months, and had him instructed sufficiently concerning the chief articles of doctrine. The bishop had reported everything to the king, who did not deign to reply. In 1538 a commission had been sent by him to England; and another in the present year—all to no purpose. He assured the English ambassador that "he received the living Word of God according to the Augsburg Confession, and thus publicly professed it, without which there is no true knowledge of God or hope of salvation; and from this Confession he would not recede even though he were compelled to lose life, and all that he had."[10]

[9] Ib. LX: 217.
[10] Seckendorf, III: pp. 225 sq.

THE WITTENBERG FACULTY.

On October 22d, Luther, Jonas, Bugenhagen, and Melanchthon sign a paper concerning further negotiations with Henry, from which we give some extracts. Melanchthon is supposed to have composed it.

"Although in our own persons, we shrink from no dangers or labors; yet in this case, assuredly, enough has been done for the instruction and admonition of the king, for the following reasons: St. Paul says that we ought to receive the weak, but let the obstinate one go, who, he says, is condemned by his own judgment, i. e., one who publicly sins against his conscience. On the other hand, he who is called 'weak' will learn, and not persecute that which he understands, but receive, hold and advance it. Yet that the King of England is acting against conscience can be inferred from this, viz.: He knows that our doctrine concerning the use of the whole sacrament, Confession and the Marriage of Priests is true, or at least that it is not contrary to God's Word. Now he says in his Articles and in his Edict, that some of these points are contrary to God's Law. This he says undoubtedly against his conscience, for many writings have come to him written both publicly and also especially for him, which he has read. He himself has had a little book of Sarcerius translated and printed in his own language, which he has used as a prayer-book, wherein the matter is briefly presented. We understand also that he himself has spoken otherwise of this doctrine, and among other things has said of the King of France that he has done wrong in persecuting it; for he understands and knows that it is right. Besides he has many godly and learned preachers, as the deposed Bishop Latimer, Cranmer and others, whom he has heard and suffered for a period. And yet in spite of all this, he condemns this doctrine more severely than the Pope himself. We therefore apprehend that this king is of such a mind as does not seek God's glory, but, as he declared to the Vice-Chancellor, wants to do only what pleases himself, whereby he shows that he does not regard the doctrine a matter of moment, and that like Antiochus and others, he wants to establish a religion of his own.

Secondly, as it is now manifest that the king is acting against his conscience, we do not think that it is our duty to instruct him anew, but we ought to abide by the rule of Paul, which teaches that the adversaries should be admonished twice, and, if that do not help, they should be shunned as those who are acting against conscience. Such admonition has already been given.

Besides we hear that the king is a sophist and glossator, who likes to color all things with his art of making glosses. But one who has no delight in clear, plain truth, can easily twist matters, even though he has to tear his own mouth, like the pike, when torn by the hook. In Sirach 37, it is written: 'God does not give grace to one who uses sophistry, and he does not attain wisdom.' For there is no end to his hypercriticisms and distortions. Hence we cannot constantly be treating with such, and especially as experience shows how offensive this is to the Lord. Since then the king takes delight in such making of glosses, we have little hope that he will allow himself to be set right. Then too we must consider that the men who have influence with him have no conscience. The Bishop of Winchester [Gardiner] carries with him throughout the country two unchaste women in men's apparel, and yet judges that the marriage of priests is against God's law, and is so arrogant that he says that he will publicly maintain against the whole world that the proposition: 'By faith we are justified' is incorrect. He is also an extreme tyrant, as this year he has had two men burned for no other reason than alone for transubstantiation; so that the saying is true, that Lord and servant are of like mind. From all this, we infer that up to this time enough has been done; as we know that we have spoken faithfully and in a Christian way, and hold that it is no longer our duty to make further efforts, for there is little hope. Perhaps God does not want his Gospel to be maintained by a king, who has such a bad reputation. Yet we leave it to your Electoral Grace's further consideration, as to whether the attempt be made still once more. We would also not fail to make an expostulation with the king, and to admonish him again in writing. More is not our duty. For what Dr. Bucer points to: 'Go into all the world, and teach,' we are doing by our writings. To respond farther to a present call is not commanded us.

I, Philip, have written also to the same effect to Crumwell and the Archbishop of Canterbury. But letters have come to me from England to the effect that the king receives my letters with displeasure; and hence it is to be well considered as to whether though I were in England, the king would give me an audience or would not direct me as he did the former ambassadors to his proud, unlearned bishops with whom to quarrel. How acutely the king disputes concerning such matters may be learned from two arguments. Of good works he argues thus: 'Since bad works merit eternal wrath, it must follow that good works must merit eternal salvation;' and this argument I hear he will not suffer to be taken from him. The other, concerning the marriage of priests, is this: 'If he have the power to give an order that one as long as he wants to be at court is not free, he has the power also to forbid priests from marrying.' This is the very superlative of perspicacity; and hence he reviles and condemns us. Whether it be possible to dispute with one who resorts to such arguments, your Grace must consider."[11]

AN ELOQUENT APPEAL.

Under date of November 1st, Melanchthon writes Henry a letter which fills over twelve pages of the book before us. The glow of a just indignation colors every line. For once all timidity has vanished, and he is bold as one speaking as the oracle of God. The Six Articles are reviewed in detail, and their defects elaborately portrayed. We can quote only a few passages:

[11] De Wette's *Luther's Briefen*, V: 213 sqq.; C. R. III: 796 sqq.; Erl. Ed. *Luther's Works*, LV: 243 sqq.

'I am pained that you are becoming the minister of another's cruelty and godlessness. I am pained that the doctrine of Christ is being restrained, vicious rites established, and lusts strengthened. I hear that men of excellent learning and godliness, Latimer, Shaxton, Cranmer and others, are held in custody; for them I pray courage becoming Christians. And although nothing better or more glorious could happen to them than to meet death in the confession of such manifest truth; yet I do not wish your Royal Highness to be stained by the blood of such men, I do not wish the lights of your Church to be extinguished, I do not wish such concession to be made to the godlessness and venomous Pharisaic hatred of Christ's enemies, I do not wish pleasure to be afforded to the Roman Antichrist, who delights in his heart that you are taking up arms for him, and hopes by the aid of the bishops to regain easily that possession from which he was driven by your honorable and godly counsels. He sees that the bishops are for a time complying with your will, but that they are joined to the Roman pontiff. The Roman pontiffs understand these arts; before these days, they have made their way out of most severe tempests by singing.'[12]

He argues, then, concerning the articles on "Abuses." "In the decree how many things are artfully set forth! 'Confession,' it says, 'is necessary, and to l e retained.' Why does it not expressly say that, according to divine law, the enumeration of offences is necessary? The bishops knew, that this declaration is false; the words, therefore, are made general, in order that darkness may be diffused over the people. When they hear that confession is necessary, they understand that enumeration of offences is necessary. There are similar deceptions in the article 'Of Private Masses.' Even the beginning: 'It is necessary to retain private masses,' is absolutely false. Who thought thus for more than four hundred years after the Apostles, when there were no private masses? But afterward the sophisms followed, 'That by them the people might receive divine consolations

---

[12] *Corpus Reformatorum* III: 806.

and benefits.' Why do they not add what these consolations and benefits are? The bishops do not mention "application" and 'merit,' because they know that these cannot be defended. They play with words, in order that they may escape, if 'application' be found fault with. And yet they want 'application' to be understood by the people! They want the idolatrous idea to be confirmed that, for some, this sacrifice merits remission of guilt, for others, an alleviation of all calamities, and finally brings gain in business, and whatever the anxiety of men imagines.

It is a like sophism, when they say that the marriage of priests conflicts with divine law. They are not ignorant of the passage in Paul: 'A bishop must be the husband of one wife.' Hence they know that, by divine law, marriage is allowed. But when they say that to this a vow has been added, they play with words; they do not say that marriage is hindered by a vow, but they absolutely lay down the proposition, that the marriage of priests conflicts with divine law. Then what impudence and atrocious cruelty they add, when they order marriages to be dissolved, while the sacerdotal vow, even were it valid, would only bind them not to remain in the ministry, in case they married. That this is the opinion of synods and councils, is manifest. O wicked bishops, O impudence of Winchester [Gardiner] who by these deceptions imagines that he is escaping the eyes of Christ and the judgment of all the godly in the entire world!"

What more eloquent than Melanchthon's conclusions?

"Again I entreat you, for the sake of our Lord Jesus Christ, to modify and amend the decree of the bishops; and, in this, serve the glory of Christ, and have regard for your salvation and that of the churches. Be moved by the prayers of many godly men throughout the whole world, who wish that kings apply their influence to the true reformation of the Church, and to abolish godless services and to defend the Gospel. Look upon those godly men who are bound for the sake of the Gospel, and who are true members of Christ. If the decree be not changed, the cruelty of the bishops will prevail without end in the Church.

For the devil has them as the instruments of his fury and hatred against Christ; he impels them to the slaughter of Christ's members. All godly persons beg and beseech you not to prefer their godless and cruel sentences, and sophistical cavils, to our most just intercession. If they gain from you what they ask, God will undoubtedly grant you great rewards for your piety, and your virtue will be proclaimed in the writings and by the voice of the godly. For Christ will judge between those doing well and ill for his church.

As long as literature shall live, the memory of these important affairs will be transmitted to posterity. When we serve the glory of Christ, and our churches are churches of Christ, some shall never be wanting who shall be able to advocate a godly cause, to adorn with due praise those who deserve it, and to censure cruelty. Christ is going about, hungry, thirsty, naked, bound, complaining of the madness of pontiffs, of the most unrighteous cruelty of many kings, begging that the members of his body be not wounded, but that true churches be defended, and the Gospel be magnified. To recognize Him, to receive Him, to cherish him—this is the duty of a godly king, and the worship most pleasing to God." [13]

[13] *Corpus Reformatorum* III: 818.

CHAPTER XII.

A LITERARY FORGERY.

Articles falsely ascribed to Luther and Melanchthon circulated in England in 1539. Similar or identical Articles in France in 1535; also in Germany. Seckendorf's detailed examination presented in full. A genuine Paper on the same topics by the leading Lutheran Theologians in 1540. The Fate of the Six Articles. Anne of Cleves. Melanchthon writes once more to Henry. Negotiations in Contemplation. Argument of the Wittenberg Theologians on " Abuses." Cranmer intercedes for the King. Another Reaction. Anne repudiated. Fall of Crumwell. Dr. Barnes burned.

THE opponents of Lutheranism in England resorted for its suppression not only to open violence, but also to arts not unknown among politicians of the Nineteenth Century. In November, 1539, the ambassadors of the Elector of Saxony to England send to their ruler a series of articles which had been industriously circulated as the joint production of Luther and Melanchthon, signed March, 1539, and expressly recanting any statements which had been hitherto made conflicting with them. The document had been used, it is stated, to prejudice the mind of the king, against the apparent vacillation of the Reformers, and thus to determine his course in reference to the Six Articles. Already in 1535, Luther had complained that a similar forged document, composed largely of garbled statements from Melanchthon's writings had been circulated in France; and hence Walch[1] has inferred that the two papers are identical. Neither without interest in this connection, is Seckendorf's discovery[2]

[1] Luther's Works, XIX: 72.
[2] III: p. 228.

of a somewhat amended and interpolated translation into German of the articles preserved in the Archives at Weimar, with the inscription that they had been sent from the Elector to Charles V. Thus it is probable that this forgery was thrice utilized, viz.: in France, in England and in Germany. We cannot help but admire the ingenuity of the composer, so skillfully has the work been done, and so closely do single statements read like expressions occasionally used by the Wittenbergers.

As no less an English authority than Strype, in his "Memorials of the Reformation,"[3] has been misled, and this primary source of information for most English students gives currency to occasional reiteration of these charges by those not acquainted with the facts, we give the articles in full as given by Strype in the English of that time, together with Seckendorf's examination of each article separately:

"I. We confess that there ought to be a policy in the church and a regime. In the which, there must be bishops; who shall have the power of the examine, and ordinance of the ministration of the same, for to exercise the jurisdiction of the same; who shall diligently see, that the churches committed unto them, may be truly instructed with pure and sincere doctrine."

Reply: "Luther and Melanchthon never declared that such Episcopal office was necessary as is established in the Roman Church, with all its power and jurisdiction; neither did they acknowledge an essential dictinction between bishops and pastors; as is manifest from all their writings which were never recalled, and especially from the treatise 'On the Power and Jurisdiction of Bishops,' composed by Melanchthon in the year 1537 at Smalcald, subscribed by Luther, and annexed to the 'Articles,' which he himself composed. They were willing, however, to tolerate bishops, and to comply with the authority of their external administration, provided they saw to it that the Word of God was purely preached, and, abuses being removed, the sacraments be administered according to Christ's institution."

[3] I: 545 sqq.

"II. We admit that it is good and convenient, that in the church, there be a Bishop of Rome, that may be above other bishops; who may gather them together, to see the examination of the doctrine, and the concord of such, as do teach discrepancies in the church. But we admit not the pomp, riches, and pride of the Bishop of Rome; who would make realms subject unto him. The which things do neither help nor promote the gospel; because the Kings that have right thereto, may and are to rule the same."

Reply: "Luther was willing to endure the Papacy with advantage to the church, not even by human law; as is evident from the Smalcald Articles. Melanchthon, in this matter of a singular opinion, to which no one assented, thought that something could be conceded, but upon the same condition, upon which the Episcopate could be admitted."

"III. We confess, that as concerning choice of meats, holy days and ceremonies, there might an agreement be made easily, if there could be a concord in the doctrine of the church, and not such discrepance as there is. For if there were a concord of doctrine in the church, we should not think reasonable to divide us from the church, seen [seeing] that it is not possible that the world might stand without ceremonies and man's constitutions; seen that all innovations without necessity ought to be excluded; and that there is no peril, to us I mean, in the observation of the said ceremonies, and men's constitutions; for that the doctrine be purely handled."

Reply: "They did not deny that separation was necessary because of ceremonies; but regarded these no less than erroneous doctrines a sufficient cause of separation, if they tended to superstition and idolatry, and the opinion of necessity were attached to them, from obligation of conscience and of merit before God, with injury to Christian and ecclesiastical liberty, in view of which it is lawful to change rites for the advantage and profit of the church; but they never used the silly argument from the government of the world to the government of the church, knowing well what injury was introduced into the church thereby."

"IV. We judge to be profitable that *confession* and rehearsal of sins be made in the church. For taking the same away, the doctrine of remission of sins, and of the power of the Keys, should be offuscate and taken away; seeing that in the confession, among other things the people ought to be taught, whence cometh the remission of sins. Provided, that there be honest fashion to instruct the persons that be shriven, and that the consciences be not overlaid with rigorous and exact rehearsal of all sins."

Reply: "Luther never maintained the necessity of the enumeration of sins, or said that, when it was removed, the doctrine of the remission of sins was offuscate; and, therefore, did not censure other churches which, in a diverse manner, aimed at the same end, the preparation and excitation of the communicants in repentance and faith being introduced in the stead of particular confession."

"V. We believe that justification is made by faith. Because there be no works, whereby we may satisfy or obtain remission of sins. Yet nevertheless the same faith that justifies us, ought not to be idle, but adorned with good and godly deeds."

Reply: "The particle '*alone*' is craftily omitted. Nor is it more correct in denying that by certain works justification may occur. For it is indicated that there are works which do this, viz., love, with which they say that faith ought to be furnished, *i. e.*, as some say, 'informed.' Luther, however, excluded charity from the act of justification; and maintained that it was not the form, bnt the effect and fruit of faith."

"VI. We confess that free-will, holpen with the Holy Ghost, may do somewhat, whensoever we will withdraw from sin."

Reply: "It is doubtful whether the framers of these articles understood them in a sound sense; and agreed with the evangelicals concerning the co-operation of man after conversion, so as to ascribe to God alone all glory without the ascription of any merit of our own."

"VII. We confess, that after the remission of sins, the Holy Ghost is given to the man; from the which he departeth again, as soon as he committeth any deadly sin."

Reply: "It should have been added that by repentance, the forgiveness of sins and the Holy Ghost can be recovered, in order that the heresy of Novatus might not be imputed to the evangelicals, as their caluminators were wont to do."

"VIII. We use the fashion accustomed in the office of the mass. For what should avail a change of ceremonies without necessity? But we admit not the privie masses, because they have occasion of sundry abuses. Because there is an open fair or market made of celebration of masses."

Reply: "They did not say that they used 'the accustomed fashion,' *i. e.* that introduced by abuse, but they affirmed that they employed a better one, the canon which they mention, and other forms and rites conflicting with orthodoxy being removed; nor did they disapprove only of the traffic in masses, but its being regarded a propitiatory sacrifice. Accordingly they recalled the mass to the communion alone, liberty being observed in changing the rites which, from the beginning they had observed in order to avoid scandal, or in hope of harmony; and this liberty they also afterwards exercised."

"IX. We believe thus concerning the Lord's Supper: That like as Christ, in his last supper did give unto his disciples his true body to be eaten and drunken; and so he gives daily to us his disciples and loyal men, as often as we keep the supper, according to the form commanded, *Accipite et comedite*, etc., the true body and blood to be eaten and drunk. This is the mind of the three evangelists and St. Paul. And so their words do sound clearly. Wherefore, away with all such erroneous interpretations as are made upon the said words.

We be taught that Christ did give to his disciples his body and blood under both species and kinds; and that, therefore, we ought to observe the same; as we do indeed. But because one of the species hath by men's constitutions been forbidden by the Bishop of Rome, there might be a remedy found without peril or danger ; so that he that would, might have both species; and that there should be a prohibition made, that the one should insult against the other."

"Reply: "They should have added that the dogma of transubstantiation was rejected by the Evangelicals, with all its consequences of inclusion, circumgestation, and adoration of the Sacrament. It is also false that communion under both kinds or one kind, was a matter of indifference to the Evangelicals; but approved only the former, as prescribed by immutable divine law."

"X. Seen" [seeing] "that it appeareth by the holy doctors, that the holy days and feasts of saints have been accustomed to be observed ; and as we see as yet some holy canons of that matter, but it appeareth not that there is made in the same a mention of their invocation ; but it appeareth only by the same, that they be proposed unto us for an example, to learn to follow their lives and conversations, yet, nevertheless, seen that by some custom, the intercession of saints ought to be admitted, then there should be prayers made unto God, that it might like him to hear them by the intercession of some saints; we affirm for a certainty, that the saints do continually intercede for the church; albeit the Christian men ought to be taught, that they shall not convert the same hope to the saints, which they ought to have unto God. Nor do we regret images of Christ and the saints, but only the worship shown them; whence idolatry sprung."

Reply: "They never affirmed it as a certainty, or an article of faith that the saints intercede for us; Luther indeed, in the Smalcald Articles, admitted the conjecture; nevertheless he denied that they should in any way be prayed to intercede, or that God should be asked to have respect to their intercession."

"XI. Also we dampne not the monastery, or life of such as be closed in the cloisters; but only the trust that some men have put in the regular observation. Also we reject the vows which have been made upon such things as men cannot observe. Yet, nevertheless we will not the monasteries be put down for the same, but that they be turned to schools; in which good doctrine should be taught. And that the pope may dispense with vows; so that it were free for every man to keep or not keep them. And so the same should be to the quiet and tranquility of mind, and the vows should not be the snares of malice."

Reply: "The resort to cloisters, they did not approve, but condemned. They maintained that the monastic life could be tolerated, if constraint, the opinion of merit, idle begging, were absent, and other abuses were removed, and the power of entering them be free, without any regard to a Papal dispensation."

"XII. Then the marriage of priests should be in the Pope's hands, who might admit the same; and the concubinate of many should be forgiven; for we see few chaste. But if the law to contract should not have place, then, for to avoid slander, there should be none advanced to the dignities ecclesiastical, but grave persons, and of full age."

Reply: "It is apparent that here falsehoods are fabricated with respect to Luther, as though he would allow the marriage of the clergy to be referred to the judgment and dispensation of the Pope; for this he regarded a matter of divine law, not only allowed, but necessary to all who did not possess the gift of continence. The caution also with respect to ecclesiastical dignities, that they should be conferred upon none but upon men of advanced age, who could be celibate, is not Luther's."

"XIII. We think it best to dispute of Purgatory and pardons, in the schools, rather than, in the pulpit, to dispute of the same publicly, without any profit; so that the markets and bargains thereof should be avoided. For we do reject in those things and others, wherein we do not agree, the abuse rather than the thing itself. The which, nevertheless, may be discussed and amended by councils lawfully assembled."

Reply: "Purgatory itself, and the entire figment of Pontifical indulgences, Luther, with his associates, rejected, as, among other passages, is manifest in the Smalcald Articles; and, therefore, he did not forbid that they be refuted in the sermon; for he did this not only with his vow, but also in his writings."

"XIV. The Zwinglians and Œcolampadians have not yet received those artices, but the simple people shall be easily reduced, and we trust that they shall shortly do conformable thereto."

Reply: "Here Zwingli and the Œcolampadians are invidiously cited, as though only their followers, and not, likewise, the Lutherans, rejected Pontifical abuses. Then, too, it is false that the people were inclined to accept these compromises, or that, through sermons, hope was offered them for these. The contrary was found also after the death of Luther, when, the edict of Charles being published in the year 1548, a very few admitted incrustations not unlike these which were then invented in England, and, although compelled by violence to receive them, nevertheless, in a short time rejected, them."

"XV. Luther hath revoked all the books, wherein there be many things contrary to those articles, and hath retracted them with his own hands and knowledged his faults. In March 3d, MDXXXIX."

Reply: "This is so impudently false, as not to be worthy of refutation."

Some of the prejudices against Lutheranism in England on the part of the more pronounced opponents of hierarchism, have not improbably originated from the false impressions produced by this forgery. To have yielded as much as this document does, would have been to have given up half the battle to the Papacy. It was essentially, as Seckendorf intimates, what afterwards was so stoutly resisted by Lutherans in the *Interim*. It is amusing to read Strype's conclusion of the matter:

"But these steps to a good concord between the king and the Germans came to nothing; the king taking some misconceit against the Duke of Saxony, because it was said, he rather inclined to have his sister-in-law, the Lady Anne of Cleves, married in Germany than to him."

As opposed to this, we have an authentic document of January 18th, 1540, in which Luther, Melanchthon, Jonas, Bugenhagen, Myconius, Sarcerius, Bucer and others unite in stating to the Elector the conditions upon which peace may be made with "the bishops."

They say: "Since the doctrine in all articles of the confession, as it is understood and taught in our churches, is truly and properly the sure Christian doctrine of the Holy Gospel, we neither will, nor can make or assent to any change therein. Therefore, if there be a meeting, first of all the doctrine must be discussed; for if they be silent concerning this, and still hold their own, and thus treat of an external, hypocritical agreement, no firm unity would follow; but they must first consider whether this doctrine be correct, and be allowed by theirs. If, perhaps, they give heed to some articles and receive them in a measure; and say that our writings are numerous and dissimilar, and therefore, certain articles must be composed; and also, perhaps, censure some so as to patch and change them; our judgment is, that we do not allow new, obscure and uncertain articles or patch-work to be prepared, but declare to them that the sum of our doctrine is set forth in the Confession and Apology, from whose doctrine we do not think of departing. And if any one have any fault to find therewith, as though it were not sufficiently explained or were incorrect, we then offer ourselves ready, with all diligence, to show either by writing or orally, what the understanding is in our churches; and so to make answer, that undoubtedly all reasonable and God-fearing men shall be satisfied."[4]

THE SIX ARTICLES

were soon lost sight of, except as an historical land-mark. "Its operation seems to have been checked in part at least, as early

---

[4] *Corpus Reformatorum*, III: 129.

as the following year."[5] Crumwell's schemes were successful. In spite of the Elector's persistent advice to the contrary, because of which he greatly offended his relatives, the marriage of Henry with the Elector's sister-in-law, Anne of Cleves, was arranged. We need not repeat the story with which readers of English history are so familiar of the flattering portrait painted by Cranach, the impatience of Henry to welcome his bride, his trip to the coast to receive her, his terrible disappointment, his fruitless endeavor to retract from his engagement even after she had entered England for her marriage, his brutal treatment of her, his divorce on the ground "that the king" [poor innocent Henry!] "having married her against his will, he had not given a pure, inward and complete consent," and her silent dignity amidst all these wrongs. Had the Elector's advice been heeded, this mortification would not have been incurred.

THE LUTHERAN ULTIMATUM.

However opposed the Elector had been to the alliance, yet when against his will it was concluded, he was unwilling to lose any opportunity which it would afford for gaining an entrance into England of that pure faith of the Gospel which had been so often repelled by the king. Hence contrary to all former expectations of both statesmen and theologians, the pen of Melanchthon was once more called into service, during the period after the marriage and before the repudiation of Anne of Cleves. April 12th, 1540, he wrote a long letter for the Elector's use, referring to an oral statement made by Henry as to his hope that he might yet become a member of the Smalcald League, and reminding him that the League has no other object but that of "the defence of true doctrine, and cases connected therewith," and "if the king wished to enter the League for other reasons than those of religion, that this was entirely at variance with the principles of the League." The king was severely rebuked for the infamous "Six Articles," which are

[5] Hardwick's *Reformation*, p. 206.

ascribed to "the conspiracy and artifices of bishops whose minds are still imbued with veneration for Romish godlessness." As, however the execution of the "Six Articles" has been arrested, and the king, on the one hand, has expressed again his desire that true doctrine be propagated in his churches, but, on the other, has stated that the Lutherans "in some articles have advanced beyond bounds," the Elector has had some theologians prepare a memorandum of the arguments on which the articles on abuses rest for the especial consideration of the king and his theologians. A conference between English and German theologians is suggested to be held at Guelders, Hamburg or Bremen, or any other place designated by the English king. "For we greatly desire," the letter continues, "that true and godly agreement be established between the Anglican and German Churches. Such a consummation would both magnify the glory of God and invite other nations. Accordingly, in this matter, we promise our aid with all our might, both because of the glory of God and our own necessities. Since, moreover, we are now united by a new bond of relationship, we are especially desirous that this union may be of some advantage to the Church of Christ, and the State; as these ought to be the chief ends in view in the friendships of princes."[6] The memorandum accompanying the letter is as follows:

"*Writing of the Wittenberg Theologians sent to the King of England.*

OF THE MASS.

There is no controversy concerning lessons and prayers in the Mass. For since Paul also in public ceremonies wanted some holy lessons, useful for exciting minds to the fear of God and to faith, to be recited, and prayers and thanksgiving to be added, this custom is not to be abolished, but to be diligently maintained in the Church. For, first, it is especially profitable that, in the common assembly, there be prayer; because Christ expressly gave promises to the church, when he said: 'If two

[6] *Corpus Reformatorum*, III: 1007.

of you shall agree on earth, as touching anything that they ask, it shall be done for them of my Father which is in heaven. For where two or three are gathered together in my name, there am I in the midst of them.' Christ, therefore, by his most comprehensive promise, invites us to join with the Church in prayer. God wants the Church to be so bound together that one be affected by the necessity of the other, and pray for the other, and promises that he will hear these prayers. The public usage of the Church in public prayers, in the Mass and other ceremonies, ought to admonish us to learn this, and to exercise such faith. Paul also in 2 Cor. I., asks that prayers be made by many, that many in turn may thank God for hearing prayer, and for looking upon the afflicted. Then the example of the Church is most useful. For it teaches many to be themselves aroused to believe and pray, especially if in the sermons, the people be admonished concerning the promises made to the Church. For thus they will understand the examples of others, and the custom of the Church will profit them unto edification, as Paul teaches, 1 Cor. 14. Thirdly, the example of the Church serves to admonish individuals in regard to what matters they should be concerned, and what they should ask. For a people untaught, does not understand public necessities. But there it not only hears that private gifts are to be sought, but also learns that each one should participate in the public care, pray for the whole Church, that it be freed from errors, scandals, dissensions, godless services, that true doctrine be propagated, that true worship be rendered God, and we be ruled and sanctified by the Holy Ghost. It learns also that prayers for bodily things, peace, happy government, harvest, against pestilence and like ills, please God. Such prayers in public ceremonies, in the Mass and elsewhere, we hold were devoutly and necessarily instituted. For it is God's command, both that we call upon him in all dangers, and that, in the public rites, the people be taught concerning this invocation, to learn to believe God, and to seek and expect aid of God.

But concerning the use of the sacrament of the Body and Blood of the Lord in the Mass, we disapprove of those who hold that the use of the sacrament is a service to be applied for others, living and dead, and that it merits for them the remission of guilt and punishment, and this too for the work wrought. For these things are unknown to the Ancient Church, and disagree with the Holy Scriptures, and obscure the doctrine of faith, and produce confidence in the work of another. But when Christ said: 'This do in remembrance of me,' he instituted this sacrament, that there might be there the remembrance in true faith of his death and of the benefits which, by his death, he has merited. And these benefits are applied by the sacrament to the one taking it, when, by this remembrance, it excites faith, which believes that Christ truly bestows upon us his benefits, while he offers us such a testimony that he joins us to himself, that he wishes to keep us as his members, that he cleanses us with his blood. This faith, whereby the benefits of Christ are received, is the spiritual worship of God, and because, with this faith, thanksgiving should be joined, whereby hearts truly give thanks, for the forgiveness of sins and redemption, to God the Father, and our Lord Jesus Christ, the Ancient Church called this use of the sacraments, Eucharist, as Cyprian says most sweetly concerning communicants: 'Piety dividing itself between what is given and what is forgiven, thanks the bestower of so abundant benefit,' *i. e.* Piety considers both, viz., how great the magnitude of the benefit bestowed upon us, grace and life eternal, and, on the other hand, how great is the magnitude of our evils, *i. e.* of sins and eternal death. Ardent thanksgiving, therefore, arises, when we see that, by unspeakable clemency, such sins are remitted us, and besides we are presented with the Holy Spirit, and the glory of life eternal. And, in this sense, we hold that this most revered ceremony is called by the holy Fathers a *sacrifice*, who certainly did not think that this work, when applied, merits for others the remission of guilt and punishment, and that, for the work wrought, but held that, in the use of the sacrament, faith is to be exercised and thanksgiving to be rendered. Since, therefore, Christ instituted the use of the sacrament, that it might be a communion, in which the sacrament might be administered to others, and the Church, for a long time, preserved this custom, and did not have private masses, we hold that such rite, wherein there is a communion of some, is godly and in harmony with the Gospel. Then private masses were wont to be performed with the opinion concerning the use of the sacrament, that it is necessary, that this service sprang up in the Church in order to be applied to others, so that it merits for them the remission of guilt and punishment. Such masses, therefore, are to be abrogated, and in order that these scandals be removed, and the institution of Christ, viz. the communion be celebrated, we hold that no one should be compelled to celebrate private masses. For since Paul says that they who abuse the sacrament are guilty of the body and blood of the Lord, the greatest care must be taken that the godly and holy use be restored to the glory of Christ and the profit of the Church.

OF BOTH KINDS.

There is no doubt that the Ancient Church, East and West, used both kinds of the sacrament of the Body and Blood of Christ, viz. bread and wine. For Paul also testifies that this was the custom in the church of the Corinthians, and Christ, on instituting the sacrament, ordained this use not only for a part of the Church, viz. for the priests, but for the whole Church; and the declaration of Jerome and others is extant, which shows that this custom remained for a long time in the Church, and *in capitulo*. 'We have ascertained,' Gelasius declared, 'that both kinds are taken; wherefore the recent prohibition is only a human tradition.' Hence it does not have the authority to change an institution of Christ, nor are men to be compelled, because of a human tradition, to change, against conscience, a custom delivered by Christ, and employed in the Ancient Church, since it is manifest that this usage is lawful and godly.

OF THE MARRIAGE OF PRIESTS.

With respect to virginity and continence and marriage, we follow and defend the manifest declaration of Paul, 1 Cor. VII. And as Christ praises eunuchs who made themselves such for the Kingdom of God, so we also teach that the preservation of virginity is a good work and useful for assiduity in study, in meditation, in prayer, in ecclesiastical ministrations; as Paul says that the husband cares for the things which are of the world, but the unmarried for those which are of the Lord. For the husband is hindered by domestic occupations from giving that uninterrupted attention, needful for studies and public services, but the unmarried is less employed, and can apply greater energy in learning, teaching and other functions; and is less distracted by cares. Therefore it is well to choose and to have in the Church ministers entirely celibate; and they who see that they are fitted, are to be exhorted, by their diligence and temperance, to preserve the gift of God because of the advantage of the Church, and are to be taught that this office pleases God and has great rewards. But inasmuch as Christ himself testifies that not all are fit for perpetual celibacy, we hold that to those who are not fitted for celibacy, marriage neither ought, nor can be prohibited by a vow or human law; because a vow and human laws cannot free us from a divine law and a natural right. But it is a divine law that every one who does not have the gift of continence, should, in order to avoid fornication, have a wife. And the desire for marriage conformably to right reason, is a right of nature. To this natural affection, as it is called, concupiscence is now added, which inflames nature the more; so that the need for marriage as a remedy, is the greater. The law, moreover, which prohibits marriage to priests, is purely a human tradition. And further, this new tradition which prohibits marriage to priests, and dissolves contracts, has not originated from councils, but from the Roman bishops alone. Purity before God, is not to pollute the conscience, but to obey God; wherefore an impure celibacy is not purity, and marriage, since it is sanctified by the

Word of God, is purity. For we certainly know that this kind of life pleases God, and it is full of the exercises of godliness; and, accordingly, for a long time, the Church not only in the East, but also in .the West, had married priests. History also testifies that this custom was changed in Spain and Germany by violence. The Greek churches still have married priests; and, hence, marriage is not impurity, or a matter unworthy of the ministers of the churches. But what examples, what impurity, what disgrace to the churches, the law of the Bishop of Rome produced, is not obscure. Since the Divine Law enjoins marriage upon those who are not continent, we judge that the pontifical prohibition concerning celibacy, is unlawful, and that marriage is allowed priests.

OF MONASTIC VOWS.

There are many important reasons why it is necessary to support, at the public expense, studious and godly men, destined for sacred literature, in order that the teachers of the churches may be derived thence. For since the more destitute cannot, from their resources, bear the expense of studies, and the rich prefer to resort to other arts, whereby great honors, and great rewards are offered in the state; it is necessary that the Church provide that some be supported at the public expense, in order to give attention to sacred literature and other arts of which the Church has need. Unless this were done, the churches in many places would be without pastors. This duty then is incumbent upon kings and princes, that they provide that pastors be not lacking to the churches, and that they supply the expenses of teachers and scholars. For Isaiah, to this end, calls kings nursing-fathers, and queens nursing-mothers, in order to teach that kings and states ought to defend teachers, and supply the expense. Neither is it unjust that they whose studies are directed to the profit of the Church, be supported, in turn, by the Church; as Paul says: 'Who goeth a warfare at his own charges?' Apparently with this design, in the beginning assemblages were instituted in colleges and monasteries, in order that there might be a large number of those engaged in sacred literature, from whom teachers could be chosen; and to this, the laws in the code, and histories bear witness. For this purpose, therefore, it is profitable, provided the godless opinions and services be reformed, that colleges and monasteries be preserved. For it is not enough that the youth who are to be employed hereafter in the government of the Church, should learn literature, but also should be accustomed, by discipline and godly exercises, to the love of ceremonies and to godliness; for those not trained by such discipline are more profane than is expedient. Besides, the Church has need of learned and skilful pastors. But familiar conversation with men learned in spiritual matters conduces very much to the strengthening of doctrine and the confirming of judgments. For without such intercourse, no one can attain to solid learning. Moreover if pastors be altogether lacking to the churches, or the pastors be unlearned and inexperienced and mere tyros, what do we suppose will be the state of the Church? There will be devastation and barbarism, and, with literary pursuits destroyed, learning will be extinct. Paul prohibits the choice of novices, because he knew that there was need of skilful and experienced teachers. Nazianzen deplores the calamity of the Church, because they who had not previously learned, suddenly became doctors, brought forward not by their learning, but by votes. Basil says that the doctrine of the eminent fathers whom he heard, was still resounding in his ears. Wherefore it is highly desirable that there be such monasteries, in which doctrine may flourish and be propagated, youth be properly trained and be prepared for the service of the Church, in order that learned and well-trained doctors of the churches be had. Such once were the colleges of bishops, as is apparent from the accounts of Ambrose and Augustine and others, in which learning was for a long time propagated. Afterwards, when, in such colleges, the pursuits of learning were neglected, a great change of doctrine followed, which was of no little injury to the Church. Therefore, with the polity preserved, let the opinion of colleges and monasteries be reformed, let superstition be removed, let godless services be rejected and the pursuits of learning be renewed to the profit of the Church. For we hold that the following opinions are godless, viz. that monastic vows merit the forgiveness of sins and eternal life, or that they are Christian righteousness or perfection; and while lawful vows are to be observed, such monastic vows are unlawful, as are made with the false persuasion that works, devised without God's command, are not matters of indifference, but a service, and merit the remission of sins and eternal life. These vows are invalid. The objection urged from Paul concerning widows, that they have made void their first faith, even though there were vows then, cannot be accommodated to monastic vows of these times, which, when fulfilled with a godless opinion, are not vows. For they transfer the glory of Christ to human observances, and obscure true worship in the Church, viz., faith in Christ and the good works of one's calling. For who did not prefer the observances of the monks to the office of magistrate and of father? For these works, as profane and unclean, seemed scarcely excusable, and faith was obscured, because they did not teach that forgiveness of sins is gratuitously bestowed for Christ's sake, but ascribed this honor to their observances. And the rest of the Church imitated these opinions and examples, and superstitiously thought that works are services of human traditions, and merit remission of sins and life eternal. Since, however, the Gospel condemns these opinions, monastic vows, made with this persuasion, are manifestly unlawful. Besides not all are fitted for perpetual continence; while a vow should be concerning a possible matter, and, it is evident that many young men and maidens were forced into monasteries, and to make vows before the just age; how great the peril of which is, is not obscure. We must, therefore, allow those preferring to live in another kind of life, to depart from monasteries. They also do aright who leave the monks, when they are compelled in monasteries to observe godless services, as the abuse of masses, indulgences and many other things. If any, however, adapted to monastic life, prefer to live in these colleges; if their opinion and worship be reformed, and they use ordinances as indifferent matters, we do not censure them, and we judge that many holy and excellent men with this intention lived a godly life in monasteries; aye, it is even to be desired, that such colleges of doctors and godly men exist, among whom the pursuits of Christian doctrine may be cultivated to the common profit of the Church, and youths not only be instructed in learning, but, by godly exercises and this pedagogy of rites, be accustomed to godliness, yet so that they be not held entangled with vows to the peril of conscience. This kind of life, because directed to the profit of the Church, to the instruction and practice of the congregations, from which doctors of the churches can be taken, is godly and pleases God; for it would have services commanded of God. For it is God's command that those, purposing to enter the ministry, be taught and trained; and, for this reason, God approves the pedagogy of rites. There may also be colleges of nuns, where maidens learn literature and the doctrine of godliness. But young girls who desire to marry are not to be retained in cloisters, nor are any, thereafter, to be burdened with vows. For the doctrine of Paul must be retained, who advises virginity in such wise, as to be unwilling that snares be cast upon consciences."[7]

We have given this opinion of the Wittenberg theologians, that it may be seen how the entire argument was concentrated on "The Articles on Abuses," as well as to show the spirit and thoroughness of the treatment. Here were the points from which the Lutheran reformers could not recede a hair's-breadth; and which, at the same time, Henry was not ready to surrender. The doctrinal articles, as we have already learned, had been already conceded by Henry and his theologians, under the influence of the able presentations of Myconius and his colleagues. As soon as the articles on Abuses would be endorsed by the An-

[7] Ib. pp. 1010 sqq.

glican authorities, in addition to the doctrinal articles of the Augsburg Confession, a union between the Lutheran and Anglican Churches could be consummated; but until then, such thoughts were useless, and all efforts for union must be directed towards the acceptance of those unalterable scriptural principles therein set forth.

All this was in vain. Cranmer, under date of May 10th, tried to apologize for his monarch, by recounting what great things Henry had already accomplished. Had he not in a short time abolished the supremacy of the Pope, the worship of images, and monasteries? Were not these in themselves labors worthy of Hercules? The Lutherans must have patience. All their arguments will be carefully examined, but they must not be offended if, on some points, the king dissent, as he himself is a very learned man, furnished with the highest critical acumen and soundest judgment, and besides this has the aid of other learned men.[8]

The breach was soon made irreparable. Gardiner was master of the field. The repudiation of Anne of Cleves, July 10th, and the formal divorce, July 24th, were closely connected with the arrest of Crumwell, June 10th, and his execution, June 28th, and the martyrdom at the stake, July 30th, of that most pronounced, though not always judicious advocate of Lutheranism, the intimate friend and table companion of Luther and Melanchthon, who had done all that mortal could, to give England the pure Gospel and to make the Anglican a Lutheran Church, Dr. Robert Barnes. This true English Lutheran, faithful even unto death, to the principles he had learned at Wittenberg, and whose dying testimony was published with an introduction by Luther, written amidst a tempest of wrath against the royal murderer and with many tears for one whom he tenderly loved, will be noticed in the next chapter.

[8] Seckendorf, III: 261.

CHAPTER XIII.

LUTHER'S "ST. ROBERT."

The Postils of Taverner. Estimate of Crumwell. Sketch of Barnes. Connection with Bugenhagen. His XIX, Theses of 1531. His "History of the Popes" (1536), with Luther's Introduction. His efforts at liturgical reform. Controversy with Gardiner. His "Confession," at the stake. The attack upon the "Confession" by Standish, and the refutation of Standish by Coverdale. Luther's Introduction to the German translation of the "Confession." Luther's estimate of Barnes. His contrast between Barnes and Henry. Sastrow's "*Epicedion*" on Barnes. Henry demands satisfaction.

PARALLEL with the diplomatic negotiations, proceeded the literary activity of scholars, to provide for the thorough reformation of the English Church. This was not confined to the revision of translations of the Bible. We have already seen how the Augsburg Confession and Apology, the hymns of Luther and his associates, and a Lutheran system of theology in Sarcerius' "Common Places," were translated and published. Early in 1540, before the fall of Crumwell, another important work appeared. It will be remembered that in March 1539, Sarcerius wrote to Henry VIII. from Frankfort, offering to send him "Postils upon the Gospels for the Lord's Days and the Festivals; as well as upon the Epistels for the Lord's Days, dedicated to your Serenity." The works referred to were either: "Postilla in Evangelia Dominicalia" and "Postilla in Evangelia Festivalia," 1538, or "Expositiones in Epistolas Dominicales et Festivales," or probably both. When, then, early in 1540, we find a volume of Postils appearing in England from the pen of Richard Taverner, the translator of Sarcerius' "Common

Places," in the Preface to which he disclaims all originality for the most of the work, the inference is very naturally suggested that the book comes from Sarcerius. Taverner's relation to it is thus stated: "I was instantly required, to the intent the Lord of the harvest might, by this mean, thrust forth his laborers into the harvest, to peruse and recognize this brief postil which was delivered me of certain godly persons for that purpose and intent. Which thing to my little power, and, as the shortness of time would serve, I have done. And such sermons or homilies as seemed to want, I have supplied, partly with mine own industry, and partly with the help of other sober men which be better learned than myself."

So, too, in the Preface to the second volume, he says: "Sith this Postil is by me though not made, yet recognized, and in diverse places augmented." The changes, modifications and additions to Sarcerius, cannot be determined, unless the two books be placed side by side. As no copy of Sarcerius, is at hand, we cannot even affirm positively that he is the author. But the entire style and character of the Postils betray their Germanic and Lutheran origin. We need refer to but one instance, where on the Gospel for the 2nd Sunday in Advent, we find the sentence: "The ancient serpent shall be loosed for a little time, that is to say, false prophets, heretics, Anabaptists, Sacramentaries, *Suarmerians*" [Ger. "*Schwarmerei*"] seductors, "frantike spirites." It is also possible that the similar work of Antony Corvinus of Calenberg, may have been used as the basis.

But we return to the political crisis of 1540, and the catastrophes which it brought. It is foreign to our purpose to enter into a discussion concerning Crumwell, and his fall. He was no theologian, but a politician. A great friend of the Lutheran movement, there is no evidence at hand to prove that he regarded it in any other light, than as offering to England an opportunity for asserting its power in defiance of Pope and Emperor. Whether he really accepted with heart and soul the faith of the Gospel, and knew in his own inner experience what the Lutheran Reformation was designed first of all and above all to maintain and impart, must be referred to Him who would have us judge nothing before the time.

Twenty days after the execution of Crumwell, viz., on January 30th, 1540, one of the most prominent of English Lutherans bore his testimony at the stake.

Dr. Robert Barnes was born about 1495. At Cambridge he was a fellow student of Miles Coverdale, with whom, throughout his entire career, he lived on terms of intimacy, and who most earnestly defended his memory after his death. Converted to the evangelical faith through Thomas Bilney, he at first showed a fanatical radicalism, having on December 24th, 1525, preached against the observance of the great church festivals, and unseasonably reproduced Luther's sermon for the Fourth Sunday in Advent. In a previous chapter, we told the story of the recantation of Lutheranism which, in 1526, he was compelled to make under penalty of the stake. The very same year, however, it was discovered that he was surreptitiously circulating Bibles. He became an object of such close surveillance that in 1528 he escaped to Antwerp, where, it is probable that he was in intimate relations with Rogers, then chaplain there. He spent the next three years in Germany, part of the time at Wittenberg, where he resided in Bugenhagen's house, and, in order to escape detection, assumed the name of Anthonius Amarius or Antonius Anglus. Bugenhagen being in Hamburg, to promote the Reformation there in 1529, probably met Tyndale, living then in Hamburg, and if Foxe's statement be correct, that Barnes' friend, Coverdale was with Tyndale at that time, it again connects them. Besides, the English merchant, Humphrey Monmouth, in whose house in London, Tyndale had lived, in later years made Barnes the executor of his will.

In 1531 he published, at Wittenberg, a defence of nineteen theses, to which Bugenhagen furnished a preface. They were in substance—1. Faith alone justifies. 2. Christ made satisfaction not alone for original sin, but for all sins. 3. The commandments of God cannot be observed from our own powers. 4. Free will of its own powers can do nothing but sin. 5. The righteous sin even in every good work. 6. The true marks of the Church. 7. The power of the keys depends upon the Word of God, and not upon man's power. 8. Councils can err. 9. Communion must be administered under both forms. 10. Human ordinances do not bind the conscience. 11. Auricular confession is not necessary to salvation. 12. It is lawful for priests to marry. 13. Monks are not holier than laymen. 14. Christian fasting does not consist in distinctions of meats. 15. Christians keep holy and worship God every day, and not only on the seventh. 16. Unjust Papal excommunication does not injure those against whom it is directed. 17. The true body of Christ is in the sacrament of the altar. 18. Saints are not to be invoked as mediators. 19. The errors of the Romish Mass are enumerated.

The same year, the King felt that he needed Barnes' services in his work of reorganizing the English Church, and persuaded him to return. He was not long in England before the antagonism to Gardiner broke out in a quarrel in which Barnes' impetuosity gave him the disadvantage. As to the point of the dispute, viz., the right to sue for debt, Gardiner seems to have had the right side, but his repugnance to the bishop's course with reference to the Gospel was doubtless back of it. In 1534, he was sent by Henry to Hamburg as special ambassador, and sought to effect an alliance with the King of Denmark. In 1535, and the following year, he was, as already stated, several times at Wittenberg on the English Commission. In 1536, he published a "History of the Lives of the Popes," dedicated to Henry VIII., to which Luther furnished an "Introduction." In the Introduction Luther says: "In the beginning, not being much versed in History, I attacked the Papacy *a priori*, i. e. from the Holy Scriptures. Now I am wonderfully delighted that others are doing the same *a posteriori*, i. e. from History. And I think I am triumphing, since, as the light appears, I understand that the histories agree with the Scriptures. For what I have learned from St. Paul and Daniel as teachers, that the Pope is the adversary of God and of all, this history indicates with its very finger, pointing out not merely genus and species, but the very individual."[1]

In 1537, he was executor for an alderman, Humphrey Monmouth, the friend of Tyndale, who left a bequest for the singular purpose of paying for the preaching of thirty sermons, instead of the saying of thirty masses. In 1538 he became the first to introduce the saying of the Mass, and the rendering of the *Te Deum* in English. The next year he was on the commission for the prosecution of the Anabaptists. He was charged with having had some part in information against Lambert for denying the doctrine of the real presence, although this in no way convicts him of having any share in his condemnation and execution for denying transubstantiation. In 1539, he was again in Germany, as agent for Crumwell in effecting the alliance with Anne of Cleves. During Lent of 1540, in preaching in St. Paul's Cross Church with Gardiner, they fell into controversy. Gardiner preached against Justification by Faith alone, Barnes, when his turn to preach came, not only attacked the Bishop's doctrine, but even inveighed against him personally. Begging pardon first privately, which was granted, then, after asking pardon publicly, in the very same service he preached on the evangelical side. His temporary waverings can be readily explained. His ardent nature led him to act hastily and rashly, and then there was a seeming vacillation, though but for a moment, to the other side. Beneath all, there is a depth of character unaffected by transient and superficial agitations. He had to pay the penalty at Smithfield, after the bill of attainder against him had been passed in Parliament.

At the stake, he made a glorious confession of Christ before many witnesses. He bore his testimony against the various Papal doctrines, each enumerated in its turn.

[1] Seckendorf, Index III., Anno 1536.

"I am come hither," he said, "to be burned as a heretic, and you shall hear my belief, whereby you shall perceive what erroneous opinions I hold. God I take to record, I never to my knowledge, taught any erroneous doctrine, but only those things which scripture led me unto, and that in my sermons I never maintained any error, neither moved nor gave occasion of any insurrection. Although I have been slandered to preach that our lady was but a saffron bag, which I utterly protest before God that I never meant it, nor preached it; but all my study and diligence hath been utterly to confound and confute all men of that doctrine, as are those who deny that our Saviour Christ did take any flesh of the blessed Virgin Mary, which sects I detest and abhor. And in this place there have been burned some of them, whom I never favored nor maintained, but with all diligence evermore did I study to set forth the glory of God, the obedience to our sovereign lord the King, and the true and sincere religion of Christ—and now hearken to my faith.

I believe in the holy and blessed Trinity, three persons and one God, that created and made all the world, and that this blessed Trinity sent down the second person, Jesus Christ, into the womb of the most blessed and purest Virgin Mary. And here hear my record that I do utterly condemn that abominable and detestable opinion which saith that Christ took no flesh of the Virgin. For I believe that without man's will or power, he was conceived of the Holy Ghost, and took flesh of her, and that he suffered hunger, thirst, cold, and other passions of our body, sin excepted; according to the saying of St. Peter, he was made in all things like to his brethren, except sin. And I believe that his death and passion was the sufficient ransom for the sins of all the world. And I believe that through his death, he overcame sin, death and hell, and that there is none other satisfaction unto the Father, but this, his death and passion only, and that no work of man did deserve anything of God, but his passion, as touching our justification. For I know the best work ever I did, is impure and imperfect. For although perchance, you know nothing of me, yet do I confess that my thoughts and cogitations are innumerable; wherefore, I beseech thee, O Lord, not to enter into judgment with me; according to the saying of the prophet David: 'Enter not into judgment with thy servant, O Lord;' and in another place, 'Lord, if thou straitly mark our iniquities, who is able to abide thy judgment!' Wherefore, I trust in no good work that ever I did, but only in the death of Christ. I do not doubt but through him to inherit the Kingdom of Heaven. Take me not here that I speak against good works, for they are to be done, and verily they that do them not, shall never come into the Kingdom of God. We must do them because they are commanded us of God, to show and set forth our profession, not to deserve or merit, for that is only the death of Christ.

I believe that there is a holy church, and a company of all them that do profess Christ; and that all that have suffered and confessed his name, are saints; and that all they do praise and laud God in heaven, more than I, or any man's tongue can express, and I have always spoken reverently and praised them, as much as scripture willed me to do. And that our lady, I say, was a virgin immaculate and undefiled, and that she is the most pure virgin that ever God created, and a vessel elect of God, of whom Christ should be born."

"Then, there was one," says Foxe, "that asked him his opinion of praying to saints." Then said he:

"Now of saints you shall hear my opinion: I have said before some what I think of them; how that I believe they are in heaven with God, and that they are worthy of all the honor, that Scripture willeth them to have. But I say, throughout all scripture we are not commanded to pray to any saints. Therefore, I neither can, nor will preach unto you that saints ought to be prayed unto; for then should I preach unto you a doctrine of mine own head. Notwithstanding, whether they pray for us or no, that I refer to God. And if saints do pray for us, then I trust to pray for you within this half hour, master sheriff, and for every Christian man living in the faith of Christ, and dying in the same, as a saint. Wherefore, if the dead may pray for the quick, I will surely pray for you."

When this testimony of Barnes at the stake was published, it was at once attacked by a hierarchical writer, John Standish, to whom Barnes' old college friend, Miles Coverdale, vigorously replied. Standish examines Barnes' confession, sentence by sentence, and Coverdale just as minutely treats every statement of Standish. The reply may be found in the second volume of Coverdale's works, published by the Parker Society. In the Preface, he says: "If Dr. Barnes died a true Christian man, be ye sure his death shall be a greater stroke to hypocrisy, than ever his life could have been. If he was falsely accused to the King's highness, and so put to death, woe shall come those accusers, if they repent not by times. And if Dr. Barnes in his heart, mouth and deed committed no worse thing toward the King's highness, than he committed against God in these his words at his death, he is like at the latter day to be a judge over them that were cause of his death, if they do not amend."

Standish contemptuously termed Barnes' doctrine as the doctrine of the Germans. Coverdale is perfectly willing to bear the reproach, and answers:

"As touching the Germans, their doctrine is, that when the servants of God have done all that is commanded them, they must acknowledge themselves to be unprofitable; to have occasion continually to cry unto God, and to say: 'O forgive us our trespasses;' to acknowledge that in their flesh dwelleth no good thing; yea, and to confess, that though they 'delight in the law of God after the inward man, yet there is another law in their members which striveth against the law of their mind.' . . . This is now the doctrine of the Germans; and thus taught also St. Augustine. . . . Such doctrine now, though it be approved both by the holy scripture and by St. Augustine, yet because the Germans teach it, it must needs be condemned of you for an error. I wonder ye condemn them not also for holding so little of the Pope's church, of his pardons, of his purgatory; for putting down his religions, his chauntries, his soul-masses and diriges, his trentals, pilgrimages, stations, etc.; for ministering the sacraments in their mother tongue, for setting their priests daily to preach the only word of God, for bringing no new customs into the church; for avoiding whoredom and secret abomination from among their clergy, as well as among other; for bringing up their youth so well in the doctrine of God, in the knowledge of tongues, in other good letters and honest occupations, for providing so richly for their poor, needy, fatherless and aged people, etc."[2]

The Confession of Barnes was published in German at Wittenberg, in the very year of his martyrdom. Luther's introduction is of the highest interest. The following is the substance of it:

"This Dr. Robert Barnes, who, when with us, in his remarkable humility, would not allow himself to be called Doctor, called himself Antonius; for which he had his reasons. For previously he had been imprisoned in England by the holy bishops, the St. Papists, and had escaped with great difficulty. This Doctor, I say, we knew very well, and it is an especial joy to us to hear, that our good pious table companion, and guest of our home, has been so graciously called upon by God to shed his blood, for His dear Son's sake, and to become a holy martyr. Thanks, praise and glory be to the Father of our dear Lord Jesus Christ, that He has permitted us to see again, as in the beginning, the times, wherein Christians who have eaten and drunk with us, are taken before our eyes, and from our eyes and sides, to become martyrs, i. e. to go to Heaven and become saints. Twenty years ago, who would have believed that Christ our Lord would be so near us, and, through His precious martyrs and dear saints, would eat and drink and speak and live at our table and home? . . . When this holy martyr, St. Robert, perceived at last that his King (by your permission) Harry of England, had become hostile to the Pope, he returned to England, in hopes that he

[2] *Remains of Bishop Coverdale*, pp. 384–86.

might plant the Gospel in his fatherland; and in fact he was successful in making a beginning, To speak briefly, it pleased Harry of England to send him to us at Wittenberg concerning the matrimonial question on which thirteen universities had given their decision, and all had given Harry the right to repudiate his Queen, Catherine, the aunt of the Emperor Charles, and to take another.

"But when we had disputed, at great length, and, at a great expense to His Electoral Prince of Saxony, we found at last that Harry of England had sent his embassy, not because he wanted to become evangelical, but in order that we at Wittenberg might endorse his divorce. I was, therefore, displeased that I and the other theologians had spent so many weeks in useless labor with them concerning religious matters, and I told them: 'Four points your king will not admit: The two forms of the sacrament—the marriage of priests, the doing away with the Mass, and with Monasticism.' 'Yes,' I continued, 'we have spent too long time in defiling ourselves, when we ought to have known from the very beginning, that, while your king takes the Pope's money, he retains his government. Harry, therefore, is Pope, and the Pope is Henry in England.'

"Dr. Robert Barnes, himself, often told me: 'My king does not care for religion.' But he so loved the king and his country, that he was ready to endure everything, and always was meditating how to help England. He always had in his mouth the words, '*My* king;' as his confession shows that even unto death he showed all love and fidelity towards 'my king,'—a service which Harry ill deserved. Hope deceived him; for he was always hoping that his king would at last turn out well.

"Among other things, we often disputed why the king presumed to bear that abominable title: 'Defender of the faith, and after Christ Supreme and Immediate Head of the Anglican Church.' But as this was generally the answer: *Sic volo, sic jubeo, sit pro ratione voluntas*, it could no where be better seen that Squire Harry wanted to be God, and to do as he pleased.

"The reason why he was martyred is still concealed. For Harry must be ashamed of himself. Nevertheless, what many trustworthy persons say is like him, viz., that Dr. Barnes (like St. John the Baptist against Herod) testified against Harry and would not consent to his disgraceful deed in repudiating Fraulein von Jülich [Anne of Cleves,] and taking another. For whatever Squire Harry wants, he makes an article of faith, both for life and death. But we let Harry go to his Harries, and with his Harries, where they belong. We ought to thank God, the Father of all mercies, that He can use such devils and masques of devils in so masterly a way, for our salvation and that of all Christians, and for the punishment both of themselves and of all who are unwilling to learn to know God; as he has always done through great tyrants. Yet, as St. Paul says, Rom. viii, all that occurs and is done and is suffered, must work for good; and, on the other hand, everything must serve for evil to those who persecute God's children. So also is it with this incendiary Harry, who, by his wickedness, is doing so much good. Let us praise and thank God; this is a blessed time for elect saints, but a sorrowful time for the devil, and the blasphemers and enemies of God, to whom it shall still be worse."

But Luther was not the only one from whose pen Henry had to suffer as a penalty for this crime. A young scholar at Lübeck, John Sastrow published a poem: "Epicedion Martyris Christi, D. Roberti Barnes, Angli," in which he compared Henry to Busiris. The sensitive King sent a legation to Lübeck, demanding reparation. The Council excused Sastrow on the ground of his youth; but the printer, John Balhorn, was banished, and, when Henry was satisfied by such a vindication, Balhorn was permitted after a few months to quietly return.[3]

---

[3] *Bilder aus der Deutschen Vergangenheit, von Gustav Freitag*, II : 197.

CHAPTER XIV.

CLOSING EVENTS OF HENRY'S REIGN.

The Paradoxes of Smithfield. Tracts of Melanchthon circulated in England. Imprisonment of Publishers, and Arrest of Readers. Enforcement of the Six Articles. Popular Opinion neutralizes them. Two irresistible forces. The young men of the Universities. The Diffusion of the Bible. Gardiner's Obstructionist Policy overcome. Spasmodic Efforts at Persecution. Plots against Cranmer and the Queen. Negotiations again proposed. The Augsburg Confession once more. The English Embassy of 1544. Henry's Argument concerning the *Variata*. Bucer intercedes for Henry. The Elector of Saxony immovable. Henry's Advances repulsed by the Frankfort Convention of 1546. His Efforts with the Elector Palatinate. Proposition of "The League Christian." His Death.

WHEN Dr. Barnes was burned at Smithfield, there was another circumstance, beyond the culmination of Henry's wickedness in endeavoring to get rid of a troublesome witness of the true faith, that might well attract attention. Three Protestants, including Dr. Barnes, were burned; three Papists were hanged. "This was caused," says the English Church historian of the next century, Fuller, "by the difference of religions in the king's privy council, wherein the Popish party called for the execution of the Protestants, whilst the Protestant lords in council (out of policy to repress the others' eagerness, or, if that failed, out of desire to revenge it) cried as fast that the laws might take effect on the Papists. And whilst neither side was able to save those of his own opinions, both had power to destroy those of the opposite party. They were dragged on hurdles, two and two, a Papist and a Protestant. A stranger standing by did wonder (as well he might) what religion the king was of, his sword cutting on both sides."[1] Thus the fact is illustrated, which is often forgotten, that doctrinal indifferentism when it gains the power, is just as relentless and cruel in its persecutions, as is the narrowest adherence to traditional principles.

Lutheranism, however, was not completely crushed, and new witnesses were being prepared to replace those who who were martyred. Though the stream had to force its way under ground, it is destined soon to reappear. Thomas Walpole was brave enough to translate into English Melanchthon's long letter to the king noticed before, where the reader may remember that Melanchthon arraigns the bishops with a severity that he rarely used. Its thorough discussion of "The Six Articles," which were now to be again enforced, made it especially timely; and an evangelical publisher, Richard Grafton, the intimate friend of Coverdale, was ready to assume the risk of its publication, although in 1540 he had spent six weeks in the Tower of London for publishing Matthews' Bible. About the same time, an English translation of one of Melanchthon's arguments sent Henry "On Marriage of Priests," made by Louis Beauchame, was published by Hoffe at Leipzig, doubtless for circulation in England. The circulation of the former is at last discovered by detectives. Translator and publisher are both arrested and imprisoned. Besides these, a Mrs. Blage, a grocer's wife in Chepe, who had given a copy to Cottiswood, a priest; Cottiswood who had given a copy to a fellow-priest, Derrick, and Derrick himself, all are summoned before the Privy Council, and receive a warning concerning their offence.[2]

It was determined again to rigidly enforce "The Six Articles." The Bishop of London, Bonner, who, until he rose to position, had seemed to be on the Lutheran side, now began that career of persecution, which, under Queen Mary, rendered him so odious as the murderer of hundreds, and, under Queen Elizabeth, justly sent him to the Tower to spend the last ten years of his

[1] Vol. II : p. 105.
[2] Dixon, II : 261.

life in imprisonment. Two hundred arrests were made in London alone. Among the first brought to trial, was a boy of fifteen, Richard Mekins, whose conviction Bonner is said to have secured by threatening the jury, and who was either burned or hanged at Smithfield for "participating in the heresies of Barnes." But except in this case, the juries were intractable. The leaven had spread so far, that they would not convict for offences against the Six Articles. Three of those arraigned were imprisoned. Outside of London, there were five executions.

Nothing, however, could check the Reformation. Two elements, working silently, were far mightier than the throne and the hierarchical bishops combined. The young men of the Universities for some years already had been preponderatingly on the Evangelical side; the English Bible was making its influence felt thoughout the entire kingdom. In 1536, the very year in which he had Taverner translate the Augsburg Confession, and endeavored to have it approved in England, Crumwell had secured the issuing of the following injunction from the king: "That every parson or proprietary of any parish church within the realm, before August 1st, should provide a book of the whole Bible, both in Latin and English, and lay it in the chair for every man that would look and read therein; and discourage no man from reading any part of the Bible, either in Latin or English, but rather comfort, exhort and admonish each man to read it as the very Word of God, and the spiritual food of every man's soul." Day after day, the churches were crowded, while the few better educated ones among the people, continued to read to the attentive multitudes of illiterate men and women about them.

Cranmer, in 1542, endeavored in the Convocation to have a thorough revision of existing versions made. When this work was obstructed by Gardiner, he determined to put it in charge of a commission from the two Universities; and when the Convocation showed an unwillingness to submit to this, because the young men of the Universities were nearly all advocates of the New Learning, the Primate threatened to prorogue the Convocation. Even the year before, viz., in 1541, it was determined to remove images from the churches, and to reform the Liturgy. Several attempts were made to revive the execution of the Six Articles. Each time a few martyrs fell, and once Cranmer himself was summoned before the Council, and his enemies were triumphing in anticipation of their victory; but his hold upon the king was still too strong. The famous scene of Cranmer's producing the king's ring, which Shakespeare places during the life of Anne Boleyn, is generally accepted as properly belonging here. The king's last queen, Catharine Parr, was an adherent of the evangelical faith, and the story runs that she herself narrowly escaped being carried by the plots of the Romanizing element to the fate of Anne Boleyn; but that, when the critical moment arrived, she had regained the graces of her vacillating husband. Those who had plotted against her, and who had come to Henry, at his appointment, to carry out their schemes, were glad to leave precipitately.

Near the close of the reign, we again find external political complications causing a re-opening of negotiations with the continental Lutherans, and the Lutheran princes and states, at that very dark hour when perils were impending on all sides, insisting once more on the complete acceptance of the Augsburg Confession as an indispensable condition for even the consideration of an alliance.

ANOTHER ENGLISH EMBASSY.

The Peace of Crespy, between Francis I. and Charles V., September 18th, 1544, had left the King of England in an embarrassing predicament. As an ally of the Emperor, he had an army on French soil, which had recently taken Boulogne, and with elation was pressing its advantages, when Charles V. undertook to make a separate peace, leaving Henry either single-handed to conduct the war, or to find his way out of it as best he could. At the same time, the Lutheran princes and States, by whose co-operation Charles V. had been able to undertake the French war, were threatened by the new alliance of the two monarchs, until then at war with one another, but who were now ready to listen to the urgent appeals of the Pope to turn their arms against the Lutheran heresy. Under these circumstances the negotiations that had so often failed before, were once again attempted. Walter Bucler and Christopher Mount were sent to Germany with instructions undated, but believed to have been written about November 14th, 1544, five days before the summons to the Council of Trent was issued by Paul III., directing them to confer with Duke Maurice of Saxony, and Philip, Landgrave of Hesse, suggesting that overtures for some marriage connection with England be made with some German prince. The Elector John Frederick was not to be overlooked, but Henry's experience in the past doubtless satisfied him that from that source he had least to hope, and, hence, though the very head of the Smalcald League, his name appears only in a subordinate position.

But it was impossible to make any progress without the consideration of the question of religion. Accordingly, in February, 1545, Henry himself writes, authorizing them to offer either of his daughters, Mary and Elizabeth, in marriage to the Duke of Holstein, and then gives more specific instructions concerning any doctrinal tests:

"In case the sayd Landgrave shall make any mocion touching the matiers of religion, desyring that there might be some accord and agreement upon the same, mencioning peraventure the return again from hens of their last ambassadie in vain; to that our sayd servaunts shall answer, that ther is no Prince nor man in the woorlde that desyreth more the glorye of God, and meaneth more the true setting furth of His Woord than we do. And to thintent the same may appere unto them, albeit it be true in dede that certayn of the Commissioners, beyng here to commyn uppon maters of religion, the same entring conference furst with certayn of our learned men, and after beyng admitted to commun with Ourself, stoode more ernestly and vehemently uppon theyr Confession, then to Us was thought reasonable, or that the trowth could beare, like as sythens that time it doth well appere, for that there be diverse of the same thinges wherein they stack them fast, moved onely as said thereto, bycause theyr preachers had set fourth and tawght the same by *theyr said Confession, and now have somewhat more moderately, as theyr books do testifie, set furth the same.*"

The king, by these last words, evidently was endeavoring to turn to his account the *Variata* editions of the Augsburg Confession of 1540 and 1542. His argument is, that if Melanchthon himself had found it advisable to make changes in the Confession, this proved only that Henry was right in insisting at the Conference of 1538 that there be some modifications, and that the course of the Lutheran commissioners at London, had been repudiated. It shows Henry's shrewdness, and would have been unanswerable where the *Variata* had actually been adopted.

He continues: "And upon this manner of proceeding they departed, without any such conclusion as with sum indifferent" [viz., unprejudiced] "handling might have succeeded to the assured conjunction of Us and our dominions on both partes, and thuniversall weall and quiet of all Christendome; yet forasmuch as we having oon commun and certain enemie, the Bishop of Rome, unto whose faccion no smale Princes be addicted, being both of us a like zele and meaning for the right and sincere setting furth of Godes glorie and his holy woord, . . . there be no nations in christendome so like to agree as we be, if the forsayed amitie beyng agreed uppon, for that must necessarily be passed out of hand, and *not be delayd for the disputacions of the matters of religion which will require a tract of time.*"[3] The king is a true type of a modern unionist. He pleads for union first, and wants to postpone to the remote future any understanding as to the doctrinal relations of the parties concerned, forgetting that it is only on doctrinal grounds, that the Lutherans are in dissent from Pope and Emperor, and for such reasons are in jeopardy.

[3] *English State Papers, Henry VIII.*, vol. X: pp. 282 sqq.

There were some who regarded this proposal on the part of the English King with favor. "Great hope," says Seckendorf "seemed to spring afresh. Christopher Mount had much to say concerning the extraordinary kindness which Henry showed Anne of Cleves since the divorce, the magnificent style in which he supported her, the frequent presents he sent, his constant solicitude for her health, etc. The execution of Crumwell was charged against the nobles, that of Barnes to his abusive attack upon Bishop Gardiner, the failure of the negotiations of 1538 to the fact that the Lutherans were represented by stiff and obstinate disputants like Burkhard and Myconius, instead of by Melanchthon and Bucer. Bucer also interposed, with the plea that while all things were not right in England, yet that Henry was nearer the Lutheran princes than any other king. Seckendorf well notes that he forgets Denmark and Sweden. But the Elector of Saxony was again immovable. "He regarded the King of England an enemy of the Gospel, who had no other aim in Reformation than himself to become Head of the Church, to which he had not been called of God, and who meanwhile raged tyrannically against godly Christians and lived shamefully, seeking in all things only his own advantage."[4] At the convention of Frankfort in January, 1546, where there were present not only the members of the Smalcald League, but also the deputies of Lutheran princes and representatives of States not included in the League, as of the Elector of Brandenburg, the Archbishop of Cologne, the Duke of Prussia, Nürnberg and Ratisbon, Henry's propositions met with no favor.

A few months later, (May, 1546,) Henry sent John Masone to Heidelberg to confer with the Elector Frederick II. of the Palatinate, who had lately become a convert to Lutheranism, and arrange a marriage between his daughter Mary and the Elector's nephew, Duke Philip. The answer of the Elector shows the same spirit as throughout inspired the Elector of Saxony. Masone reports :

[4] III: p. 552.

"Concerning religion he hath framed his conscience thoroughly to Confessionem Augustanam, and hath so accepted the same as he trusteth not to varrye from it during life, which determination he hath not rashly entered into, but with long tyme and great deliberation. And to say the trewthe, if he were determined to sende any man, unto your Majestie in those matters, *he wotheth not where to fynde any such indifferent man*, as your Majestie seemeth to require, his hole provynce as well the Nobles as the clergye and others being so thoroughly bent in one trade. . . . The Emperour, at his late being at Spire, was in hande with them for the lyke, and hadd for answer that their doctryne hadd often inoughe ben disputed upon, and was wel knowen throughe the worlde, and they intended to bring that mattier no more in questyon, wherein by soamuch tyme and great deliberation they were thoroughlye persuaded."[5]

The King is persistent. A league must be formed. Froude has asserted that he assured Cranmer, that he was ready to make further concessions, and to take measures for a more radical reform. At any rate, his next proposition was for the formation of "The League Christian." The Lutheran commissioners were to select the names of ten or twelve learned men; from this number, Henry would select one half; and then, they, with a similar commission of English theologians, would come to a final settlement of a doctrinal basis. The King himself was to participate in the deliberations. It was too late. The breaking out of the Smalcald war early in the summer interrupted all negotiations; and a few months later, January 28th, 1547, the reign of Henry VIII. was at an end.

[5] *State Papers, Henry VIII.*, vol. XI: pp. 147 sqq.

CHAPTER XV.

NEW DIFFICULTIES IN THE REIGN OF EDWARD VI.

Decline of Lutheranism in Germany. The Results of the Battle of Mühlberg. The Interim. Melanchthon wavers. The Firmness of the Elector of Saxony. Influence of the Elector in England. Edward's congratulatory Letter. The Elector's Reply. The Augsburg Confession, still the only Basis. League with the Germans contemplated. John Frederick to be its Head. Deaths of the King of England, and the Elector of Saxony.

THE death of Henry VIII. removed the great barrier that had stood in the way of the English Reformation. The two parties that had been held together by his arbitrary measures, were now to come to an open rupture. Cranmer was free to pursue his own course. All Romish interests were suppressed during the reign of Edward VI., as, from the Roman Catholic point of view, Mary was the rightful heir, and Edward, a usurper. The king's uncle, the Duke of Somerset, "the Protector," was known as an ardent friend of the Reformation; but he concerned himself almost exclusively with the political affairs of the kingdom, leaving to Cranmer the task of the ecclesiastical administration.

Could this change have been foreseen at any time during the preceding period from 1535, the prediction would have been made that the Church of England would now, at last, become Lutheran. If we seek the reasons why this expectation was not fulfilled, we must consider first of all the condition, at that time, of the Lutheran Church in Germany. Never was it less able to assert itself or to impress its influence upon those without. To human eyes, it really seemed as though it were on the very verge of destruction. Looking back, we can scarcely imagine that only seventeen years had passed since the Diet of Augsburg, so great has been the fall. The transition has been even more rapid. For only a few years before, with five out of seven of the German electors on the Lutheran side, the prospect for its complete triumph was exceedingly encouraging.

Henry VIII. died January 28th, 1547. Eleven months before, the Reformation had lost its great pillar, when Luther died, February 18th, 1546, and the accomplished but vacillating Melanchthon succeeded to a position, for which his gifts, however eminent in other spheres, did not fit him. External dangers were rapidly gathering. The loyalty of the Lutheran princes of the Empire had induced them to participate in the war against Francis I., and, after they had conquered the foe whose activity had kept the Emperor's hands from them, he was at last able to make an attempt to suppress the Lutheran heresy. This might readily have been repelled, if Duke Maurice of Saxony, influenced by motives of personal hostility against his cousin, the Elector John Frederick, had not energetically thrown himself upon the side of the Emperor, even though professing to be true to that faith, for whose destruction the war was waged. April 24th, 1547, less than three months after the accession of Edward VI., the battle of Mühlberg was fought, and the heroic and godly Elector, next to Luther perhaps the greatest figure of the days of the Reformation, and the head of the Smalcald League, who for so many years had been insisting on the acceptance of the entire Augsburg Confession, as interpreted by the Apology, as the condition of any further negotiations with England, was taken prisoner, deprived of his electoral dignity, despoiled of half his dominions and kept in degrading imprisonment for the next five years. Two months later the Landgrave of Hesse met a similar fate. When Melanchthon heard of the Elector's defeat, he at once wrote to Cruciger (May 1st): "I see that a change of doctrine, and new distractions in the Church will follow,"[1] and fled, first to Brunswick, and then to Nordhau-

[1] *Corpus Reformatorum* VI: p. 532.

sen. After Wittenberg was captured by the Emperor, and placed in charge of Maurice, Melanchthon was prevailed upon to return, although the Elector John Frederick, through his sons, besought him to aid in establishing a new University at Jena, one of the cities still left the Elector. Maurice's exceeding kindness and his presents, as well as his assurances that he was still devoted to the Lutheran faith, seem to have almost reconciled Melanchthon to the changed circumstances. Among the homes offered him elsewhere at this time was one in England. October 25th, 1547, he writes:[2] "To-day I have answered the Bishop of Canterbury who invites me to England."

Then came the persecutions connected with the forcing of the *Interim* upon Lutheran people. Charles V. dissatisfied with the uncompromising spirit manifested by the Council of Trent, and hoping still to maintain the unity of his Empire by a compromise making some concessions to his Lutheran subjects, caused a document (the Augsburg Interim) to be prepared by Agricola, in connection with two Roman Catholic theologians, which, in effect, reintroduced, with a few modifications, the abominations of the Papacy. It forced hundreds of Lutheran ministers into exile, and entailed the greatest distress in various communities, especially at Magdeburg and Augsburg. It was during this persecution, that John Brentz showed himself such a hero in Württemberg. Even the Elector Maurice was indignant, and would not accept it save with certain restrictions. But this did not prevent Melanchthon from a second exile, as the Emperor demanded that, because of his opposition, he must be surrendered or banished. Maurice devised another expedient in the Leipzig Interim, which was preponderatingly Lutheran in its statements, but was so worded as to give the least offence to its opponents, and which enjoined the use of a number of ceremonies, made more acceptable by an evangelical explanation, that heretofore had been regarded badges of the Papists.

Melanchthon was free to express his preference for what he

[2] Ib. p. 714.

regarded a more correct statement of doctrine and prescription of usage, but at the same time declared (January 6th, 1549,) that it "made no change in the Church,"[3] that its prescriptions were "tolerable"[4] and that "it is the better course to treat some follies moderately."[5] He in no way foresaw the storm which his disposition to suppress a protest would call forth.

The Leipzig Interim found no favor anywhere and all attempts to introduce it, had to be abandoned. It is worth while noting that the entire history of the Interims shows that the controversy which had just ceased in England, had been transferred to Germany; and that the policy of yielding certain matters to the Papists, to secure outward unity, was only the repetition of the course of Henry VIII. The Six Articles and the Augsburg Interim belong together; while the Leipzig Interim was also a recession from the principle which demanded unconditional subscription to the Augsburg Confession as the condition of union. Just when the English Church was ready for the entrance of the full truth, those who were regarded the representatives of Lutheranism, themselves waver. Is it wonderful, therefore, that a more radical element soon enters, by its more positive and decided testimony to take the place of such uncertain and wavering Lutheranism? Let any one who who has the curiosity, look into the Calendar of State Papers of the reign of Edward VI., and he will note what pains the authorities in England were then taking to be promptly and fully informed concerning what was transpiring on the Continent, and how the weekly and almost daily dispatches of such ambassadors as Christopher Mount, Sir John Masone and Sir Richard Morysinne, supply, not only most valuable information concerning the ecclesiastical complications of Germany, but even the details of the current gossip of courts and cities. We can imagine the pain and consternation, with which English Lutherans looked on the defection of those, from whom

---

[3] VII: 292.
[4] Ib. 274, 275.
[5] Ib. 275.

they had hoped for encouragement and sympathy in the better times that had now come for them in England.

One great figure, however, stood forth as a beacon light amidst the storm. One heart rose superior to the crisis. The clearness of the testimony of the imprisoned Elector, upon whom even sentence of death had been passed, carried with it a moral weight that was felt throughout Christendom. Summoned before the Emperor in 1548, he was offered the most favorable terms, in case he would desist from his error, and submit to a council." His answer is worthy of everlasting remembrance : " I stand before your Imperial Majesty a poor prisoner. I do not deny that I have confessed the truth, and for it have lost possessions and property, wife and child, land and people, in short everything that God has given me in the world. I have noting left but this imprisoned body, and even this is not within my power, but within that of your Majesty. By the truth which I have confessed, I will abide, and will suffer, as an example, whatever else God and your Imperial Majesty may impose."[6] The better feelings of the Emperor, we are told, overcame him, and he turned away to hide his emotion. When the *Interim* was published, another persistent effort was made to secure the Elector's subscription. But he was immovable. " From his youth he had been instructed according to the doctrine contained in the Augsburg Confession. As in his conscience he was convinced of its truth, should he yield, he could not show himself grateful for such distinguished grace, nor could he expect the inheritance of everlasting life which Christ promised those who would confess him. But if he were to accept the *Interim, he must deny the Augsburg Confession, whereby he would sin against God for time and to eternity*. Nothing could be more pleasing to him and his unwieldy body (for he was corpulent) than freedom, yet, then, he could not testify with a good conscience before God's judgment seat that he had sought for no comfort of this poor temporal life, but only for God's glory and the inheritance of life everlasting."[7] He

---

[6] *Salig's Historie des Aug. Conf.*, I : 580.
[7] Ib.

wrote also a paper to be preserved as his testimony after his death, beginning: "I a poor prisoner in Babylonian captivity, in order that every one may know that, with God's help, I will not during my life receive the *Interim*, but will abide faithful to the Augsburg Confession, and the other articles agreed upon at Smalcald."[8]

When Maurice at last could no longer suppress his indignation at the manner in which the Emperor had used him as a tool to destroy the Lutheran faith, and in which the most sacred pledges were wantonly broken, he sought to repair, to an extent, the wrong in which for years he had participated. Finding an ally in the King of France, he so suddenly made war, that the Emperor, surprised, routed and almost captured at Innspruck in 1552, was glad to conclude, the same year, the Peace of Passau. But even before peace was forced, the Emperor to conciliate his subjects liberated the Elector, who, nevertheless, preferred for awhile to remain with his late captor. When he finally returned to Saxony, his course became a regular triumphal procession, as the people turned out in mass, to honor one who had been greater in defeat, than he could have been even in victory. "Everywhere," says Salig, "he was embraced as a father of his country and a faithful defender of the Augsburg Confession, who, through no trouble and suffering, could be alienated from the truth."[9] Melanchthon promptly wrote a long letter of congratulation. "The memory of your confession, your troubles and liberation, is useful to the Church both now and to posterity. As that of the Israelites in the fiery furnace, or of Daniel among the lions, so also your example will, in many ways, profit others for the true knowledge of God. This honor is much to be preferred to bloody victories and triumphs."[10] The Elector in his courteous reply administers a significant rebuke, when he intimates that the great theologian had culpably wavered and declares how he had wished

---

[8] *Cyprian's Historia der Aug. Conf.*, p. 279.
[9] *Salig*, I: 680.
[10] *Corpus Reformatorum*, VII: 1083.

from his heart that no change whatever had been attempted in the doctrine as set forth by Luther in 1537 at Smalcald and received by all preachers and pastors of the Augsburg Confession. "We have no doubt," he says, "that if such had been the case, the divisions and errors that have occurred among the teachers of the above mentioned Confession, would, with God's help, have been removed." [11]

In England also, the release of the Elector was hailed as a great victory for the Gospel. The despatches show that he was then regarded as the leader of the Lutheran cause. King Edward VI. also wrote a congratulatory letter. The reply of John Frederick (August 22d, 1552) shows that he still had in mind his old terms of agreement with England. It would be a great gratification to have the very letter; but, in its absence, the abstract given in the "Calendar of English State Papers" [12] must answer: "Returns thanks for his Majesty's letter from Petworth of 25th of July, delivered to him by Sir Richard Morysinne, and for his ready good will towards him. Commends his Majesty's efforts on behalf of the Gospel religion, and urges him to continue these. And whereas his Majesty had exhorted him to exert himself towards procuring a suspension of controversies among the professors of Protestantism, declares that of all things the most difficult is to settle religious differences, especially at this advanced age of the world, when every one thinks he has found the truth, lest the old serpent should bite the heel of him who tramples on him. These dissensions arise in consequence of many being misled by philosophical speculations and civil wisdom, withdrawing *from the Confession of Augsburg*, which had been approved by the consent of the most eminent theologians. To which, if they had firmly adhered, as they ought, neither that most mischievous Zwinglian sect, nor the Anabaptists, nor the Antinomians, nor the Adiaphorists, and authors of change in religion, would have disturbed, as they have done, the best con-

---

[11] Ib. p. 1109.
[12] *Calendar*, Edward VI. (Foreign) p. 219.

stituted churches, and inflicted a wound that seems almost incurable."

Again it began to look as though an Anglo-German Lutheran alliance might yet be made. With John Frederick liberated, they had now a leader who could be trusted, especially as he was supported by by Francis Burkhard who, in 1538, with Myconius, had so nearly gained the victory in the negotiations in London. Hence we find, in the "Calendar" of May 25th, 1553,[13] the record that commissioners appointed for the purpose recommend to the Royal Council the formation of "a league with the Germans, including the Emperor," and "suggest that for the naming of the matter, John Frederick is the fittest person to hear of it first; because as he cannot but like, so he is better able to further it, than they, having a man, Francis Burkhard, who has been thrice in England, as fit as any in Germany to handle the subject."

But this was not to be. Providence again mysteriously interfered. Within less than six weeks, (July 5th, 1553) the young King of England died, and the reign of Bloody Mary began. On the third of March following, the heroic Elector, broken down by the severe sufferings through which he had passed, was added to "the noble army of martyrs" in the Church Triumphant. When Amsdorf visited him on his death-bed, to receive his confession and impart the consolations of the Gospel, he heard this dying testimony: "This I know: Whether I live, I live unto the Lord, or whether I die, I die unto the Lord. Of this I am certain."[14]

[13] Ib. *Domestic Series.*
[14] *Salig,* I: 681.

CHAPTER XVI.

CONFLICT OF THEOLOGICAL PARTIES IN ENGLAND DURING THE REIGN OF EDWARD VI.

Effect of the deaths of Fox and Barnes. Reaction against Transubstantiation. Ridley and Hooper, Zwinglians. Bullinger's Influence. John a Lasco, and his congregations. Polanus and the Flemish weavers. Peter Martyr at Oxford. His theological position. Bucer at Cambridge. Was he a Lutheran? Löscher's Argument. Correspondence between Bucer and Brentz. Bucer on the Real Presence. His Doctrine compared with that of Martyr. Switzerland free from the desolations of Smalcald War. English Negotiations with the Reformed Cities. Bullinger and Lady Jane Grey. Calvin's Correspondence. Cranmer yields. His course explained. When and how he became a Calvinist? His Catechism. Indication of process of change afforded by Zürich Letters.

IN the last chapter, we noted how the cause of Lutheranism in England was weakened by its sad condition on the Continent at the time of the Smalcald War and the Interim. But there were other reasons, why it did not gain the ascendency. The stricter Lutherans of the type of Bishop Fox, and Dr. Barnes, had departed. Cranmer, whose connection with Lutheranism in Germany had been maintained, largely, through his intimate correspondence with Osiander, felt the weakening influence of the latter's defection on the doctrine of Justification, even though he had no sympathy for his relative's error; and, doubtless, was influenced by Osiander's increasing bitterness against the Wittenberg theologians. Melanchthon, to whom he had looked for advice, was also found at this time untrustworthy. A reaction against Romish transubstantiation had manifested itself for years in the denial of the doctrine of the real presence, one extreme violently asserted inevitably producing the other, especially as the leaven of Anabaptism was to a greater or less extent diffused. No sooner had the reign of Edward begun, than iconoclastic zeal was ready to tear the crucifixes, out of churches, and otherwise to manifest feeling that had been suppressed so long. Prominent leaders of the English Reformation had not realized the importance of the issue involved concerning the Lord's Supper. Long before this, Tyndale had advised Frith not to allow it to be a matter of discussion. "Barnes will be hot against you. My mind is, that nothing be put forth till we hear how you have sped. I would have right use preached, and the presence to be an indifferent thing, till the matter might be reasoned in peace at the leisure of both parties."[1] As early as 1545, Nicholas Ridley, afterwards Bishop of London, especially distinguished as a preacher, and probably the most learned divine in the English Church after the death of Bishop Fox, had been influenced by one of Zwingli's treatises against Luther and by the study of Ratramnus to reject both the Roman Catholic and the Lutheran doctrines. John Hoper or Hooper, afterwards bishop of Gloucester and then bishop of Worcester, a former Cistercian monk, "infected with Lutheranism by books brought from Germany," had been driven by the persecutions concerning "The Six Articles," from England to Switzerland, where he became intimate with Bullinger, the scholar and successor of Zwingli, first at Basle, and afterwards at Zürich. The death of Henry VIII., and accession of Edward, brought him back to England, not only as a zealous advocate of Zwinglianism, but also as an obstinate polemic, giving great trouble to Cranmer and Ridley, and most of all to Peter Martyr, then Professor at Oxford, who dreaded lest the Continental Reformers should be held responsible for his extreme position. Although imprisoned, because, when nominated as bishop, he both refused to wear Episcopal robes at consecration, and in a tract bitterly attacked this custom as one which he regarded a relic of the Papacy, he yet had sufficient influence to overcome the opposition against him, and to secure a prominent

·Jenkyn's *Cranmer's Remains*, I: XX.

place the councils of the English Church. He diligently circulated the theological writings of his friend Bullinger. Blunt traces to his influence the order which Cranmer actually sent the Dean of St. Paul's in 1552, "to forbid playing of organs at divine services." Hooper's disposition towards Lutheranism may be learned from a letter to Bullinger (January 25th, 1546) in which he says: "The Count Palatine has lately provided for the preaching of the Gospel throughout his dominions: but as far as relates to the eucharist he has descended, as the proverb has it, from the horse to the ass; for he has fallen from Popery into the doctrine of Luther, who is, in that particular, more erroneous than all the Papists." (Original Letters, I. 38). How bitter was the prejudice of Bullinger against Lutheranism, may be learned from another letter in the same collection (p. 251), in which Richard Hilles writes concerning a student at Strassburg, that Bullinger had written requesting that his lodging be changed, since Mr. Marbach, with whom he boarded was "not one with whom the father of Lewis would like his son to have any intercourse," the reason being "that Marbach is altogether a Lutheran." It is interesting to note the answer: "If we consider this, there is no reason for your friend Lewis again to change his lodging; since he will have just such another, if he should lodge with any learned man in this place."

With the *Interim*, there were learned divines glad to find a refuge in England; and whom Cranmer was glad to call to assist him in his great work. Protestants in large numbers had congregated in London, driven from various portions of the Continent. In 1549, there were no less than four thousand Germans there. John a Lasco, was made Superintendent of the several congregations of foreigners, all apparently worshipping in one church. A Lasco was a Polish nobleman, not an exile, but absent from his country by leave of his King, in order to preach the Gospel. He was an intimate friend of Erasmus, whose library he had generously purchased, allowing the owner the use of it for the rest of his life. He had been converted to the Reformed faith, and induced to devote himself to the ministry by Zwingli at Basle. He was an intimate friend and correspondent of Melanchthon. He is described by Goebel,[2] as "in science an Erasmian, in faith a Lutheran, in cultus a Zwinglian, in church organization a Calvinist, as a dogmatician loose and indefinite." On the doctrine of the Lord's Supper, he was either Calvinistic or Zwinglian. He supported Hooper in his controversy, being especially extreme in his opposition to clerical vestments and to kneeling at the communion.

There was a congregation of foreigners at Glastenbury in Somersetshire, consisting chiefly of weavers who had been driven by the *Interim* from Strassburg. Of this congregation, which doctrinally seems to have been in sympathy with a Lasco, Valerandus Pollanus was pastor.

Peter Martyr, Paul Fagius and Martin Bucer, all from Strassburg, were welcomed to professorships of theology, Martyr at Oxford, and Fagius and Bucer at Cambridge. V. E. Löscher, Walch and Buddeus, all maintain that up to this time Martyr had been a Lutheran,[3] and a letter of Bucer to Brenz which we shall shortly quote, seems to confirm it. However this may be, in a public disputation at Oxford in 1549, into which he was forced by Richard Smythe, an advocate of transubstantiation, he virtually yielded the doctrine of the real presence, much to Bucer's dissatisfaction. Even this Buddeus[4] explains as only a

[2] Herzog *Real Encyclopædie*.

[3] Buddeus, *Isagoge*, 1120: "It has been observed by learned men, that in the beginning he did not differ much from the position of Luther, which also pleased the English, until at last he went over to the side of Calvin." Even of his answer to Bishop Gardiner, of 1562, Walch (*Bibl. Theol. Sel.* II: 439) says: "Previously he was not alien to the true doctrine, but now seems to approach the opinion of those who deny the real presence." The Calvinistic element in England, regarded him in the same light. Burcher to Bullinger (October 29th. 1548): "The Archbishop of Canterbury, moved, no doubt, by the advice of Peter Martyr, and other *Lutherans*." Or. Letters, II: 542.

[4] *Vita Petri Martyris*, per Josiam Simler, in Gerdesius' *Misscellanea Groningana*, III: 38, 48. *Melchior Adam's Vita Germ. Theol.* II: 13 sqq.

temporary inconsistency. Martyr was the spiritual father of Bishop Jewel, whose "Apology" is almost a symbol in the Anglican church. Jewel was Martyr's pupil, and took down the discussion with Smythe. Driven from England on the accession of Mary, the charge of disloyalty to the Augsburg Confession was made against him at Strassburg. His answer shows how he wished to be regarded as subscribing to the confession, while, he tried to read into it a Calvinistic interpretation. Writing to the Senate, " he professed that he cheerfully embraced the Augsburg Confession, and whatever does not differ therefrom, *provided it be correctly understood;* and that, if there were need, he would maintain them with all his might." Concerning the Wittenberg Concord between Luther and Bucer, he replied "that to this he had not subscribed; that it could not be conceded by the Word of God and conscience, that those destitute of true faith, in partaking of the sacraments, receive the true body of Christ." As years advanced, his opposition to Lutheranism increased, and in 1561, in negotiations at the Colloquy of Paissy, with the King of Navarre, "when he was asked his judgment concerning the Augsburg Confession, he answered that the Word of God seems to us sufficient, as it clearly contains all things which pertain to salvation. For even if that Confession be received, reconciliation with the Romanists will not follow; since they proscribe it as heretical." [5] He ended his life as Professor at Zürich.

Fagius was known to have very decided Lutheran sympathies, but was more distinguished as an Old Testament scholar than as dogmatician, or ecclesiastical leader, and died before he could enter upon his duties.

Bucer had endeavored to mediate between Lutheranism and Zwinglianism. In 1536, however, he had come to an understanding with Luther and Melanchthon in "the Wittenberg Concord," in which the Lutheran doctrine of the Lord's Supper was subscribed, Bucer reserving the nature of the communion of the unworthy as a point not yet settled in his mind. In subse-

[5] *Isagoge* p. 1120.

quent years, he does not seem to have materially varied from this position. Löscher, in his *Ausführliche Historia Motuum*, devotes an entire chapter, to prove that "although with considerable weakness, he is, nevertheless, to be reckoned among evangelical Lutherans."[6] Hardwick pronounces him "a moderate Lutheran, and, as such, decided in his opposition to the school of Hooper."[7] It is certain, however, that the very point in which he failed at Wittenberg in 1536, continued to render the transition to the Calvinistic doctrine very easy. Possibly he attempted to render the Lutheran doctrine more acceptable to Calvinists by concessions, or possibly he was never entirely in the clear as to what was involved in statements which he maintained. In "the Sententious Sayings of Master Martin Bucer upon the Lord's Supper,"[8] of 1550, written while professor at Oxford, there is much that, if taken by itself, would seem to be an entire surrender to Calvinism, e. g., (22) "There is no presence of Christ in the Supper, but only in the lawful use thereof, and such as is *obtained and gotten by faith only*." (33): "I define or determine Christ's presence, howsoever we perceive it, either by the sacraments or by the word of the Gospel, to be *only the attaining and perceiving of the commodities we have by Christ*, both God and man, which is our Head reigning in heaven, dwelling and living in us, *which presence we have* by no worldly means, but we have it *by faith*." A letter, however, of Bucer to Brentz, May 15th, 1550,[9] apologizing for Peter Martyr's discussion is in a different key. He writes, as in full harmony with Brentz, whose strict Lutheranism has never been questioned, and as though discussions were in progress, in which the Lutheran doc- was vigorously assailed, and he were being overpowered. This is the letter: "With respect to the book of Dr. Martyr, I undoubtedly have as much regret as any one else; but the discus-

[6] *Ausführliche Historia*, II: 27.
[7] *History of Reformation*, p. 220.
[8] Strype's *Memorials of Archbishop Cranmer*, II: 597 sqq.
[9] *Anecdota Brentiana*, p. 304.

sion was announced and the proposition formulated before I had arrived in England. At my advice, he has introduced much in his preface, whereby he expresses more fully his faith in the presence of Christ. With the heads of government, they have much weight who contract their ministry within a narrow sphere, and are not anxious about restoring the discipline of the church; the violence of these has also to certain extent influenced this friend of ours. While he was with us, all things were presented more correctly and amply. In wishing to prevent us from including in the bread, our Lord taken from Heaven, and from giving him to men to be eaten without faith, which none of us imagines, they fall into the error of including him in a fixed place in Heaven, although for this they are absolutely without Scripture testimony, and of his presentation and presence in the Supper they speak so feebly (yea they do not even mention these words), that they seem to hold that in the Supper nothing but bread and wine are distributed. Our simple position, as held by me, no one as yet has reproved, nor have I heard of any one able to refute it by any firm declaration from Scripture. Neither as yet has any such attempt been made. Their chief argument is: 'The mysteries of Christ ought to be intelligibly explained.' They would be correct in saying this, if they were to add: 'To faith, not to reason.' They now assume that it can in no way be understood how Christ is now circumscribed in a physical place in Heaven; and since he is thus in Heaven (which they assume not only without any warrant, but even without any firm reason), it cannot be understood how the same body of Christ is in Heaven and in the Supper. When, then we say that in the Supper none should suppose a local presence of Christ, they again say that the body of Christ cannot be understood to be anywhere, unless its presence be that of local circumscription. The substance of their argument, therefore, is: 'Reason does not perceive what you teach concerning the presentation and presence of Christ in the Supper, and hence it is not true. The Scripture passages which seem to prove it, must be understood otherwise.' Let us pray for them. Thus far I have met no true Christians who were not entirely satisfied with our simplicity in this matter."

So important was Bucer, until his death in February, 1551, as one of the chief advisers of Cranmer in the determination of the formularies of this period, that we add yet the explanation of his inconsistencies given by Löscher: "We must not deny that he resorted to many worldly counsels from carnal prudence, mingled with love for peace, which were of great damage to the Evangelical Lutheran Church, that he had too little zeal for truth in the doctrine of the Lord's Supper, that in the side-questions pertaining to the Lord's Supper he was still not in the clear, that he always had a *penchant* for seeking to reconcile the two contradictories. 'The body of Christ is substantially present, etc.,' and 'The body of Christ is not substantially present, etc.,' an impossible work, at which, nevertheless, he labored until the close of his life. Yet these points must not be mingled with the chief question, in the investigation of historical truth."[10]

It is certain, however, that the Anti-Lutheran element in England regarded him an exponent of Lutheranism, and were anxious that he should be displaced, as the following shows:

"Bucer has a most dangerous relapse into his old disease. Richard writes that there is little or no hope of his recovery. In case of his death, England will be happy, and more favored than all other countries, in having been delivered in the same year, from two men of most pernicious talent, namely Paul Fagius and Bucer." (Burcher to Bullinger, April 20th, 1550).[11] So after Bucer's death: "The death of Bucer affords England the greatest possible opportunity of concord. If you know any one qualified for so important an office, pray inform me." (Or. Letters, p. 678).

There were political considerations which increased the influ-

---

[10] *Ausfuhr. Histor.* II: 26 sq. For additional information concerning Bucer's theological position, see my edition of "Book of Concord," Vol. II: p. 253 sqq., and the authorities there cited.

[11] *Original Letters*, II: 662.

ence of the anti-Lutheran element in the Church of England. While Lutheranism seemed to be almost ruined by the Smalcald war and the *Interim*, there was peace in Switzerland. Francis I. held the Roman Catholic cantons back from supporting Charles V., and, however much they sympathized with the Emperor, they were powerless to aid him. Hence Zürich and Geneva knew nothing of the persecutions that overwhelmed Wittenberg and other Lutheran centers. The English court sought, therefore, an alliance with the Reformed cities. Thus, October 20th, 1549, Edward VI, writes to the Senate of Zürich: "We have understood by the frequent letters of our faithful and beloved servant, Christopher Mount, both your favorable disposition towards us, and ready inclination to deserve well of us. In addition to which, *there is also a mutual agreement between us concerning the Christian religion* and true godliness, which ought to render this friendship of ours, by God's blessing, yet more intimate."[12]

Those high in position in the State were also in frequent correspondence with the Reformed leaders in Switzerland. Bullinger was directing the studies of Lady Jane Grey. Thus, July 12th, 1551, she writes to him in reference to her Hebrew, and pays this tribute to the Swiss theologian: "Oh, happy me to be possessed of such a friend, and so wise a counsellor, and to be connected by ties of intimacy and friendship with so learned a man, so pious a divine, and so intrepid a champion of true religion."[13] Calvin was in correspondence with the Lord Protector,[14] the young king,[15] and Cranmer,[16] giving them in long and tedious letters, a great deal of advice. There are published in the "Original Letters," chiefly from the archives at Zürich, no less than one hundred and seventy letters written to Bullinger alone, during the six years of Edward's reign, by friends in Eng-

[12] *Original Letters* relative to the English Reformation, Vol. I: 1.
[13] Ib. p. 5.
[14] Ib. Vol. II: p. 704.
[15] Ib. p. 707.
[16] Ib. p. 711.

land, most of whom were exerting all their power to transplant thither the theology of Switzerland. Every change and wavering in Cranmer that can in any way be noticed, is promptly and faithfully reported at headquarters in Zürich.

It is no wonder, then, that a man of the temperament and disposition of Archbishop Cranmer, pressed on every side, gradually yielded to Calvinism, just as during Henry's reign he had so often allowed his better judgment to succumb for a time to Romanizing tendencies. His change must not entirely be ascribed to vacillation amidst fixed principles. In himself there existed simultaneously the contradictory positions, which had never been thoroughly fought over in his own experience. We would not question his sincerity; but again and again when he firmly maintained a doctrine, he seems not to have understood it in its relations. With Fox and Crumwell and Barnes to aid him, he was a Lutheran; deprived of them, he drifted between the conflicting elements, in hope of a better day when he thought he would be able to act with less embarrassment. But when these came with new complications, "he considered," says Dr. Jenkyns, "the exchange from the long established and absolute sway of Henry, to the new and unsettled authority of Edward, as a loss, rather than a gain to the cause of the reformation. He may perhaps have been mistaken in this view; the flexibility of the son may in truth have been no less favorable to the construction of a new system, than the obstinacy of the father to the demolition of the old one. But the inference is almost unavoidable, that the difficulties of his situation under Henry were less, and under Edward greater, than is usually supposed."[17] The precise time when the Archbishop became a Calvinist on the doctrine of the Lord's Supper cannot be accurately determined. He himself stated that it was through Ridley's arguments that the change in his opinion began.[18] Although in the

---

[17] *Remains of Thomas Cranmer*, D. D., I: p. xliv.

[18] "Dr. Ridley did confer with me, and by sundry persuasions and authorities of doctors, drew me quite from my opinion." *Examination*, Jenkyns IV: 97.

preface to the Embden edition of the defence, generally ascribed to his intimate friend, Sir John Cheke, tutor to Edward VI., this change is assigned to the year 1546, this probably marks only the beginning, especially as the Nürnberg *Kinderpredigten*, improperly known as the Catechism of Justus Jonas' because of Jonas' Latin version, which he translated in 1548, and, which in English, is usually designated Cranmer's Catechism, not only teaches most emphatically the Lutheran doctrine, but also contains *verbatim* Luther's Small Catechism. Here the Zürich letters are of service:

1548, August 1st. Traheran to Bullinger: "All our countrymen who are sincerely favorable to the restoration of truth entertain in all respects like opinions with you. I except the archbishop of Canterbury, and Latimer, and a very few learned men besides." [19]

August 18th. John ab Ulmis to Bullinger: "He has lately published a Catechism, in which he not only approved that foul and sacrilegious transubstantiation of the papists in the holy supper of our Saviour, but all the dreams of Luther seem to him sufficiently well-grounded, perspicuous and bold." [20]

October 29th. John Burcher to Bullinger: "The archbishop of Canterbury, moved no doubt by the advice of Peter Martyr and other Lutherans, has ordered a catechism of some Lutheran opinion, to be translated and published in our language. This little book has occasioned no little discord." [21]

September 28th. Traheran to Bullinger: "Latimer has come over to our opinion respecting the true doctrine of the Eucharist, together with the archbishop of Canterbury, and the other bishops, who heretofore seemed to be Lutherans." [22]

November 27th. "Even Cranmer, by the goodness of God, and the instrumentality of that most upright and judicious man,

[19] *Original Letters*, I: p. 320.
[20] Ib II: p. 381.
[21] Ib. p. 643.
[22] Ib. I: p. 322.

Master John a Lasco, is in a great measure recovered from his dangerous lethargy." [23]

December 27th. Hooper to Bullinger: "The archbishop of Canterbury entertains right views as to the nature of Christ's presence in the Supper, and is now very friendly towards myself." [24]

December 31st. Traheran to Bullinger: "The archbishop of Canterbury, contrary to general expectation, most openly, firmly and learnedly maintained your opinion on this subject. I perceive that *it is all over with Lutheranism*, now that those who were considered its principal and almost only supporters, have altogether come over to our side." [25]

[23] Ib. II: p. 383.
[24] Ib. I: p. 73.
[25] Ib. p. 323.

CHAPTER XVII.

LUTHERAN SOURCES OF THE BOOK OF COMMON PRAYER.

Uniformity of Worship in the Western Church, prior to the Reformation, only relative. Influence of Reformation on present Roman Order. Groups of Liturgies. Sources of the Roman Liturgy. Confession of the Opening of the Reformation. The old English Orders. The three-fold task of the Reformers of the Service. Introduction of the Vernacular. Development of the Lutheran Service. Luther's Reformation of the Service. Principles laid down in his *Formula Missae* of 1523. The old Worship, not to be abolished. Scripture-lessons, Sermons and Hymns to be in German. Luther's German Mass of 1526. German, Latin, Greek, Hebrew may all be used in the same service, if there be those who understand them. Translation of New Testament of 1523. Hymns, mostly of 1524. Formula of Baptism, 1523. Translation of revised Mass, 1526. Bugenhagen's order of 1524. The Nürnberg Service. Volprecht. Doeber's Mass, 1525. Osiander's Order of Baptism, 1529. Brandenburg-Nürnberg Order, 1533. Reformation of Cologne, 1543 (Bucer, Melanchthon, Sarcerius). Its Sources. Order of Morning Service in three typical Lutheran Liturgies. The tentative Order of Bucer in the Strassburg Agende of 1524.

IF, however, those who controlled the work of the reorganization of the English Church, after many vacillations, at last failed in a full appreciation and confession of the Lutheran faith, the results of the first glow of awakening love for the Gospel in England and of years of contact and negotiation with the leaders of the Lutheran Reformation in Germany, have not been without fruit, but have left their permanent record in the great ecclesiastical documents which are the glory and pride of the English Church, and upon which its very existence depends. Turn where we may in the history or the worship of the English Church and its descendants, we meet at every step with what they owe to that memorable time, and to the incomplete and greatly embarrassed work of the first English Lutherans. We have already traced the origin of the English Bible to German soil, and Lutheran influences. We now enter upon the examination of the influence of Lutheranism upon the worship of the English Church.

It is a great misconception to imagine that prior to the Reformation, the worship in the Western Church, was uniform. Uniformity of worship, like the subjection of the churches of the various countries to the see of Rome, was a gradual growth. The uniformity in the Romish Church of to-day, is, in large measure, the result of the Council of Trent, and even now, is not entirely absolute, as *e. g.* the continuance of the Mozarabic Liturgy at Toledo in Spain still attests. Liturgiologists classify the various liturgies into groups, and in the Gallican group trace a very decided oriental influence, some conjecturing that their origin was at Ephesus. The Roman Liturgy, Mss. of which as far back as the Ninth Century remain, representing or purporting to represent the Liturgy, as current under Leo I. (440–61, *Sacramentarium Leonianum*) Gelasius (492–96, *Sacr Gelasianum*) and Gregory the Great (590–604), continued to press its way, especially in accordance with the schemes of Gregory, in some places entirely supplanting other liturgies, in others adopting some of their features, and in still others only engrafting some of its own features upon liturgies which it could not supplant. Hence at the opening of the Reformation, there was much confusion. Nürnberg and Bamberg are only thirty-three miles apart; and yet the Nürnberg Missal of 1484 differs from the Bamberg Missal of 1492 in the very first Gospel lesson that is given, viz. that for the First Sunday in Advent, where Nürnberg had yielded to the prevailing practice of Rome by surrendering Matth- 21 : 1 sqq. for Luke 21 : 25 sqq., a change which affected the Gospel for every Sunday in Advent. The old conflict between the Gallican and the Roman Missal had not been fully decided; and, therefore, some of the discrepancies in the services of Lutheran churches in various lands, may be traced back to discrepancies in the Ante-Reformation services which they undertook to reform.

In England also, when the Reformation opened, the various dioceses had divergent orders, as the proportion of Rome or Gallican elements was more or less decided. The chief of these are the Missals according to the use of Sarum (Salisbury), Bristol, York, etc., the former of which dating back to 1085, is the best representative of liturgies of the English type.

Upon the basis of these liturgies, therefore, the Reformers both on the Continent and in England, had alike to labor in providing for the reformation of public worship. They had a threefold work to perform: *first*, to translate the service which up to this time had been exclusively Latin; *secondly*, to correct Romish errors by omission and amendment; *thirdly*, to supplement what was lacking, by reintroducing whatever was wholesome in the service of the Early Church that had fallen into disuse, and by inserting whatever changed circumstances rendered needful, in order to guard against prevalent abuses.

As long as public worship was congregational, it had been conducted in the language of the people; only when it ceased to be congregational, and became a work of the priests for the congregation, could a language unknown to the people become that of the entire service. The dominancy of the Romish, over the provincial liturgies, and the fact that all the culture of the West was Latin, explain how it supplanted all other languages.

Luther soon felt the necessity of reintroducing the vernacular. We can trace his desire for it, to a statement in his sermon of 1520 on the Mass. During his absence at the Wartburg, Carlstadt having radically changed the service, on his return he began to reform it upon conservative principles. Even then, he recognized the fact that it was impossible at one stroke, to attain everything desirable, and that the work must be gradually wrought. This is shown very clearly in his " Formula of the Mass " of 1523, where he begins by saying: "I have not exchanged old things for new, always hesitating, both because of minds weak in faith, who could not be suddenly freed of what is old and established by custom, and with whom so recent and unusual a mode of worshipping God could not be introduced; and especially because of frivolous and fastidious spirits, who, without faith, and without mind, rush forward, and delight in novelty alone, and then grow nauseated with whatever ceases to be new; as the latter class of men give more trouble than others, in other matters, so, in holy things, they are most troublesome and intolerable, although, while ready to burst with wrath, I am compelled to endure them, unless willing to remove the Gospel itself from the public. But since there is now hope, that the hearts of many have been illumined and strengthened by the grace of God, and the subject itself demands, that scandals be removed from the Kingdom of Christ, something must be attempted in Christ's name. . . . First of all, we, therefore, profess that it has never been our intention to entirely abolish all worship of God, but only to reform that in use, which has been corrupted by the worst additions, and to demonstrate its godly use."[1] He asks, therefore, only that the Scripture-lessons and sermons be in German, and that after the Gradual, and the *Sanctus* and *Agnus Dei* in the Communion Service, German hymns, as far as possible, be sung. But he realizes the poverty of the German as yet in hymns; and hence he felt himself so soon constrained to provide by his own pen, for this want in public worship

Three years later, (1526), in his German Mass he has directed that the most of the liturgical acts shall be in German, but "for the sake of the youth," wishes part of the service still to be in Latin. For, it must not be forgotten that the pupils of the schools, where the Latin was faithfully taught, up to through the Gymnasia, were compelled to take their places in the choirs, and daily, at Matins and Vespers, to chant the Psalms, as well as to

---

[1] A full translation of Luther's *Formula* may be found in Lutheran *Church Review* for 1889 and 1890.

aid in the regular Sunday services. So, too, the Apology says: "We retain the Latin language, on account of those who are learning and understand Latin, and we mingle with it German hymns, in order that the people also may have something to learn, and by which faith and fear may be called forth. It has nowhere been written or represented that the act of hearing lessons, not understood, profits men, or that ceremonies profit, not because they teach or admonish, but *ex opere operato*, because they are thus performed or looked upon. Away with such pharisaic opinion!" But wherever a language be understood and edify, there Luther would give it a place in the service: "Were I able, and the Greek and Hebrew were as common as the Latin, and had in them as much fine music and song as the Latin has, Mass would be held, sung and read one Sunday after the other, in all four languages, German, Latin, Greek, Hebrew. I have no regard for those who are so devoted to but one language, and despise all others; for I would like to educate youth and men, who might be of service to Christ and converse with men, also in foreign lands, so that it might not be with us, as with the Waldenses and Bohemians, who have so confined their faith to their own language, that they cannot speak intelligently and clearly with any one, until he first learn their language. But the Holy Ghost did not so in the beginning. He did not wait, until the whole world came to Jerusalem and learned Hebrew, but he gave various tongues for the ministry of the Word, that the Apostles might speak wherever they went. This example I prefer following; and it is also proper that the youth be practiced in several languages; for who knows how God may use them in time?"

Accordingly he provided for the service in German, first of all by his translation of the New Testament of 1523; then, by his hymns, the first of which were composed the same year, and twenty-one of the thirty-seven which he wrote having originated in 1524; by his German forms for Baptism (*Taufbüchlein*) of 1523; and his translation of the revised Masss in 1526. His colleague, Bugenhagen, was likewise active in similar work, by his Order of Service of 1524. On the Twentieth Sunday after Trinity, 1525, the Mass was said for the first time in German at Wittenberg.

Nürnberg, whose intimate relations with the English Reformation, because of the connection between Osiander and Cranmer, has been already noticed, requires special consideration in this connection. Here Wolfgang Volprecht, Prior of the Augustinian cloister, (d. 1528) on Maunday Thursday 1523, administered the communion in both forms to members of his order, and on Easter, 1524, to three thousand persons. In 1525, Doeber's Evangelical Mass was introduced. In 1529, Osiander published an Order of Baptism, partly translated from the Bamberg Order, and partly taken from Luther's *Taufbüchlein*. In 1533, the very important *Brandenburg-Nürnberg* Agende was published, having been prepared, as we have before seen, by Osiander, with the assistance of Brentz, and having been submitted to, and received the endorsement of the Wittenberg Faculty. It is the model, after which many succeeding Lutheran liturgies were constructed, holding a place, in the first rank, for conservatism, purity of doctrine and correctness of usage. Altogether between 1523 and 1555, Augusti asserts that there were published one hundred and thirty-two Lutheran Agende and Kirchenordnungen. Their great variety is partly explained by historical and local relations, but, at the same, indicates that the Lutheran Church lays less emphasis upon external uniformity, than upon fidelity to the common Evangelical principle. These orders may be distributed into three classes : 1. Those pure in doctrine, but adhering most strictly to the received Roman forms. Of these, Mark-Brandenburg, of 1540, the Pfalz-Neuberg and the Austrian of 1571, are types. 2. Those of the Saxon Lutheran type, among which Luther's Formula of the Mass is most prominent. Among them are the Prussian (1525), the various orders prepared by Bugenhagen, as Brunswick (1528), Hamburg (1529), Minden and Göttingen (1530), Lübeck (1531), Soest (1532),

Bremen (1534), Pomerania, (1535), the Brandenburg-Nürnberg (1533), Hanover (1536), Herzog Heinrich of Saxony (1539), Mecklenburg (1540), etc. 3. Those which mediate between the Lutheran and the Reformed type, as Bucer's in Strassburg; the Württemberg Orders, and, to a greater or less extent, the orders of S. W. Germany in general.

Of these, there is one that exerted an especial influence above all the rest, upon the orders of the English Church, viz., the Liturgy for the Reformation of Cologne of 1543. Hermann the Archbishop and Elector of Cologne, having become a convert to the Lutheran faith, expected to reform the churches in his realm according to the Lutheran doctrine; and, at his request, a Church Constitution, with orders of Service, was drawn up by Bucer, and thoroughly revised by Melanchthon, with the aid of Sarcerius and others. It is derived chiefly from the Brandenburg-Nürnberg order of 1533, and the orders of Herzog Heinrich, of Saxony, prepared by Justus Jonas in 1536, and published, after revision by Cruciger, Myconius, etc., in 1539, and of Hesse Cassel, (Kymens) of 1539. Carefully guarding against any explicit statements of a polemical character towards both the Romanists and the Reformed, it did not meet with the favor of Luther, who demanded that beyond the positive presentation of doctrine in the service, the negative should also be unmistakably expressed, and, therefore, had not patience to read it thoroughly.

The Order of Morning Service, (*Hauptgottesdienst*) as given in these typical Lutheran liturgies, is as follows:

I. LUTHER'S GERMAN MASS, (1526).

1. A Spiritual Song or Psalm in German, as "I will bless the Lord at all times." (Ps. 34).

2. Kyrie Eleison, three, not nine times.

3. A Collect, as follows:

"O God, the Protector of all that trust in Thee, without whom nothing is strong, nothing is holy," etc.

4. The Epistle.

5. A German Hymn: "*Nun bitten wir den Heiligen Geist,*" or some other.

6. The Gospel.

7. The Creed in German: "*Wir glauben all in einem Gott.*"

8. Sermon on the Gospel for the day.

9. Paraphrase of the Lord's Prayer, and Exhortation to the Communion.

10. Words of Institution.

11. *Agnus Dei* in German: "*O Lamm Gottes unschuldig.*"

12. Distribution.

13. Collect:

"Almighty God, we thank Thee that Thou has refreshed us with this salutary gift, and we beseech Thy mercy graciously to strengthen us in faith towards Thee, and in fervent love towards one another," etc.

XIV. Benediction.

II. BRANDENBURG—NÜRNBERG, (1533.)

1. When the priest comes to the altar, he may say the *Confiteor.* 2. *Introit* or German Hymn. 3. *Kyrie.* 4. *Gloria in Excelsis.* 5. "The Lord be with you," etc. 6. One or more collects, according to the occasion. 7. A chapter from the Epistles of Paul, Peter or John. 8. Hallelujah, with its versicle, or a Gradual, from Holy Scripture. 9. A chapter from the Gospels, or Acts. 10. The Creed. 11. Sermon. 12. Exhortation. 13. Words of Institution. 14. Sanctus. 15. Lord's Prayer. 16. "The Peace of the Lord," etc. 17. Distribution, accompanied by the singing of the "*Agnus Dei.*" 18. Prayer of thanksgiving: "Almighty and everlasting God, we heartily thank Thee," etc.

"Almighty God, we thank Thee," as in Luther's German Mass. 19. Benedicamus. 20. Benediction.

"The Lord bless thee," etc.; or, "God be merciful unto us, and bless us," etc.; or, "God, the Father, Son and Holy Ghost, bless and keep us;" or "The blessing of God the Father, and of the Son and of the Holy Ghost, be and abide with us all. Amen."

III. SAXONY (*Herzog Heinrich*, 1539).

1. Introit *de tempore*. 2. Kyrie Eleison. 3. Gloria in Excelsis. 4. Creed (*Wir glauben*). 5. Sermon. 6. Salutation. 7. *Sursum Corda*. 8. Prefaces. 7. Sanctus. 8. Admonition with Paraphrase of Lord's Prayer, or Lord's Prayer unparaphrased alone. 4. Admonition with Words of Institution, or Words of Institution alone. 10. *Agnus Dei*, on Festivals, or if there be many communicants. 11. At close of Communion, Thanksgiving Collect:

"Almighty God," as in Luther's Mass, or "*Ach du lieber Herre Gott.*" 12. Benediction.

IV. REFORMATION OF COLOGNE, (1543).

1. Public Confession.

"I will confess my transgression, etc. Almighty and eternal God and Father, we confess and lament that we are conceived and born in sin, and are full of ignorance and unbelief of Thy divine Word; that we are ever inclined to all evil and averse to all good; that we transgress thy holy commandments without end; and that thereby we have incurred everlasting death, and our corruption ever increaseth. But we are sorry, and crave Thy grace and help. Have mercy upon us all, O most merciful God and Father, through Thy Son, and Lord Jesus Christ. Grant unto us Thy Holy Spirit, that we may learn our sins, and thoroughly lament and acknowledge our unrighteousness; and with true faith accept Thy grace and forgiveness in Christ, our Lord, Thy dear Son; so that we may die more and more unto sin, and live a new life in Thee, and may serve and please Thee, to Thy glory and the profit of Thy Church. Amen.

2. *Consolation of the Gospel.*

Hear the Consolation of the Gospel: John 3: 16; 1 Tim. 1: 15; John 3: 35, 36; Acts 10: 43; 1 John 2: 1, 2.

3. *Absolution.*

Our Lord Jesus Christ hath left to his Church the great consolation in that he hath enjoined his ministers to remit sins unto all those who are sorry for their sins, and in faith and repentance desire to amend, and hath promised that unto all such, their sins shall be forgiven in Heaven. Upon this gracious command and consolation of our Lord Jesus Christ, I announce unto all those who are penitent for their sins, console themselves in our Lord Christ, and thus desire to amend their lives, the remission of all their sins, with the assurance of divine grace, and eternal life, through Jesus Christ, our Lord. Amen.

4. Introit. 5. Kyrie. 6. Gloria in Excelsis. 7. "The Lord be with you." 8. Collect. 9. Epistle. 10. Hallelujah, Gradual or Sequence. 11. Gospel. 12. Exposition of Gospel (Sermon). 13. General Prayer:

"Almighty and everlasting God and Father, Thou hast commanded us through Thy dear Son and his Apostles, to come unto Thee in His name, and hast promised, that whatsoever we, when thus assembled, ask Thee in his name, Thou wilt graciously grant ; we pray Thee, in the name of Thy Son, our Lord Jesus Christ, first that Thou would graciously forgive us all our sin and misdeeds which we confess unto Thee," etc.

14. Creed, during the singing of which the offerings are gathered. 15. Warning against unworthy reception of the Lord's Supper. 16. "The Lord be with you," etc. 17. "Lift up your hearts," etc. 18. "Let us give thanks," etc. 19. "It is truly meet, right and salutary," etc. 20. Sanctus. 21. Words of Institution. 22. Lord's Prayer. 23. "The Peace of the Lord," etc. 24. Distribution, during which the *Agnus Dei* is sung. 25. "The Lord be with you," etc. 26. Collects, as in Brandenburg-Nürnberg. 27. Benediction, as in Brandenburg-Nürnberg.

To these, we add Bucer's tentative, but still earlier work, in the Strassburg Mass of 1524, although published without authority. This is of especial interest, because of Bucer's connection both with the Reformation of Cologne, and the Revision of I Edward VI.

1. In the Name of the Father, and of the Son and of the Holy Ghost. Amen. 2. Kneeling. I said, I will confess my sins unto the Lord. And Thou forgavest, etc. I, a poor sinner, confess to God Almighty, that I have grievously sinned by trangression of his commandment, that I have done much which I should have left undone, and that I have left much undone which I should have done, by unbelief and want of confidence towards God, and by lack of love toward my neighbor. For this, my guilt, whereof God knows, I grieve. Be gracious, be merciful to me, a poor sinner. Amen. 3. This is a faithful saying, and worthy of all acceptation, etc. This I believe. Help, Thou, mine unbelief, and save me. Amen. 4. The priest then says to the people: God be gracious, and have mercy upon us all. 5. The Introit, or a Psalm. 6. Kyrie Eleison. 7. Gloria in Excelsis. 8. Salutation. 9. Collect, or Common Prayer. 10. Epistle. 11. Hallelujah. 12. Gospel. 13. Sermon. 14. Apostles' or Nicene Creed. 15. Admonition to Prayer. 16. Sursum Corda. 17. Prefaces. 18. Sanctus with Benedictus. 19. Prayer: Almighty, Merciful Father, as Thy Son our Lord Jesus Christ hath promised that what we ask in His Name, etc. 19. Words of Institution. 20. How great is Thy goodness, in that Thou not only hath forgiven us our sins, without any merit of our own, but that Thou hath given us as an assurance thereof, the memorial of the Body and Blood of our Lord Jesus Christ in the bread and wine, as Thou art wont to seal other promises by outward signs. Therefore we have now great and irrefutable assurance of Thy grace, and know that we are Thy children, Thine heirs, and coheirs with Christ, and that we may pray freely as Thine only begotten Son hath taught us, saying: *Our Father*, etc. 21. Lord, Deliver us from enemies, seen and unseen, from the devil, the world and our own flesh. Through Christ, our Lord. Amen. 22. *Agnus Dei.* 23. Lord Jesus, Christ, Thou Son of the Living God, who, by thy Father's will, and with the working of the Holy Ghost, hath, by Thy death, brought the world to life; deliver us, by this Thy

holy Body and Blood, from all our unrighteousness and wickedness, and grant that we may alway obey Thy commandments, and never be separated from Thee eternally. Amen. 24. Admonition to the profitable remembrance of Christ's Death. 25. Distribution, with the words alone of the Evangelists or Paul. 27. Thanksgiving Hymn:

> " Gott sei gelobet und gebenedeiet
> Der uns selber hat gespeiset
> Mit seinem Fleische und mit seinem Blute, et." (Luther).

CHAPTER XVIII.

THE LITANY OF THE ENGLISH CHURCH.

Provision for the reading of Scripture Lessons in English. Introduction of Homilies. Purification of the Mass, a gradual Process. Revision of the Litany. The old English Litany (1410). Luther's Revision (1529). Cranmer's of 1544, from the Reformation of Cologne (1543), and this from Luther. Earlier Revision of Marshall (1535), also follows Luther. Luther's and Marshall's in parallel columns. Hilsey's Revision of 1539, dependent on Marshall. Luther's changes in the Litany, transferred to England, examined in detail. Dr. Blunt's singular mistake.

As with the German, so with the English Reformation, the first step in reforming the service, was to provide what is the chief part of the service, the Holy Scriptures, in the language of the people. We have noted the difficulties attending the translation of the Bible, and how it gradually overcome opposition. First we find a proclamation of the King, of November 14th, 1539, (1538) "allowing private persons to buy Bibles, and keep them in their houses."[1] Eighteen months later, May 5th, 1541 (1540), all curates were commanded, under penalty of a fine of forty shillings a month, to set up Bibles in their church, in a convenient place for the people to read. In St. Paul's, London, six Bibles were thus provided.[2] But in accordance with his vacillations, two years later, the king took measures again to suppress their circulation, and Grafton, the publisher, was committed to the Fleet for six weeks, and released only on condition that he would "neither sell nor imprint any more Bibles, till the King and clergy should agree upon a translation. . . And from hence-

---
[1] Strype's *Cranmer*, III: 387.
[2] Strype's *Cranmer*, I: 191 sq.

forth the Bible was stopped during the remainder of King Henry's reign." [3]

In 1542, however, the Convocation ordered that "one chapter of the New Testament in English" should be read every Sunday and holidays, and "when the New Testament was through, then to begin the Old." [4] Provision was made for Homilies at the same time. Every morning and evening, one chapter of the New Testament was to be read in each parish. Provision was also made that "all mass books, antiphoners, porturses in the church of England should be corrected, reformed and castigated from all manner of mention of the Bishop of Rome's name; and from all apocryphas, feigned legends, superstitions oraisons, collects, versicles and responses." [5]

Nothing, however, in the way of liturgical reform was effected during Henry's reign, except in the Litany. The Litany was the processional prayer of the Early Church, used especially on occasions of great or impending calamity, appointed as early as A. D. 450 by Mamertus, Bishop of Vienna, for the three days before Ascension Day, known as Rogation Days. It was used also at other times, especially during Lent, and had a powerful hold upon the people. It was not strange, therefore, that in 1544, Cranmer undertook to revise it; for it had forced itself into the language of the people long before the Reformation, filled, however, with all the abominations of the worship of saints.

In an English Primer, according to Dr. Maskel's conjecture of about 1410, it is found, in a form, of which the following are some of the petitions:

"Lord: Have mercy upon us.
Christ: Have mercy upon us.
Christ: Hear us.
God the Father of Heavens: Have mercy upon us.

[3] Ib. p. 194.
[4] Strype's *Henry VIII.*, I: 602.
[5] Ib. p. 601.

God the Son, azenhier of the world: Have mercy upon us.
God, the Holy Ghost: Have mercy upon us.
The Holy Trinity of God: Have mercy upon us.
From fleshly desires: Good Lord, deliver us.
From wrath and hate and all evil will: Good Lord, deliver us.
From pestilence of pride and blindness of heart: Good Lord, deliver us.
From sudden and unadvised death: Good Lord, deliver us.
From lightning and tempest: Good Lord, deliver us.
From covetousness of vain glory: Good Lord, deliver us.
By the privity of thine holy incarnation.
By thy holy nativity.
By thy blessed circumcision and Baptism.
By thy fasting and much other penance doing.
By thy blessed burying.
By thy glorious rising from death.
By thy marvelous stigying to Heaven.
By the grace of the Holy Ghost, the Comforter.
In the hour of our death.
In the day of doom."

They are accompanied by such petitions as:
"St. Mary: pray for us.
Holy Virgin of virgins: pray for us.
St. Michael: pray for us.
St. Gabriel: pray for us.
St. Raphael: pray for us.
All holy angels and archangels: pray for us.
All orders of holy spirits: pray for us.
St. John the Baptist: pray for us.
All holy patriarchs and prophets: pray for us.
St. Peter, Paul, Andrew, John, James, Philip, etc.
All holy apostles and martyrs."

Down to
"St. Mary the Egyptian, Perpetua, Anne, Catherine, Margaret, Agatha, Agnes, Felicitas," etc.

As early as 1521, when Luther was summoned to Worms, a Litany (*Litany for the Germans*)[6] was adapted at Wittenberg

[6] This is found in Luther's Works, Walch's Ed. XV: 2174 sqq. *Litanei, das ist, demüthiger Gebet zu dem dreieinigen Gott, für Deutschland, gehalten in einer gewissen berühmten Stadt in Deutschland am Aschermittwoch.*

into a prayer for Luther's cause. Its petitions are not altogether free from the Romish leaven and sound very strangely: "Christ, hear the Germans." God, the Father in heaven, have mercy upon the Germans." "St. Raphael, pray for the Germans." "All holy angels and archangels, pray for the Germans." "From all evil, help the Germans." "From those who come to us in sheep's clothing, but inwardly are ravening wolves, help the Germans." "From the horrible threats, bulls and banns of the Pope, protect the Germans, Lord God." "From all godless and heretical doctrine, cleanse the schools, dear Lord God. "From all unspiritual questions, protect the theologians, dear Lord God." "From all evil suspicions against Lutheranism, free the minds of the great." "We, Germans, do beseech Thee to hear us." "To guard and protect Martin Luther, the firm pillar of the Christian faith, as he will soon enter Worms, from all Venetian poison." "To support that valiant German Knight, Ulrich von Hutten, Luther's trusted friend, in his good purpose, and render him steadfast in the work undertaken for Luther." "To testify to the Italians, Lombards and Romans, that Thou art Lord God." "And graciously to hear us, Germans." The accompanying Psalm begins: "Make haste, O God, to deliver us Germans." This may be characterized as a popular adaptation of the of Litany, in violation of churchly taste and character. Nevertheless it indicated that the Litany could readily be utilized in the service of the purified faith. Before March 13th, 1529, Luther had revised the Litany, in both German and Latin, and introduced it, as revised, into the service at Wittenberg. He writes that the Latin was commonly chanted after the sermon on Sunday by the school boys. He is quoted as saying that it was, next to the Lord's Prayer, the best that could be prayed. Cranmer follows Luther closely, either immediately, or through the Litany in the Reformation of Cologne, which is Luther's. "The whole Litany very much resembles that of Hermann, the reforming Archbishop of Cologne."[1] He "had before him the litany formed upon the

---

[1] *The Prayer Book Interleaved*, p. 77.

same ancient model, by Melanchthon and Bucer (1543) for Hermann."[8] Both the writers from whom these statements are derived, have overlooked Luther's earlier work, of which Cranmer probably heard during his abode in Germany. Dr. Blunt knows of Luther's Litany, but thinks that its date was 1543.

The relation of Cranmer's work to Luther's, becomes manifest when we examine the manner in which the Reformed Anglican Litany attained its present form. In 1535 already, a translation of the chief parts of the service, as a private attempt at its reformation, known as Marshall's Primer, was published. It retains, in the Litany, the intercession of saints. With these omitted, it will be seen at a glance how closely it corresponds to Luther's Latin Litany.

Luther, 1529.	*Marshall, 1535.*
Kyrie, Eleison.	Lord, have mercy upon us.
Christe, Eleison.	Christ, have mercy upon us.
Kyrie, Eleison.	Lord, have mercy upon us.
Christe, Eleison.	
Pater de coelis Deus,	God the Father of heavens, have mercy upon us.
Fili redemptor mundi Deus,	God the Redeemer of this world, have mercy upon us.
Spirite sancte Deus, Miserere nobis.	God the Holy Ghost, have mercy upon us.
	The Holy Trinity in one Godhead, have mercy upon us.
Propitius esto.	Be merciful to us,
Parce nobis, Domine.	And spare us, Lord.
Propitius esto,	Be merciful to us,
Libera nos, Domine.	And deliver us, Lord.
Ab omni peccato,	From all sin,
Ab omni errore,	From all error,
Ab omni malo,	From all evil,
Ab insidiis diaboli,	From all crafty trains of the evil,
	From the eminent peril of sin,
	From the posession of devils,
	From the spirit of fornication,
	From the desire of vain glory,
	From the uncleanness of mind and body,
	From unclean thoughts,
	From the blindness of the heart,

[8] Procter's *History of Book of Common Prayer*, p. 17.

Luther, 1529.	Marshall, 1535.
A subitanea et improvisa morte,	From sudden and unprovided death,
A peste et fame,	From pestilence and famine,
A bello et caede,	From all mortal war,
A seditione et simultate,	
A fulgure et tempestatibus,	From lightning and tempestuous weathers,
	From seditions and schisms,
A morte perpetua;	From everlasting death;
Per mysterium sanctae incarnationis tuae,	By the privy mystery of thy holy incarnation,
Per sanctam nativitatem tuam,	By thy holy nativity,
Per baptismum, jejunium et tentationes tuas,	By thy baptism, fastings and temptations,
Per agoniam et sudorem tuum sanguineum,	By thy painful agony in sweating blood and water,
Per crucem et passionem tuam,	By the pains and passions on thy cross,
Per mortem et sepulturam tuam,	By thy death and burying,
Per resurrectionem et ascensionem tuam,	By thy resurrection and ascension,
Per adventum Spiritus Sancti, Paracleti;	By the coming of the Holy Ghost;
In omni tempore tribulationis nostrae,	In the time of tribulations,
In omni tempore felicitatis nostrae,	In the time of our felicity,
In hora mortis,	In the hour of death,
In die judicii,	In the day of judgment;
Libera, nos, Domine.	Deliver us, Lord.
Peccatores,	We sinners,
Te rogamus, audi nos;	Pray thee to hear us, Lord.
Ut ecclesiam tuam sanctam Catholicam regere et gubernare digneris;	That it may please thee, Lord, to govern and lead thy Holy Catholic Church;
Ut cunctos Episcopos, Pastores et Ministros ecclesiae in sano verbo et sancta vita servare digneris;	That thou vouchsafe that our bishops, pastors and ministers of thy Church, may in holy life, and in thy sound and whole word, feed thy people;
Ut sectas et omnia scandala tollere digneris;	That thou vouchsafe that all perverse secrets and slanders may be avoided;
Ut errantes et seductos reducere in viam veritatis;	That thou vouchsafe, that all which do err and be deceived may be reduced into the way of verity;
Ut Satanam sub pedibus nostris conterere digneris;	That thou vouchsafe, that we may the devil, with all his pomps, crush under foot;
Ut operarios fideles in messem tuam mittere digneris:	That thou vouchsafe to send us plenty of faithful workmen into thy harvest;

Luther, 1529.	Marshall, 1535.
Ut incrementum Verbi et fructum Spiritus cunctis audientibus donare digneris;	That thou vouchsafe, Lord, to give the hearers of thy word lively grace to understand it, and to work thereafter by the virtue of the Holy Ghost; That all extreme poverty, thou please, Lord, to recomfort;
Ut lapsos erigere, et stantes confortare digneris;	That they which are weak in virtue, and soon overcome in temptation, thou, of thy mercy, wilt help and strengthen them;
Ut pusillanimos, et tentatos consolari et adjuvare, digneris;	
Ut regibus et principibus cunctis pacem et concordiam donare digneris;	That thou vouchsafe to give universal peace amongst all kings and other rulers;
Ut Principem nostrum cum suis praesidibus dirigere et tueri digneris;	That thou vouchsafe to preserve our most gracious sovereign lord and King, Henry VIII, his most gracious queen Anne, all their posterity, aiders, helpers and true subjects;
Ut Magistratui et plebi nostrae benedicere et custodire digneris;	That our ministers and governors may virtuously rule thy people;
Ut efflictos et periclitantes respicere et salvare digneris;	That thy people in affliction, or in peril and danger, by fire, water, or land, thou wilt vouchsafe to defend and preserve;
Ut praegnantibus et lactentibus felicem partum et incrementum largire digneris;	That teeming women may have joyful speed in their labor;
Ut infantes et aegros fovere et custodire digneris;	That all young orphans and sick people, thou please, Lord, to nourish and provide for;
Ut captivos liberare digneris;	That all being captive, or in prisons, thou wilt send deliverance;
Ut pupillos et viduas protegere et providere digneris;	
Ut cunctis homnibus misereri digneris;	That unto all people, Lord, thou wilt show thine inestimable mercy;
Ut hostibus, persecutoribus, et calumniatoribus nostris ignoscere et eos convertere digneris;	That thou wilt forgive all warriors, persecutors, and to convert them to grace;
Ut fruges terrae dare et conservare digneris;	That the fruits, Lord, on the earth, may give good increase, and that thou wilt conserve them;
Ut nos custodire digneris; Te rogamus, audi nos.	That Thou, Lord, wilt hear our Prayer; We pray Thee to hear us. O the very Son of God, We pray Thee to hear us.
Agne Dei, qui tollis peccata mundi, Miserere nobis.	O Lamb of God, which taketh away the sins of the world, Have mercy on us.

Luther, 1529.	Marshall, 1535.
Agne Dei, etc.	O Lamb of God, etc.
Miserere, etc	Have mercy on us, etc.
Agne Dei, etc.	O Lamb of God, etc.
Dona nobis pacem.	Give peace and rest upon us.
Christe, Exaudi nos.	
Kyrie, Eleison.	
Christe, Eleison.	
Kyrie, Eleison. Amen.	
Pater noster, etc.	
Vers. Domine, non secundum peccata nostra facias nobis.	O Lord, hear thou my prayer
Ans. Neque secundum iniquitates nostras, retribuas nobis.	That my calling may come unto thee.
Deus misericors Pater, qui contritorum non despicis gemitum, et moerentium non spernis affectum, adesto precibus nostris quas in afflictionibus, quae jugiter nos premunt, coram te effundimus, easque clementer exaudi, etc.	O Omnipotent and merciful God, the Father eternal, which dost not despise us sinners, bewailing with contrite heart for offending the high majesty, we pray thee, by thy holy grace and mercy, to draw us near to thee, to hear our prayers, to forgive our offences, and to comfort us in our afflictions, etc.
Vers. Peccavimus, Domine, cum Patribus nostris.	We have sinned with our forefathers.
Ans. Injuste egimus, iniquitatem fecimus.	Iniquity have we wrought with unjust living.
Deus, qui deliquentes perire non pateris, donec convertantur et vivant, debitam, quaesumus, peccatis nostris suspende vindictam, et praesta propitius, ne dessimulatio cumulet ultionem, sed tua pro peccatis nostris misericordia semper abundet.	Lord, God, which dost not suffer sinners to perish and die in their works, but rather wilt that they shall convert and live, we humbly pray thee to forgive us now, while we have time and space. And give us grace that we do not abound in sin, nor in iniquity, no more, lest Thou, Lord, be wroth with us, etc.
Luther adds three collects: "Omnipotens aeterne Deus, cujus Spiritu;" "Omnipotens Deus, qui nos in tantis periculis constitutos;" and "Parce, Domine, parce peccatis."	Marshall adds one collect: "O most high and mighty Lord God and King of peace," etc., for the King and counsellors, etc.

In 1539, Bishop Hilsey, of Rochester, at the commandment of Crumwell, prepared a "Primer," giving us the first official form of the Reformed English Litany. It very closely follows Marshall, reducing the number of saints, but including the archangels, apostles, evangelists and a few martyrs, confessors and virgins. In other respects, the correspondence with Luther of

1529, while not as close, in general continues. The closing collects differ.

In the Litany prepared in 1544, which is that of the Book of Common Prayer, the simple Kyrie was omitted, and a beginning made with its expanded paraphrase, to which "miserable sinners" was added, the dogmatic statement of the procession being inserted in the third petition. The *Ne reminiscaris* was transferred from the close of the Penitential Psalms, to the beginning of the deprecations. The deprecations themselves are multiplied from the pre-Reformation English Litanies. Luther's Litany, after the Roman, furnished: "From Sin." Luther's German Litany of 1529, suggested the double translation of "Insidiis" as "crafts and assaults" (*Trug und List*) "of the devil," and, as in 1535, the translation of "*perpetua*" as "*everlasting*" (*für den ewigen Tod*). A more accurate rendering of the Latin of 1529, than that of Marshall gives "*From battle and murder.*" "Sudden and unforseen death," found even in Sarum, however, has been changed into "Sudden," while Luther's German, followed by Reformation of Cologne, has made it "*bösen schnellen Tod.*" The Obsecrations almost precisely reproduce Luther's Latin, adding however "Circumcision," changing "Temptations" into the singular, and omitting "Comforter" from "By the coming of the Holy Ghost." The intercessions are expanded, and the order is changed for apparent reasons. While Luther's Litany defers praying for temporal rulers until the tenth intercession, the Litany of 1544, according to Henry's pretensions as Head of the Church, inserts five petitions for him before that for bishops and pastors. In the American "Book of Common Prayer," this inversion has not been changed, and prayers for temporal, are made in Episcopal churches before those for spiritual rulers, even with the assumption which the change declares no longer received. The "Bishops, Priests and deacons" of the Prayer Book are the "*Bishoffe, Pfarrherr und Kirchendiener*" of Luther's German. Concerning the petition: "To give to all thy people an increase of grace," Blunt says: "A beautiful combination of the passage about the good ground with James 1: 21 and Gal. 5: 22. Its date is 1544." Cf. however Luther (1529) above: "*Ut incrementum Verbi*," etc. So also all the clauses which he is unable to trace to earlier English Litanies or Roman use, and assigns to 1544; but which are found already in the Primer of 1535. Marshall's probable misunderstanding of Luther's Latin is rectified in the petition: "That it may please Thee to strengthen such as do stand, and to comfort and help the weak-hearted, and to raise up them that fall." So also Luther is again more accurately rendered in the "To beat down Satan under our feet," and while not precisely, yet far more nearly than in 1535, in the clause: "To succour, help and comfort." Of the intercession: "To defend and provide for the fatherless children and widows, and all that are desolate and oppressed," Blunt says: "One of the tenderest petitions in the Prayer Book, and full of touching significance, as offered to Him who entrusted His Mother to His Apostle. It was placed here in 1544 (the words being clearly suggested by such passages as Ps. 146: 9; Jer. 49: 11)." Again Luther has been overlooked, even though Hermann of Cologne, is referred to: "*Ut pupillos et viduas protegere et providere.*" So in the next petition, "expressing" as the same author says, "the same all comprehensive charity," Cranmer turned from Marshall to Luther, and translated literally: "That it may please thee, to have mercy upon all men." The same may be said of the next petition.

The versicle and collect that directly follow the Litany, are from Luther. Dr. Blunt gives the form of the collect from the Sarum Mass in his parallel with the English; but Cranmer followed Luther with all his variations from that text. Into that collect, Luther inserts, or follows another text that inserts: '*Misericors Pater*" and the English Litany reads: "O God, Merciful Father." Sarum reads: *quas pietati tuae pro tribulatione nostra offerimus;* Luther: *quas in afflictionibus quae jugiter nos premunt coram te effundimus;*" and then, the English

Litany: "That we make before thee in all our troubles and adversities whensover they oppress us." Sarum reads:— "*Implorantes ut nos clementer respicias;*" Luther: "*Eosque clementer exaudi;*" and then, the English Litany: "And graciously hear us." It is certainly very patronizing for Dr. Blunt to remark: "Hermann's and Luther's form is very like ours."[9] But it is still more surprising to read his remark: "It is somewhat doubtful whether in the case of the Litany, our English form was not in reality the original of that in Hermann's book!!" In a foot-note, he adds that "Cranmer had married a niece of Osiander, who is said to have prepared the Nuremberg formularies *for Luther,*" etc. Can it be, that any one could think of tracing the liturgical reformation of the Lutheran Church, in this way, to an English source? It certainly is inverting history!

The English Litany thus formed was set forth for public use, June 11th, 1544. With it ended the work of liturgical reform in the reign of Henry VIII., the Primer of 1545 excepted, which has significance only as an aid to the more thorough preparation of what was to follow, and not for its influence on public worship.

[9] Introduction to "*Annotated Book of Common Prayer,*" p. xxvii.

CHAPTER XIX.

THE COMMUNION SERVICE OF THE ENGLISH CHURCH.

The Order of March 1548. First Exhortation traced to Cassel Order of 1539. Second, from Volprecht of Nürnberg, 1524. Idea of the Admonition from the Cassel Order. Prayer of Confession from the Cologne Order. Absolution compared with that of Cologne, in parallel columns. Origin of the Formula of Distribution. Expansion of this in 1549. Later Calvinistic Modifications. Hilles' Testimony of 1549.

THE death of Henry, and the accession of Edward, at length gave Crumwell the opportunity to carry out his plans of a thorough reform of the liturgical and doctrinal formulas. After giving his first attention, in lack of a ministry properly trained in purity of doctrine, to the preparation of "Homilies," to furnish the churches with sound preaching, and, of a Catechism, for the instruction of children, he began the reformation of the Communion Service. For this purpose, a commission of bishops assembled in January, 1548; and early in March, the results of their deliberations were published, that the formula might be introduced the succeeding Easter. It was a mere temporary provision to supplement the Latin Mass; but has left its impression upon the service afterwards provided. It begins with an exhortation to be made by the minister, "the next Sunday, or holy day or at the least one day before he shall minister the communion." This exhortation is constructed after the model of the first exhortation in the Reformation of Cologne, which, in turn, was taken from the Cassel Order of 1539. The second exhortation, the third in the Book of Common Prayer, was constructed after the model of the second in the Reformation of Cologne, which is the Nürnberg Exhortation of Volprecht (1524). Then followed a warning: "If any man here be an open blasphemer, an advouterer, in malice or envy, or any other notable crime," etc, which follows the idea of the conclusion of the Cassel Exhortation, where the offences against each commandment are briefly enumerated, and those guilty of such sins, and impenitent, are urged not to come to communion. The prayer of confession is an adaptation of that in the Reformation of Cologne, as contained in the order given above. The "Absolution" is a free rendering of the Reformation of Cologne.

| Unser lieber Herre Jesu hat seiner Kirchen den hohen trost verlassen, das er seinen dieneren befohlen hatt, allen denen, welche ihre sünden leidt sindt, im glauben und vertrauen, und sich zu besseren begehren die sünd zuverzeihen, etc. | Our blessed Lord, who hath left power to his Church, to absolve penitent sinners from their sins, and to restore to the grace of the Heavenly Father such as truly believe in Christ, etc. |

The "comfortable words" are taken from the same source, where, however, they precede the Absolution. "The prayer of humble access" seems to have been derived from another source. The formula of distribution adopts from the Nürnberg formula, the clauses "which was given for thee," "which was shed for thee," etc., unknown to the Mass, Roman and Sarum. This addition was in accordance with Luther's declaration in the Small Catechism, that the words "given and shed for you," were besides the bodily eating and drinking the principal parts of the Sacrament, and with the prescription of the Reformation of Cologne that "ministers should always admonish the people with great earnestness to lay to heart the words 'given for you,' 'shed for you for the remisssion of sins.'" In other respects the formula resembles that of Schw.-Hal. (Brentz) of 1543: "The body of our Lord Christ, preserve thee unto everlasting life. The blood of our Lord Christ cleanse thee from all thy sins. Amen;" the English formula of 1548 being: "The body of our Lord Jesus Christ, which was given for thee, preserve thy body unto everlasting life. The blood of our Lord Jesus Christ, which was shed for thee, preserve thy soul to everlasting life."

The Communion Service of the English Church. 243

This form was expanded into that of the Book of Common Prayer of 1549, where the Communion Service takes the following form:

1. Collect for Purity. (From Sar. and Rom. Missals.) 2. Kyrie. 3. Gloria in Excelsis. 4. Salutation and Response. 5. Collect for day, with one for the King. 6. Epistle. 7. Gospel. 8. Nicene Creed. 9. Exhortation (based on Volprecht's). 10. Passages of Scripture, instead of Offertory. 11. Salutation and Response. 12. Sursum Corda. 13. Preface. 14. Sanctus. 15. Prayer of Consecration, including words of institution (modelled after Sarum, and also following, in part, Cassel and Cologne), closing with the Lord's Prayer. 16. Pax. 17. Christ our Paschal Lamb, is offered up, etc. 18. Invitation. 19. Confession (Cologne). 20. Absolution (Cologne). 21. Comfortable Words (Cologne). 22. Prayer of Humble Access (Eastern). 23. Distribution, during which the Agnus Dei is sung. 24. Scripture passages after Communion. 25. Salutation. 26. Prayer of Thanksgiving from the Brandenburg-Nürnberg Order.

Brandenburg-Nürnberg, 1533.	*1st Edward*, 1549.
O Almechtiger ewiger Gott, wir sagen deiner Götlichen miltigkeit lob und danck, das du uns mit dem haylsamen flaysch und blut, deines aynigen Suns Jesu Christi, unsers Hernn gespeyst und getrenckt hat, etc.	Almighty and everlasting God, we most heartily thank thee, for that thou hast vouchsafed to feed us in these holy Mysteries, with the spiritual food of the most precious body and blood of thy Son, our Saviour Jesus Christ, etc.

The increasing influence of Calvinism is shown in 1552 by the insertion of the Ten Commandments, probably as Procter supposes from the formula of Pollanus, but having the precedent of the Lutheran Order of Frankfort, 1530, and the change of the words of distribution into "Take and eat this, in remembrance that Christ died for thee, and feed on him in thy heart by faith, with thanksgiving." "Drink this, in remembrance that Christ's blood was shed for thee, and be thankful." In 1559 both formulas were combined. In 1552 the Lord's Prayer was transferred to the post-communion service, and the *Gloria in Excelsis* placed after the *Brandenburg-Nürnberg* Thanksgiving Collect.

It is certainly not remarkable that in June 1549, four days before the first Book of Edward appeared, Hilles wrote to Bullinger concerning the "Order of Communion:" "We have a uniform communion of the eucharist throughout the entire realm, yet after the manner of the Nürnberg churches and some of the Saxons. The bishops and magistrates, present no obstruction to the Lutherans."[1] The most un-Lutheran part is the Consecratory Prayer, where prayer for saints, and other Romanizing elements still remain, the formula of Cologne being followed only in its beginning.

[1] *Original Letters*, CXXI.; also in *Procter*, p. 26.

CHAPTER XX.

THE MORNING AND EVENING SERVICES OF THE ENGLISH CHURCH.

The Ancient Matin Service. The Lutheran Revision of the Matin Service. Luther's Explanation of its parts. The typical Lutheran Matin Service and that of Edward VI.; in parallel columns. The earlier English Matin Service. The Vesper Service of I Edward VI. Kliefoth's Explanation of the Structure of the Lutheran Matin and Vesper Services. I. Edward's Substitution of Psalms for Introits according to Luther's *Formula Missae* of 1523. Not followed by the Lutheran churches. Loss of Introits by English Church. The Collects in the Lutheran Orders. Why the English Church anticipated the Lutheran, in revision of the ancient Collects. New Collects. Gospels and Epistles in the two systems. Minor Variations explained. How the English Orders sometimes follow Luther, where he has not been followed in the Lutheran Church.

IN noticing the later changes in the Communion Service, we have anticipated the historical order. The commission which prepared the temporary order for communion, continued its labors, and by the close of the year had the entire book ready to be submitted to the King, by whom it was laid before Parliament, and was finally published, Pentecost, 1549 (June 9th). The chief members of the commission besides Cranmer, "were probably Ridley, Goodrich, Holbeach, May, John Taylor, Haynes and Cox." (Procter.)

The "Order for Daily Morning Prayer" of the English Church does not grow, like the *Hauptgottesdienst* of the Lutheran Church, entirely from the Communion Service or Mass of the Ancient Church but from its Matin Service, to which it appends that of the Mass. The Matin was the early service before day, provided not for the laity, but for the clergy alone. From the very beginning, Luther pointed out the great profit which would be derived by an adjustment of it to the uses of schools, (1523). "For Matins, of three lessons . . are nothing but words of divine Scripture; and it is beautiful, yea, necessary that the boys be accustomed to reading and hearing the Psalms and the lessons of the Holy Scriptures." (1526): "Early, about five or six, several psalms are sung as at Mass; then there is a sermon on the Epistle for the day, chiefly for the sake of domestics, that they may be cared for and hear God's Word, since they cannot attend other preaching. Afterwards there is an antiphon, and the *Te deum laudamus, Benedictus*, with the Lord's Prayer, Collects and the *Benedicamus domine.*"

This simple service is almost precisely that of the Prayer Book of 1549. It is interesting to compare it with the old Lutheran Matin Service given in Löhe's Agende.

Lutheran.	*1st Edward* VI.
[Schleswig-Holstein (Bugenhagen, 1542) begins with, Creed; Lord's Prayer]	
O Lord, Open thou my lips	Lord's Prayer.
And my mouth shall, etc.	O Lord, open thou my lips
O God, make speed to, etc.	And my mouth shall show, etc.
O Lord, make haste to, etc.	O God, make speed to save me.
Gloria Patri.	O Lord, make haste to help me.
Hallelujah.	Gloria Patri.
Venite, Ps. XCV.	Hallelujah.
Gloria Patri.	Venite, Ps XCV.
Hymn	Gloria Patri.
O satisfy us early with thy, etc.	
And we will be glad, etc.	
One to three psalms.	Certain psalms.
Gloria Patri at end of each.	Gloria Patri at end of each.
First Lesson.	Old Testament Lesson.
["Ordinarily from the Old Testament," Prussian KO, 1525.]	
Te Deum.	Te Deum or Benedicite.
Second Lesson.	New Testament Lesson.[1]
Benedictus.	Benedictus.
Kyrie.	Kyrie.
Lord's Prayer.	Creed.

[1] Cf. direction from Schleswig-Holstein, 1542: "The Lessons should be taken only from the Bible, i. e. from the Old and New Testaments"

Morning and Evening Services of English Church.

Versicle and Response.	Lord's Prayer.
Salutation and Response.	Versicles and Responses.
Several Collects, the first being for the day.	Salutation and Response.
	Collect of day, followed by collect for peace and for grace.
Salutation and Response.	
Benediction.	

Let this be compared with the far more complex Matin Service in Bishop Hilsey's Primer of 1539, or Henry's of 1545, and the determining influence of the Lutheran liturgies will be apparent.

The same may be said of the Order for Evensong of 1549. We give it for comparison with the Vesper Service, familiar to many of our readers from its place in the Common Order of the Lutheran Church:

Lord's Prayer. O God, make speed to save us. O Lord, make haste to help us. *Gloria Patri.* Hallelujah. Psalms in Order. Old Testament Lesson. *Magnificat.* New Testament Lesson. *Nunc Dimittis.* Same suffrages as at Matins. Collects.

Concerning the structure of the Lutheran Matin and Vesper Services, which have been thus followed by the Church of England, Kliefoth[2] has some observations that may be of importance to our readers:

"The Matins begin with an introduction consisting of the *Domine labia mea, Deus in adjutorium* and *Venite,* in which God is, on the one hand, invoked to grant his aid against all enemies and hindrances to the preaching of his Word; and the congregation, on the other hand, is invited, by such proclamation and confession, to call upon the Lord. Then follows the psalmody, consisting of Psalms 1–109 in order, and when they are finished, beginning anew. While, however, the contents of the psalms are general and always identical, regard to the facts of salvation which the day affords in accordance with the order of the Church Year, is had by the antiphons which they include. Following the psalmody is the reading of Scripture; the entire Scripture is read continuously, but, again, with regard to

[2] *Liturgische Abhandlungen,* VIII., 179 sqq.

the Church Year, the chief facts or fundamental thoughts contained in what is read being always presented by the responsories. But after the congregation has been fed by the Word of God in the two-fold form of psalmody and lesson, it allows the Word of God to bring forth fruit; and such fruit appears in the hymnody. The *Te Deum* and the *Benedictus*, or a hymn and the *Benedictus*, or a hymn and the Athanasian Creed are sung; for in singing the Athanasian Creed or *Te Deum* or *Benedictus*, we make confession of our acceptance of the salvation which has been heard from the Word of God, and bring the sacrifice of the fruit of our lips; since when a hymn or the *Te Deum* or the *Benedictus* is sung, God and his salvation is praised and the sacrifices of thanksgiving are offered. At the same time, this hymnody gives Matins the character of Morning Worship, since a morning hymn is naturally chosen. But a Christian not only has to thank and praise God; hence, following the hymn is the act of supplication; in the *Kyrie*, God's mercy is implored, the Lord's Prayer, the common prayer of all children of God is prayed, and finally everything is summarized in the Collect, which, since it is *de tempore*, recurs again to the particular fact of salvation given in the Church Year, and presented already by the antiphons of the psalms and the hymn. Nothing then remains, but finally in the *Benedicamus*, to implore God's blessing. All this is both liturgically and musically connected in the closest and most beautiful manner; between the various parts, there ascends unto Heaven, at intervals (after the *Deus in adjutorium*, after the Psalms, after the responsories, after the *Benedictus*) the *Gloria Patri*, bearing the whole as a morning offering to the throne of grace. The Matin Service, therefore, can be simply arranged in the succession of: "Introduction, Psalmody, Lessons, Hymnody, Prayer and Conclusion."

We find precisely the same succession in Vespers. The distinction is confined to the somewhat briefer arrangement of the introduction, the use of the Vesper (Ps. 110–150) instead of the Matin psalms, and the difference of Hymnody. The last is the most important distinction between Vespers and Matins, as it is given thereby the character of an Evening Service of Prayer. In Vespers, it is not the jubilant *Te Deum*, nor the morning hymns, but the *Magnificat* and the *Nunc Dimittis* and evening hymns, that are sung; and the *Nunc dimittis* is a hymn of parting, for the close of the day, as well as for the close of life. Thus there is in Lutheran Matins and Vespers, a structure just as thoughtful, as in the chief service. It has here just as fixed an order and organization, and, yet, with this, provision is made for the richest impartation of the entire divine word, and the most careful adaptation to the peculiarities of the seasons and days of the Church Year."

Next to the orders for "Matins and Evensong throughout the year," the Liturgy of 1549 gives the variable parts of the service for each day of the Church Year.

The Introits are not those of the Roman or Sarum Missals, but entire psalms, viz., 1. Sunday in Advent, Psalm 1. 2d, Ps. 120. 3d, Ps. 4. 4th, Ps. 5. Christmas Day, At First Communion, Ps. 98; At Second Communion, Ps. 8. St. Stephen's Day, Ps. 52, etc.

This change was made according to Luther's advice in 1523, when in his "*Formula Missae*," he writes: "*We would prefer psalms.*" In this, however, he was not followed by the Lutheran churches generally. The liturgy of Schwabach Hall of 1526, however, directs that for the Introit, psalms be sung. In the Lutheran Church, the retention of the Introit was attended with no little difficulty. It was sung neither by the pastor, nor by the people, but by the choir; as announcing to both the leading thought that the Lord had for his Church on that day. There was much trouble encountered in its translation. In the Latin, each Introit had its own musical arrangement, and to such a degree was the effort made to give each word and shade of thought its proper tone, that it is impossible to sing the Introits translated into German, according to the setting which they have in Latin.[3] For a time in some orders, the Introit of the leading

[3] Kliefoth's *Liturgische Abhandlungen*, VI: 224.

festivals was used on the Sundays belonging to the period of which it was the center, thus rendering such difficulties less numerous. But they all were finally overcome; and the Lutheran Service rejoices in the retention of the old Introits. In the English Church, the substitution of the Psalms was unsatisfactory, for the reason that no series of Psalms can be used to express the precise thought of each Sunday and, therefore, in the revision of 1552, they fell out. Wheatly has some just observations on the defect caused by this suppression of the Introits.*

As with the Introits, so with the Collects, the Lutheran Orders encountered peculiar difficulties in adapting them to the revised service. They are in the original so condensed, and so much of the form often depends upon alliteration and other peculiarities not readily translatable, that time was required for this work. Besides this, in a number, though, as Luther remarks in his *Formula Missae*, not in most of those for Sunday, unevangelical doctrine had entered, of which they had to be purged. In the Roman Church, contrary to the order of Gregory where but one occurs, three Collects were read together, the first being that of the day. Luther insisted that there should be one Collect, and, for the time, thought that this, instead of being varied every Sunday, should be more frequently repeated, in order that the people, by becoming familiar with it, might the more heartily enter into its spirit. The Brandenburg-Nürnberg Order contains, therefore, eighteen Collects, without designation of day, one each for the Birth of Christ, the Passion of Christ, Easter, Ascension Day, Whitsunday, Trinity, the Coming of God's Kingdom, the Doing of God's Will, and two *Pro pace*. Soon the attempt was made to compose anew Collects for each Sunday, the most noted being those of Veit Dietrich, pastor of St: Sebald's Nürnberg, (Wittenberg, 1541,) and of Johann Matthesius, (Nürnberg, 1568,) a rich collection for all Sundays and Festivals appearing also in the *Oesterreich unter Ems* Order of 1571. The Lutheran Church was, therefore, anticipated by the Church of England,

* *Rational Illustration of Book of Common Prayer*, p. 205.

in the work of the more complete revision of the old Collects. This was undoubtedly owing partly to the far greater ease with which translations of prayers could be made from Latin into English, than from Latin into German, the Latin elements in the English offering much aid; for it must not be forgotten that, in devotional language, only the very simplest words are allowable, and a single technical and scientific term, on the one hand, or a colloquial phrase, on the other, would mar an entire Collect. The compilers of the Book of 1549, however, also followed the example of the Lutheran reformers of the Service, in substituting for the old Collects a number which they either composed or, in some cases, probably derived from Lutheran sources. The new Collects of 1549 are those for I., II. Advent, Second for Christmas day, Quinquagesima, Ash Wednesday, I. Lent, I., II. p. Easter, Sts. Thomas, Matthias, Mark, Philip and James, Barnabas, John the Baptist, Peter, James the Apostle, Matthew, Luke, Simon and Jude and All Saints', Days, changes being made in those for Sexagesima, Sunday p. Ascension, Conversion of St. Paul and St. Bartholomew.

The Gospels and Epistles of I. Edward VI. and of the Lutheran Orders, exhibit only a few variations. Some of these are more noticeable in the Second Book (1552), as *e. g.* where in the First Book, provision is made for two communion services on Christmas and Easter, double sets of lessons are given, in the Second Book, with only one Communion Service, the lessons for the second Christmas Service, and for the first Easter Service are adopted, while the permanent lessons in the Lutheran Church become those for first Christmas Service, and the second Easter Service. These differences thus are entirely those of a later time. Luther in 1524[5] gave Heb. 1: 1–12, and John 1: 1–14, as the lessons for High Mass, on Christmas the Day after the proper lessons for Tit. 2: 11–15 and Luke 2: 1–14. The use of Sarum shows the former lessons as those for Christmas at Midnight, and the latter as those for the third mass.

[5] *Erl. Ed.* LXIII: 175.

The Gospels and Epistles of the four Sundays in Advent in the Lutheran and Anglican Churches differ from those in the Roman Missal, the latter omitting the pericope of our Lord's trumphal entry, and the corresponding epistle on I. Advent, and transferring thither the lessons for II. Advent; and then transferring to II. Advent, those of III. Advent; to III. Advent, those of IV. Advent; and as those for IV. Advent, prescribing Luke 3 : 1 sqq. for the Gospel, and 1 Cor. 4: 1 sq. for Epistle,—a modern change on the part of Rome, contrary to the testimony of the older Orders. So too especially in the latter part of the Church Year, Rome has made many changes in the lessons of the Ancient Church, which the Lutheran Church has retained.

On the Sunday after Christmas, I. Edward introduced, instead of the Gospel of both the Sarum and Lutheran Orders, the Gospel for Christmas eve, and the Midnight Christmas Service, Matth. 1 : 1 sqq., services for which the English Reformers made no provision, but whose Gospel they deemed it important to retain. For Palm Sunday, Luther in 1524 prescribed two Gospels,[6] one for the day generally used in the Lutheran Church; the other for the Mass; Matth. 26, 27, adopted by I. Edward, and also even to the present used in many Lutheran churches, as part of the Passion History. If we find a divergence on XXV. Sunday p. Trinity between the lessons of the two Churches, a reference to Luther, 1524, shows that those prescribed by him are the same as those of I. Edward, viz., Epistle: Jerem. 23: 5–8; Gospel: John 6; 5–14.[7] That is, the difference is, that the English Reformers followed Luther's " Register of Epistles and Gospels," while the Lutheran Orders followed those adopted by Luther in his Postils.

[6] *Erl. Ed.* LXIII: 192.
[7] Ib. p. 218.

CHAPTER XXI.

THE ORDER OF BAPTISM IN THE ENGLISH CHURCH.

Archbishop Laurence's Testimony. The English Introduction, with Lutheran Sources. The Rubrics traced to Lutheran Orders. The English Baptismal Exhortation, with its original in parallel columns. Palmer's difficulty explained. A prayer from Luther. Blunt, Palmer, Procter on the Prayer. Höfling's Investigations. The Sign of the Cross and accompanying words, from the Cologne Order. The Exorcism, from Luther. Palmer on the Lutheran origin of what follows. History of closing Collect. An Address, from Osiander. Development of Address in Brandenburg-Nürnberg, Cassel, Würtemberg and I. Edward VI. Baptism in Private Houses. Conditional Baptism.

CONCERNING the Order for the Ministration of Baptism, Archbishop Laurence says:[1] "The office of our own Church is principally borrowed from the Lutherans." Dr. Blakeney, with like frankness: "The address is borrowed, to a great extent, from the Reformed Service of Cologne. . . The first prayer is derived from a form which is attributed to Luther. . . In the selection of the Gospel, our Reformers have followed not the Sarum office . . but the Cologne. . . The collect is taken from the same service,"[2] etc. So Blunt, Campion and Beaumont, Warren, etc., etc. That Archbishop Laurence is right in saying that it was *principally* borrowed, from the Lutherans, will be manifest on an examination of the Order of 1549.

[1] *Bampton Lectures*, p. 183.
[2] *The Book of Common Prayer in its History and Interpretation*, p. 510 sqq.

"OF THE ADMINISTRATION OF PUBLIC BAPTISM, TO BE HELD IN THE CHURCH.

" It appeareth by ancient writers, that the Sacrament of Baptism in the old time, was not commonly ministered but at two times in the year, at Easter and Whitsuntide, at which times it was openly ministered in the presence of all the congregation."

> *Schw. Hall* (1526, Brentz): "In the first churches, only two times were appointed for Baptism, Easter and Pentecost."
>
> *Cologne* (1543): "It is known that the ancients baptized only on Easter and Pentecost."
>
> *Nassau* (1536, Sarcerius): "Baptism should be administered on festival days, before the assembled congregation."

"Which custom (now being grown out of use) although it cannot for many considerations be well restored again, yet it is thought good to follow the same as near as conveniently may be: Wherefore the people are to be admonished, that it is most convenient that Baptism should not be ministered, but upon Sundays and other holy days, when the most number of people may come together."

> *Cologne*, (1543): "But since it perhaps would not be so suitable to restore such times to their old position, Holy Baptism, if the children be not sickly, and there be anxiety about deferring it unto the holy day, must not be given until the holy days when the people and church of God are together."
>
> Cf. *Würtemb.* (1553 but, doubtless, from an earlier Order): "Nevertheless we deem it more profitable that, except from the necessity of their weakness, children should be presented for Baptism, not at the time when there are no church assemblies, but on a Sunday, or other festival days, or upon a weekday, where there be preaching, or a large number of people come together."

"As well for that the congregation there present may testify the receiving of them, that be newly baptized, into the number of Christ's Church, as also because in the Baptism of Infants, every man present may be put in remembrance of his own profession made to God in his Baptism."

> *Schw. Hall* (1526): "Whereby they not only do a kindness unto the child by public prayer, but every one is admonished of his Baptism, that he direct his life accordingly."

Sax. Vis. Articles (1528): Thus Baptism is not only a sign to children, but also draws and admonishes adults to repentance." Cf. *Würtemb.* (1553).

For which cause also, it is expedient that Baptism be ministered in the English tongue.

Schw. Hall (1526): "It is not only useless, but unreasonable to baptize in a strange language."

Würtemb. (1537): "Baptism should be ministered in German."

"Nevertheless (if necessity so require) children ought at all times to be baptized, either at the church or else at home."

Schw Hall (1526): "Baptism may, as necessity requires, be administered at all times and places"

Nassau (1536): "Baptism should be administered on festival days before the assembled congregation, but dare not be denied sick children."

Cologne (1543): "Where there be not danger of death . . where the child be not sickly. . . But if this cannot be, the child shall be baptized at any time when brought. For, without Holy Baptism, they must not be allowed, so far as we concerned, to depart."

The rubric directs that information of the desire to have the child baptized, be given, "over night or in the morning," while the Reformation of Cologne prescribes that it be given "in good time." The question is first asked whether the child be baptized or not, evidently in order that where Lay or *Noth-taufe* have occurred, parents may be prevented from any such erroneous practice as that of a supposed rebaptism. Such practice the Prussian Order of 1525 explicitly forbids, as "a blasphemy of holy baptism." Hence the Brandenburg-Nürnberg Order of 1533 explicitly states: "The priest shall first ask, whose the child is, what it shall be named, and whether it have received *Jachtaufe*," (Lay Baptism), and the Reformation of Cologne: "The pastors should ask whether in haste they have before received Baptism, or, as it is called, *genothtauft sein*. For if this have occurred according to the proper order, the pastors should maintain the order."

The service begins with an Exhortation, which most English

writers trace to the Reformation of Cologne. It is unworthy of Blunt's scholarship that he tries to resolve the connection of the two formulas into a mere suggestion. Nor does he seem to be acquainted with more than the opening sentence. The exhortation is older than the Reformation of Cologne. In its first form, it was prepared by Luther in 1521, was repeated in a number of the older Orders, as the Saxon of 1539, and the Pomeranian of 1542, and was amplified and combined with a similar Exhortation from Brandenburg-Nürnberg of 1533, in Mark-Brandenburg, 1540, Schw. Hall, 1543, Ott-Heinrich, 1543, and Reformation of Cologne, 1543. This Exhortation, in the various forms in which it occurs in the Lutheran Orders, may be found in Höfling's *Das Sacrament der Taufe*.[3] The compilers of the English formula seem to have had Luther's original formula before them, which they greatly condensed.

Luther (1521).	*I. Edward VI., (1549).*
Dear friends in Christ: We hear daily out of the Word of God, and learn by our own experience, that we all from the fall of Adam, are conceived and born in sin, wherein, being under the wrath of God, we must have been condemned and lost eternally, except we be delivered by the only begotten Son of God, our Lord Jesus Christ.	Dear beloved: Forasmuch as . . . . all men . . . . be conceived and born in sin, and that no man born in sin can enter into the Kingdom of God, except he be regenerate and born anew of water and the Holy Ghost;
I beseech you, therefore, that, from Christian love, ye earnestly intercede for this child with our Lord God, that ye bring it to the Lord Jesus Christ, and unite in imploring for it the forgiveness of sins and entrance into the Kingdom of Grace and Salvation.	I beseech you to call upon God the Father, through our Lord Jesus Christ, that of his bounteous mercy, he will grant to these children that thing which, by nature, they cannot have, that is to say, that they may be baptized with the Holy Ghost, and received into Christ's holy church, and be made lively members of the same.

Palmer says of this: "We can perhaps scarcely find any parallel to this amongst the primitive rituals of the church, except in those of the churches of Gaul. The Gothic and ancient Gallican liturgies published by Thomasius and Mabillon, prescribe an ad-

[3] Vol. II: 64 sqq.

dress or preface of this kind at the very commencement of the office of baptism."[4] But the example which he gives shows only a very remote resemblance. It is: "Beloved brethren, let us in the holy administration of the present Mystery, humbly beseech our Almighty Creator and Saviour who has deigned by his grace to restore the adornments of nature, lost by the fall, to impart his virtue to these waters, both that the presence of the Triune Majesty may assist in producing the effect of most holy regeneration," etc. The reader will see how little influence such an Exhortation could have had, either on Luther, or on the English reformers.

Concerning the prayer which followed, there can be no question that it comes from Luther. Blunt says:[5] "This prayer is not derived from the old office of the English Church, but is probably of great antiquity. Luther translated it into German from the ancient Latin [?] in 1523, and it appears again in his revised baptismal book of 1524. From thence it was transferred to the Nürnberg office, and appears in the Consultation of Archbishop Hermann in 1545 [?]. The latter was translated into English in 1547, and the prayer, as it stands in the Prayer Book of 1549, is almost identical with this translation as given above," i. e. the prayer in I. Edward. This prayer was somewhat abbreviated in II. Edward, 1552, and, therefore, also in the English Book as now known. Palmer, after all his labor to find the "original," from which Luther translated, gives a prayer from the Gothic Missal, in which there is one clause of eight words similar: "O God who didst sanctify the river Jordan for the salvation of souls." Procter[6] frankly says: "The first prayer seems to have been originally composed by Luther."

Höfling, after the most thorough search among the Mediaeval Agende, has failed to find a trace of this prayer. Its absence

[4] *Origines Liturgicae*, II: 172.
[5] *Annotated Book of Common Prayer*, p. 218.
[6] On the *Book of Common Prayer*, p. 364.

from the Romanizing Protestant liturgies is also significant. He concludes, therefore, that, although in Luther's *Taufbüchlein* of 1523, everything else has been translated, "the hypothesis of Luther's authorship has most foundation. This excellent prayer has also, within the sphere of the Lutheran Church, not merely the most extensive diffusion, but also the most permanent acceptance and adoption."[1]

As given in the first English Prayer Book, it reads:

"Almighty and everlasting God, which of thy justice didst destroy by floods of water the whole world, for sin, except eight persons, whom of thy mercy (the same time) thou didst save in the Ark; and when thou didst drown in the Red Sea wicked King Pharao, with all his army, yet (at the same time) thou didst lead thy people the children of Israel, safely through the midst thereof; whereby thou didst figure the washing of thy holy baptism; and by the baptism of thy well-beloved Son Jesus Christ, thou didst sanctify the flood Jordan and all other waters to this mystical washing away of sin; we beseech thee (for thy infinite mercies) that thou wilt mercifully look upon these children, and sanctify them with thy Holy Ghost, that by this wholesome laver of regeneration, whatsoever sin is in them, may be washed clean away; that they, being delivered from thy wrath, may be received into the ark of Christ's Church, and so saved from perishing: and being fervent in spirit, steadfast in faith, joyful through hope, rooted in charity, may ever serve thee: And finally attain to everlasting life, with all thy holy and chosen people."

The use of the sign of the cross at this point, the manner in which it was made and almost the very words follow the Reformation of Cologne. The precious collect that follows is from the old offices: "*Deus, immortale praesidium.*" "*O God, du unsterblicher Trost.*" "Almighty and immortal God, the aid of all that need," etc. In the ancient service, it belonged to the order for the Baptism of adults. Luther transferred it to Infant Baptism.

[1] *Das Sacrament der Taufe*, Vol. II: p. 53 sq.

Even the Exorcism which Luther transferred from the Order for Adult Baptism, is retained. The single sentence of the Reformation of Cologne, and Brandenburg-Nürnberg, was not sufficient, and to it was added the substance of Luther's vigorous formula of 1524:

Luther, *1523*.	I. Edward VI., *1549*.
Darum, du leidiger [Vermaledeyter, Mk-Br., 1540] Teufel, erkenne dein Urtheil, etc.	Therefore, thou cursed spirit, remember thy sentence, etc.

Blunt, who regrets its omission in later editions, throws the blame upon "the half-sceptical *Germanism* of Bucer!"

The Gospel read was, in the ante-Reformation offices, from Matth. 19: 13-15. The English Reformers followed the Reformation of Cologne, which in turn followed Luther, in substituting Mark 10: 13-16.

Palmer[8] explains what immediately succeeds: "The address and collects which follow the Gospel, and terminate the Introduction of the baptismal office, do not occur in the ancient offices of the Ancient Church, as far as I can perceive. . . The forms themselves are in part taken from the Ritual of Hermann of Cologne." He should have said, that the Collect "Almighty and everlasting God, heavenly Father" is a literal translation, only a qualifying clause of the Lutheran Order being suppressed.

The rest of the service is almost precisely that of Luther. The closing Collect which at one time was the subject of much controversy in the Church of England, originally was used in the baptism of proselytes in connection with the chrism that followed baptism:

"Almighty God, Father of our Lord Jesus Christ, who hath regenerated thee of water and the Holy Ghost, and hath given unto thee remission of all thy sins, anointeth thee with the unction of salvation unto everlasting life, in the name of Jesus Christ, our Lord. Amen."

"Almighty God, grant unto them, remission of all sins, send,

[8] II: p. 176.

Lord, upon them, the Holy Ghost, the Comforter, and give them the spirit of wisdom and understanding," etc.

Luther, in 1523, when his revision of the old order, was as yet only tentative, retained the chrism and therefore left the Collect in its first form, only translating it. This Order was retained by Mk-Brandenburg, 1540, and Ott-Heinrich, 1543. The English Commission retained the chrism, modifying the form only by the change of the conclusion into "vouchsafe to anoint thee, with the unction of his Holy Ghost, and bring thee to the inheritance of everlasting life." Luther, however, in 1526, had omitted the chrism, and amended the Collect accordingly, being followed in this by Brandenburg-Nürnberg, into the simpler form: "And who hath forgiven thee all thy sins, strengthen thee by his grace unto everlasting life." Had the more thorough Lutheran revision been followed by Cranmer and his associates, the subsequent revision in the English Prayer Book, which has greatly marred it, might have been prevented.

The address to the Sponsors, while derived partially from the Sarum and York Uses, is far more dependent upon the formula originally introduced by Osiander in 1524, into his *Taufbuche*,[9] and thence adopted by the Brandenburg-Nürnberg Order of 1533. The Cassel Order of 1539, shows other points of resemblance, which reach a more complete development in the Würtemberg Order of 1553.

I. Edw. (1549). "Forasmuch as this child hath promised by you his sureties to renounce the devil and all his works, to believe in God and to serve him; ye must remember, that it is your parts and duties to see that this infant be taught, so soon as he shall be able to learn what a solemn vow, promise and profession, he hath here made by you. And that he may know these the better, ye shall call upon him to hear sermons, and chiefly ye shall provide that he may learn the Creed, the Lord's Prayer and the Ten Commandments in the vulgar tongue, and all other things which a Christian ought to know and believe to his soul's

---

[9] Richter's *Kirchenordnungen*, I: 10.

health; and that this child may be virtuously brought up to lead a godly and a Christian life; remembering always that baptism doth represent unto us our profession, which is, to follow the example of our Saviour Christ, and to be made like unto him; that, as he died and rose again for us, so should we, who are baptized, die from sin, and rise again from righteousness; continually modifying our evil and corrupt affections, and daily proceeding in all virtue and godliness of living."

Brandenburg-Nürnberg, (1533): "I beseech you from Christian love, as to what ye have now done in Baptism, in the place of this child, that if it be deprived of its parents by death or other misfortune, before it come to the use of reason, ye diligently and faithfully instruct and teach it, first the Ten Commandments, in order that thereby it may learn to know God's Will, and its sins; then, the Creed, whereby we receive grace, the forgiveness of sins, and the Holy Ghost; lastly, also the Lord's Prayer, in order that it may call upon God, and pray to him for aid to withstand Satan, and to lead a Christian life, until God shall fulfil that which he has now begun in Baptism, and it shall be eternally saved."

If we find nothing in Brandenburg-Nürnberg, corresponding to the closing words from "Remembering," etc., any one who is familiar with the close of Luther's treatment of Baptism, in his Catechism, knows whence they are derived.

The corresponding Würtemberg admonition of four years later is so rich and beautiful that it is here added. It almost precisely corresponds with the Cassel Order of 1539, and therefore, in its most essential features, was in the hands of the English Commission.

"Ye all, parents and relatives of this child, and as many as be here present, should now acknowledge and regard this child since Holy Baptism, as none else than a child of the Almighty, and a member of our Lord Jesus Christ, whom also the angels of God's serve, in no wise doubting that whatsoever ye do this child, whether ill or good, that ye do God Himself, and our

Lord Jesus Christ. Nor should effort or labor be spared by any one, according to his calling and relation with this child, to bring it up well for the Lord and to instruct and teach it, to observe all that the Lord has commanded us to be observed; and accordingly, ye parents, relatives and sponsors should spare no pains, and have the child, so soon as it have attained the proper age, faithfully brought to the church for catechetical instruction, in order that it may learn thoroughly what great and inexpressible gifts have been bestowed and transmitted it in Holy Baptism, and then, in the church, willingly and cordially and cordially confess and affirm for itself its faith, and in act and deed renounce the devil and the world, with all their works and lusts, and declare that it will abide by the Lord and his Holy Church, in entire obedience to his Holy Gospel, live faithfully to our Lord Christ unto the end, and, as a living member of Christ, and faithful branch of Christ's vine, bring forth much fruit to the glory of God, and the advancement of his Holy Church. Amen."

Passing to the Order "Of them that be in Private Houses in time of Necessity," the dependence is no less manifest. Without entering into all the details of the service, a few of the main features may suffice.

I. Edward: "They shall warn them that without great cause, and necessity, they baptize not children at home in their houses. And when great need shall compel them so to do, that then they minister on this fashion :

First let them that be present call upon God for his grace, and say the Lord's Prayer, if the time will suffer. And then one of them shall name the child, and dip him in water, or pour water upon him, saying these words : 'I baptize thee in the name of the Father, and of the Son, and of the Holy Ghost. Amen.' And let them not doubt but that the child so baptized is lawfully and sufficiently baptized, and ought not to be baptized again, in the church. But yet nevertheless, if the child which is after this sort baptized, do afterwards live, it is expedient that he be brought into the church, to the intent that the priest may examine and try whether the child be lawfully baptized or no."

Compare this now with *Reformation of Cologne* (1543, on the basis of the Saxon Order of 1539, the Würtemberg of 1536, and Hamburg of 1529):

"The pastors should instruct the people in their sermons, that they should not readily hasten to *Nothtaufe*, unless extreme necessity require, that baptism be administered, and if so that they must first call upon our Lord God, pray the Lord's Prayer, and then baptize the child, as Christ commanded his apostles, in the name of the Father, and of the Son and of the Holy Ghost, nothing doubting that the child is properly and sufficiently baptized, and should not be baptized again in the church, or otherwise. Yet such child if it live, should be brought into the church, that the pastor may ask the people whether they be certain that the child have been properly baptized."

Reformation of Cologne, (*1543*.)	*I. Edward*, (*1549*.)
The Pastor shall ask further:	The Priest shall examine them further:
Through whom was this done? And who were present?	By whom the child was baptized? Who was present, when the child was baptized?
Whether they who baptized the child, called properly upon the name of the Lord?	Whether they called upon God for grace and succour in that necessity?
And baptized the child with water?	With what thing or what matter they did baptize the child?
In the name of the Father, and of the Son and of the Holy Ghost?	With what words the child was baptized?
Whether they know that these words were used according to Christ's command?	Whether they think the child to be lawfully and perfectly baptized?
Now, my dear friends, I declare that ye have done right and well, in doing all this in the Name, and according to the command of our Lord Jesus Christ.	I certify you that in this case ye have done well, and according unto due order, concerning the baptizing of this child.

The rest of this service is a repetition of what is found in the order for Public Baptism. The form for "Conditional Baptism:" "If thou be not baptized already," etc., is not in accordance with the Cologne Order, although the act is. It was prescribed in the ancient orders, and afterwards endorsed by the Council of Trent. The old Lutheran Orders vary. The Reformation of Hesse (1526) and Hamburg (1529) presents it, while that of Schleswig-Holstein (1542, Bugenhagen) expressly forbids it. Cologne and Saxony, simply say that the child shall be baptized, precisely as though it were known to be not baptized.

CHAPTER XXII.

THE ORDERS FOR CONFIRMATION, MARRIAGE, VISITATION OF THE SICK, BURIAL.

Rome's Exaltation of *Confirmation* to a Sacrament, explained. Chemnitz on Confirmation. Examinations in Lutheran and English Orders. Catechisms of the two Orders. The Anglican Collect derived from the Cologne and Cassel Orders. The Act of Confirmation and its Words. The *Marriage* Ceremony. The old English Orders. Amendments and Additions from the Lutheran Orders. The "Visitation of Sick" and "Burial" as likewise modified. Dr. Cardwell's Testimony.

CONFIRMATION, although now universally practiced in the Lutheran Church, and highly esteemed as a most valuable ecclesiastical rite, for a long time fell into disrepute, in the reaction from the Romish overestimate of its importance, and the errors and superstitions connected with it. Rome, without any Scriptural authority, urged its necessity, and raised it, to the place of a Sacrament; made the chrism an essential, if not the most important part; and so exalted it, as to disparage the efficacy of Baptism. How thoroughly Rome undermines the value of Baptism, both by her doctrine of Penance and of Confirmation, is not generally understood. Baptism, with her, is the sacrament for the beginning of the Christian life; but its influence is evanescent, and other sacraments bring comfort to the more mature Christian. The great end of its teaching to those who have been baptized, is not, therefore, daily to return to God's covenant in baptism; but to seek new ordinances in which a new covenant is made. As Chemnitz has stated, the error was "that in Baptism, the Holy Spirit is given solely for regeneration, but that, for other necessary gifts, he is not given in Baptism, but only in Confirmation."[1]

The disuse of Confirmation, therefore, speedily followed, when there was an embarrassment in retaining it without continuing in the minds of the people the false estimate. Nevertheless, it did not become entirely obsolete throughout the Sixteenth Century. The writer above mentioned, the greatest theologian of the Lutheran Church, in his "Refutation of the Council of Trent," presents the Lutheran view of Confirmation, as follows: "Our writers have frequently shown, that, with the useless, superstitions and unscriptural traditions removed, the rite of Confirmation may be used after a godly manner, and in harmony with Scripture, so that they who have been baptized in infancy (for such is now the state of the Church), when they have attained to years of discretion, may diligently be instructed in a fixed and simple catechism of Church doctrine. And when they seem to have attained the elements in a moderate degree, they are afterwards presented to the bishop and the Church; and there the child, baptized in infancy, is first admonished, in a brief and simple exhortation, concerning his baptism, viz., how, why and into what he was baptized, what the Holy Trinity conferred and sealed upon him in Holy Baptism, viz., the covenant of peace, and the compact of grace; how renunciation of Satan, profession of faith and promise of obedience were there made. 2. The child makes a public profession of its own before the entire Church. 3. He is asked concerning the chief topics of Christian doctrine, and answers to each; or if he do not understand, is more correctly instructed. 4. He is admonished, and, by this profession, proclaims that he dissents from all heathen, fanatical and profane opinions. 5. An earnest exhortation is added from the Word of God, to persevere in the covenant of Baptism, and in that doctrine and faith, and by advancing to be gradually confirmed. 6. Public prayer is made for these children that God would deign to govern, preserve and confirm them in this profession.

[1] *Ex. Concil. Trid.* I: 296.

To which prayer, the laying on of hands may, without superstition, be added. Nor is the prayer vain; for it is based on the promises concerning the gift of perseverance and the grace of Confirmation. Such rite of Confirmation would confer great profit for the edification of the young and the entire Church."

Although this was published nearly thirty years after I. Edward, it shows the estimate of Confirmation which thus far had obtained. Even Confirmation by a bishop or superintendent is here allowed, although, in the same connection, the error of the Council of Trent, is shown, in anathematizing all other than episcopal Confirmation; for if any priest, or, even in case of necessity a layman, may baptize, while only a bishop may confirm, Confirmation, the human rite, is elevated above Baptism, the divine ordinance.

The order for Confirmation, of the English book, agrees with the preceding Lutheran Orders, in requiring a knowledge of the Creed, the Lord's Prayer and the Ten Commandments. No one, in either communion, was to be admitted without an examination concerning these parts of the Catechism. See Luther's vigorous language, in the beginning of his Preface to the Small Catechism. So Brandenburg-Nürnberg: "Those who neither can, nor will learn the Ten Commandments, Creed and Lord's Prayer, shall not be admitted to the sacrament." Hence the most diligent examination is uniformly required before the first communion. The Private Confession, then prevalent in the Lutheran Church gave pastors the opportunity for such examination, and hence rendered the desire for such public rite as that of Confirmation less urgent. Afterwards there came a time when Private Confession had fallen into disuse; and then, the need of some such ceremony as Confirmation, on the eve of the first admission to communion, asserted itself, and brought about its restoration. Nevertheless, as the above extract from Chemnitz indicates, the public examination was by no means unusual, provision being made for it especially in such Orders as furnish the Common Prayer so much material, as the Cassel Order of 1539, and the much quoted Reformation of Cologne. "Before all the congregation" (Cassel, Cologne), "public in the church before the people" (Ott-Heinrich, 1543) is the very language of those old Orders.

I. Edward places the examination in charge of the bishop. Cologne says that "this work would be especially appropriate to the bishops, if the dioceses were not so large," and assigns it to a "Visitator," the pastor, however, asking the questions. Mark-Brandenburg (1540), notwithstanding its Romanizing reputation, says: "Since, thank God, the population in our lands is great, and the bishops few, so that there will be too many for them to hear and instruct each one, they may commit this to their pastors. Nevertheless we think it well, that whenever Confirmation by the pastors occur, some one of those learned be with them to see that the pastors attend to it properly, and do not reintroduce former abuses or carelessness;" and the Reformation of Cologne: "It is not the prerogative of bishops, so that no one else may administer it, as baptism which is more, is administered by ordinary ministers, yea, in case of necessity, by any Christian." It is assigned to bishops only "that they may learn to know their hearers and especially the young people." It would not be difficult to reconstruct the first three rubrics of the first English book from the Cologne Order, and the final one is thoroughly Lutheran in doctrine, although we cannot trace its origin. The Catechism which follows "to be learned of every child, before he be brought to be confirmed of the bishops," we treat of in a separate chapter. It is sufficient here to say, that Cologne is again followed by the introduction of the Catechism in this place, as well as in its subject matter. Of the two Collects in the first English Order, the first was the second prayer in connection with the unction at Adult Baptism in the ante-reformation Orders; and the second, "Almighty, everlasting God," is conceded by most English authorities to be from the Cologne Order. The prayer from the Eighth Century of Egbert, bishop of York, which Palmer gives as its source, has only the faintest resemblance. It is found also in the Cassel Order of 1539, and, thence, has been traced by Höfling[2] to Bucer. In various revisions, it is generally found in the Lutheran formularies, and "can with difficulty be supplanted by any other, since it is excellent."[3] The act of Confirmation in I. Edward, was according to that of the ancient form: "I sign thee with the sign of the holy cross," etc., and was replaced in II. Edward (1552) by the prayer said by the bishop while his hands rested upon the one confirmed: "Defend, O Lord, this child with thy heavenly grace, that he may continue thine forever and daily increase in thy Holy Spirit, more and more, until he come unto thy everlasting kingdom." This also comes from the Cassel and Cologne Orders: "Receive the Holy Ghost, as thy protection and defence against all evil, and thy strength and aid unto all good, from the gracious hand of God the Father, Son and Holy Ghost. Amen."

The Marriage ceremony in the English Book, is to a large extent from the old English, with very important additions introduced from the Lutheran Orders. The opening address, which has been left unchanged in succeeding revisions in England, has been much condensed in the American edition. In the Sarum Order, the address read:

"Brethren, we are gathered together in the sight of God, and his angels, and all the saints, in the face of the Church, to join together two persons,—to wit., this man and this woman, that, whatsover they have done aforetime henceforth they may be one body, yet two souls, in the faith and law of God, ["to knyt these two bodyes togyder." York Use] to the end they may together attain eternal life."

This was condensed into an introduction:

"Dearly beloved friends, we are gathered together here in the sight of God, and in the face of his congregation to join together this man and this woman in holy matrimony."

The resemblance to the Introduction of the Reformation of Cologne fully justified the retention of the old formula. It ran:

[2] II: 366; Löhe's *Agende*, II: 47.
[3] Ib.

"Ye appear before God our Heavenly Father, and Christ Jesus, our Lord, and his Church," etc.

What follows is chiefly a condensation of the long address in Schwab-Hall of 1543, no precedent for it being found in the older English Orders. It follows the order and uses the very language of this liturgy of Brentz.

ENGLISH PRAYER BOOK (1549): "Which is an honorable estate instituted of God in Paradise,[4] in the time of man's innocency, signifying unto us the mystical union that is betwixt Christ and his Church;[5] which holy estate Christ adorned and beautified with his presence, and first miracle that he wrought in Cana of Galilee,[6] and is commended of St. Paul to be honorable among all men; and therefore is not to be enterprised or taken in hand unadvisedly, lightly or wantonly,[7] to satisfy men's carnal lusts and appetites,[8] like brute beasts that have no understanding, but reverently, discreetly, advisedly, soberly and in the fear of God.[9] One cause was the procreation of children, to

[4] SCHW-HALL, (1543): "For the Marriage estate has not been devised by human reason, but was found and instituted by God himself in Paradise."

[5] From Collect at close of Osiander's (1526) and Luther's (1529). Brandenburg-Nürnberg, (1533), Schw. Hall, (1543), Cologne, (1543), and most Lutheran Orders: "Wherein the Sacrament of Thy dear Son, Jesus Christ and the Church, his Bride, is signified unto us." There is a similar Collect in Sarum, from the Gelasian Sacramentary: "Who hast consecrated the state of matrimony to such an excellent mystery, that in it is signified the sacramental union and marriage of Christ and the Church."

[6] Schw. Hall: "This estate, the Son of God, our Lord Jesus Christ, so highly esteemed, that not only when bidden, with his Mother and disciples, did he honor the marriage with his first miracle." Cassel, (1539), Cologne, (1543): "Who also honored and richly adorned the marriage estate by his presence."

[7] Osiander (1524), Brandenburg-Nürnberg (1533): "To the end that this may not be done without understanding of the Word of God, as do unbelievers."

[8] Schw. Hall, (1543): "For it has not been instituted for worldly or carnal wantonness."

[9] See 4.

be brought up in the fear of and nurture of the Lord, and praise of God. [10] Secondly, it was ordained for a remedy against sin, and to avoid fornication, that such persons as be married might live chastely in matrimony, [11] and keep themselves undefiled members of Christ's body. [12] Thirdly, for the mutual society, help and comfort, that the one ought to have of the other, both in prosperity and adversity." [13]

The Exhortation that, "if any can show just cause, why they may not, lawfully, be joined together, let him now speak," is partly according to the older English Orders, but the words: "Or else hereafter forever hold his peace," come from Osiander's Orders of 1526, followed by Brand-Nürnb. (1533), Mark-Brandenburg (1540), Ott-Heinrich (1543), Cologne (1543), etc.: "If any one hath aught to say thereon, let him speak in time, or afterward be silent, and refrain from interposing any hindrance." In the Lutheran Orders, however, this declaration is made in connection with the publication of the banns. The questions addressed bride and groom, follow the York and Sarum Orders, the earlier Lutheran forms being much briefer, although, in this, the later Orders of the Sixteenth Century more nearly approach the English. The Lutheran custom generally provided for the use of the ring, but without any words concerning the ring, on the part of those being married. Osiander (1526) fol-

---

[10] Schw. Hall: "That therein children might be brought up by their parents to the glory and knowledge of God, and the doctrine of the true Christian faith might be transmitted from children to children's children, and be diffused and maintained throughout the world, unto the Last Day. For God has not created man to live a beastly life here on earth, and to care only for that which is earthly, but that he may learn to know God."

[11] Schw. Hall: "God has appointed and ordained matrimony, that every form of unchastity might be avoided."

[12] Schw. Hall: "And besides God wishes the love and communion of his Son, our Lord Jesus Christ with the Christian Church, as his Bride, to be thus known and represented."

[13] The thought probably enters here, as Schw. Hall ends with the prediction of the cross, and the divine comfort under it.

lowed by Brandenburg-Nürnberg, etc., prescribes that first the groom shall say after the minister: "I, N., take thee N. to my wedded wife, and plight thee my troth," and then the bride also, in the same way, plights her troth to her wedded husband.

We are compelled here to dispel an illusion which has misled some of the English writers on the Prayer Book. Palmer[14] says: "The succeeding rites in which the priest, with a certain formulary, joins their right hands together, and afterwards pronounces the marriage to be complete, are perhaps peculiar to the Church of England." Blunt: "This is a noble peculiarity of the English rite, though probably derived originally from Archbishop Hermann's Consultation." The hint thus given, however, at once destroys the idea of peculiarity. The sentence "What God hath joined together, let no man put asunder," is found in every Lutheran Order which we have examined, from Osiander's of 1526, on: "*Was Gott zusammen gefüget hat, sol Kein Mensch scheiden.*"[15] Nor have we to search long for the declaration, unknown to the old Orders.

Luther's Traubüchlein, 1529.	*English Book.*
Weil dann Hans N. und Greta N. einander zur Ehe begehre, auch die Ehe Einander versprochen, und solches hie öffentlich für Gott und seinen Gemein bekennet, darauf die hände und Trauringe einander gegeben haben, so spreche ich sie ehelich zusammen, im Namen Gottes des Vaters, und des Sohnes, und des Heiligen Geistes. Amen.	Forasmuch as N. and N. have consented together in holy wedlock, and have witnessed the same here before God and this company; and thereto have given and pledged their troth either to other, and have declared the same by giving and receiving gold and silver, and by joining of hands, I pronounce that they be man and wife together; In the Name of the Father, etc.

In accordance with Osiander's Order, and the Lutheran Orders in general, following it, Psalm 128 was designated as the first to be sung. Cologne give Ps. 127 first, and then Ps. 128.

The English Service closes with a long Address to "All ye which be married, or which intend to take the holy estate of

[14] 2: 217.
[15] *Annotated Book of Common Prayer*, p. 270.

marriage upon you," which is only an elaboration of the portion of the Address in Luther's Order, beginning: "Since ye both now are given in marriage, in God's name, hear first the command of God touching this estate," etc.

In the Order for "Visitation of the Sick," the most important feature derived from a Lutheran source is the "Exhortation." The ancient Exhortation from the old Orders quoted by Palmer, Blunt, Procter, etc., has little more resemblance to that of the English book, than that it is an exhortation to a sick person. The compilers of the English book adopted that in the Reformation of Cologne, originally found in the Saxon Order of 1539, condensing and very freely rendering it, rather following the thought than the words. The two exhortations begin:

Saxon, 1539.	English, 1549.
Dear friend: Since our Lord Jesus Christ hath visited you with bodily sickness, in order that you may take to heart God's will, know: First, that such bodily sickness come to us from God for no other causes, etc.	Dearly beloved: Know this, that Almighty God is the Lord over life and death. . . Wherefore whatsoever your sickness is, know you certainly that it is God's visitation. And for what cause soever this sickness is sent unto you, etc.

The Order for the "Burial of the Dead," has been much changed in the English book, since I. Edward VI. Prior to the same period, the Lutheran Orders also have a relatively less complete development. The essential features however are the same. They retain from the old Orders: "I am the resurrection and the life," "In the midst of life, we are in death," "Blessed are the dead that die in the Lord,"—and the lesson 1 Cor. 15: 20 sqq. The first Collect: "Almighty God, we give thee hearty thanks," which Palmer declares to be of modern origin— we find in the Reformation of Cologne. The concluding Collect for the forgiveness and peace of the departed is not found in any Lutheran authorities examined, as it retains Romish error. The first Collect, now found in the Anglican Order, was in I. Edward VI., in the "Celebration of the Holy Communion when there is a burial of the dead." It occurs in the burial service of Lower Saxony (1585), as "*O Herr Jesu Christe, der du bist der Aufer-*

stehung u. das Leben," from which it would be interesting to trace it to its source.

Such was in general the First Book of Edward VI. Dr. Cardwell is right in saying: "The new Liturgy was greatly indebted, wherever it deviated from the ancient breviaries, to the progress made upon the continent in religious worship." After alluding to its indebtedness to the Reformation of Cologne, he adds: "In the Occasional Offices, it is clear on examination that they were indebted to the labors of Melanchthon and Bucer, and through them to the older Liturgy of Nürnberg, which those reformers were instructed to follow." [16]

[16] *The Two Liturgies of Edward VI. contrasted*, Preface, xv. sq.

CHAPTER XXIII.

THE SECOND PRAYER BOOK OF EDWARD VI.

The Calvinistic Reaction. The "Censures" of Bucer and Martyr. Orders of Pollanus and A Lasco. The "Confession" introduced. Its derivation. Mistake of English Liturgiolists. Traced to Bucer's Strassburg Order of 1524. Revisions of Bucer's Formula by Calvin and Zwingli. Source of the "Absolution." Other changes. The Ten Commandments in the Communion Service. The General Prayer. The original in its unabbrevated form in Cassel, Cologne, and Calvin's condensation, given in full. Results of the Revision of 1552. Hardwick's Testimony.

THE Book of 1549 was found in some of its features to be unsatisfactory. As shown in the preceding pages, a number of causes combined to increase the influence of Calvinism in England. Cranmer himself first wavered and then succumbed. The first book was too Lutheran, and besides, like in all such movements, much was suggested by the experience of its use. The history of the revision does not concern us; we have to do only with the results attained. The general facts are well known. Cranmer was again at the head of the commission. Bucer and Martyr, then Professors at Cambridge and Oxford, prepared "Censures" of the First Book, (published about January 1552) while the French Order of Pollanus, and the German of A Lasco had also been published and afforded suggestions. Coverdale had translated it into Latin for Calvin's examination. The new book thus prepared was issued in September 1552. The Preface disclaims any very important changes from the First Book.

The first difference appears in the introduction of a confessional service before the regular morning service. The ancient Orders provided such service for the priest who was to minister,

(275)

in order that, before coming to the holy mysteries, he might himself privately confess and be absolved. The public service of the Mass, however, began with the Introit, and in this the Lutheran Orders had made no change, although subsequently becoming general, especially when private confession lost its position, or a corresponding Saturday evening service was disused. The English authorities are much perplexed as to the origin of the Confessional Service introduced in 1552, and still retained. The usual explanation is that it was suggested by the Orders of Pollanus and A Lasco. "The hint was taken from two books of Service, used by congregations of refugees in England."[1] The formula of Pollanus has been traced by Archbishop Laurence[2] to Calvin. Pollanus had succeeded Calvin as pastor at Strassburg, and had thence emigrated with his congregation to Glastonbury in Somersetshire. The formula is the same as that prescribed by Calvin for the church of Geneva in 1545.[3] It resembles that prepared by Zwingli for Zürich and Berne in 1536.[4] But its sources are still more remote. In June 1524, Bucer, whose influence on the Book of Common Prayer enters at so many points, had prepared a Reformation of the Mass, which he published, as his biographer Baum says, without the knowledge or consent of the clergy of Strassburg, who, in a radical reaction against Rome, were opposed to any fixed form.[5] This Order was, at the close of the same year, reported in abstract to Luther by the council of the city, as in use in their churches. It is here given with the others above mentioned.

STRASSBURG ORDER (1524).

"In the Name of the Father, and of the Son, and of the Holy Ghost. Amen.

Confess unto God the Lord; for he is good, and his mercy is

---

[1] *Procter*, p. 48.
[2] *Bampton Lectures*, p. 209.
[3] *Niemyer's Coll. Conf.*, p. 171.
[4] Ib. p. 73.
[5] Baum's *Capito and Bucer*, p. 266.

unto everlasting. I said I will confess my transgressions unto the Lord; and Thou forgavest the iniquity of my sin.

I, a poor sinful man, confess unto God Almighty, that I have grievously sinned by the transgression of his commandments, that I have done much that I should have left undone, and that I have left undone much that I should have done, by unbelief and distrust of God, and weakness of love towards my fellow-servants and neighbors; for which, as I acknowledge myself guilty before God, I grieve. Be gracious unto me; be merciful unto me, a poor sinner. Amen.

This is a faithful saying and worthy of all acceptation that Christ Jesus came into the world to save sinners, of whom I am chief This I believe. Lord, help my unbelief and, save me. Amen.

The priest then says to the people: God be gracious and merciful unto us all. Amen."

Then come the Introit and the Mass proper.

CALVIN'S ORDER (1545).

"Our help is in the Name of the Lord, who made heaven and earth. Amen.

Brethren, let us each place himself before the Lord, and confess his sins, following me in these words:

O Lord God, Eternal and almighty Father, we acknowledge and frankly confess before Thy Holy Majesty that we have been conceived as miserable sinners, and have been born in iniquity and depravity, prone to wickedness, useless unto every good work, and that, being vicious, we do not cease to transgress Thy holy commandments. Wherefore we would receive destruction from Thy just judgment. But, Lord, we sincerely lament that we have offended Thee; we condemn ourselves and our offences, seeking in true penitence for Thy grace to relieve our misery. Deem us, therefore, O Most kind and merciful Father, worthy of Thy mercy, for the sake of Thy Son, our Lord Jesus Christ. Blotting out all our offences and washing away all our filth, increase in us daily the gifts of Thy Holy Spirit, so that, from our hearts, acknowledging our iniquity, we may be more and more dissatisfied with ourselves, and thus be aroused to true repentance; and mortifying ourselves, with all our sins, may bring forth fruits of righteousness and innocency grateful unto Thee, Through Jesus Christ our Lord."

Then follows a Psalm. There is no absolution.

The form of Pollanus (1551) varies only in a few words, but adds: "Absolution. Here the Pastor recites to the people in the Name of the Father, and of the Son, and of the Holy Ghost, a passage of Holy Scripture concerning the remission of sins."

Upon the basis, then, chiefly of the Strassburg form, together with that of Calvin and of the Reformation of Cologne, used in the Preparatory Service, the English Confessional Prayer was constructed. "We have erred and strayed like lost sheep" was probably suggested by the shorter Prayer, before Communion, of the Cassel and Cologne Orders.[6] The Absolution was taken from that in the Preparatory Service of the Reformation of Cologne, Bucer's earlier and later work being thus combined.

The other important changes in the Matin Service, were in making the *Jubilate* alternate with the *Benedictus*, and in changing the Apostles Creed from directly after, to directly before the *Kyrie*. By those who refer to the American "Book of Common Prayer," this cannot be traced, since the American revisers have still further mutilated the old Matin Service by omitting the Kyrie and the Lord's Prayer; the latter, doubtless, because it had already been used, out of its place, after the Absolution.

In the Communion Service, the *Kyrie* disappears, and the *Gloria in Excelsis* is transferred to the Post Communion Service. The Ten Commandments, we have seen above, are inserted, not simply as Blunt suggests after "the jejune liturgy of Pullain" (Pollanus), since they are found in the Roman Mass, and the Liturgy of Frankfort-on-the-Maine of 1530.[7] "Glory

---

[6] "*Deine zerstreuete Schäflein.*"
[7] Richter's *KO*. p. 141.

be to thee, O Lord," after the reading of the Gospel, is omitted. The Nicene Creed reappears, as the proper Creed for the Communion Service. The direction that the sermon shall follow the Creed, disappears. The Admonition of I. Edward, is transferred to a later place; so also the Salutation, *Sursum Corda*, and the words: "It is meet, right and our bounden duty." What in I. Edward VI. is in another place as the "Consecratory Prayer," is now changed into a prayer for the Church and rulers—the Cassel-Cologne Order being more closely followed, and the Romanizing taint of the First Book being excluded. This Cassel-Cologne prayer was already outlined by Bucer in his Strassburg Mass of 1524. We translate it, unabridged, from Cassel (1539) as the form, in which Cranmer and his associates used it.

" Almighty, Everlasting and Gracious God and Father, Thou hast commanded us through Thy dear Son and Lord Jesus Christ, and his holy apostles, to assemble ourselves before Thee in His Name, and hast promised that whatsoever we thus unitedly pray Thee in His Name, Thou wouldst graciously give. We pray Thee, therefore, through the same Thy dear Son, our only Saviour; first, that Thou wouldst graciously forgive us all our sins and offences, which we here all confess and acknowledge before Thee, and that Thy just wrath, which, by our grievous transgressions, we have merited, Thou wouldst graciously turn away from us, for the sake of the Blood and precious Satisfaction of Thy Son, our Mediator. Strengthen also Thy Holy Spirit within us, that we may wholly surrender ourselves to Thy good pleasure, that, now and ever, we may pray Thee in all true faith for ourselves and others, and may richly obtain Thy help and grace.

We pray Thee also especially for Thy Church and congregation. Deliver it from all wolves and hirelings, who desolate it, and, by their corruptions, array themselves against Thee. Grant and sustain godly and faithful pastors, through whom all Thy scattered sheep may be brought back unto Thy dear Son, the Chief Shepherd and Bishop of our souls, and into his true communion, that there may be one Shepherd and one fold.

We pray Thee for all rulers, Emperors, Kings, princes and lords, and especially for those of our land, and the counsellors and magistrates of this city. Grant and increase unto them all grace to rule, that they may acknowledge and embrace Christ Thy Son our Lord, as One to whom Thou hast given all power in Heaven and Earth, and that they may so govern their subjects, as Thy creatures and children; that we, here and everywhere, may lead a quiet and peaceful life in all godliness and honesty.

We pray Thee further, Holy Father, for all men, even for those estranged from Thy Kingdom. Draw unto Thy Son our Saviour, all those who flee from Him, and those whom Thou hast drawn to Him and enlightened, grant that they now may know to find in Him alone the forgiveness of sins and all good. Strengthen them, in this knowledge, and make it ever more active within them, unto all good works.

We pray Thee also, Gracious God and Father, for all upon whom Thou hast imposed any special chastisement. Whether it be by poverty, exile, sickness, or any other distress and trial, give them to recognize Thy gracious fatherly hand, comfort and deliver them from all evil, and grant that they may acknowledge and consider in every chastisement, that they have deserved what is far more grievous, and thus may be turned the sooner and the more completely from all evil unto Thine alone good will.

Finally, we pray Thee, Everlasting and Faithful God and Father, that, as we are here assembled in Thy Divine Presence, for Thy Holy Word, Prayer and the Holy Sacraments, enlighten the eyes of our understanding, and grant we may acknowledge and remember, that we, alas! of ourselves and from our parents, are of such perverse and condemned nature, that in our flesh and blood, we cannot inherit Thy Kingdom of righteousness and blessedness: that we can deserve nothing but eternal wrath and all misery; but that Thou, Gracious God, out of thy boundless mercy, didst regard our misery and corruption, and didst will that Thy Eternal Word, Thy dear Son, shouldst become flesh and our brother, whereby flesh and blood again might become holy, and we, poor condemned men, might be renewed and sanctified again through Him, unto Thine image and unto all Thy divine will and good pleasure. Therefore he giveth us to eat and to drink, in his Holy Sacrament, that very holy flesh and blood which he hath offered upon the cross unto the Father for our sins, and whereby he hath paid the ransom for all our sins, and reconciled us unto Thee, in order that he might live in us, and we, in him, might live a holy and godly life. Grant, Heavenly Father, that we may acknowledge all this, in true living faith, and, now and at all times, meditate thereon, that, renouncing reason and all wicked lusts, we may devote ourselves entirely unto Thy dear Son, our Lord and Saviour, seek and obtain all help and consolation in Him alone, and in His death and resurrection; and may now receive his holy Body and Blood with all thankfulness, and worship and praise Thee, because of His bitter suffering and death, His Heavenly governance, and the gift of Himself which he makes unto us, for food and drink, unto life everlasting."

The prayer ends with a brief paraphrase of the Lord's Prayer. Both in Cassel and Cologne, there is a shorter form of this prayer.

"Merciful God, Heavenly Father, Thou hast promised that if we come together in the Name of Thy dear Son, our Lord and Saviour, Jesus Christ," etc.

Calvin has appropriated the thoughts, but rewrought the language in the form, prepared for Geneva (1545), which begins:

"Almighty God, Heavenly Father, Thou hast promised us that Thou wilt hear the prayers which we offer Thee in the Name of Thy dear Son and Lord Jesus Christ; and we have learned both of Him and of His Apostles, that we should come together in one place and in his Name, the promise being given that He will be present with us to intercede with Thee for us, and obtain all things which, with one consent, we ask of Thee on Earth.

First, Thou hast commanded us to pray for those whom Thou hast appointed over us as rulers and governors; then to approach Thee as suppliants for all things necessary unto Thy people and all mortals. Since, then, we have come into Thy presence, relying upon Thy holy commands and promises, assembled in the Name of Thy Son our Lord Jesus Christ, we, as suppliants, sincerely beseech Thee, O God and Father, in the Name of the same, our only Saviour and Mediator, so deign to forgive our sins and to turn our hearts unto Thee, that we may call upon thee,," etc.

Calvin presents, at length, the topics, in the same order, as in Cassel, except that he prays for rulers before praying for the Church. His prayer ends also with the Confession of sin, original and actual, and the paraphrase of the Lord's Prayer. From these sources, therefore, the prayer was condensed:

"Almighty and Everliving God, which by thy holy apostle hast taught us to make prayers and supplications, and to give thanks for all men; we humbly beseech Thee most mercifully to receive our prayers which we offer unto Thy divine Majesty," etc.

The latter part of the prayer in I. Edward, containing the Words of Institution, is transferred to another part of the service. The modification here of the formula of distribution has been noticed in a preceding chapter.

The only change in the Vesper Service, was in the insertion of "O Lord open thou my lips," etc., from the Matin Service, the omission of the Hallelujah, and the provision that the Psalm *Cantate Domino* (XCVIII.) may alternate with the *Magnificat* and the *Deus Misereatur* (Ps. XVII.) with the *Nunc Dimittis*. The Athanasian Creed was retained as in I. Edward VI.

In the Baptismal Service, the Exorcism was omitted, the sign of the cross changed to after the baptism, Luther's Collect abbreviated, the thanksgiving Collect rewrought, the Lord's Prayer and Creed after the Exhortation omitted, several Collects from the former Order for Consecration of the Font introduced, etc. In the Burial Service, prayers for the dead were suppressed, etc., details interesting in the history of the Book, but whose examination lies outside of the scope of our undertaking. The result of the revision was, on the one hand, to remove a number of Romanizing elements, but, on the other, to sacrifice much of its Lutheran to a Calvinistic Spirit, and to make changes which seriously impaired the service as an organism.

Archdeacon Hardwick has well said : " His " (Cranmer's) " Lutheran predilections are also manifested in the formation of the First Service Book of Edward VI., put forth in the month of June, 1549; for, like the corresponding work of the Saxon Reformers, our own is derived almost entirely from the ancient or mediæval Liturgies, and, in no inconsiderable degree, through the medium of a Lutheran compilation, itself based upon the older Offices of Nuremberg."[8]

[8] *History of the XXXIX Articles*, p. 80.

CHAPTER XXIV.

AN EXCURSUS ON THE TYPICAL LUTHERAN CHIEF SERVICE.

Application of the Evangelical Principle to the Sphere of Worship. The distinctive features of the Lutheran Service. The Sacramental and Sacrificial factors with respect to the Roman, the Reformed and the Lutheran Services.
THE "COMMON SERVICE" examined. Preparatory Service of *Confession*. Its Origin; its Structure. The *Declaration of Grace*. No Absolution. The Declaration analyzed.
THE SERVICE PROPER. First Act—THE WORD: Part I. A. *The Introit*. Agreement of Lutheran Orders. Origin. Structure. When and by whom chanted. B. *The Kyrie*. Relation to Introit. No Confession of Sin. C. *The Gloria in Excelsis*. Significance of its place. Its Structure. Its Origin. Part II. A. *The Salutation*. Where only to be used. B. *The Collects*. The *Oremus*. Why called Collect. Origin. Structure. C. The *Epistle*. The New Testament Law. D. *The Hallelujah*. Significance of its place. Luther's Rule. Graduals, Sequences, etc. E. *The Gospel* Origin of attending Responses. Part III. A. *The Creed*. Variations in its place, and its significance as so changed. Lutheran Orders prefer the Nicene Creed. B. *The Sermon*. The Explanation of the Gospel. *Votum*. C. *Offertory*. Improperly so called. D. *General Prayer*. Analogy of Roman Mass. Emphasizes the Church as the Communion of Saints. Various forms used. Luther's Litany greatly enriches the ancient Litany. Structure. Not a mere penitential prayer.
Second Act—THE COMMUNION: The Lutheran Conception of the Communion, in its relation to the Word. Communion, not to be separated from the Preaching Service. Part I. INTRODUCTION. A. *Salutation* B. *Preface*. C. *Sanctus* Structure and Significance Meaning of the "*Benedictus*." D. *Exhortation*. Origin (Volprecht, Nürnberg, 1525) Unliturgical. Why retained? Part II CONSECRATION. A. *The Lord's Prayer*. Not properly consecratory. Why the Lord's Prayer is

used? B. *Words of Institution.* Meaning of their recitation in this place. C. *The Pax.* Luther's Explanation. Part III. THE DISTRIBUTION. A. *Agnus Dei.* Origin. The *Dona nobis;* when introduced, and what it signifies. B. *Distribution Proper.* Meaning of the words. Luther's addition. Benediction. Is "true" to be used? Consecration not complete until in the Distribution. Part IV. *Post Communion.* A. *The Nunc Dimittis.* In the oldest, but not the most Orders. Significance. B. *Versicle.* C. *Collect.* D. *Benedicamus.*

The First Part of Service, variable; the Second part, fixed. Exceptions. Kliefoth's Comments. Simpler Services for villages and country churches. A typical Simple Service.

THE tracing of the relation between the Orders of Edward VI. and those of the Lutheran Church, having led to the incidental discussion of various details of the latter, it may not be out of place to introduce here a brief presentation of the Chief Service (*Hauptgottesdienst*), as it has attained a fixed form, where the reformation of the ancient Orders of public worship upon the principles laid down by Luther and his associates, has been carried out. We, of course, fail to find any form so rigidly fixed, and uniformly used, as the Roman Order. In the various Lutheran countries, the application of the same principles was modified by varying circumstances, as Romanizing or Reformed influences, or, as in South-Western Germany, even the prejudices diffused by Carlstadt, through his connection with Strassburg, are traceable. Then, as even the principles themselves were more strongly or more feebly apprehended, there were varying results. The application and elaboration of the evangelical principle,[1] within the sphere of worship, could not be realized at one

[1] This principle within the sphere of worship, is that the public worship does not in itself convey the forgiveness of sins, and the blessings of salvation. These are found only in the gracious assurances of the Gospel, which are appropriated only by faith. This principle had to assert itself against the Romish error that the public service was an institution appointed by God, directly conditioning salvation. The Public Service, according to the evangelical principle is not a means of grace, as Rome makes it; but a means, through which the means of grace, Word and Sacrament, are brought to men. In it, the Holy Spirit comes to men, as Word and Sacrament are administered;

stroke, but only through a gradual process. In the consideration of a typical Lutheran service, we must constantly eliminate from any given Orders the factors pertaining to historical and local relations, and having, therefore, only transitory significance. We will follow here "The Common Order of Service," which three of the Lutheran General Bodies in America, have agreed upon as exhibiting the Consensus of the pure Lutheran liturgies of the Sixteenth Century.

Preliminary, however, to the examination of the Service, it is important to keep in mind a principle marking the worship of the different Confessions, which Dr. Kliefoth has discussed at length in his *Liturgische Abhandlungen*, and whom we shall mainly follow here. In all true worship of God, two things are implied, viz., God offers and communicates, and man not only receives what God offers, but also returns something to God. The former is the sacramental; the latter, the sacrificial element in worship. A sacrament may, in a wide sense, be defined as "a ceremony in which God gives that which the promise attached thereto offers." Thus Baptism is no act of ours, but one which God brings to us, and through which he bestows upon us the blessings announced at the institution of Baptism. The Son of God was not content with providing for us salvation by his sacrifice on the cross; but he has ordained means whereby the efficacy of his sacrifice, is applied. The Lord's Supper was insti-

and men, in turn, through the Holy Spirit, attending Word and Sacraments, receives what the Holy Spirit offers. The perfection of the liturgical Service depends, therefore, upon the provision made for this constant reciprocation, God giving and man receiving, like the two sides of one breath. There could be no such conception of the Service where everything was spoken in a language not understood. Nor could it occur, where the doctrine of the constant presence of the Holy Spirit with the Word and Sacraments was denied, and an inner Word made the more prominent and important. All questions, then, concerning places, times, forms and books of worship, fall under the category of adiaphora; they are of value, not in themselves, but in the degree that they promote true worship, *i. e.* edification from Word and Sacrament, and invocation of God based thereon. Cf. Koestlin's *Geschichte des Christlichen Gottesdienstes* (Freiburg, 1887), pp. 152 sqq.

tuted not that we might thereby bring anything to Christ, but that he might bring something to us. So the reading and preaching of the Word, bring with them the very grace which the Word proclaims.

The sacrificial element is when we bring something to God. There are two forms of sacrifice, the propitiatory and the eucharistic. Under the New Testament, there is but one propitiatory sacrifice, viz., that of our Lord and Saviour Jesus Christ, made by both his active and passive obedience throughout life, and finally offered once for all upon the altar of the cross. Eucharistic sacrifices are those of prayer, praise and thanksgiving, made in response to what is given us in Word and sacraments.

In every true act of worship, there is a reciprocation between the sacramental and sacrificial elements. God gives through Word and sacraments; and we give back to him in prayer and praise. The fundamental element in every Service must be the sacramental; for God must give to us, before our faith can render worship, good works, etc. Hence the fundamental principle of Lutheran worship is that the individual Service must never consist merely of sacrificial parts, but must always have something sacramental, *i. e.* the application of Word and Sacraments. For the sacramental is the divine address; and the sacrificial, the human answer.

In the Romish worship, the sacramental element was crowded out by the sacrificial. The Mass, instead of being a sacrament, was made a sacrifice; and that, too, a propitiatory sacrifice. By becoming a sacrifice, it ceased to be a real means of grace. God's act, they changed into man's work. Man's believing and thankful reception they transformed into a meritorious transaction whereby to purchase grace. Hence participation in the Eucharist was regarded unimportant. If it be a sacrifice made for us, even our presence is unnecessary. So the Word need not be understood when read. Presence, at its public reading, whatever the language, becomes a propitiatory act.

In the Reformed Church, the sacramental was also crowded

out by the sacrificial element; but in another way. In antagonizing the Romish propitiatory-sacrifice, they make the Service almost entirely Eucharistic-sacrificial. As is well known, Zwingli denied the reality of means of grace. The application of grace is conceived of as occurring immediately from Spirit to spirit. The constant presence of the Holy Spirit with the Word and Sacraments is denied. All liturgical acts are expressions of faith already wrought. The sacraments offer nothing from the Lord, but the faith or piety of those celebrating them. The Word does not bring the Spirit; but the Spirit brings the Word. Through the exposition of the Word, the preacher simply gives testimony as to his faith. Believers come together chiefly by common prayer, confession, praise, thanksgiving, etc., to exercise their faith.

The Lutheran Church, laying emphasis upon both elements, provides for both, throughout every part of her Service. They interpenetrate each other, the sacramental always evoking the sacrificial-eucharistic, and the sacrificial-eucharistic never occuring except as the sacramental has preceded. And yet, as we shall see, certain parts of the Service are predominantly sacramental, and others predominantly sacrificial.

With this principle understood, we proceed to the presentation of the Service:

I. THE PREPARATORY SERVICE

A. *Confession.*

In the name of the Father, and of the Son, and of the Holy Ghost. Amen.

Beloved in the Lord! Let us draw near with a true heart, and confess our sins unto God, our Father, beseeching him, in the name of our Lord Jesus Christ, to grant us forgiveness.

Our help is in the name of the Lord.

Who made heaven and earth.

I said, I will confess my transgressions unto the Lord.

And thou forgavest the iniquity of my sin.

Almighty God, our Maker and Redeemer, we poor sinners confess unto thee, that we are by nature sinful and unclean, and that we have sinned against thee by thought, word and deed. Wherefore we flee for refuge to thine infinite mercy, seeking and imploring thy grace, for the sake of our Lord Jesus Christ. O most merciful God, who hast given thine only begotten Son to die for us, have mercy upon us, and for his sake, grant us remission of all our sins; and, by thy Holy Spirit, increase in us true knowledge of thee, and of thy will, and true obedience to thy word, to the end that by thy grace we may come to everlasting life, through Jesus Christ, our Lord. Amen.

This does not belong to the Service properly so called. The Service of the Mass does not have it as such. The *Consensus* of the Lutheran liturgies of the Sixteenth Century does not contain it. It has its origin in the *Confiteor* or *Praeparatio in Missam*, said by the officiating priest for himself, first secretly, but in course of time, publicly, before beginning the service.[2] Thence revised, so as to exclude the Roman errors, it was transferred to a number, but not the majority, of the Lutheran services. Thus the Brandenburg-Nürnberg Order begins: "When the priest comes to the altar, he may say the *Confiteor*, or whatever his meditation suggests." Even an earlier Order (Strassburg, 1524) prescribes it in a form similar to that here given.[3] The form adopted is that of Mecklenburg, 1552.[4] The structure of the Confession is not manifest in the English translation. The German is: "*Ich armer sündiger Mensch*," showing that it is the officiating minister, who begins under the deep sense of his unworthiness of that which his office communicates (Is. 6 : 5 sq.). Then, in the second part of the prayer, the people join, or as in the Meckenburg Order, a second minister. There is also progress in the thought. The first is a general prayer for God's mercy; the second, passing to what is more specific, presents the plan of salvation, with the prayer that God would fulfil his

---

[2] Confiteor Deo Omnipotenti, beatae Mariae semper virgini, beato Michaeli archangelo . . omnibus sanctis et vobis, fratres, quia peccavi nimis cogitatione, verbo et opere. Mea culpa, mea culpa, mea maxima culpa. Ideo precor beatam Mariam semper virginem—et vos fratres orare pro me ad Dominum, Deum nostrum. Then his fellow ministrants continue : Misereatur tui Omnipotens Deus, et dimissis peccatis tuis perducat te ad vitam aeternam.

[3] See above Chapter xxii.

[4] *Richter*, II :122.

promises connected with that plan. The second petition has almost the force of an absolution by his congregation, of the minister who has prayed the first petition, and, at the same time, joins therewith the congregation's prayer for the same blessing. In the first petition, a most important addition has been made to the *Confiteor* of the Roman Order, in that Original Sin is included, and made prominent. The German traces sin from the act to its source in Original Sin; the English begins with the source, and shows how it has developed in outward manifestations.

B. *The Declaration of Grace.*

Almighty God; our heavenly Father, hath had mercy upon us, and given His only Son to die for us, and for His sake forgiveth us all our sins. To them that believe on His Name, He also giveth power to become the sons of God, and bestoweth upon them His Holy Spirit. He that believeth, and is baptized shall be saved. Grant this, O Lord, unto us all. Amen.

In this form, the declaration is found in Mecklenburg, 1552. It is often, but improperly, called an absolution. An absolution is, however, the individualization of the general promise of the Gospel, the application to the individual of the forgiveness which is offered to all. Such absolution cannot be spoken to an entire congregation, or even to two or three persons, but only to one. In a wide sense, the term general, as distinguished from private or personal, absolution may be used. But such general absolution occurs wherever the Word of God is preached. Any other form of general absolution detracts either from preaching, on the one hand, or from the personal absolution on the other. The subject was involved in controversy at Nürnberg in 1533, where Brentz and Osiander objected to the custom which previously obtained.[5] Brentz urged that it could not be a true absolution, since it is nowhere read in Scripture, that a mixed assembly could be absolved, in which are found unbelievers, fanatics, impenitents, adulterers, usurers, drunkards, murderers, and where none asks for absolution; that such absolution would be

---

[5] For details see *Kliefoth*, II: 335 sqq.

either conditional, *i. e.* I absolve you, if you have repentance and faith, or unconditional, *i. e.* I absolve, you whether you have or have not repentance and faith. But a conditional absolution is no absolution; and an unconditional absolution of such kind, "is a lie and blasphemy." Luther and the Wittenberg Faculty tried to mediate between the two sides.[6] But Brentz more consistently carried out the Lutheran principle. In the Reformed churches, the public absolution is not objectional, since, according to the Reformed conception, the absolution does not communicate that which it announces.

We have here, therefore, not an absolution, but only a declaration of the Order of Salvation, and its general offer to the sinners who have confessed. A more admirable and thoroughly logical statement could scarcely be framed:

1. *God's General Benevolence. His Antecedent Will.*

(*a.*) His pity for fallen man. "Hath had mercy upon us," *i. e.* from all eternity, as he foresaw our fall.

(*b.*) His provision for man's recovery. "And given his only son to die for us."

(*c.*) The fruits of this mercy and redemption. "For his sake forgiveth us all our sins." All being redeemed by Christ, all through Christ are potentially forgiven. There is forgiveness for all, though all do not avail themselves of it.

2. *God's Special Benevolence. His Consequent Will.*

(*a.*) The Manner; (*b.*) The Means, by which the forgiveness provided for all is bestowed. The manner—Faith, Regeneration, the Holy Spirit. The means—Faith, Baptism.

3. *Prayer* that the Holy Spirit may work this faith, and apply to each heart the forgiveness which, for Christ's sake, belongs to it.

In Döber's Mass (1525) where the outlines of this form are found, it ends: "Be it to each according to his faith. Pray God for me. I also will do likewise." (Löhe).

---

[6] See De Wette's *Luther's Briefen*, IV: 480 sqq.

THE SERVICE PROPER.

Löhe has said that every complete Service is a mountain with two summits: The preaching of the Word is one, the administration of the sacrament is the other. As Sinai is higher than Horeb, so the latter rises above the former. We reach both by a gradual ascent.

First Act—The Word.

Part I. A. *The Introit.* The normal Lutheran service always begins with the Introit. "In this there is complete agreement among all Lutheran Orders until the middle of the XVII. Century" (Kliefoth), the only exceptions being in the occasional use of introductory hymns or psalms, and the confessional service just considered. To what has been already said in chapter XX., we add the following:

The Introits appear first in Gregory the Great, and in the essential form which they have since had. Every Introit consists of three parts: An Antiphon, a Psalm and the Gloria Patri. The Antiphon presents, by means of a brief passage of Scripture (with a few exceptions from the Psalms), the leading thought of the particular day. The Psalm is a brief passage from the Psalms, in which the joy of the heart at what the Antiphon announces, finds expression. Originally an entire Psalm was chanted here. This usage can be traced from the fact that, of the sixty-one Introits included in the appended table, fifty-two have as the Psalm-verse, the first verse of the Psalm used, the intention generally being that the entire Psalm should follow. Where the verse is not the first of a Psalm, the Introit, as a rule, has begun with the first verse, or first and second verses, which is then followed by the rest of the Psalm.

TABLE OF INTROITS.

	Antiphon.	Psalm.
I. Sunday in Advent.	Ps. 25: 1–3 a.	25: 4.
II. " " "	Zach. 9: 4. / Is. 30: 30. / Is. 30: 29.	80: 1.
III. " " "	Phil. 4: 4-6.	85: 1.
IV. " " "	Is. 45: 8.	19: 1.
Christmas.	Is. 9: 6.	98: 1.
Sunday after Christmas.	(Ps. 93: 5, 2).	95: 1.
Circumcision.	(Ps. 8: 1, 4).	Is. 63: 16.
Epiphany.	Mal. 3: 1.	Ps. 72: 1.
I. Sunday after Epiphany.	Is. 6: 1. / Rev. 19: 6.	100: 1.
II. " " "	Ps. 66: 4.	66: 1, 2.
III., IV., V. " "	Ps. 97: 7, 8.	97: 1.
VI. Sunday " "	Ps. 77: 18.	84: 1.
Septuagesima.	Ps. 18: 5, 6.	18: 1, 2.
Sexagesima.	Ps. 44: 23–25.	44: 1.
Quinquagesima.	Ps. 31: 2, 3.	31: 1.
Ash Wednesday.	Ps. 57: 2; 1 b.	57: 1 a.
I. Sunday in Lent.	Ps. 91: 15, 16.	91: 1.
II. " " "	Ps. 25: 6, 2 b., 22.	25: 1.
III. " " "	Ps. 25: 15, 16.	25: 1.
IV. " " "	Is. 66: 10.	122: 1.
V. " " "	Ps. 43: 1, 2.	43: 3.
VI. " " "	Ps. 22: 19, 21.	22: 1.
Monday in Holy Week.	Ps. 35: 1, 2.	35: 3.
Tuesday and Thursday in H.W.	Gal. 6: 14.	46: 1.
Wednesday in Holy Week.	Phil. 2: 10, 8.	5: 1, 2.
Good Friday.	Is. 53: 3–6.	5: 1, 2.
Easter.	Ps. 139: 18, 5, 6. / or, / Luke 24: 6 a., 5 b., 6 b., 7.	139: 1, 2. / / 8: 5 b., 6 a.
First Sunday after Easter.	1 Pet. 2: 2.	81: 1.
Second " " "	Ps. 33: 5, 6.	33: 1.
Third " " "	Ps. 66: 1, 2.	66: 3.
Fourth " " "	Ps 98: 1 a., 2 b.	98: 1 b.
Fifth " " "	Is. 48: 20.	100: 1.
Ascension Day.	Acts 1: 11.	47: 1.
Sunday after Ascension.	Ps. 27: 7, 9.	27: 1.

Excursus on the Typical Lutheran Chief Service. 293

	Antiphon.	*Psalm.*
Whitsunday.	Wisd. 1 : 7 a. Ps. 68 : 3.	68 : 1.
Trinity Sunday.	Partly from Job 12 : 6. Partly ecclesiastical. or, Is. 6 : 3. Rom. 11 : 36.	8 : 1 8 : 1.
First Sunday after Trinity.	Ps. 13 : 5, 6.	13 : 1.
Second " " "	Ps 18 : 18 b., 19.	18 : 1, 2 a.
Third " " "	Ps. 25 : 16, 18.	25 : 1, 2 a.
Fourth " " "	Ps. 27 : 1, 2.	27 : 3.
Fifth " " "	Ps. 27 : 7, 9 b.	27 : 1 a.
Sixth " " "	Ps. 28 : 8, 9.	28 : 1.
Seventh " " "	Ps. 47 : 1.	47 : 3.
Eighth " " "	Ps. 48 : 9, 10.	48 : 1.
Ninth " " "	Ps. 54 : 4, 5.	54 : 1
Tenth " " "	Ps 55 : 16, 18 a, 19 a., 22 a	55 : 1
Eleventh " " "	Ps 68 : 5 b., 6 a., 35 b	68 : 1
Twelfth " " "	Ps. 70 : 1, 2 a.	70 : 2 b.
Thirteenth Sunday after Trinity.	Ps. 74 : 20 a., 21 a., 23 a.	74 : 1.
Fourteenth " " "	Ps. 84 : 9, 10 a.	84 : 1.
Fifteenth " " "	Ps. 86 : 1 a., 2 b., 3.	86 : 4.
Sixteenth " " "	Ps. 86 : 3, 5.	86 : 1 a.
Seventeenth " " "	Ps. 119 : 137, 124.	119 : 1.
Eighteenth " " "	Eccles. 36 : 16, 17 a.	122 : 1.
Nineteenth Sunday after Trinity.	Ps. 35 : 3 b. Ps. 34 : 17. Ps. 48 : 14 a.	78 : 1.
Twentieth Sunday after Trinity.	Dan. 9 : 14 b. Song of the Three Children [3 : 20. Ps. 119 : 124. Ps 51 : 1.	48 : 1.
Twenty-first Sunday aft. Trinity.	Esther 13 : 9, 10, 11.	119 : 1.
Twenty-second " " "	Ps. 130 : 3, 4.	130 : 1, 2 a.
Twenty-third " " "	Jer. 29 : 11, 12, 14.	85 : 1.
Twenty-fourth " " "	Ps. 95 : 6, 7.	95 : 1.
Twenty-fifth " " "	Ps. 31 : 9 a., 15 b.	31 : 1.
Twenty-sixth " " "	Ps. 54 : 1, 2.	54 : 5.

Twenty-seventh or whenever last Sunday occurs, repeat Introit for Twenty-third.

The Introit was chanted as the minister entered the church. Some derived the name, from the fact that originally a Psalm was sung by the choir, as the people entered. The Antiphon was chanted by the choir, representing the chorus of angels that chanted at Bethlehem, or, as Gerbert suggests, the chorus of Old Testament prophets,[1] and the Psalm formed the response of the congregation. The chanting of the Introit by the congregation, was deemed inappropriate, since it is its office to announce to the congregation what God has for it on that day. The opening word for the Introit gave the name of the day. Hence *Cantate*, *Rogate*, *Jubilate*, Sundays. The *Gloria Patri* follows every Psalm, and hence its position here, after the Psalm-verse. Originally its form was: "Glory to the Father, through the Son, in the Holy Ghost," or "Glory to the Father, in the Son, and the Holy Ghost." But from the time of the Arian controversy, it assumed its present form. So also "As it was in the beginning," etc., was added first in the East, and afterwards in the West, as the Council of Vaison (A. D. 529) declares: "Because of the craftiness of heretics, maintaining that the Son of God was not always with the Father, but had begun to be in time."

B. THE KYRIE. The glory of the divine goodness manifested by what the Introit has announced, has been celebrated in the Gloria Patri. But the greater the manifestation of divine goodness, the deeper the humiliation. The Kyrie is not a confession of sin, but a confession of wretchedness to be borne as a consequence of sin now forgiven, as long as life lasts, Rom. 7: 24. When the blind man cried out "Thou Son of David, have mercy on me," Matth. 9: 27, he did not confess his sins, but prayed that his infirmity might be removed. So we also pray for the removal of the blindness which obstructs from us the full light of heavenly grace. Even amidst the glory of New Testament light, the sighing of the Old Testament prophets is heard.

[1] "The choir as the voice of the Church Universal, specifically of the O. T. Church." Schoeberlein *Liturgische Ausbau*, p. 246.

Is. 33: 2: "O Lord be gracious unto us; we have waited for thee." From the Kyrie, the Litany seems to have originated, (Calvor). According to pre-Reformation practice, the Kyrie is sometimes said in Greek in our Lutheran churches. The reason may be learned from that suggested by Bona for its use in Greek in the Roman Mass. "The Latins say the *Kyrie* in Greek; they also say *Amen, Hallelujah, Sabaoth*, and *Hosanna* in Hebrew, perhaps to show that there is one Church, consisting first of Hebrews and Greeks, and then also of Latins." He adds that thus the mysteries of the faith are transmitted in the three tongues in which the superscription above the cross was written, and quotes from Augustine (Epistle 178), that "just as by the term *Homöousion* one substance of the Trinity is believed by all the faithful, so by the *Kyrie Eleison* the nature of one God is besought by all Latins and barbarians, to be merciful." In perfect harmony with this, Bugenhagen says in the Brunswick Order of 1531: "It would be well that, as we do not change the Hebrew words '*Amen,*' '*Hallelujah,*' '*Hosanna,*' after the example of the Holy Apostles, who although in the New Testament, they wrote Greek, did not change those words; so also we would translate the *Kyrie Eleison* and *Christe Eleison*, which are Greek, into German. . . By Greek writing, the whole New Testament has been produced, and we dare not so completely cast aside everything that is Greek. You can easily understand, unless you obstinately despise it, when you are once told that '*Kyrie Eleison*' means 'Lord, have mercy,' and '*Christe Eleison,*' 'Christ, have mercy.' But if you want to be so rigidly German, you must not even say 'Christ, have mercy,' but '*Du Gesalbter*, have mercy.'"

C. The GLORIA IN EXCELSIS. The minister now comforts the congregation. He has gone down with them into the depths of their wretchedness, and now, from these depths, he looks up, and bids them look up with him, "unto the hills whence cometh their help." At once, faith in the hearts of the people is roused to action, and takes the word from God's lips. First, in the song of the angels, they celebrate the divine goodness. Then again, the contrast between God's Love and their disposition towards it, awakens within the *Gloria* a second *Kyrie*. Then once more, the thought of their own need is forgotten, as the song of triumph in the three-fold ascription of Glory to Christ alone, ends the strain. The "Gloria Major" is without doubt one of the very oldest hymns of the Christian Church. It is sometimes, though without sufficient evidence, ascribed to Bishop Telesphorus (127–138), by others, to Hilary, bishop of Poictiers (†368), although it is probably earlier. It is found in the "Apostolical Constitutions" (Second or Third Century), which sufficiently establishes its Eastern origin. It occurs there in the following form: "Glory be to God in the highest, and upon earth peace, good-will among men. We praise Thee, we glorify Thee, we worship Thee by Thy great High Priest; Thee, who art the true God, who art the One Unbegotten, the only accessible Being. For Thy great glory, O Lord and heavenly King, O God the Father Almighty, O Lord God, the Father of Christ, the immaculate Lamb, who taketh away the sin of the world, receive our prayer, Thou that sittest upon the cherubim. For thou only art holy, Thou only art the Lord Jesus, the Christ of the God of all created nature, and our King, by whom glory, honor and worship be to Thee." Luther says that it neither grew, nor was made upon earth, but came directly from Heaven.

With the *Gloria in Excelsis*, the first part of the act of the Word ceases. The congregation has been prepared for the Word itself, and then proceeds to its reception. The sacrificial element has thus far prevailed. Now the sacramental is to preponderate.

Part II.—A.—THE SALUTATION introduces the sacramental part of the Service, whether it be the administration of Word or Sacrament, that is to follow. Through his minister, Christ salutes us when about to make his abode within us. Thus the angel to the virgin, Luke 1 : 23. The Response follows Ruth 2 : 4, or 2 Tim. 4 ; 22. The Salutation and Response are not, however, confined to the sacramental act. As seen in the Matin and Vesper Services, they belong to the Collects. "By this frequent repetition of this greeting and Response, the bonds of love and unity between pastor and people are tied anew." (Löhe). "The meaning is: 'May the Lord abide in you, and give efficacy to your petitions' (Durandus), or the priest says that he is at peace with both clergy and people (Damianus), or the attention is aroused to prayer (Rupertus); for it is not God nor Christ, but 'the Lord be with you,' since 'Lord' signifies power (Turrecrem)." (Gavanti). The minister prays for his people. The people pray for their minister; and then they unitedly pray for one another.

B. THE COLLECTS. The "Let us pray," indicates that the people are to join in the prayer, which may be done either silently or in subdued voice. Again we refer to what is said in Chapter XX. As the Collect is to be a prayer of the people, the earlier Lutheran Orders evidently restricted the number, in order that those well known to the people might be used. As originally in the Gregorian Order, only one Collect was to be used. The meaning of the term is not certain. It is either the united or the collected prayer of the entire congregation—the minister has prayed for his people in the Salutation, and they have prayed for the minister in the Response—or a prayer made by a collected congregation, or a prayer that collects and concentrates the thought of Gospel and Epistle. Its office here is to prepare the congregation for the reception of the special Word, pertaining to the day, announced by the Introit, and now about to be read.

The Collects for the Sundays and chief festivals are almost entirely of Pre-Reformation origin, from the Leonine (440), Gelasian (492), and Gregorian (596) Sacramentaries.

The following may be noted, as *Leonine:* III. Sunday after Easter, IV. XII. and XIII. after Trinity. *Gelasian:* II., III., IV. Advent, Christmas Eve, Christmas Day, I. Other Collect for Advent, Palmarum, Easter Eve, Easter Day, II., IV. V. after Easter, Sunday after Ascension, I., III.. V., VI, VII., VIII.,

IX., X., XI., XIV., XV., XVII., XVIII., XIX., XX. after Trinity. *Gregorian:* I. Advent, Sunday after Christmas, II. Other Collect for Advent, Epiphany, I., II., III., IV., V. after Epiphany, Septuagesima, Sexagesima, Quinquagesima, II., III., IV., V. Sundays in Lent, Monday, Tuesday and Wednesday in Holy Week. Other Easter Collects, I. after Easter, I. for Ascension, Whitsunday, Monday, in Whitsun-week, XVI., XXI., XXII., XXIII , XXIV. after Trinity.[8] In comparing them with the Anglican Collects, it must be remembered that, after the Third Sunday after Trinity, the Anglican Collects fall one Sunday behind, and that elsewhere, as in the first three Sundays in Advent, the Anglicans have composed new Collects, while we retain the ancient Collects.

The structure of the Collect is always the same. It embraces one main petition, consists of but one sentence, asks through the merits of Christ, and ends with an ascription to the Holy Trinity. Its parts as well analyzed by English writers, such as Neale,[9] are: 1. Invocation. 2. Antecedent Reason. 3. Petition. [4. Benefit]. 5. Conclusion, The fourth part is not always found. The conclusions are uniform even when not so designated. If to the Father: "Per Dominum nostrum Jesum Christum, Filium tuum, qui tecum vivit et regnat in unitate Spiritus sancti, Deus per omnia saecula saeculorum ;" if to the Son : "qui vivis et regnas cum Deo Patre in unitate," etc. "That no prejudice may be shown the other persons of the Godhead, not addressed in the prayer." (Gavanti).

There are no versicles for the Collects at this part of the service. The Collect is followed by the "Amen," to be said or

---

[8] From Gerbert's *Monumenta veteris Liturgiae Alemannicae,* supplemented by Muratori's *Liturgia Romana.*

[9] The distribution can be traced, as far back as Thomas Aquinas (*Summa Summarum.* 2, 2. Q. 83, Art. XVII.,) who tries to apply to it 1 Tim. 2: 1. He says: "In the Collect for Trinity Sunday, '*Almighty and Everlasting God*' pertains to the raising of the mind to God; '*Who hast given unto us Thy servants,*' pertains to thanksgiving; '*We beseech Thee that Thou wouldest keep,*' pertains to petition; '*Through our Lord,*' to supplication."

sung by the congregation, according to 1 Cor. 14: 10; Neh. 8: 6.

THE LESSONS. That there are two lessons, the Epistle and the Gospel, is traceable to the Service of the synagogue, where on every Sabbath, a lesson from the Law and one from the prophets, was read. The entire Pentateuch was divided into sections corresponding to the weeks of the year, so that it was annually read through.

C. THE EPISTLE is the Word of the Christian Law; with all its greater depth and breadth as set forth in the New Testament. In his first liturgical writing, the *Formula Missae*, Luther has not understood this, when he attacks the selections made, on the ground that they are not such epistle lessons as treat of faith and Christ.

"The Epistle which is read before the Gospel pertains to the ministry of John." (Gerbert *Monumenta Veteris Liturgiae*, III: 151). The Epistle is taken sometimes from the Old, and sometimes from the New Testament. For John was the way between those who preceded and followed, intermediate between Apostles and Prophets. For the Law and Prophets were until John. 'What is the Law,' asks Justin' Martyr. 'The Gospel which is proclaimed. What is the Gospel The Law which is fulfilled.' St. Augustine: 'In the Old and New Testaments the things are the same; but there they are adumbrated, here revealed; there prefigured,' here manifested. On Lord's Days the Epistle is conformed to the Law from the New Testament, since now we are under the law of grace, which, since the resurrection, the Lord's Day represents, and which now illumines the whole world. The Epistle precedes: 1. Because it designates the office which John exercised before Christ; for he went before the face of the Lord to prepare his ways. (Rupert, Innocent, Alex. de Ales., Durand.) 2. Because the Apostles were sent two and two before the Lord. (*Alcuin*). 3. Because God does not make the manifestation of his power and goodness all at once; but first less, and afterwards more. What he spoke himself contains more perfect manifestation than what he spoke by the Apostles. 4. That the mind of the hearers may advance from the reception of what is less to what is greater, and thus gradually ascend from the lowest to the highest (Walafried Strabo.) (J. S. Durantus, *De Ritibus Ecc. Catholicae.*) [9]

D. *Hallelujah.* With the consciousness of the forgiveness of sins imparted by the preceding part of the Service, the congregation receives even the Law with joy. Having in view the Gospel which is still to be read, the Law has lost its terrors; it is written in the heart, Heb. 8: 10, and hence is greeted with an exultant "Hallelujah."

This is an inheritance from the Jewish Church, and hence comes appropriately after the Christian Law. So often does it occur in Ps. 113–118, that this section of the Psalms is often called "The Great Hallelujah." It is probable that the latter portion of this (Ps. 115–118) was chanted by our Lord as "the hymn," at the last passover. Thus it points to his sacrifice. In Rev. 19: 1, it is the triumphant hymn of the hosts of Heaven. Hence it is not translated, since it belongs no more to any particular language of earth, but to the vocabulary of spiritually minded men and angels. This explains Luther's rule that it must never be omitted from the service. "*Allelujah enim vox perpetua est ecclesiae, sicut perpetua est memoria passionis et victoriae ejus.*" Later Lutheran usage, following that of the early Church, has sanctioned its suppression during the Passion Season, upon the principle that Luther's rule, if strictly applied, would forbid all penitential services.

In connection with the Hallelujah, a prolific musical and poetical growth of graduals, sequences, proses, tracts and hymns arose. They prolonged and complicated the Service. Even Cardinal Bona maintains that "some very foolish ones crept in." [10] But the chief objection was the doctrinal impurity by which they were pervaded. Some of our best hymns came from this source. Luther translated a number of them; and if a pure

---

[9] *Editio Lugduni*, 1675, p. 241.
[10] *Rerum Liturgicarum Libri*, III: 141.

hymnody of sufficient extent could have arisen, the Hallelujah would have had more extensive supplement than now. In his *Formula Missae*, Luther specifies a few whose retention he approved.

E. *The Gospel.* Here we find not only the summit of the First Act reached, but the saving deed which the day celebrates, is clearly declared. It is no longer the Apostolic doctrine concerning Christ, but it is Christ Himself who is evidently set forth. We see Him in all his concrete personality move before us; we hear his very words. Hence we rise in reverent adoration. In former days, men of war unsheathed their swords and listened with drawn weapons, ready to defend the truth of that which was heard. Elsewhere, weapons previously in hand, were laid down, in adoration of the Great Conqueror, before whose words all earthly power must yield. The infirm laid away their staffs, and listened with uncovered heads. In the Ethiopic Order, the Gospel was introduced by the words: "Arise and hear the Gospel and good message of our Lord and Saviour Jesus Christ."

F. "Glory be to Thee, O Lord," not only expresses the first bound of joy at the very announcement of a message from the Lord, but also enables the congregation to rise without any awkward break in the Service.

"Praise be to Thee, O Lord," is usual in our Lutheran liturgies. It is an appropriate doxology in response to the Gospel, and marks the close of the second part of the Act of the Word. Those who superficially object to it, that it sounds as though the people were thankful that an end had come to the lesson, may answer whether then the singing of a doxology at the close of the Service, would not mean that the people are thankful that a tedious sermon has ended. Profane criticism can ridicule anything sacred.

PART III. A. THE CREED. This is introductory and subordinate to the Sèrmon. In a few Orders, it directly follows; but in most, it precedes. In the latter case, its office is to give a summary of the faith as a whole before the minister expands the part contained in the Gospel for the day. The whole horizon of the faith sweeps before the view, and, then, the hearers are prepared to enter the one limited part. 'Where it follows the Sermon, as in the Reformation of Cologne, it is as the affirmative answer to the Sermon. Another explanation is sometimes given: "The Creed is recited after the Gospel, that while, by the Holy Gospel, there is faith unto righteousness; by the Creed, there may be confession with the mouth unto salvation." (Durandus). "After Christ has spoken to his people, it is proper for them to express their belief the more ardently and intently, as it is written in the Gospel of John that they did, who had heard the word from the Samaritan woman." (Gerbert).

The Creed generally prescribed in Lutheran Liturgies, is the Nicene. There is precedent for the Apostles' Creed, and that, too, in the earlier Orders, Doeber's (1525) and Bugenhagen's, of the same year; but this is rare. The Apostles' Creed, as the Baptismal Confession, belongs properly to the Baptismal Service, and the subordinate weekly and daily services. The Nicene Creed is the Communion Confession, and belongs whenever this is administered; the two Creeds corresponding to the two Sacraments. Luther's metrical version of the Nicene, was more common and occasionally, even the Athanasian was used, as on Trinity Sunday and at Ordinations. The *Te Deum* also was used at times. Because of its confessional character, the latter was sometimes called the "Ambrosian-Augustinian Symbol."

B. THE SERMON. A number of our Orders provide for this under the direction: "Explanation of the Gospel." The whole Service is thrown into confusion, if that towards which its several parts lead be neglected, and some other than the focal topic be introduced. Not that which for the moment is nearest the heart of the minister, nor that which is nearest the heart of the individual members, but that which is so arranged that the entire contents of the divine Word are unfolded and communicated in a complete cycle, will afford most permanent edification, and maintain the interest of devout people. The service of the minister on the pulpit ends with the *Votum*, intended to summon the people to join in the succeeding psalmody, with which they are occupied, while he descends from the pulpit, and takes his place before the altar.

C. THE OFFERTORY. This is so different from the Offertory in the Roman Mass, that it seems scarcely proper to retain the name. As we use it, the reference is to psalmody, "adapted either to the Sermon, or to repentance, or to the Holy Supper." (Calvor).

D. THE GENERAL PRAYER. Here the analogy of the Roman Mass has been followed. The General Prayer has its origin in the long series of petitions attached to the Roman Offertory, which were mostly connected with the worship of saints, prayers for the dead, etc. The Lutheran Church, going back to a purer tradition, and eliminating these elements, found this the proper place to pray for all sorts and conditions of men. For the cry of repentance has led to the thought that there are others comprehended in the same sin, the same redemption, and the same forgiveness.

The office of the General Prayer is, therefore, to present most forcibly the Church as the communion of saints, where the end of all our prayers for men, is that they may be brought to repentance and faith, and, through repentance and faith, experience the fullness of the divine blessings, both temporal and eternal. Luther presented, as a proper form for general prayer, a paraphrase of the Lord's Prayer, expanding its petitions at length, and was followed in this by a number of Orders. Elsewhere the Litany or the *Te Deum* was used, or several Collects were combined, as in the Brandenburg-Nürnberg of 1533. The first General Prayer of the Common Service is, except the first paragraph, in the Strassburg Order of 1598, and is probably considerably older. In its main features, it is found in the Austrian Order of 1571.

The Litany, presented for use in many of the Orders, where there is no communion, was greatly changed by Luther in his revision of 1529, as shown above in Chapter XVIII. He transposed "from all sin" to before "all evil;" inserted "by thine agony and bloody sweat," "in all time of our tribulation, in all time of our prosperity;" changed to its present form, "to preserve all pastors and ministers," etc.; and either originated or greatly enlarged all the intercessions of the same group. In the second group, only the first intercession is in the Roman Mass; the rest are by Luther. The third group is entirely by Luther. In the fourth, he amended "*omnibus benefactoribus*" so as to read "*hostibus, persecutoribus et calumniatoribus nostris*," i. e. where the old Litany reads: "To repay everything good to our benefactors," Luther reads: "To forgive our enemies, persecutors and slanderers, and to turn their hearts." This is a fulfilment of the passage: "Ye have heard that it hath been said by them of old, etc., but I say unto you," Matth. 5 : 21 sqq. The prayers at the close of the Litany, he reduced to the form of Collects, and greatly changed. Thus, except at the beginning, it is almost a new Litany. Its structure has been analyzed as follows: 1. The Simple Kyrie. 2. Invocations. 3. Deprecations, beginning "from." 4. Obsecrations, beginning "by" and ' in." 5. Intercessions, through the prayer for "enemies." 6. Supplications, for "fruits of the earth," and "answer to prayer." 7. The expanded Kyrie. 8. Simple Kyrie. 9. Lord's Prayer. 10. Versicles, and Collects. "It is the general prayer of the Christian Church under all necessities and conditions. We must carefully avoid narrowing its significance. It is not *e. g.* a mere penitential prayer; like every true prayer, it contains this element, but is not confined to this. It is a prayer in every necessity, not only against sin, but also against all evil. It is not a mere cry of anguish, belonging only to times of trouble; it is a prayer not merely against all evil, but for all good. The Pomeranian Agende goes so far as to prescribe the Litany for the Saturday Vesper Service in the place of the *Magnificat*, and to have it sung in one and the same week-day Service with, and, that too, even before the *Te*

Deum." [10] Luther pronounced it, next the Lord's Prayer, the very best that could be made.

SECOND ACT. THE COMMUNION.

On the relation of the Communion, to the rest of the Service: "To Luther, Word and Sacraments are the objective foundations of the Church, and, accordingly, the objective factors of the Service, as the means of grace whereby the individual comes into possession of the blessings of salvation; the Lord's Supper especially as a sacrament is regarded not merely the highest and most impressive announcement and assurance of grace, but also as the objective sealing of grace. Hence the Lord's Supper forms the summit of the Service, as well on its objective, as on its subjective side: inasmuch as in the celebration of the sacrament the gracious declaration of the Gospel is completed and given especial power, and the appropriation of salvation on the part of the congregation is accomplished. Hence while the Service has indeed to Luther the office of instructing in salvation, so far as he keeps the preaching of the Word in view, he regards it also as a sealing of salvation, a communication of grace, not merely in the Lord's Supper, but also in the Word. He, therefore, finds the sum and summit of the entire Service in the Communion, in the Eucharist." [11]

For this reason, the separation of the communion from the preaching Service, is entirely foreign to the spirit of the Gospel as apprehended by the Lutheran Church. The "Communion Address," which replaces the Sermon in some churches, is an importation from the Reformed Church, and cannot be liturgically justified. There is no proper Service, without the preaching of the Word; [12] there is no complete Service, without Word and Sacrament.

Part I. *Introduction*—A. SALUTATION, as in beginning of Act I., Part I. "May he be present by his grace, who is always

---

[10] Kliefoth's *Liturgische Abhandlungen*, VIII. (V) p. 71.
[11] Koestlin's *Geschichte des Christlichen Gottesdienstes.*
[12] See Luther's *Von Ordenung Gottesdiensts.*

present by his Omnipotence. For not all are with him in the manner in which he said: "Lo, I am with you alway, nor is He with all, in the manner of which we say: 'The Lord be with you.'" (Durandus).

B. THE PREFACE. This is the oldest and most unchanged form of the Service. It was in use already in the time of Tertullian. It begins with the *Sursum Corda*, continues in the *Gratias*, and is then embodied in the *Dignum et justum*, with special ('*proper*') prefaces for the chief festivals, chiefly from the Gregorian Sacramentary.

(*a*). The SURSUM CORDA, found in the Greek form: ἄνω τὰς καρδίας· μηδὲν γήϊνον ἡγήσασθε. "Lift up your hearts; think of nothing earthly." An exposition of this is given by Cyprian in his treatise "On the Lord's Prayer:" "When we stand praying, beloved brethren, we ought to be watchful and earnest with our whole heart intent on our prayers. Let all carnal and worldly thoughts pass away, nor let the soul at that time think on anything, but the object only of its prayer. For this reason also the priest, by way of preface before his prayer, prepares the minds of the brethren by saying 'Lift up your hearts,' that so upon the people's answer: 'We lift them up unto the Lord,' he may be reminded that he himself ought to think of nothing but the Lord. How can you ask to be heard of God, when you yourself do not hear yourself?" Cyril: "It is necessary at that important hour to lift our hearts to God, and not to sink them to earth and earthly things. In this sentence, therefore, we are commanded to relinquish, in that hour, all cares and domestic anxieties, and to have the heart in Heaven with God, the Lover of the human race." Augustine: "The hearts of believers are in Heaven, because daily directed towards Heaven, when the priest says: 'Lift up your hearts,' and they confident reply: 'We lift them up unto the Lord.'"

(*b*.) Augustine's explanation of the GRATIAS, is: "That we lift up our hearts to the Lord is by God's gift; for which gift, then, we are bidden to give thanks to our Lord God."

(*c.*) DIGNUM: "To praise God above all things is meet, so far as God is concerned; for he is our Lord God; it is just, so far as we are concerned; because we are his people. It is *meet*, because Thou hast made us by Thy pure will; it is *just*, because Thou hast redeemed us by Thy pure mercy; it is *right*, because Thou dost gratuitously justify us; it is *salutary*, because Thou dost perpetually glorify us." (Innocentius, quoted by Durandus).

C. THE SANCTUS. Having offered numerous petitions for the Church on earth, the congregation of believers now unites with the Church in Heaven which does not need its prayers, in the angelic trisagion. For it is about to sit in heavenly places with Christ Jesus. The *Benedictus* from the Great Hallelujah (Ps. 118: 26) of the Passover, added to the *Sanctus*, tells that Christ is now coming to his people through his real presence in the Lord's Supper. They are to eat and drink in remembrance not of an absent, but of a truly present, though unseen Lord. Hence they exclaim: "Blessed be he that cometh in the name of the Lord—Hosanna." As the *Sanctus* emphasizes the divine, the *Benedictus* emphasizes the human nature of of our Lord. Luther separated the *Sanctus* from the *Preface*, in order probably to bring the *Benedictus* directly before the Consecration. The *Hosanna* is found in the earliest Communion Service on record, viz , that in "The Teaching of the Twelve Apostles." (Chapter IX., § 6).

D. THE EXHORTATION. Composed by Volprecht of Nürnberg, 1525, is unliturgical, and causes a break in the Service; since this is not the place for preaching. It was prepared to answer the necessity for instructing the people, who had been raised under Romish error, concerning the true significance of the Lord's Supper. In the original, it is much longer. The edifying character of its teaching has made it especially dear to the Lutheran Church, and, even when not used, its presence in the book gives an excellent practical exposition of the doctrine of the Lord's Supper. The Exhortation took the place of the *Sancta Sanctis*, τὰ ἅγια τοῖς ἁγίοις, of the early Church, *i. e.* "Holy things for holy persons." "If any one be not holy, let him not approach. He does not say 'absolutely free from sin,' but 'holy;' for not absolute freedom from sin, but the presence of the Spirit, makes holy." (Chrysostom).

PART II. CONSECRATION.

The Consecration properly speaking consists only of the Words of Institution. *Accedit verbum ad elementum et fit sacramentum.* But without prayer, we cannot come at Christ's invitation, to partake of what He is about to give.

A. THE LORD'S PRAYER. This prayer is not really consecratory, so far as the elements are concerned; but it is consecratory of the believers who are ready to receive the heavenly blessings. We have heard: "Blessed is he that cometh in the name of the Lord;" and in the Lord's Prayer, we go forth to meet the coming King. "That a prayer given by the Lord is preferred to any furnished by the Church, is explained because at this center of the communion act, we prefer to deal with the Lord alone and to use no words other than his." [13] The doxology to the Prayer is here omitted. That it is not simply the prayer of the officiating minister is manifest from the *Oremus:* "Let us pray." [14] The Lord's Prayer, however highly prized in the Lord's Supper, is not an essential part; and, hence, is omitted in a few Orders.

B. THE WORDS OF INSTITUTION. As they here occur, they are not offered to the congregation to awaken their faith; but are recited to the Lord, in connection with the Lord's Prayer, as a part of the act of prayer. Hence the minister turns, not towards the congregation, but towards the altar, as he reads the words. The significance of the entire act is as though he were to say: "O Lord, we come at Thine invitation; for here are Thy gracious words, unto which Thou wilt assuredly be faithful." Great stress is laid upon the neces-

---

[13] Kliefoth, VIII. (V.) 96.
[14] See above, Act I., Part II., B.

sity for clearness and distinctness in the utterance, as over against the inaudible mumbling of the Romish administration of the Mass. The raising of chalice and paten was intended to render everything visible as well as audible.

C. THE PAX. Of this, Luther says: "It is truly the voice of the Gospel announcing the forgiveness of sins, the only and most worthy preparation for the Lord's Table, provided it be apprehended by faith, in no respect different than if it proceeded from the mouth of Christ. Hence I want it announced with face towards the people. It is an absolution of the communicants from sin," *i. e.* "Come hither, and receive from God's own Word, and through the pledges of the very body and blood, which have been given for thy sins, the peace of God which is in reality made ready for thee."

PART III. THE DISTRIBUTION.

A. The AGNUS DEI, sung during the Service, is said to have been introduced by Pope Sergius I. (687–700). It is based on John I: 29. The *Dona nobis pacem* ("Give us thy peace") has been introduced since the XI. Century; and is a reminiscence of the wars and general disorder of that disturbed period. In the Lateran Church at Rome, Alt says that the old form, without the *Dona*, is still maintained; as the Church should be an image of the heavenly Jerusalem, where already all is peace. In the Lutheran Service, it is a beautiful response to the *Pax:*

God's Word: "The Peace of the Lord be with you alway."

Man's Answer: Ah, Lord, Thou knowest how we need what Thou dost here offer. "O Lamb of God, have mercy on me." "Grant me this, Thy peace."

B. THE DISTRIBUTION PROPER. Then the Lord says: "Here is that for which thou prayest. Thou hast been redeemed by Christ's blood. Here is the very Body and the very Blood which purchased thy forgiveness and salvation. Just as certainly as they are here offered thee, just so certainly art thou a redeemed sinner, for whom God has only thoughts of love. Come, receive what God has provided thee. "Take and eat, this is the Body of Christ, given for thee." Take me at my word, and receive my peace.

"Given for thee," is an addition to the formula, referred to Luther.[15] The Catechism tells us that the "for you," are "the chief things in the sacrament," and "require truly believing hearts." "For thee," as a formula of distribution is preferable to "for you," since it is the office of the sacrament to individualize grace.

The Benediction is found in Luther's German Mass of 1526. "Preserve you in true faith," is better than "in *the* true faith," as the reference is to the personal faith of the believer.

The introduction in the same Orders of "true" before Body and Blood, is traced no further than a Brandenburg-Nürnberg Agende of 1591, and then to the Coburg of 1626.[16] The introduction of a confessional statement reflecting the violent controversies of the times, seems out of place, in that moment, when, of all others, the soul is alone with its Saviour. The acceptance of what such formula declares, should be presupposed in every administration.

The sacramental union occurs in the sacramental action, and, therefore, neither until, nor after the taking and eating. The consecration is, therefore, not completed until in the distribution. In his earlier liturgical writings, Luther advises strongly that the bread shall be consecrated and distributed before the wine is consecrated. He argues that this occurred at the institution of the Lord's Supper. This practice preserves the unity of the consecration and distribution. It is adopted in the communion of the sick.

PART IV. POST COMMUNION.

A. The *Nunc Dimittis* is found at this part of the Service in the oldest Lutheran liturgies (Bugenhagen, 1524; Döber, 1525; Strassburg, 1525), although not generally adopted in the XVI.

---

[15] It is not however without precedent in the Oriental Liturgies, although not in this precise form: "Which shall be given for you." (Mozarabic).

[16] Kliefoth VIII., (V.) p. 125

Century. Casaubon, quoted by Calvör, traces it to the Liturgy of Chrysostom, adding: "In most Protestant churches, the entire action of the celebration of the Lord's Supper, is concluded with this hymn, which the people chant on bended knees—which is a most beautiful and holy institution."

The peace offered in the "*Pax*," prayed for in the "*Agnus Dei*," received in the "*Distribution*," is now thankfully acknowledged, "Now lettest Thou Thy servant depart in peace." The child of God is as near Heaven as he can be in this life; nearer yet he one day shall be, when this sinful flesh is entirely put off. He is ready for the blessed exchange this very moment, as he also is ready for everything assigned by his Lord. Whithersoever the Lord sends him, will he go; whatsoever the Lord commands him, will he do. For the peace of God is his; and the salvation of God is a possession, whereof he is so fully conscious that he can exclaim: "Mine eyes have seen Thy salvation."

The use of the *Nunc Dimittis* accords with the practice at the institution, Matth. 26: 30: "When they had sung a hymn, they went out into the mount of Olives."

B. THE VERSICLE. The *Nunc Dimittis*, however, is individual. The thanksgiving is yet to be rendered by the entire congregation. This is introduced by the versicle, which appears first in the Coburg KO of 1626, and afterwards was generally introduced into Lutheran liturgies.

C. THE COLLECT. That adopted in the "Common Service" is from Luther's German Mass of 1526, replacing the Post-Communion of the Roman Mass which abounded in doctrinal corruptions. That heretofore used in the English churches of the General Council is from the Brandenburg-Nürnberg Order of 1533, which, as seen elsewhere, has reappeared, in a revised form, in the Book of Common Prayer.

D. THE BENEDICAMUS is found already in the liturgy of Chrysostom. The Romish Mass has it: "Benedicamus Domino."

"Deo Gratias." "*Gott sei gelobet und gebenedeiet*" is a German metrical rendering.

Of the Service as a whole, it may be said that the First Act is variable, the Second invariable in its parts. In the First, there is a constant change according to the day or season of the Church Year. In the Second, whatever be the day or season, the uniformity is almost complete. The only exception to the variations of the First Act, is the permanence of Kyrie, Gloria in Excelsis, and Creed. The only exceptions to the permanence of the Second Act, are the "Proper" Prefaces, and, where the music is thoroughly elaborated, the melodies of the *Sanctus*, *Agnus Dei* and *Benedicamus*, changing according to the season of the Church Year.

"In a series of acts, covering thousands of years," says Kliefoth, "God has borne his testimony to men, and has spoken to them in thousands of words. So also every one of the people that enters God's house, brings with him an entire world of cares and blessings, joys, necessities, and sins. Varied, too, and manifold, are the ways in which the Word of God finds men, and man finds himself related to the Word. It is right, therefore, that the Act of the Word should present the saving deeds of God to men in their ever fresh richness, and thus lead men to salvation. But all the acts of God, and all the cares and hopes of the human breast, have one goal; so also all divine services and all divine dealings with men, lead to but one goal: Redemption through the Blood of Christ. Hence it is proper, that the act of the Service which gives his Blood, and, in it, the forgiveness of sins, life and salvation, should also be externally one and the same, offering the one thing for all in but one form."[17]

Another general remark is necessary. From the very beginning, the Lutheran Orders recognize that a difference must be made between the cities where the necessary musical resources are at hand for the full rendering of the Service, and the vil-

[17] VIII. (V.) 148 sq.

Excursus on the Typical Lutheran Chief Service. 313

lages and country where they are absent. Care was taken that a modified Service should be provided, in which the structure of the full Service and the significance of its parts were preserved unbroken. The following is a type: 1. German Hymn. 2. Kyrie. 3. Hymn—metrical version of the *Gloria in Excelsis*. 4. Salutation. 5. Collect. 6. Epistle. 7. Hymn. 8. Gospel. 9 Metrical rendering of the Creed. 10. Sermon. 11. General Prayer. 12. Hymn. 13. Preface. 14. Exhortation. 15. Lord's Prayer. 16. Words of Institution. 17. Distribution during the singing of "Christi, Du Lamm Gottes." 18. Post Communion. 19. Benediction. 20. Closing Hymn. (Lüneberg, Calenberg, etc.)

CHAPTER XXV.

THE ANGLICAN CATECHISMS.

Cranmer's Catechism of 1548, a translation of the Nürnberg Catechism of 1533. Changes by Cranmer. Cranmer's Version of Luther's Catechism, in full. The Nürnberg Catechism's theory of "Apostolic Succession."—Archdeacon Hook's mistake. Becon's Catechism dependent on Luther. The Catechism of Dr. John Brentz (1527), the Cassel Catechism (1539), Revision of the Cassel Catechism in Reformation of Cologne (1543). The Church Catechism compared with those of Brentz, Cassel-Cologne and Luther. Catechisms of Ponet and Nowell.

THE Church Catechism is a part of the Book of Common Prayer, being included in the Order for Confirmation. But so important is the history of the development, that it requires separate treatment. We have already noticed the "Bishop's Book" or "Institution of a Christian Man" of 1537, and shown its dependence on Luther's Catechisms.

CRANMER'S CATECHISM.

In 1548 Cranmer made another attempt to supply the want of a popular book of religious instruction, which was published under the following title:

"CATECHISMUS;

That is to say a shorte Introduction into Christian Religion for the synguler commoditie and profyte of childre end yong people. Set forth by the moste reverende father in God Thomas Archbyshop of Canterbury, Primate of all England and Metropolitane. Gualterus Lynne excudebat, 1548."

It was introduced by a dedicatory letter to to Edward VI., in which, after referring to the deplorable ignorance of the people, and the king's desire to remedy it, he continues: "I knowing my selfe as a subjecte greatly bounden to set forward the same, am persuaded that thys my smal trauyall in thys behalfe taken, shall not a lytle helpe the sooner to brynge to passe your godly purpose." Although the sub-title, *i. e.*, the title above the Preface, in the words, "oversene and corrected by the moste reverende father in God, the Archebyshoppe of Canterburie," gives the hint that it was not original, Burnet has entirely overlooked this, in the statement that the Catechism "was wholly his own without the concurrence of any others." At his examination on his trial at Oxford, Cranmer testified that he had translated the Catechism from Justus Jonas; in his "Defence" concerning the Lord's Supper, he speaks of it as "a catechism by me translated," while the testimony of one of his chaplains, Dr. Rowland Taylor, that "he made a catechism to be translated into English," seems to imply that the translation was made under his supervision. Bishop Gardiner already gives the key to this Catechism of Justus Jonas, when in his "Explication and Assertion of the true Catholique Faith, he says: "Justus Jonas hath translated a catechisme out of Douch into Latin, taught in the city of Noremberge in Germanye, where Hosiander is chiefe preacher—which catechisme was translated into English in this auctor's name about two yeares paste."[1]

The Latin Catechism of Justus Jonas mentioned is that whose title is given in Feuerlin's Bib. Symb. (p. 260):

"1122. Catechismus pro pueris et juventute in Ecclesiis et ditione Ill. Principum Marchionum Brandeborgensium et inclyti senatus Norimbergensis breviter conscriptus, e germanico latine redditus per Justum Jonam, addita epistola de laude Decalogiæ. Viteberg, 1539, 8."

Strype's statement[2] that it was made by Justus Jonas, Jr., is incorrect. It is nothing more than the Sermons on the Cate-

---

[1] Quoted in Burton's Cranmer's Catechism, Oxford, 1829, pp. v. vi. A more accessible editon of Cranmer's Catechism, with the part concerning the Sacraments and the Power of the Keys omitted, and the orthography modernized, was published by the Presbyterian Board of Publication, Philadelphia, 1842, in their series of writings of the British Reformers, among the selections from Cranmer.

[2] Strype's *Cranmer*, I: 227.

chism, originally appended to the Brandenburg-Nürnberg *Kirchenordnung* of 1533, and frequently republished since. The *Kirchenordnung* was the joint work of Osiander and Brentz. It is not improbable that it was in preparation while Cranmer was an inmate of Osiander's house.

The changes made by Cranmer are very slight. The chief are the addition of fourteen pages on, "Thou shalt not make unto thee any graven image,"—foretokening the adoption of the Calvinistic division of the commandments—and of a page on the Introduction to the Lord's Prayer; the omission of nineteen lines on the Second, of three lines on the Fourth, and of a page on the Seventh commandment; of six lines and a repetition, on the Third Article of the Creed, and of a paragraph of fifteen lines, on Baptism. When it is borne in mind that, in the edition mentioned, the English Catechism fills two hundred and fourteen pages, it will be noticed that the Archbishop left the body of the Brandenburg-Nürnberg Explanation untouched.

A striking feature of the Brandenburg-Nürnberg Explanation is, that at the close of each sermon the words of Luther's Small Catechism are always recalled, as the sum of what has been said. Its method is synthetic. Instead of beginning with Luther, it discusses the various parts contained in each answer, and then only at the conclusion brings them together. We give as an example the close of the Sermon on Baptism:

"Wherefore, good children, learne these thinges dilygentlye, and when ye be demaunded, What is baptisme, Then you shal answer, Baptism is not water alone, but is water inclosed and joyned to the word of God and to the covenante of God's promise."

By bringing these summaries together, we may, therefore, construct Luther's Catechism, in the earliest English form, thus far discovered, as follows:

CRANMER'S LUTHER'S CATECHISM.

I. THE TEN COMMANDMENTS.

I.

In this precept we be commaunded to feare and love God with al oure harte, and to put our whole trust and confidence in him.

II.

We ought to love and feare God above al thyng, and not to abuse his name to idolatrie, charmes, periure, othes, curses, ribaldrye, and scoffes, that undre the pretence and coloure of his name we begile no man by swearynge, forswearynge, and lyinge, but in al our nedes we should cal vpon hym, magnifie and prayse him, and with oure tongues confesse, utter and declare our faythe in him and his doctrine.

III.

We ought to feare and love our Lord God above all thinges, to heare diligently and reveiently his holy worde, and with all diligence to follow the same.

IV.

We ought to love and dreade our Lorde God, and for his sake to honoure oure parentes, teachers, masters and governors, to obey them and in no wise despise them.

V.

We ought to love and dreade our Lorde God above all thinges, so that for hys sake we hurt not our neyghbour, nether in his name, goodes, cattel, life or body, but that we ayde, comforte, and succour him in all hys necessities, troubles and afflictions.

VI.

We ought above all thynges to love and dreade our Lord God, and for his sake to lyve chastly in wil, worde and dede, and every man is bownde to love and cheryse his wife.

VII.

We ought to feare and love our Lord God above al thinges, and for hys sake willingly to absteine from our neyghbor's goodes and cattell, to take nothing from him, but to helpe him in his neede, and to defende and augment his ryches and commodities.

VIII.

We ought to feare and love oure Lorde God above all thynges, and for his sake to absteyne from all lyinge, backe bytynge, slaunderynge, and yll reportynge, by the whiche oure neyghbour's good name, fame and credit may be impeched or decayed, and rather to excuse, hydde or gentely to enterprete another manne's faute, then maliciously to make the wourste of the same, and wyth the loude trumpe of our tongue to blaste it abrode, to the knowledge of all the towne or place wherein we dwel.

IX.

We oughte to feare and love our Lorde God above all thynges, and for hys sake so to chastise oure eyes and lustes, that we desyer not oure neyghboure's house, nor other thynge belongynge unto hym, but helpe him (as muche as shall lye in us), to retayne and kepe hys landes, goodes and all that is his.

X.

We ought to feare and love our Lord God above al thinges, and for his sake willyngly to absteyne from our neighbour's wife, familie, goodes and cattel, and to helpe hym as muche as lyeth in vs, that he may kepe and possesse the same.

II. THE CREED.

I.

I beleve that God the Father hath made me and al creatures in heaven and earth, that he hath gyven to me and conserveth my bodye and soule, reason, senses, eyes, cares, and all my other members. And I beleve that the same almightye Lorde and God doth dayly gyve to me and to us all, meat, drynke, cloth, wife, children, house, lande, riches, cattell, and all thynges necessarye to the mayntenaunce of our lyves, and that he doth dayly defende, kepe and preserue vs from all perell, and delyver vs from all evel. And all thys he dooth of hys owne mere mercie and goodnes, without our worthynes or deseruynges. For the which benefites it is our dutie to render to hym continuall and everlastyng thankes, to obey hym in all thynges, and to take hede thatt we be not unkynde to hym, that hath shewed so greate kyndnes towardes vs.

II.

I beleve that Jesus Christ, veray God, begotten of God the Father, and and verye manne, borne of the Virgin Marie, is my Lorde, whiche by hys precyouse bloode and holy passyon, hath redeemed me, a myserable and damned wretch, from all my synnes, frome death eternall, and from the tyrannie of the Devell, that I should be his own true subject, and lyve within his kyngdome, and serve hym, in a newe everlastynge lyfe and iustice, even as oure Lorde Christe, after he rose from deathe to lyfe, lyveth and raygneth everlastyngly.

III.

I beleve, that neither by man's strength, power or wysdome, neyther by myne owne endeavor, nor compass of myn owne reason, I am able to beleve in Jesus Christ, or come unto hym. But the Holy Goost did call me by the worde of the gospell, and with the giftes of his grace, he hath hitherto endowed me, and halowed me, and in the true faith, he hathe hitherto preserved and confirmed me, and this he hath not done only to me, but also he calleth and gathereth togyther in the unitye of one faith and one baptisme, all the vniversal churche, that is here on earth, and he halloweth, kepeth and preserveth the same, in the true knowlege of Christ, and faith in his promyses. And in this churche, he giveth free and generall pardon, to me and to al that beleve in him, of al our synnes, offences and trespasses, and at the last day he shall rayse me, and all other that be deade, and all that dyed in the true faith of Jesus Christ, he shall glorifye in the lyfe everlastyng.

III. THE LORD'S PRAYER.

The name of God of it selfe is holy, but here we do aske, that it be halowed of vs. And when you be asked, how it is halowed of us, answere, whan the worde of God is puerly and syncerelye taught, when we leade our lyfe in this worlde holyly and godly, as it becommeth the veray true children of God. Here in this point succour us, good Lorde, helpe us, O heavenly Father. For he that either teacheth or liveth otherwise than the worde of God requireth, he dyshonoreth and polluteth the worde of God.

II.

The kyngdom of God commeth of it selfe, without our prayer, but here we pray that it may com to vs. Whiche commeth to passe, whan the heavenly Father gyveth vs his spirite, to beleve his holye word, to lyve wel and godly, here in his churche, for a tyme, and after in heaven for ever.

III.

Althoughe God's holy wyll be done without our praier, yet we pray that it may be done in vs, and fulfylled amonge vs here in earth. Whiche is done, whan God doeth overthrow and destroy the wicked counsels of the Devell, of worldley people, and of oure owne fleshe (which do all that lieth in theim, to let and hynder the kyngedome of God, and the halowynge of his name) and doeth kepe vs in the true knowledge of hys worde, in the lyvely fayth of Christ, in hys love and obedience of his commandments. For this is the holye and perfecte wyll of God, whiche God graunte vs to keape nowe and ever. Amen.

IV.

God doeth sufficientlye provyde for vs meate and lyvyng without our desyre, nevertheIesse we desyre hym, to graunt vs, that we maye knowe that we have all thynges at his handes, that we may gyve to him due thankes for the same. And yf further anye man wyll aske you, what is mente by his worde, oure dayly breade, you answere that by dayly breade is understande all thinges necessarie for oure lyvynge, as meate, drynke, clothe, house, lande, cattell, monye, housholde stuff, a good wyfe, obedient children, trustye servantes, good governors, a well ordered common wealth, common pease and tranquilitie, seasonable wether, holsome ayer, health of body, constant frendes, honest neighbours, and suche lyke thynges, whereby we maye leade in thys worlde a godly and quiet lyfe.

V.

Herein we desyere that our heavenly Father wil not lnke upon our synnes, and for them, cast vs awaye. For we have not deserved those greate gyftes and grace whiche we desir at God's hands, nor be not worthye to have the same, but we desyer God, that althoughe we dayly offend him, and deserve grevous punishmentes for our synnes, yet he of hys mere grace and mercie wil heare our prayers, and frely forgyve us oure offences And we offer our selves for his sake from the botome of our heartes to forgyve them that have offended vs.

VI.

God tempteth no man. But here we praye, that God wil kepe and defende vs, that the Devel, the world and the fleshe deceave us not, and leadde us not into ungodlynes, ydolatrie, blasphemie, desperation, and other horrible synnes. And althoughe we be tempted with these synnes, yet we desyer God, that at length we may overcome them, and triumphe over them, by the helpe and assistence of the Holy Gost.

VII.

Herein we generally desyre our heavenly Father, to delyver us from all evell and perell, bothe of body, soule, lande, catell and riches. And that when we shall lye on oure deathbed, he wyll than graunt us a good houre, that we maye departe oute of this vale of miserie, in his favour, and from this transitorie lyfe, enter into life everlastynge. The whiche God graunte us all. Amen.

IV. BAPTISM.

I.

Baptism is not water alone, but it is water enclosed and ioyned to the worde of God, and the covenante of God's promyse. And these be the wordes, whereby our Lorde Jesus Christ did ordeine baptisme, which be written in the laste chapter of Saint Mathew. Go and teache al nations, baptisynge them in the name of the Father, and the Sonne, and the Holy Ghost.

II.

And when you shal be asked what auayleth baptisme? you shal answere: Baptisme worketh forgyvnes of synne, it delyvereth from the kyngdome of the

Devel, and from death, and giveth lyfe and everlastyng salvation, to all them that beleue these wordes of Christ, and promyse of God, which are written in the laste chapter of Sainct Marke his gospell, He that wil beleue, and be baptised, shall be saved. But he that wil not beleue shall be damned.

III.

Yf a man aske you, how can water brynge to passe so great thynges? ye shall answer. Uerely the water worketh not these thynges, but the worde of God, whiche is joyned to the water, and fayth whiche dothe beleue the worde of God. For without the worde of God, water is water, and not baptisme, but when the worde of the lyuing God is joyned to the water, then it is baptisme, and water of wonderful holsomnes, and the bath of regeneration, through the Holy Ghost, as Sainte Paul writeth. God saved vs by the bath of regeneration, and renewyng of the Holy Ghost, whom he powred upon vs, plenteously by Jesus Christ our Saviour, that we beyng made righteous by his grace, maye be heyres of everlastyng lyfe

[In another connection: "But peradventure some wil saye. Howe can water worke so greate thynges? To whome I answere, that it is not the water that dothe these thinges, but the almyghtie worde of God (whiche is knyt and joyned to the water), and faith, which receyueth God's worde and promyse. For without the worde of God, water is water, and not baptisme. But when the worde of the living God is added, and ioyned to the water, then it is the bathe of regeneration, and baptisme water, and the lyuely sprynge of eternall salvation, and a bathe that wassheth our soules by the Holy Ghoste, as saynct Paule calleth it saying: God hath saved vs thorowe hys mercye, by the bathe of regeneration, and renewyng of the Holy Gost, whome he hath poured vpon vs plenteously, by Jesus Christ oure Savioure, that we beynge made ryghtuous by his grace, maye be heyres of everlasting lyfe. This is a sure and trewe worde."]

IV.

Yf a man aske you, what doth the baptisynge in the water betoken? aunswere ye, it betokeneth, that olde Adam with all synnes and euel desyers, ought daylye to be kylled in vs, by trewe contricion and repentance; that he may rise againe from death, and after he is risen with Christ, may be a new man, a new creature, and may liue everlastyngly in God, and before God, in rightuousnes and holynes. As saincte Paule wryteth, saying. All we that are baptized, are buried with Christ in to death, that as Christ rose agayne, by the glorie of his Father, so we also should walke in newnes of lyfe.

V. THE LORD'S SUPPER.

Yt is the trew body and trew bloude of our Lorde Jesus Christe which was ordeyned by Christ him selfe, to be eaten and dronken of vs Christen people, vnder the forme of brede and wyne. Furthermore, yf any man wil aske ye, wher is this written? ye shall answer. These be the wordes which the holy Evangelistes Mathewe, Marke, Luke and the Apostle Paul do writ. Our Lorde Jesus Christ the same nyght, etc.

II.

Furthermore yf any man aske ye, what auayleth it, thus to eate and drynke? ye shall answer. These wordes do declare what profit we receave thereby, my bodye which is given for you, my bloude whiche is shed for you, for the forgyuenes of synnes. By the whiche wordes Christe declareth, that by this sacrament and wordes of promyse, are gyuen to us, remission of synnes, lyfe and salvation. For whereas forgyuenes of synne is, ther is also lyfe and salvation.

III.

Againe yf a man wil go further with you, and aske you. How can bodily eatyng and drynkynge have so greate strength and operation? ye shall answer. To eate and to drynke, doth not worke so great thynges, but this worde and promyse of God, my bodye which was giuen for you, my bloude whiche was shede for you, for the remission of sinnes. This worde of God is added to the outward sygnes, as the chiefe thing in this sacramente. He that beleueth these wordes, he hath that thing, whiche the wordes do promyse, that is to saye, forgyvenes of his synnes.

IV.

Besydes this, yf a man aske of you, who be they, that do worthily receave this sacrament? ye shal answere. That fastyng, abstinence and suche other lyke, do perteyne and are profitable for an outward discypline or chasticement of the bodye. But he receaueth the sacrament worthily, that hath faith to beleve these wordes. My bodye whiche was gyven for you, my bloude whiche was shed for you, for the remission of synnes. But he that belueth not the wordes, or doubteth of them, he receaueth the Lorde's supper unworthily. For this worde, gyven for you, doth require a faithful and beleuyng harte.

How little this origin of Cranmer's Catechism has been known to the more distinguished scholars of the English Church, may be illustrated by a singular error of the late Dr. W. F. Hook, Dean of Chichester, author of the " Lives of the Archbishops of Canterbury," (12 vols , 8vo.), " Church Dictionary," etc. In his sermon on " A Call to Union on the Principles of the English Reformation," published in Vol. II. of " Tracts for the Times," he cites Cranmer with the greatest assurance, as an advocate of the doctrine of Apostolical Succession, and attempts to substantiate his position by a quotation in the Appendix (p. 103 sqq.), from what he calls "Cranmer's Sermon on the Apostolic Succession and Power of the Keys." To one not understanding the historical relations, he must seem to prove his point. But alas! the words are not Cranmer's. They are only a section of this Lutheran Catechism, translated from the German with almost verbal exactness. The reader, familiar with Luther's writings, at once sees at the basis of the Brandenburg-Nürnberg explanation of this section, a portion of Luther's argument in his book "*Von der Winkelmesse*," published the same year, 1533, translated into Latin also by Justus Jonas, and in another part of which he maintains the identity of bishops and presbyters. It is the strong emphasis that those who preach must be rightly called, and that the Apostolic mode of recognizing this call, and formally inducting men into office was only by the laying on of hands, and, as Luther says, "neither by chrism or butter," that misled Dr. Hook. The following passage of "Cranmer" could not be misleading, when used under the circumstances of the time and place of its composition in Germany, though when tranferred to another land and tongue, and applied in other relations, a more careful guarding of some of its statements would be necessary. As it is, nothing is intimated of "an Episcopal Succession."

Darnach haben die Apostel andern frommen heyligen leuten solchs predigampt auch mitgethailt und befohlen, sonderlich an den orten, da schon Christen waren, und Prediger bedorfften, und doch die Apostel selbs bey ihnen nicht bleyben konten, dann sie musten immer weyter ziehen, und an andern orten auch predigen. Wo sie nun fromme heylige leut funden, die zum Predigampt tüglich waren, denselbigen legten sie die hende auff, und theyleten ihn den heyligen Geist mit, wie sie ihn von Christo zü solchem ampt auch hetten empfangen, dieselbigen waren dann auch richte ordentliche beruffene Prediger, gleich so wol als die Apostel selbs, wie das alles der heylig Paulus in den Episteln zum Timotheus klärlich anzeygt. Und ist also das Predigampt, das Christus unser Herr selbs angefangen, eingesetzt, und verordnet hat, immer von einem auff den andern kommen, durch das aufflegen der hende, und mittheylen des Heiligen Geists, bis auff dise stund. Und das ist, auch die rechte weyhe, damit man die Priester weyhen sol, und allweg geweyhet hat, und sol noch also bleyben, *dann das, was man sonst für andere Ceremonien darbey hat getrieben, die sein on not, von menschen erfunden, und hinzu gesetzt worden.*

BECON'S CATECHISM.

Dr. Burton[3] has conjectured that Cranmer's Catechism was translated for him by one of his chaplains, and mentions Taylor, Ponet or Poinet, and Becon, as possible translators. Both Ponet and Becon have left catechisms of which they were themselves the authors. As the former gives no indication of any influence on the part of Luther's Catechism, or the Brandenburg-Nürnberg Explanation, and the latter shows their traces on almost every page; of these three, Thomas Becon was probably the chaplain who performed the work, or aided the Archbishop in it. He was born in 1511. B. A. Cambridge, 1530–31; was a diligent hearer of Hugh Latimer; took orders in 1538; was brought before Privy Council in 1541, on charge of heresy, and recanted, but under an assumed name continued by his pen to disseminate the principles of the Reformation. Was again compelled to abjure in 1543. His books were prohibited by a proclamation, July 8th, 1546. Chaplain to Cranmer from March 24th, 1547. In the tower after Mary's accession from August 16th, 1553—March 22d, 1554. An exile at Strassburg and Marburg. Books again prohibited by a proclamation, June 13th, 1555. Returned to England at Elizabeth's accession, and, after being rector in a number of parishes, died July 2d, 1567.[4] His works in two volumes were republished by the Parker Society in 1844. While his career shows great weakness and vacillation in the presence of danger, his writings are among the most profoundly spiritual which the English Church has produced. His Catechism, prepared for his children, is without date, and while its very first words are: "Though I be small in quantity," contains more

---

[3] Cranmer's *Catechism*, viii.
[4] Cooper's *Athenæ Cantabrigienses*, Art. Becon.

matter[5] than our entire "Book of Concord," and is, in fact, an extended system of theology. It is evidently of later origin than Ponet's, as it shows the change in the order of parts, which it enumerates, as: I. Repentance. II. Faith. III. Law. IV. Prayer. V. Sacraments. VI. Offices of all degrees. It is an independent development by one in whose mind and heart, Luther's explanations, often in their very words, are deeply fixed and who with great freedom, expands and developes what he has drawn from this source and thoroughly assimilated.[6] The traces of the Calvinistic movement, however, are very apparent.

On the Lord's Supper, the Calvinistic influence leaves only a few traces of Luther. The last part of Becon's Catechism is occupied with the *Haustafel*, amplified and explained.

THE CHURCH CATECHISM,

which appeared originally in the liturgy of Edward VI. of 1549, and which, with the addition of Bishop Overall on the Sacraments made in 1604, is contained in the Book of Common Prayer, belongs to another class of Catechisms. It is a Catechism of the Brentian type, which begins with Baptism, and then deduces, from the profession made in Baptism, the several parts of the Catechism. John Brentz, the Suabian Lutheran Reformer published a Catechism, probably first in 1527-28. Another German edition was published in 1536. The first Latin edition (1551-2) is before us, from which we translate:

BRENTZ'S CATECHISM.

What is your religion?
The Christian religion.
Why?
Because I believe in Jesus Christ, and was baptized in the name of Jesus Christ.
What is Baptism?
A sacrament or divine seal, whereby God the Father, through Jesus Christ,

---

[5] In Parker Society edition 4to pp. 8vo. 58 lines to the page.
[6] The evidence for this will be found in *Lutheran Church Review*, for July, 1888, pp. 174 sqq.

with the Holy Ghost, surely testifieth that God is propitious to him who is baptized, and out of gratuitous kindness forgiveth him his sins for Christ's sake, and adopteth him as son and heir of all heavenly benefits.

Recite the passages of Scripture which prove the institution of the sacrament.

Matt. 28: 19, 20; Mark 16: 15, 16.

Recite the Symbol of faith.

I believe in God the Father, etc.

Of what profit is this faith?

That, for the sake of Jesus Christ, I am reckoned by it, righteous and holy before God, and there is given me the spirit of prayer and of calling upon God as Father, and of ordering my life according to God's commandments.

In what prayer, are you wont to call upon God?

The Lord's Prayer, which Christ hath taught us.

Recite the Lord's Prayer.

Our Father, etc.

What are the Commandments of God?

Those contained in the Ten Commandments.

Recite the Ten Commandments.

I am the Lord thy God, etc.

For what purpose were the Ten Commandments given?

First, that from them we may learn to recognize our sins. Secondly, that from them we may learn what works please God, and are to be done, that we may lead an honorable life.

Can we, by our works, perfectly fulfil God's commandments?

In no way. For our works are not perfectly good, and we have been conceived and born in sin. But to provide for our salvation, our Lord God hath given us his Only-begotten Son, Jesus Christ, who did no sin and most perfectly fulfilled all of God's commandments. If, therefore, we believe in Jesus Christ, God with his gratuitous favor reckons us for Christ's sake, just as though we ourselves had fulfilled all of God's commandments.

Why ought we to do good works?

Not that, by our works, we may make satisfaction for sins and merit life eternal, For Christ alone hath made satisfaction for our sins, and merited for us life eternal. But we should do good works, that by them we may attest our faith, and render thanks to our Lord God for his benefits.

What must be done to strengthen our faith in adversity, and receive consolation in affliction?

We must use the Lord's Supper.

What is the Lord's Supper?

A sacrament or divine seal, whereby Christ truly presenteth, offereth and giveth us, with the bread and wine, his Body and Blood, and certifieth to us that our sins are remitted us, and that the right to life eternal belongeth to us.

Recite the Words of Institution.

Our Lord Jesus Christ, etc.

What are the Keys of the King of Heaven?

The Ministry of proclamation of the Gospel concerning Jesus Christ.

Recite from the Evangelists some passages, in which Jesus Christ hath instituted the Ministry of preaching his Gospel.

Luke 10: 16; Matth. 16: 19; John 20: 22, 23.

A comparison made with variations of the older editions, as given in Höfling's *Sacrament der Taufe*, II.: 326, 327, shows no important changes, so far as the subject here treated is concerned. The Catechism of Brentz was adopted by, and included in the Church Constitution for Schwabisch-Hall of 1543.

In 1539, when a Church Constitution was prepared for the Lutheran churches in Cassel (Hesse Cassel), an Order for Confirmation was inserted, including a brief Catechism to be used, at a public examination, immediately preceding and in connection with the Confirmation. In 1543, this Cassel Order for Confirmation was adopted, with some slight changes, in the famous book prepared by Melanchthon and Bucer for the Reformation of Cologne, which became so important in the preparation of the Book of Common Prayer, Bucer himself being Professor at Cambridge while the work was in progress. This Catechism follows the model of Brentz.

THE CASSEL CATECHISM.

Art thou a Christian?

Yes.

Whence dost thou know this?

Because I have been baptized in the name of God the Father, Son and Holy Ghost.

What dost thou believe of God the Father, Son and Holy Ghost?

All that the Articles of the Creed contain.

How do they run?

I believe in God the Father, etc.

What dost thou mean, then, in confessing God the Father, Son and Holy Ghost?

That there are three persons and yet one God, of one nature and power.

Why dost thou say: God is Almighty and that he is Creator of all things?

That God is, doeth and giveth all good, hath made all things from nothing, and maintaineth and preserveth them; He also is present, by His power, to all things, and worketh all in all, from His only good and righteous will and counsel.

What dost thou understand in the Second Article, of Christ our Lord?

That, through Adam, we are so corrupt that no angel or man could pay the price of our sins, but the Eternal Word and Son of God, had, and willed to become, flesh, and was born a true man, yet without all sin, by the Holy Ghost of the Virgin Mary. By his death, He hath paid the price for all our sins, and by His resurrection and ascension hath placed us again in a heavenly nature to whom the Father hath given all power in Heaven and on earth, etc.

After a similar long explanation of Article III, the question is asked:

Art thou in the church and congregation of Christ?
Yes.
How didst thou enter therein?
By Holy Baptism.
What is it?
The washing of regeneration, wherein I was washed from inborn sin, incorporated with Christ my Lord, and clothed in Him.
Wilt thou remain in this fellowship?
Yes, by the help of God, eternally.

Questions are then asked and answered concerning the duties which this fellowship within the church through baptism brings. Then follow several concerning the Lord's Supper, and the duties pertaining to its fellowship. There is no allusion to either the Ten Commandments or the Lord's Prayer.

HERMANN'S CONSULTATION.

The Cassel Catechism, as revised and introduced into the Consultation of Cologne, translated into English, and published in 1548, varies somewhat from the above, as may be learned from extracts given in Blunt's Annotated Book of Common Prayer, and Campion's and Beaumont's Prayer Book Interleaved.

Demaunde. Dost thou profess thyself to be a Christian?
Answer. I profess.

D. What is it to be a Christian?
A. To be borne agayne in Christ, and to have remission of synnes, and participation of everlastyng lyfe through him.
D. Whereby trustest thou that these thynges be given thee?
A. Because I am baptized in the name of the father, the sonne, and the holye gost.
D. What belevest thou of God the father, the sonne, and the holy gost?
A. The same that the articles of our crede do comprehend.
D. Rehearse them.
A. I do believe in God, etc.

* * * * * * * * * *

D. Doeth that please thee then, and doest thou allowe it, and wilt thou continue in the same, that thy godfathers promysed and professed in thy name at holy baptisme, when in thy steede they renounced Satan, and the world, and bound thee to Christe and to this congregation, that thou shouldst be thorowlie obedient to the Gospel?
A. I allow these things, and by the healpe of our Lord Jesus Christe, I will continue in the same unto thende.

We give the old English rendering, quoted by the English writers on the "Book of Common Prayer," in order that it may appear in what form it was present to the compilers of that book, although a comparision of the original, with the Cassel Catechism shows no variation in the introductory questions. The same writers might have added, that, after the question, whether the catechumen would abide by all that was promised by his sponsors, the Order of Hermann continues:

Q. Dost thou renounce, now and here, before the eyes of God and his Church, with thine own heart and mouth, Satan and all his works? *Ans.* I renounce. *Q.* Also the world and all its lusts? *A.* I renounce. *Q.* And dost thou surrender thyself in all obedience to our Lord Jesus Christ, and his holy Church? *A.* I surrender. *Q.* How wast thou first received by God unto sonship, and into his Church? *A.* By Holy Baptism, * * . *Q.* Wilt thou continue in this fellowship of the Lord unto thine end? *A.* Yes, by the Lord's help, unto eternity.

If now we turn to "The Church Catechism," found in the Book of Common Prayer," its close dependence upon the Brentian type of Lutheran Catechisms is very manifest. It is in vain for the writers of the Church of England to plead that the compilers of "The Book of Common Prayer," found only the hint there.[7]

The order of parts first of all shows this:

Church Catechism. 1549.	Brentz.	Cassel-Cologne.
Baptism.	Baptism.	Baptism.
Creed.	Creed.	Creed.
Commandments.	Lord's Prayer.	
Lord's Prayer.	Commandments.	
1604.		
Baptism.		
Lord's Supper.	Lord's Supper.	Lord's Supper.

But beyond this, the thought that underlies the entire development, if compared with the Catechisms above given, will be seen to be taken from them. Even where Brentz and the Cassel Catechism have nothing to say concerning the relation of sponsors to Baptism, the thought with which the Church Catechism opens, comes from Hermann's Consultation. We can trace also some of the very brief explanations, back through Cranmer's, to Luther's Catechism.

FIRST COMMANDMENT.

Cranmer's Luther.	Church Catechism.
We be commanded to feare and love God with al oure hearte and to put our whole trust and confidence in him.	My duty towards God is to believe in him, to fear him, and to love him with all my heart, [and] to put my whole trust in him.

SECOND COMMANDMENT.

Cranmer's Luther.	Luther.	Church Catechism.
To call upon hym, magnifie and prayse him.	To call upon him . . . and worship him, with prayer, praise and thanksgiving.	To worship him, to give him thanks, and to call upon him.

[7] "The idea is probably due to Hermann's *Consultation*. No part, however, of our Catechism was borrowed from this source." Procter, History of the Book of Common Prayer, p. 389. "As the same arrangement is found in Hermann's Consultation, the notion of an authoritative form of instruction to be thus inserted in the Ritual, was probably derived from that source. *There is no resemblance, however,* between the English and foreign formularies." Trollope on the Liturgy, p. 233.

THIRD COMMANDMENT.

Cranmer's Luther.	*Church Catechism.*
To heare diligently and reverently his holy worde, and with al diligence to folow the same.	To honor his holy Name and his Word, and to serve him truly all the days of my life.

FOURTH COMMANDMENT.

Cranmer's Luther.	*Church Catechism.*
To honoure oure parentes, teachers, masters and governors, to obey them and in no wise despise them.	To love, honor and succour my father and mother . . . to submit myself to all governors, teachers, spiritual pastors and masters.

EIGHTH COMMANDMENT.

Cranmer's Luther.	*Church Catechism.*
To absteyne from all liynge, backbytyng, slaunderynge.	To keep my tongue from evil-speaking, lying and slandering.

PONET'S AND NOWELL'S CATECHISMS.

The Church Catechism, being only a formula for the public examination of catechumens belonging to the Order for Confirmation, was deemed inadequate for full instruction, and, hence, as the Calvinistic tendency strengthened, there were various efforts to provide a substitute for Cranmer's ample Lutheran explanation. The first of these, known as Edward VI.'s Catechism, is generally ascribed to Bishop Ponet or Poinet. It was first published in 1553, in connection with the Articles of Religion of 1552. Ponet, one of Cranmer's chaplains, was bishop of Rochester after 1550, and in 1551 succeeded Gardiner as Bishop of Winchester. He fled to Strassburg on the accession of Mary, where he died in 1556. The Catechism is even polemical in its attitude towards Lutheranism, devoting a large page and a quarter to discussing the impossibility of the presence of the Body of Christ on earth. It treats in order, the Ten Commandments, the Creed, and the Lord's Prayer. Although published by authority, it did not answer its purpose, and soon was lost in obscurity. Before its republication in the "Liturgies of Edward VI.," issued by the Parker Society, it was almost impossible even for scholars to find a copy.

A far more important work is the Catechism of Alexander Nowell (1507–1601), Dean of St. Paul's and Prolocutor of the Convocation under Elizabeth that revised the Articles of Edward VI. There are, in fact, three Catechisms which bear his name, but his Large Catechism is what is generally so known. It was published in 1570, and follows the order of the Ten Commandments, Creed, Lord's Prayer and Sacraments. It combines theological exactness with catechetical skill. It appropriates some of Poinet's material, but is still more dependent upon Calvin's Institutes, whose order it follows, and whose very language it frequently uses, as we could readily show. In some parts it is not without controversial bitterness and unfairness, where it touches points on which the antagonisms to Lutheranism are especially prominent. Bishop Overall's additions in 1604 to "The Church Catechism," were derived from Nowell. It is a significant fact that the English translator of this Catechism, in 1570, Thomas Norton, was the translator also of the first English edition of Calvin's Institutes. It is worthy of examination whether there be not a close relationship between Nowell's work and Calvin's Catechism of 1536, which was afterwards supplanted by the *Catechismus Genevensis* (1538.)

CHAPTER XXVI.

THE HOMILIES OF 1547.

Taverner's Postils, a temporary Expedient. Preparation of an authorized Book. Reasons for its Unpopularity. Merits and Defects. Permanent Results. Symbolical Authority. Homily on "The Salvation of Mankind" examined. Sources whence it was compiled. Indebtedness of other Homilies. Homilies of the Reign of Queen Elizabeth.

THE line of the liturgical development of the English Church, has led us some years beyond the period of the English Homilies Taverner, as we have seen, had already made a temporary effort to supply the lack of preaching, by the preparation of "Postils," to be used for this purpose. A more formal and complete work was to appear later. Ordered by Convocation in 1542, it seems to have been completed in 1543, and, then, after awaiting revision for several years, finally appeared in the summer of 1547. A second edition was issued the same year. One of the Homilies was to be read "every Sunday at high mass," "except a sermon be preached," and, then, the Homily had to be read the succeeding Sunday. When the Homilies had all been read, the clergyman was to begin the volume anew, and read and re-read it, until he received further instructions. The book, though highly commended by Bucer, from Strassburg, did not prove popular. Sometimes when read, "there would be such talking and babbling in the church, that nothing could be heard. And if the parish were better affected, and the priest not so, he would 'so hauk and chop it,' that it were as good for them to be without it, as for any word that could be understood."[1] No

---
[1] Strype's *Memorials of the Reformation*, II: 49.

wonder. For, first, the book reflected the inconsistent position of the English Church, the advocates of the various tendencies having taken part in its preparation, and the evangelical position of Cranmer being balanced by the hierarchical position of Bonner. Even though there be few direct antagonisms, the very mode of treatment was affected. Secondly, the Homilies are not popular, but largely didactic in their character. The doctrinal Homilies are essays in Dogmatic Theology, burdened with technical terms and abounding in arguments from the Fathers: and even those of a more practical nature show the hand of the student cloistered among books, rather than that of one who had much experience in the care of souls. There is, in this respect, a great contrast between them, and the expositions of doctrine for plain pastors which are found in the introduction to so many of our Lutheran Church Orders. Thirdly, they entirely ignored the Church Year, and caused an interruption of the true idea of the Service, which, even though it may be borne occasionally, nevertheless, when occurring as a rule becomes awkward and tedious. They exhibit no progressive unfolding of the life of Christ. Compared with the earlier effort of Taverner, there was here by no means an improvement.

Although, the Homilies did not long serve the purpose for which they were composed, and as sermons were failures; yet their importance as theological treatises, must not be overlooked. Art. XXXIV, of the Church of England and of the Protestant Episcopal Church of America, gives them, with the later Homilies of Queen Elizabeth, symbolical authority; and Art. XI. gives still more emphasis to one particular Homily. To the study of this Homily, thus officially endorsed, which was constructed from Lutheran material, John Wesley ascribed the origin of the Methodistic movement. Cranmer seems to have endeavored in those which he prepared, to clearly explain and defend at length the cardinal doctrines of Sin and Grace, and especially that of Justification by Faith alone without works. No document that has come into our hands, shows that he has merely translated. Yet his close dependence not only in order of treatment, and of thought, but also in language, cannot be questioned. The order with which the opening Homilies are arranged, shows that Osiander's influence has wrought here, as elsewhere, upon his relative. If the Homilies begin: I. The Reading and Knowledge of Holy Scripture; II. the Misery of all Mankind; III. the Salvation of all Mankind; IV. True and Living Faith; the *Brandenburg-Nürnberg* Instruction proceeds: I. Of Doctrine; the Old and New Testaments. II. Penitence, the Law; III. the Gospel, etc. In many of the Homilies, we do not claim any Lutheran elements. Patristic and scholastic learning, rather than the "New Learning," are frequently manifested. But examining especially that on the "Salvation of Mankind by only Christ our Saviour," we at once find that we are treading the same ground as that traversed when the "Common Prayer" was examined.

The opening sentence of the Homily is taken directly or indirectly from the Schwabach Articles of Luther and Melanchthon of October 15th, 1529.

Schwabach Articles. (Art. V.)	*Homily.*
Because all men be sinners, subject to sin and to death, besides to the devil, therefore can no man by his own strength or good works, deliver himself thence, so that he may again be made righteous or godly; yea, he cannot even prepare or dispose himself for righteousness, but the more he attempts to deliver himself, the worse it is for him. But that the only way to righteousness and deliverance from sin and death is, if, without all merits or works, we believe in the Son of God who suffered for us... For God regards as righteous and godly all those who have this faith in his Son, that, for his Son's sake, they are received into grace.	Because all men be sinners and offenders against God, and breakers of his Law and commandments, therefore can no man by his own works, acts and deeds (seem they never so good) be justified, and made righteous before God; but every man of necessity is constrained to seek for another righteousness or justification, to be received at God's own hands, in such things as he hath offended. And this justification or righteousness, which we so receive of God's mercy and Christ's merit, embraced by faith, is taken, accepted and allowed of God, for our perfect and full justification.

Cf. also Apology of Augsburg Confession, p. 90: § 40. The close of the paragraph introduces the very language of Art. III.

of the Augsburg Confession, supplementing it, however, by a clause referring to the "Active Obedience" of Christ. This is a matter of much interest, since the doctrine of the "Active Obedience" has generally been traced to Flacius in 1552, who is said to have formulated it, in order to counteract the error of Osiander on Justification.[2] This Homily of 1547, however, says that God sent his only Son "to fulfil the Law for us and to make a sacrifice," and a few pages later : " Christ is now the righteousness of them that truly do believe in him. He for them paid their ransom by his death. *He for them fulfilled the Law in his life.* So that now in him, and by him, every true Christian man may be called a fulfiller of the Law; forasmuch as that which their infirmity lacked, Christ's justice hath supplied." But the doctrine of the "Active Obedience," was derived from the Reformation of Cologne, which, in turn, had taken it from *Brandenburg-Nürnberg* of 1533, where even Osiander had assisted in formulating the following : " First, he directed all his life according to the will of the Father, did for us what we were obliged, and yet were unable, to do, and fulfilled the Law and all righteousness for our good, as He himself says, Matth. 5: 17, and Paul says, Gal. 4: 4; 1 Cor. 1: 30; Phil. 3: 9. Secondly, he took upon himself all our sins, and bore and suffered all that was due us, John 1: 29; Is. 53; 4-6; Rom. 8: 32; Gal. 3: 13."

The statement of the Augsburg Confession that Christ was "a sacrifice not only for original guilt, but also for all actual sins," carries Cranmer at once, in thought, to Art. IX. of the Confession.

Aug. Conf., Art. IX.	*Homily.*
Children are to be baptized, who by baptism, being offered to God, are received into God's favor.	Infants being baptized . . are, by this sacrifice washed from their sins, brought to God's favor.

And then to Art. XII.

[2] See Schmid's *Dogmatik*, English Translation, First Edition, pp. 377 sqq., Second Edition, pp. 360 sqq.

The Homilies of 1547.

Aug. Conf., Art XII.	*Homily.*
Such as have fallen after baptism, may find remission of sins at what time they are converted.	They which in act or deed do sin after baptism, when they turn again to God unfeignedly, they are likewise washed by this sacrifice from their sins.[3]

Then after two passages of Scripture are cited, another of Melanchthon's statements appears.

Melanchthon's *Loci Comm.* (*De Evangelio*).	*Homily.*
Justification is given freely, that is, not on account of our worth, yet there must be a ransom for us.	Although this justitfication be free unto us, yet it cometh not so freely unto us, that there is no ransom paid therefor.

After proving and illustrating this statement, Cranmer continues:

" The Apostle toucheth specially three things, which must go together in our Justification ; upon God's part, his great mercy and grace; upon Christ's part, justice, *i. e.* the satisfaction of God's justice or the price of our redemption by the offering of his Body, and shedding of his Blood . . ; and upon our part, true and lively faith."

The Apology (1531) had said:

" As often as we speak of Justifying Faith, we must keep in mind that these three objects concur: the *promise* and that too *gratuitous*, and *the merits of Christ*, as the price and propitiation. This promise is received by *faith*" (p. 92 : § 53). "Which" [faith] "yet is not ours, but by God's working in us." continues the Homily. "It is not my doing, not my presenting or giving, not my work or preparation," says the Apology (p. 91 : § 48). "Faith doth not shut out repentance, hope, love," says the Homily. "Love and works ought to follow faith. Wherefore, they are not excluded," says the Apology. "It excludeth them," says the Homily, "so we may not do them, to this intent, to be made good by doing of them." "Confidence in the merit of love or of works," says the Apology, "is excluded in Justification."

[3] Cf. above chapter. The Ten Articles.

It is unnecessary to illustrate further. The Homilies "Of our Salvation" and "Of Faith," are almost mosaics of passages from approved Lutheran authorities. We would not infer that they were mechanically joined together; but that they were deeply fixed in the mind of the writer, were thoroughly assimilated and flowed forth almost spontaneously from his pen Nevertheless this, in no way diminishes the extent of the indebtedness.

We recognize also many corresponding similarities in the Homily "Of Good Works," and, to a less extent, in that "Of Christian Love and Charity." Those first mentioned, are worthy of far wider study than has been accorded them. They are among the most valuable memorials which the struggle of the Gospel for the English Church, has left to succeeding generations, and, as models of a pure and eloquent English style, are scarcely to be surpassed. Among those added in the next reign, were the two of Taverner on the Death and Resurrection of Christ. The great devotion of the author to Lutheranism has been previously shown, in connection with what has been said concerning his translation of the Augsburg Confession and the Apology.

CHAPTER XXVII.

THE THIRTY-NINE ARTICLES.

Archdeacon Hardwick's Researches. Dr. Schaff's "Creeds of Christendom." Retrospect to Preparatory Work in the preceding Reign. The XLII. Articles of 1552. Revision under Queen Elizabeth. Table showing the parts of each article taken from the Augsburg Confession, Apology, Smalcald Articles and Würtemberg Confession.

THE minute investigations which Archdeacon Hardwick has made, and whose results are embodied in his well-known "History of the Articles of Religion," relieve us of the necessity of any extended examination. So thorough has been his work, and so full his treatment of the relation of the articles of his Church to the Augsburg and Würtemberg Confessions, that, it will supply the most needed information concerning what yet remains. He has overlooked, however, the connection of the Articles with the Apology and Smalcald Articles. The first volume of Dr. Schaff's "Creeds of Christendom" also presents a very satisfactory summary. The pamphlet of Dr. Morris has collected the statements of many English writers on the fact, which no scholar, or well-informed person will any longer venture to dispute, that the Thirty-Nine Articles are of Lutheran origin.

We have above traced the history of the Wittenberg negotiations of 1535-6, the Ten Articles of 1536, the Memoranda of 1538, etc. After the accession of Edward, Cranmer seems to have delayed the preparation of a Confession, possibly in the hope that the various Protestant communions might be induced to unite in one common Confession against Rome.

The first sketch of the English Articles was made in the summer of 1551, chiefly, as cotemporaries affirm, by Cranmer himself. This rough draft was submitted to the bishops throughout the country, and after receiving their suggestions, was submitted to two learned laymen, Sir William Cecil and Sir John Cheke. Then it was submitted to the King, and referred to his six chaplains, among whom was John Knox. Revised again by Cranmer, the Articles finally were issued with authority in 1553.[1] In the previous year, however, they seem to have been privately circulated. They are known as the XLII. Articles of 1552.

Ten years later, after the accession of Elizabeth had restored the Reformation in England, Archbishop Parker undertook a revision of the XLII. Articles, in which he made free use of the Würtemberg Confession[2] prepared by Dr. John Brentz in 1551, and published under the authority of Duke Christopher, for submission to the Council of Trent. The document, thus completed, is known as the XXXIX. Articles of 1562. It omitted the 10th, 16th, 19th and 41st articles of 1552, and introduced as new articles, the 5th, 12th, 29th and 30th. The Convocation did not ratify the last three, and the 29th was omitted during printing, making the number actually only thirty-eight. But in 1571, when the final revision occurred, the 29th was reintroduced, and then the entire document, receiving the sanction of Parliament, was made obligatory upon the clergy. The following table will show the relation of the several Articles to the Lutheran formularies.

I. Aug. Conf., Art. I. ; XIII. Articles, 1538.

II. Aug. Conf., III. ; XIII. Articles 1538; Revision of 1562 introduced : "Begotten from everlasting of the Father, the very and eternal God of one substance with the Father," from the Würtemberg Confession.

[1] For details, see *Hardwick*, pp. 84 sqq.
[2] "All the alterations are drawn chiefly from the Würtemberg Confession," Adolphus, *Compendium Theologicum*, p. 438.

III. and IV. Each following a clause in Aug. Conf., Art. III., but not identical with the Confession.

V. Würtemberg Confession, Art. III. Not in 1552.

VI. [V. of 1552.] ⸻

VII. [VI. of 1552.] ⸻

VIII. [VII. 1552]. Articles of 1536, I. Saxon Arts., (1551, Melanchthon), I.

IX. [VIII., 1552]. Aug. Conf., II.; XIII. Articles (1538), II.

X. [IX]. Former Sentence from close of Art. III,, Würtemberg Confession; "the latter almost verbatim from St. Augustine."

XI. Aug. Conf. IV.; Arts. of 1536, V.; XIII. Arts., IV. See preceding chapter on Homilies.

XII. Hardwick refers this in part to the Würtemberg Confession. It is nearer the argument of the Apology which in fact it condenses, and may possibly be connected with the Homilies. Almost the very words of Apology however reappear, p. 139: § 172.

XIII. [XII]. Also condensing the thought of the Apology, pp. 89; 147 sqq.; 230.

XIV. [XII]. Apology, 285: 24, 25.

XV. [XIV]. Amplifying a thought of Aug. Conf., Art. II.

XVI. [XV]. Partly from Aug. Conf., Art. XII.

XVII. ⸻

XVIII.⸻

XIX. [XX]. Aug. Conf., Art. VII; XIII. Arts., V.

XX. [XXI]. Cf. Aug. Conf., Art. XXVIII. Melanchthon's Appendix to Smalcald Articles, II.

XXI. [XXII.]⸻

XXII. [XXIII]. Possibly from Smalcald Articles, Part II: Art. II., § 12. "Purgatory and every solemnity, rite, and profit connected with it, is to be regarded nothing but a spectre of the devil. ("*Mera diaboli larva*)" Eng. Art: "*Res est futilis.*"

XXIII. [XXIV]. Based on Aug. Conf., Art. XIV.; XIII. Arts., X.

XXIV. [XXV]. Cf. Apology, 259: 4

XXV. [XXIV]. Based on Aug. Conf., Art. XIII.; XIII. Arts., IX.

XXVI. [XXV]. Aug. Conf. Art. VIII; XIII. Arts., X.

XXVII. [XXVIII]. The Articles of 1536 and 1538, based on Augsburg Confession and Melanchthon "Against the Anabaptists," were probably, as Hardwick supposes, before the compiler; but there was a very decided weakening to conform it to the Calvinistic doctrine.

XXVIII. (XXIX) ——————(Calvinistic).

XXIX. § ——————Calvinistic. First published in 1571.

XXX. Cf. Aug. Conf., Art. XXII. Added in 1562.

XXX. (XXX). Based on Aug. Conf., Art. XXIV: 22–27.

XXXII. (XXXI) Cf. Aug. Conf., Art. XXIII: 3 sqq.

XXXIII. (XXXII). ——————

XXXIV. (XXXIII). Based on Aug. Conf. Art. XV. Cf. Apology, Art. XV: 1, 3, 8, 51.

XXXV. (XXXIV) ——————

XXXVI. (XXXV). ——————

XXXVII. (XXXVI). Partly from Aug. Conf., Art. XVI.

XXXVIII. (XXXVII). Partly from Aug. Conf., Art. XVI, and its explanation by Apology, Art. XVI: 36, 61, etc.

XXXIX. (XXXVIII). From same Article.

The suppressed Art. XLI. of 1552 was based on Aug. Conf., Art. II.

CHAPTER XXVIII.

THE SUBSEQUENT HISTORY.

The Refugees of Mary's reign. The Congregations of Exiles at Frankfort-on-the-Main. The Revised Service. John Knox. The Conflict between Puritanism and the adherents of the Prayer-Book. Dr. Richard Cox. Knox withdraws. A Question as to Lutheran Baptism. Calvin at Frankfort. His later opinion of the Augsburg Confession. An Anglican Theological Seminary at Frankfort. Kindness shown the refugees. Archbishop Grindal. Duke Christopher of Würtemberg. Bishop Aylmer at Jena; nearly becomes Schnepf's successor as a member of the theological Faculty. The Restoration under Elizabeth. Robert Brown and the "Independents." The fate of English Lutheranism. Its continued Influence. Accession of the House of Hanover. New attempts at examination of historical relations. Pufendorf's Principles. Conclusion.

THE limit fixed for this survey has been the close of the reign of Edward VI., with a reference to the permanent memorials of the Lutheran movement which remain. Another interesting field opens to the historical student in the development of the English Church among the bands of exiles scattered on the Continent during the Marian persecution. Mary came to the throne, July 5th, 1553. Before her former coronation, in October, the leaders of the evangelical movement had, with only one or two exceptions, been deprived of their positions and cast into prison. Cranmer was sent to the Tower September 14th. During the same month, Polanus with his congregation of exiles fled to Frankfort-on-the-Main. Here the chief Lutheran pastor was Hardtmann Beyer, distinguished for his courage and zeal in the days of the Interim, an alumnus of Wittenberg, and frequently mentioned in the correspondence of Luther and Melanchthon. They were kindly received, and were given the *Weissfrauenkirche* for their services, which were begun in the French language, April 21st. They were followed (June 27th) by a number of English Protestants who were given the same church for services in English at a different hour, William Whittingham, brother-in-law of Calvin, being their first pastor. One year later, (June 1555), John a Lasco and his congregation came, and they worshipped in the same place in the Dutch language. Very soon a controversy began among the English. The Calvinistic party had fretted even in England, that the revision of the Book of Common Prayer in 1552, was not more radical. A new Service was prepared. It "was concluded that the answeringe alowde after the Minister shulde not be vsed, the letanye, surplice and many other thinges also omitted. The Minister in place off the Englishe Confession shulde vse another, bothe off more effecte, and also framed according to the state and time. And the same ended, the people do singe a psalme in meetre in a plaine tune . . that don, the minister to praye for thessistance off gods holie spirite and so to proceade to the sermon. After the sermon, a generall praier for all estates and for oure countrie of Englande was also devised, at thende off whiche praier, was coined the lords praier, and a rehearsall of tharticles off oure belieff, which ended the people to singe an other psalme as afore. Then the minister pronouncinge this blessinge: The peace of God, etc."[1] John Knox was called from Geneva to take charge of this congregation, and accepted, being its pastor from November 1554 to March 1555. But this change of the Service proved too radical, and caused a reaction. More exiles sympathizing with a more conservative course arrived from England. Knox was strengthened by the interference of Calvin. In March 1555, Dr. Richard Cox arrived. He was one of the band of first English Lutherans at Cambridge, mentioned in the beginning

[1] A Brief Discourse of the Troubles begun at Frankfort, 1554. Reprint London 1846, p. VII.

of this book, and had actively co-operated in the preparation of
the principal English formularies, especially the Book of Common Prayer. He at once antagonized Knox. "The sundaie
folowinge, one off his company withowt the knowleg off the congregation gate upp suddainly into the pulpit, redd the lettany,
and D. Cox withe his companie answered alowde, whereby the
determination of the churche was broken."[2] Such is the record
of the one side. In two weeks time, Knox had left Frankfort.
Thus the struggle between Puritanism and the English Church
began in Lutheran Germany, and was to be tranferred to England for fuller development during the reign of Elizabeth. The
congregation was hopelessly divided. One party would not allow the English minister to baptize their children. They carried them to the Lutheran ministers. Then came another controversy. Peter Martyr was called upon to prepare an opinion
on the question: "*An liceat hominibus evangelicis baptismum
a Lutheranis accipi.*" "May evangelical men receive baptism
from Lutherans?" He thought not. This did not settle matters,
and he had to write again to the effect, that while "he would
not say it was unlawful, yet he disliked the practice." Here
are a few of Martyrs arguments: "Since the Lutheran faith and
ours is diverse, we cannot commit ours to be sealed by the Lutherans. . . What advantage or spiritual edification is had from
baptism sought for at the hands of the Lutherans? The salvation of your infants is not imperilled if they die without baptism,
since neither the grace of God, nor the effects of predestination
are to be bound to external things and sacraments."[3] Calvin
himself repaired to Frankfort in 1556. He avoided the Lutheran pastors, his relations towards Lutheranism having changed
some three years previously. A few years later, he wrote to the
Prince of Conde, "the Confession of Augsburg is neither flesh
nor fish, and is the cause of great schisms and debates among the

[2] Ib. XXXVIII.
[3] Strype's *Cranmer*, III.: 162 sqq.

Germans;"[4] and to Admiral Coligny:[5] "It is such a meagre composition, so feeble and so obscure, that it is impossible to stop short at its conclusions."[6] Thus Puritanism showed in its very outstart the same hostility to Lutheranism, as to the English formularies drawn from Lutheran sources.

The other portion of the congregation found, with little difficulty, sufficient material among its members for a theological faculty, and established for the time a Seminary, with Dr. Horn, previously Dean of Durham, for Hebrew; Dr. John Mullins for Greek, Dr. Traheron, previously Dean of Chichester, for Divinity.

Not only at Frankfort, but also in Reformed centers, English exiles received kind treatment. Frankfort, however, is of most importance in its historical relations. Dr. Edmund Grindal, Archbishop of Canterbury, 1576–83, bears most emphatic testimony to its influence on the later history of the English Church: "That England had so many bishops and other ministers of God's Word, which at that day preached the pure doctrine of the Gospel, was owing to Strasburgh, Zürich, Basel Worms, but *above all the rest, to Frankfort.* You received our people to harbor, and, being received, embraced them with the highest humanity, and defended them with your authority. And if we should not acknowledge and speak of this piety of yours, we were, of all mankind, the most ungrateful."[7] His biographer says: "In truth, the remembrance of the former kindness, received by him and the rest of the exiles in Germany, under Queen Mary, stuck close upon his grateful mind; and he thought he could not sufficiently express it upon all occasions."[8] Duke Christopher, of Würtemberg, the prince for whom Dr. John Brentz prepared the Würtemberg Confession, and distinguished for his decided

---

[4] Sept. 24th, 1561. Letters.
[5] May 10th, 1563. See Letters.
[6] Strype's *Memorials*, V : 71.
[7] Strype's *Grindal*, p. 16.
[8] Ib. p. 182.

Lutheran convictions, was held in particularly grateful recognition, because of his kindness to the exiles. "The Duke had been very kind unto the English exiles, having at one time bestowed among them at Strasburgh four or five hundred dollars, besides more given to them at Frankfort."[9] This act was duly acknowledged by Queen Elizabeth, when the Duke sent a representative to England in 1563, and by Bishop Grindal who entertained him and discussed with him Brentz's doctrine of the Omnipresence of Christ's humanity, which the Duke cordially approved. "But this without heat. They were contented to hear one another's arguments, and each to suffer other to abound in his own sense."[10]

Of John Aylmer, Lord Bishop of London in the reign of Queen Elizabeth, we are told that he improved the time of his exile by attending the University of Jena, and that he came near becoming the Professor of Hebrew in that institution. "He should, if he had not come away," says his biographer, "have had the Hebrew lecture there which Snepphinus [Erhard Schnepf] had, having been entertained there to read in that University both Greek and Latin, and with the good love of those famous men, Flacius Illyricus, Victorius Strigelus, D. Schnepphinus (whom they termed the other Luther), with divers others."[11]

But on the accession, of Elizabeth, all elements again were found in the Church of England, and the former system of compromise continued, postponing, although not averting, the crisis which at length came, in the entire separation of Presbyterianism, and the Westminister formularies of the next century. The "Independent" ("Congregationalist") movement of Robert Brown, which sent the Pilgrim fathers to America began as early as 1571. While it repudiated Calvin's theory of Church government, it was in other respects a development of the Calvinistic principles that had entered the Church of England

[9] Ib. p. 132.
[10] Ib.
[11] Strype's *Life of Bp. Aylmer*, pp. 10 sq.

during the reign of Edward, but whose development had been greatly stimulated by the closer contact with Calvinistic centers during the succeeding reign. Between Hierarchism and Puritanism, Lutheranism seemed to have been completely overcome. But it continued to live in the Liturgy and other formularies, and though checked in its course by foreign principles with which it is mingled, occasionally started some evangelical movement, which, however, from lack of intelligent consistency, fell short of a true and thorough reformation. Such was the Methodistic movement, which soon became one sided, and so concentrated its force only on a few points of faith and life, that John Wesley whose work was especially that of awakening and arousing the slumbering conscience, in his later years was surprised that in his earlier years he could have so warmly commended Luther on Galatians.

When the Lutheran House of Hanover was called to the English throne, again the question of the relation of the Church of England to the Lutheran Church became a matter of consideration. It was in this interest, that Theophilus Dorrington, Rector of Wittresham in Kent, published a translation of a posthumous book of Baron Pufendorf with the title: "A view of the Principles of the Lutheran Churches; showing how far they agree with the Church of England; being a seasonable essay towards the uniting of Protestants upon the accession of His Majesty, King George to the throne of these Kingdoms. London, 1714." The book was written by Pufendorf, not with respect to the Church of England, but to exhibit the reasons why there could be no union between the Lutherans and the Romish Church, and what difficulties there were in the way of a uniting of Protestants. Mr. Dorrington says in his Preface: "I thought that it might be of use to us in England, to understand and know the principles and practices of the Lutheran churches (which are the true Protestant churches beyond the seas) better than for aught I can find we commonly do."

This statement we would particularly commend to the members of the Church of England and her affiliated churches of today. The close dependence of the English Church on the work of the Lutheran Reformers, which has been above shown, certainly calls for more extensive acknowledgement and remembrance. Here in America, the two churches have again been brought into close local relation. Each must justify before God and men the reason for its separate existence; and this requires of necessity the careful and thorough review of historical relations and connections. In such review, the questions formerly at issue may be judged without that violence done conscience by the sacrilegious interference of a godless King, which English writers universally so deeply lament and condemn. The work begun by Cranmer may here be carried to its desired conclusion. The Lutheran Church should also recognize the many elements of strength and edification in the English Church; and judge with discrimination her noble formularies. Any claim, however, to the acknowledgement of a succession of bishops as a mark of the Church cannot be conceded without abandoning Art. VII. of the Augsburg Confession, upon which, even in the time of Henry VIII., there seems to have been no controversy. The various other English communions that have originated by a reaction against hierarchical elements, retained by the incompleteness of the reformation of the English Church, can be judged with the greater charity. The attainment of an ultimate union of Protestants does not lie in the way of ignoring, but of bravely facing, differences, and examining the grounds of their origin. It is to humbly contribute something to such attainment, that we have prepared the foregoing summary of facts.

CHAPTER XXIX.

BIBLIOGRAPHICAL.

Sixty-five English Lutheran Books of the XVI. Century.

No BETTER indication of the extent of the influence of the Lutheran Reformation upon that in England can be given, than that afforded by the subjoined list. It probably might be largely increased by more extensive researches:

SOME ENGLISH LUTHERAN BOOKS OF THE SIXTEENTH CENTURY.

1536. The Confessyon of the Fayth of the Germaynes, exhibited to the Most Victorious Emperour Charles the V., in the Council or Assemble holden at Augusta, the yere of our Lord, 1530. To which is added the Apologie of Malancthon, who defendeth with Reasons invincible the aforesayd Confessyon, translated by Richard Taverner, at the commandment of his Master, the ryght honourable Master Thomas Cromwel, chefe secretare to the Kynges Grace. London, Robert Redman.

1536. A compendious letter which John Pomerane—curate of the congregacion of Wittenberge sent to the faithfull christen congregacion in England. London, Richard Charlton.

1537. How and whither a christian man ought to flye the horrible plage of the pestilence. A sermon out of the third Psalme: Qui habitat in adjutorio altissimi. By Andrew Osiander. Translated out of the hye Almayne by Miles Coverdale. London, Richard Charlton.

1537. M. Luther's exposition of the Twenty-third Psalm, translated from the German by Miles Coverdale. Southwark, John Nicholson.

1537. The causes why the Germanes will not go nor consente onto the councill which Paul the 3 now Bp. of Rome, hath called to be kept at Mantua in Italy, and to begynne the 23 daye of Maye.   Southwark, James Nicholson.

Before 1548. The Apology of the Germans against the Council of Mantua. Translated by Miles Coverdale.

1538. Common places of scripture orderly and after a compendious forme of teachyng set forth. By Erasmus Sarcerius. Translated into English by R. Taverner. London, J. Byddell.

1541. A very godly defense full of lerning, defending the marriage of priests, gatthered by Philip Melancthon, and sent unto the Kyng of England, Henry the aight. Translated out of Latine into the English by Lewis Beauchame. Lipse, Printed by Ulryght Hoffe.

1542. The acts of the disputation in the cowncell of the empyre, holden at Regenspurg; that is to say, all the artycles concerning the christen relygion, both agreed upon and not agreed upon, even as they were proposed of the emperour unto the nobles of the empire, to be judged, delebered and debated, etc. Translated out of Latyne into English by Mylys Coverdale.

1544. De Libertate Christiana. The liberty of a christian Man. Cum priveligio regali. A lytle worke moost necessary to be knowen, of the freedome and bondage of the soule and body. God save the Kynge. Imprynted at the same by me John Byddell.

1545. The dysclosyng of the canon of ye popysh Masse, with a sermon annexed unto it, of ye famous clerk of worthy memory D. Marten Luther.[1] Apocal. XVIII: "Come away from hyr my people, that ye be not partakers in her synnes." Imprinted have at al Papiste, By me Hans hitprycke.

1545. The exposicion of Daniel the Prophete, gathered out of P. Melancton. Printed at Geneva, afterwards in London, Edward Whitchurch.

---

[1] Archbishop Laurence comments on this title to show how much greater in England was the influence of Luther than that of Calvin.—Bampton Lectures, p. 235.

1546. The true hystorie of the christen departynge of the reverende man D. Martyne Luther, collected by Justus Jonas, Michael Celius, and Joannes Aurifaber, whych were thereat, & translated into Englysh by Johan Bale.

1547. The Epistle of P. Melancton made unto Kynge Henry the Eighth, for the revokynge and abolishing of the six articles set forth and enacted by the craftie meanes and procurement of certeyne of our prelates of the clergie, translated out of laten into Englishe by J. C. Weesell.

1547. A Simple and religious consultation of vs Herman by the grace of God, Archbishop of Colone, and prince Electour, &c., by what means a Christian reformation, and, founded in God's Word, of doctrine, administration of the devine sacramentes, of ceremonies, and how the holy cure of soules and other ecclesiastical ministries, may be begun among men committed to our pastorall charge. Imprinted in the yere of our Lord 1547. The XXX. of October, I. P.

1548. Of the true auctorities of the churche, compyled by the excellent learned man Philippe Melancthon, and dedicate unto the noble Duke off Prussia, newly translated out of the Latin into Englyshe. Ipswich, John Owen.

1548. The Justification of Man by faith only. By Philip Melanchthon. Translated by Nicholas Lesse. Greenwich, William Powell.

1548. Conjectures of the end of the World, gathered out of the scriptures by A. Osiander, and translated by G. Joye.

1548. A declaration of the twelve articles of the christen faythe with annotations of the holy scriptures where they be grounded in. By D. Urban Regium. Richard Jugge for Geualter Lynne.

1548. The Olde Learning and the newe compared together, whereby it may be easely knowen which of them is better and more agreyng wyth the everlasting word of God. Newly corrected and augmented by Wyllyam Turner. Translated from Urban Regius. London, Robert Stoughton.

1548. A lytle Treatise after the maner of an Epistle wryten by the famouse clerk Doctor Urban Regius to his friend, about the causes of the great controversy, that hath been & is yet in the christian church.

1548. A frutefull and godly exposition and declaration of of the Kyngdom of Christ, and of the Christen lybertye, made upon the words of the Prophete Jeremye in the XXIII chapter with an exposycyon of the VIII. Psalme, intreatyng of the same matter, by the famous clerke Doctor Martyn Luther, whereunto is annexed a godly sermon of Doctor Urbanus Regius, upon the IX chapyter of Mathewe, of the woman that had an isseu of blood, & of the ruler's daughter, newly translated out of the hyghe Almayne. Imprinted for Gwalter Lynne.

1548. The chiefe and pryncyple Articles of the Christen faythe, to holde against the Pope and al Papistes, and the gates of hell, with other thre very profitable and necessary bokes, the names of tytles whereof are conteyned in the leafe next followynge. Made by Doctor Marten Luther. To the reader. In thys boke shal your fynde Christian Reader the ryght probation of the righte Olde Catholyke church, and of the newe false church, whereby eyther of them is to be knowen. Reade and iudge. London, Gualter Lynne.

1548. M. Luther's sermon of the Keys, and of Absolution, on John XX: 21, 22. Translated by R. Argentine, Ipswich, An. Scoloker.

1548. Melanchthon, his waying and considering of the Interim, translated by John Rogers. London, Edward Whitchurch.

1548. Catechism, set forth by Thomas Archbyshop of Canterbury [Translated from the Brandenberg-Nürnberg *Kinderpredigten.*]

1548. A simple and religious consultation of vs Harmâ by the grace of God, Archbishop of Colone, etc.

About 1548. Herman, archbishop of Colen, Of the right institution of baptism; also a treatise of matrimony, and buriall the dead by Wolph. Muscul. Translated by Richard Rice.

Before 1549. The Confessyon of Fayth, deliwered to the Emperour Charles the Vth. by the Lordes of Germany, written in Latyn by Phylyppe Melancthon, and translated into English by Robert Syngylton. Printed by John Mychell, Canterbury.

1549. A briefe collection of all such of the scriptures as do declare ye most blessed and happye estate of them that be vyseted with syckness and other visitations of God, and of them that be departinge out of this lyfe, wyth most godly prayers and general confessions, very expedient and mete to be read to all sicke persons, to make them wyllynge to dye. Whereunto are added two fruitfull and comfortable sermons made by the famouse clarke doctor Martin Luther, verye mete also to be reade at the burialles. Ecclesiastes VII. Imprinted on Somer's Kaye.

1550. The censure of J[ohn] B[rentz] in the cases whiche are concerning matrimony.

1556. A very fruitfull exposition upou the syxte chapter of Saynte John, divided into X Homelies or Sermons. Written in Latyn by the ryghte excellent Master John Brencius, and translated into English by Richard Shirrye, London. 9 April, 1550.

1550. A treatise of the argumentis of the old and new Tesment, by John Brentius: translated by John Calcaskie. London, Richard Charlton.

1550. A homelye of the Resurrection of Christe by John Brentius, translated by Thomas Sampson. London, Richard Charlton.

1550. A Godlye treatyse of Prayer, translated into Englishe by John Bradforde. From the Latin of P. Melancthon. [Also in 1589, John Wight, Publisher.]

1554. Preface of Melancthon to "A Faithful Admonition of a certain true Pastor and Prophet sent unto the Germans."

1561. A famous and godly history, contaynyng the lyves and actes of three renowned reformers of the christian church, Martine Luther, John Ecolampadius and Huldericke Zuinglius: the declaration of Martin Luthers faythe before the Emperour Charles the fyft, and the illustre estates of the empyre of Germanye, wyth an oration of hys death : all set forth in Latin by Philip Melancthon, Wolfgangus Faber, Capito, Simon Grineus and Oswald Miconius. Newly Englished by Henry Bennett, Collesian. London, John Sampson.

1566. P. Melancton upon the VIII chapter of Paules epistles to the Romanes, Whether it be mortall sin to transgress civil lawes.

1569. The Miseries of schoolmasters, uttered in a Latine Oration made by the famous clearke, Philip Melanchthon. London, Henry Denham.

1570. Newes from Niniue to Englande brought by the prophete Jonas. By Brentius; translated by Thomas Tinime, Minister.

1573. An Exposition of Solomon's Booke, called Ecclesiastes or the Preacher. By Martin Luther. London, John Day.

1573. A Commentarie of M. Doctor Martin Luther on the epistle of St. Paul to the Galatians. London, Thos. Vautrollier. [In the library of British Museum, there are English editions of Luther on Galatians of 1577, 1580, 1588, 1616.]

1577. M. Luther's Exposition on 130 Psame. Translated by Thos. Potter. London, Hugh Shyngleton.

1577. A commentaire upon the fiftene psalmes callel Psalmi Graduum, that is Psalmes of Dygrees: faithfully copied out of the lectures of D. Martin Luther.—Translated out of the Latin by Henry Bull. Cum priveligio. London, Thos. Vautrollier.

1577. A commentarie of M. Doctor Martin Luther upon the epistle of Paul to the Galathians first collected and gathered word by word out of his preaching, and now out of Latine faithfully translated into English for the unlearned. Diligently revised, corrected and newly imprinted again. Cum priveligio. London, Thos. Vautrollier. [See above 1573.]

1577. A newe worek concernyng both parties of the Sacrament to be receyved of the lay people as well as under the kynde of breade, with certen other articles, of bysshops, the chapters whereof are conteyned in the next leafe: made by Philip Melanchthon and now translated out of the Latyn. London, Richard Jugge. [Of this translation, there were earlier editions, Basle, probably 1543, and London, probably 1560. See catalogue of books published prior to 1640, in Library of British Museum].

1578. A very comfortable and necessary sermon in these our dayes, made by the right reverend father and faithful servant of Jesus Christ Martin Luther, concernyng the coming of our Saviour Christ to iudgement, and the signes that go before the last day. Whiche sermon is an exposition of the Gospell appointed to be read in the church on the second Sunday in Advent, and is now newly translated out of the Latin into English, and somethyng augmented and enlarged by the translator with certaine notes in the margent. Imprinted cum gratia et priveligio—Majestatis, London, John Byddell.

1578. M. Luther on Is. ix: 2-7; being a prophecie of Christ, wherein the conquest of Christ and his members over sin, Death and Sathan is declared. London, H. Bynneman for Gregory Seaton.

1578. Special and chosen sermons of D. Martin Luther, collected out of his writings and preachings. Englished by W. C. (Will Gace). [These 34 sermons are dedicated "To—Syr Thomas Heneage." He was fined for printing this book without license, xs. Another edition 1581.]

1578. A Right Comfortable Treatise containing fourteen pointes of consolation for them that labor and are laden. Written by D. Martin Luther to Prince Frederick Duke of Saxony, he being sore sicke, thereby to comfort him in the time of his great distress, Englished by W. Gace. [Another edition 1580.]

1578. The sermon which Christ made on the way to Emaus to those two sorrowful disciples, set down in a dialogue by D. Urbane Regius, wherein he hath gathered and expounded the chief prophecies of the old Testament concerning Christ. London, John Day. [Another edition 1612.]

1579. Phil. Melangton, his praiers, translated by Richard Robinson. London, Henry Denham.

1580. A Right Godly and Learned discourse upon the booke of Ester. Written in latin by J. Brentius, and new turned into English by J. Harrison. London.

1581. A commentarie or exposition upon the twoo Epistles generall of Saint Peter and that of Saint Jude. First faithfullie gathered out of the Lectures and Preachings of that worthie Instrumente in Goddes Churche, Doctour Martine Luther. And now out of the Latine, for the singuler benefite and comfort of the Godlie, familiarle translated into Englishe by Thomas Newton. Imprinted for Abr. Veale in Paule's church yard.

1581. A Manuell of christian praiers by divers devout and godly men, as Calvin, Luther, Melangton, etc., augmented and amended by Abr. Fleming. London, Henry Denham.

1581. Singuler and fruitfull manner of prayer used by D. M. Luther, paraphrastically written on the Lordes praier, beliefe and the commandements.

1582. A descouerse and batterie of the great Fort of unwritten Traditions, otherwise, An examination of the Councill of Trent, touching the decree of traditions. Done by Martinus Chemnitius in Latine, and translated into Englishe by R. V. London, Thos. Purfoot.

1583. A declaration made by the Archbishop of Collen, opon the deede of his marriage. Sent to the States of his Archbishoprike According to the coppie Imprented at Collen, 1583. London: Printed by John Woolfe, 1583.

1588. Luther's sermon on the Angels. London, Hugh Syngelton.

1588. An instruccyon of christen faythe how to be bolde upon the promyse of God and not to doubte of our salvacyon, made by Urbanus Regius. Translated into englyshe. Dedicated by J. Fox the translator. Londown, Hugh Syngelton

1590. A homelie or sermon of the good and evill Angell; on the 18 Mat., ver. 10, Preached at Zelle in Saxony, 1537. By Urbanus Regius. First translated by Richard Robinson, citizen of London. Licensed in 1582. [Another edition in 1593.] John Charleswood, London.

1584. Solace of Sion, and Joy of Jerusalem, being an expositon on the LXXXIII Psalm. Translated into English by R. Robinson.

1596. The force of Faith, containing a most sweet and comfortable treatise of the divine talke between Christ and the woman of Canaan. Also a Dialogue between a sorrowfull sinner, and God's word concerning him. Written in Latin by Nicholas Selneccerus. Translated by R. M. Printed for Chr. Hunt.

WITHOUT DATE.

A fruitfull sermon of D. Martin Luther concerning Matrimony, taken out of the Epistle to the Hebrews.

Declaration of the Order that the churches in Denmarke and many other places in Germany do use, not onely at the holye Supper, but also at Baptisme. By Miles Coverdale. Printed beyond the sea.

A brefe and playne declaratyon of the dewty of married folkes, gathered out of the holy scriptures, and set forth in the almayne tonge by Hermon Arcbyshop of Cologne, whiche wylled all the hosholdes of his flocke to have the same in their bedchambers as a mirror or glasse dayly to loke in, etc. Newly translated into ye Englishe tonge by Hans Dekyn Imprynte—in Temestrete by Hughe Syngyleton, at the dobbel hoad, over agaynst the Stylyarde.

INDEX.

Absolution, 93, 278.
Abuses, Articles of Augsburg Confession on, 133, 141, 150, 156, 177 sq.
Active Obedience of Christ, 336.
Adiaphorists, 204.
Adult Baptism, 258 sq.
Aepinus, John, Superintendent at Hamburg (b. 1499, d. 1553), 128, 148.
Agende, Mediæval, 257.
Agnus Dei, 221, 309.
Agricola (Schneider) John, (of Eisleben, b. 1492, d. 1566), 13, 76, 123, 200.
Alcuin (b. 735, d. 804) 299.
Alesius, Alexander, Professor at Leipzig, (b. 1500, d. 1565), 57, 76, 85, 87, 128, 151.
Allen Thomas (d. 1558), 9.
Alva, Duke of, (b. 1508, d. 1582), 143.
Amsdorf, von, Nicholas (b. 1483, d. 1565), 205.
Anabaptism, 68, 77, 89, 90, 139, 180, 183, 204, 267, 342.
Anderson, Christopher, (b. 1782, d. 1852). His "Annals of the English Bible," 17 sq.
Annaberg (town in Saxony), 141.
Anne Boleyn, (b. 1507, d. 1536), 32, 41, 43, 44, 74-76, 193.
Anne of Cleves (b. 1515, d. 1557), 152, 167, 168, 178, 183, 189, 196.
Anti-Christ, 134, 135, 156.
Antinomians, 204.
Antiphons, 291.
Antwerp, 125, 181.
Apology of the Augsburg Confession (1531), 52, 63, 67, 68, 70, 72, 80, 83 sq., 89, 91-96, 103, 109, 110-112, 127, 138, 167, 179, 199, 335, 341 sq.
Apostolical Constitutions, The, 296.
Apostolical Succession, 323 sq.
Aquinas, Thomas, (*Doctor angelicus*, b. 1227, d. 1274), 41, 298.
Argentine R., 353.

(359)

Arthur, Prince, brother of Henry VIII., (b. 1486, d. 1502), 40.
Arthur, Thomas, (d. 1532), 7, 9, 12.
Articles, on Abuses, see Abuses.
    Six, The (1539), 145 sq., 150–155, 159, 167 sqq., 191 sqq., 201.
    Ten, The (1536), 80, 88–104, 128, 138, 139.
    Thirteen, The (1535), 63.
    Thirteen, The (1538), 136–139.
    Thirty-Nine, The (1563), 136, 339–42.
    Forty-two (1553), 340.
Augsburg, 200.
Augsburg Confession, (1530), 52, 63, 67 sq., 70–3, 75, 80, 83 sq., 91–3, 96 sq., 101, 103, 109, 111, 127, 132 sq., 136–9, 141, 146, 148, 150, 152, 167, 178 sq., 192, 195, 197, 199, 201–4, 210, 336–42, 349, 350, 354.
Augsburg, Diet, (1530), 142.
Augusti, Prof. C. J. W. (b. 1771, d. 1841), 223.
Augustine, St. (b. 354, d. 430), 306, 341.
Augustinianism, 2.
Aurifaber, Johann (b. 1517, d. 1568), 352.
Austrian "Order of Service," (1571), 250, 303.
Authorized Version, (1611), 147.
Aylmer, John, Bishop of London, (b. 1521, d. 1594), 347.

Balhorn, John (Printer), 189.
Bamberg Missal, 219.
Bamberg Order, 223.
Baptism, Order of, 253–8.
    Ten Articles on 90.
    Tyndale on, 37.
Barlow, Wm., Bishop of St. David's, afterwards of Chichester, (d. 1568), 83.
Barnes, Robert (b. 1495 martyr, d. 1540), 7, 8, 9, 11, 12, 49, 55–60, 67, 76, 116, 118, 127, 132 sq. 149, 151, 178, 181–92, 196, 206 sq., 215.
Basle, 346.
Baum, John William (Biographer of Bucer), 276.
Baumbach von, Ludwig, 149.
Beauchame, Louis, 191.
Becon, Thomas, (b. 1511, d. 1567), 324 sq.
Benedicamus, 311 sqq.
Benger, Elizabeth Ogilvy (b. 1778, d. 1827), **75.**
Berne (Switzerland), 276.
Beyer Hardtmann (b. 1516, d. 1577), 343.
Bible, English, 14, 115–26, 145–7.

Billican, Theobald (d. 1559), 13.
Bilney, Thomas (b. 1500, martyr 1531), 6 sq., 11 sq., 181.
Bishops, Luther and Melanchthon on, 160.
Bishops' Book of 1537, 104-14, 314.
Blakeney, Richard Paul (b. 1820, d. 1884) 253.
Blage, Mrs. 191.
Blaurer, Ambrose (b. 1492, d. 1567), 148.
Blunt, John Henry (b. 1823, d. 1884), 101, 208, 234, 238-40, 253, 257, 259, 272 sq., 328.
Boleyn, Anne, see Anne Boleyn.
Boleyn, Sir Thomas (b. 1477, d. 1539), 44.
Bona, Giovanni, Cardinal (b. 1609, d. 1674), 300.
Bonner, Edmund, Bishop of London (b. 1490, d. 1569), 191 sq., 334.
Boyneburg, a, George, LL. D. (a Hessian diplomatist), 129.
Bradford, Rudolph, 10.
Bradwardin, Thomas of, Archbishop of Canterbury (b. 1290, d. 1348), 2.
Brandenburg, Elector of (1546), 196.
Brandenburg-Nürnberg *Kinder Predigten* (1533), 4, 316.
Brandenburg-Nürnberg Order (Osiander, Brentz, 1533), 47, 142, 223-5, 243, 250, 255 sq., 259 sqq., 267, 270 sqq., 282, 289, 303, 310, 316, 335 sq.
Bremen, 169.
Brentz, Dr. John, the Swabian Reformer (b. 1499, d. 1570), 13, 46 sqq., 72, 200, 209, 211, 222, 242, 270, 289 sq., 325, 340, 342. 354, 355, 357. His Catechism, 325-7.
Bristol, Use of, 220.
Browne, Robert, Founder of "Independents" (b. 1550, d. 1631), 347.
Browne, Sir Thomas (b. 1605, d. 1682), 138.
Brunswick, 199.
Bucer (*Kuhhorn*) Dr. Martin (b. 1491, d. 1551), 13, 48, 72, 152, 155, 167, 196, 209-213, 224, 227, 234, 259, 269. 274 sqq., 278 sq., 327, 333.
Bucler, Walter, 194.
Buddeus, Dr. J. F. (b. 1667, d. 1729), 209.
Bugenhagen, Dr. John, Pomeranus (b. 1485, d. 1558), 13, 58, 153, 167, 187 223, 240, 302, 310, 350.
Bull, Henry (d. 1575) 355.
Bullinger, Henry, the Swiss Reformer (b. 1504, d. 1574), 207 sq., 213-17, 244.
Burcher, 213 sq.
Burials, Orders for, 273 sq. [205.
Burkhard, Francis, Vice-Chancellor (b. 1504, d. 1560), 72, 129, 149, 153, 196,
Burnet, Gilbert, Bishop of Salisbury (b. 1643, d. 1715), 48, 59, 67, 100.

Calenskie, John, 354. [349.
Calvin, Dr. John, (b. 1509, d. 1564), 214, 275, 277 sq., 281, 337, 344 sq., 347,
Calvinism, 243, 342, 344, 347.
Calvör, Kaspar (b. 1650, d. 1725), 295, 303.
Cambridge, University of, 3, 6, 8, 10, 11, 14 sq., 43 sq., 48, 61 sq., 117, 125, 181, 192, 209, 275, 327, 344.
Camerarius (Liebhard), Dr. Joachim (b. 1500, d. 1574), 46, 56, 76.
Campeggi, Lorenzo Cardinal (b. 1474, d. 1539), 42.
Campion and Beaumont's " Prayer-Book Interleaved," 253, 328.
Cardwell, Dr. Edward (b. 1787, d. 1861), 87 sqq.
Carlstadt (Bodenstein) Dr. Andrew (b. 1483, d. 1541), 13, 220, 284.
Cassel (Hesse) Catechism (1539), 327 sq.
Cassel (Hesse) Order (1539), 224, 241 sq., 260 sq., 267 sqq., 278-81, 327.
Catechism in Confirmation, 267.
        Anglican, 314.
        Calvin's, 332.
        Genevan, 332.
        Luther's, 104-9.
        Nowel and Ponet's, 331. [188.
Catherine of Aragon, Queen of England (b. 1486, d. 1536), 40 sqq., 49 sq., 76,
Catherine de Medici (b. 1519, d. 1589), 52.
Catherine Parr, Sixth Queen of Henry VIII. (b. 1513, d. 1548), 193.
Celius, Michael, Court-Preacher at Mansfeld, (1546), 352.
Cecil, Sir William, 340.
Cellarius (Kellner) Martin (b. 1499, d. 1564), 13.
Ceremonies, 161-163.
" Charity," in Justification, 96.
Charles V., Emperor (b. 1500, d. 1558), 41, 43, 134, 142, 144, 148, 160, 166, 188, 193, 200, 202 sqq., 214.
Chemnitz, Dr. Martin (b. 1522, d. 1586), on Confirmation, 285.
Cheke, Sir John (b. 1514, d. 1557), 216, 340.
Christ, Vicarious Satisfaction of, 93, 114, 181, 184.
Christopher, Duke of Würtemberg (b. 1515, d. 1568), 342, 346 sq.
Chrysostom, John (b. 350, d. 407), 308.
Church, The, Definition of, 84, 110, 185.
        Marks of, 182.
Clark or Clerke, John (at Cambridge, 1525), 10, 11, 44.
Clement VII. (Pope 1523-34), 42, 52.
Coburg Order (1626), 310.
Cochlæus (Dobeneck) John (b. 1479, d. 1552), 17, 19, 35.
Colet, John, Dean of St. Paul's (b. 1466, d. 1519), 2, 15.

Index.

Coligny, Admiral (b. 1517, martyr 1572), 346.
Collects, 250, 251, 297, 311.
Cologne, Hemann of (b. 1477, d. 1552, Elector and Archbishop, 1515-1546),
    196, 224, 233 sq., 239 sq., 253, 328, 336, 352, 353, 357 sq.
    Order of (1543), 224, 226 sq., 241 sq., 244, 253-9, 263 sq., 268-74,
    278-80, 302, 327 sq., 336.
Commission, English to Wittenberg (1536), 55-73.
    Lutheran to England (1538), 127-139.
    English and Lutheran, at Frankfort (1539), 148 sq.
Common Prayer, Book of, 11, 124, 218-34, 243.
Communion in Both Kinds, 164, 178 sqq., 182.
Communion Service of Edward VI., 278.
    in Lutheran Orders, 305
Conde, Prince of, 345.
Conditional Baptism, 263 sq.
Confession, Augsburg, see Augsburg.
    Saxon, see Saxon.
Confession, to a Priest, 92, 153, 156, 162.
Confessional Basis, 52, 58 sqq., 63, 67, 70-3, 80, 103, 132 sqq., 141, 169 sqq.,
    177, 194 sq., 197, 203.
Confessional Service of II. Edward VI. (1552), 276.
Confirmation, 265-9.
Confiteor, The, 288 sq.
Congregationalists, 347.
Consecration of Elements, 308.
Convocation, English, 77, 81, 83, 88, 100, 115, 116, 192, 231, 342.
Corvinus, Antony (b. 1501, d. 1553), 52, 180.
Cottiswood, 191.
Councils, not infallible, 182.
Cox, Dr. Richard, Bishop of Ely (b. 1499, d. 1581), 11, 44, 245, 344 sq.
Cranach, Lucas (b. 1472, d. 1533), 168.
Cranmer, Thomas, Archbishop of Canterbury (b. 1489, martyr 1556), 43 sqq.,
    57, 61 sq., 74, 76 sq., 79 sq., 83, 85, 89, 97, 100-05, 112, 115, 122,
    131 sq., 134, 136, 141, 150 sq., 153, 155 sq., 178, 192 sq., 197 sq., 200,
    206, 214, 215-7, 223, 231, 233 sq., 239 sq., 245, 275, 279, 314 sqq., 334,
    336, 339 sq., 343.
Creed in the Service, 301 sq.
Creed, Catechetical Exposition of, 106 sqq.
Crespy, Peace of (1544), 193.
Crome, Edward (d. 1562), 9.
Crook or Croke, Richard (b. 1489, d. 1558), 48.

Cross, Sign of, 258.
Cruciger, Caspar (b. 1504, d. 1548), 5-8, 124, 129, 199, 224.
Crumwell, Thomas (b. 1490, d. 1540), 43, 49, 59, 67, 77-80, 82, 86 sq., 128, 140 sq., 145, 147, 150 sqq., 155, 168, 178-81, 183, 192, 196, 215, 237, 241, 350.
Cyprian, Bishop of Carthage (b. 200, d. 258), 306.
Cyril of Jerusalem (b. 315, d. 386), 306.

Dachstein, Wolfgang, German Hymn-writer (d. 1530), 124.
Damianus, Peter (b. 1007, d. 1072), 297.
Days, Distinction of, 182.
Decius (Hovesch) Nicholas, German Hymn-writer (d. 1541), 123, 124.
Demaus on Tyndale's Relation to Luther, 24 sq.
Denmark, Alliance with, 182.
Derrick, 191.
Dietrich, Veit (Luther's amanuensis, afterwards pastor of St. Sebald's, Nürnberg, b. 1507, d. 1549), 129, 250.
Dixon, R. W., Dean (b. 1833), 95, 102.
Döber's Mass, 223, 290, 302, 310.
Dorrington, Thomas, 348.
Dürer, Albrecht (b. 1471, d. 1528), 45.
Durandus, William (b. 1237, d. 1296), 297, 299, 302, 306 sq.

Eadie, John (b. 1810, d. 1876), 18, 35, 117, 146.
Easter, a season for Baptism, 254.
Edward VI. (b. 1537, d. 1553, reigned from 1547), 9, 11, 198-205, 214 sq., 241, 314, 343.
    First Book of, 243 sq., 246, 249, 251-3, 257, 200, 202 sq., 282.
    Second Book of, 251, 257, 269, 275, 281, 344.
Egbert, Archbishop of York (d. 767), Prayer of, 268.   347.
Elizabeth, Queen (b. 1533, d. 1603, reigned from 1558), 126, 191, 194, 342,
Ellis, Sir Henry (b. 1777, d. 1869), 86.
English, Melanchthon speaks, 144.
Erasmus (Gerard) Desiderius (b. 1465, d. 1536), 3, 7, 15, 23, 43 sq., 105, 208.
Ethiopic Order, 301.
Evening Service, 245-52.
Excommunication, Papal, 182.
Exhortation in the Communion Service, 307.
Exorcism, 259, 282.
Extreme Unction, 84.

Faber, Jacob, Stapulensis (b. 1450, d. 1536), 43.
Fagius (Bücher) Paul, (Prof. in Cambridge, b. 1504, d. 1549),

Faith, 92, 96, 109, 181.
    and Works, Tyndale on, 31 sq.
Fasting, 182.
Ferdinand I., of Germany (b. 1503, d. 1564), 53.
Fisher, John, Bishop of Rochester (b. 1459, d. 1535), 5, 6, 12, 42.
Flacius Illyricus (b. 1520, d. 1575), 347.
Forgery, A Literary, 159-178.
Forty-two Articles, 136.
Fox, Edward, Bishop of Hereford (b. 1496, d. 1538), 61 sq., 67, 70, 75, 78, 80, 83, 86 sq., 89, 97, 101, 104 sq., 128, 130 sq., 134, 149, 150, 152, 207, 215.
Foxe, John (b. 1517, d. 1587), 12, 15, 98, 181, 185.
France, Spurious Articles in, 159.
Francis I. (of France, b. 1494, d. 1547; King from 1515), 41 sq., 52 sq., 80 134, 145, 153, 193, 199, 203, 214.
Frankfort on the Main, Conferences at, 1536—72, 128.
                                      1539—144, 148.
                                      1546—196.
                Exiles at, 343, 344, 346 sq.
                Order of (1530), 243, 278.
Frederick III., the Wise, Elector of Saxony (b. 1463, d. 1525), 142.
Frederick II., Elector Palatine (b. 1482, d. 1556), 196.
Freedom of the will, 84, 162, 182.
French Lutherans, 52.
Frith, John (b. 1503, martyr 1533), 11, 38, 78, 207.
Froschauer, Christopher (Publisher at Zürich, b. 1485, d. 1564), 116.
Froude, J. A. (b. 1818), quoted 4, 79, 82, 95 sq., 197.
Fuller, Thomas (b. 1608, d. 1661), 88, 99, 190.
Gace, William (Translator), 356.
Gallican Liturgies, 219.
    Missals, 219.
Gardiner, Stephen, Bishop of Winchester (b. 1495, d. 1555), 75, 78 sq., 83, 98, 101 sq., 104 sq., 127, 150, 154, 157, 178, 182 sq., 192, 196, 315.
Gavanti, Bartholomew (b. 1570, d. 1638), 297 sq.
Geikie, Cunningham (b. 1824), 101.
Gelasius I. (Pope 492-6), 219, 297.
Geneva, 214, 276, 281, 344.
George of Anhalt, Bishop and Prince (b. 1507, d. 1553) 72.
George I. of England (b. 1660, d. 1727, reigned from 1714), 348.
Gerbert, Martin, Baron of Homan (b. 1720, d. 1793), 294, 298, 299, 302.
Gerdesius, Dr. Daniel (b. 1698, d. 1765), 143.

Germans, The, Coverdale on, 186.
           Fox on, 87.
           Litany of, 232 sq.
Germany, the house called, 8.
           Orders of South-Western, 284.
Ginsburg, Christian D., 117.
Glastenbury, 209, 276.
Gloria in Excelsis, 295.
    Patri, 294.
Glosses, Tyndale's, 29 sqq.
Gochius, John (d. 1475), 13.
Goebel, Maximilian, 209.
Good Works, 37, 95, 155, 182, 185.
Goodrich, Thomas, Bishop of Ely (b. 1480, d. 1554), 83.
Gospels and Epistles, 252.
Grace, Declaration of, 289 sq.
Gradual, The, 221.
Grafton, Richard (Publisher, d. 1572), 145, 191, 230.
Gratias, The, 306.
"Great Bible, The," (1539-41), 118.
Gregory the Great (b. 550, d. 604), 219, 250, 291, 297.
Greiser (Greiter) Matth., (d. 1550), 124.
Grey, Lady Jane (b. 1537, d. 1554), 214.
Grindal, Edmund, Archbishop of Canterbury (b. 1519, d. 1583), 346 sq.
Guelders, 169.

Hallam, Henry (b. 1777, d. 1859), 23.
Hallelujah, The, 300.
Hamburg, 17, 116, 128, 151, 169, 181 sq., 263.
Hanover, House of, 348.   [339, 342.
Hardwick, Charles, Archdeacon (b. 1821, d. 1859), 79, 100, 111, 211, 282,
Hare, Julius Clark (b. 1795, d. 1855), 96.
Heath, Nicholas (b. 1501, d. 1579), 61 sq., 67, 70, 74-6, 146, 149 sq.
Hegenwald, Erhard, M. D., (Würtemberg Hymn-writer), 124 sq.
Heidelberg, 196.
Heilmann, 142.
Henry II, King of France (b. 1518, d. 1559, reigned from 1547), 52.
Henry VIII, King of England (b. 1491, d. 1547, reigned from 1509), 1, 39-44, 46, 48-60, 62-69, 71-80, 89, 95 sq., 99, 105, 112-14, 128 sq., 132-6, 140, 144 sq., 148-58, 168 sq., 177-9, 182, 187-99, 207, 215, 231, 238, 241, 349.

Index. 367

Herford, Charles H., 124.
Hermann, Archbishop of Cologne, see Cologne.
Hermann, Rychard (Merchant), 74.
Herzog, Heinrich, of Saxony, Order of (1539), 224, 226, 256, 273.
Hesse Cassel, Order of (1539), see Cassel.
Heynes, Simon (d. 1552), 9, 10, 245.
Hilary of Poictiers (d. 366), 296.
Hilles, (Hills or Hils) Richard, (London Merchant), 208, 244.
Hilsey, John, Bishop of Rochester (d 1538), 83, 237, 247.
Höfling, Dr. J. W. F. (b. 1802, d. 1853), 256 sq., 269, 327.
Hoffe, Ubright (Leipzig Publisher), 191.
Holbeach, Laurence, 245.
Holstein, Duke of (1545), 194.
Homilies of the Church of England, 231, 241, 333-8.
Hook, Dr. W. F., Dean of Chichester (b. 1768, d. 1875), 322. [217.
Hoper or Hooper, John, Bishop of Worcester (b. 1495, martyr 1555), 207-11,
Horne, Dr. Robert, Dean of Durham, Bishop of Winchester (b. 1519, d. 1579), 346.
Hymns from the German, 119-123.

> *Christ lag in Todesbanden.*
> *Durch Adam's Fall ist ganz verderbt.*
> *Ein feste Burg ist unser Gott.*
> *Es ist das Heil uns Kommen.*
> *Gelobet seist du Jesu Christ.*
> *Gott der Vater wohn uns bei.*
> *In Gott gelaub ich.*
> *Komm, Heiliger Geist, Herre Gott.*
> *Mensch, wilt du leben seliglich.*
> *Mit Fried und Freud, ich fahr dahin.*
> *Mitten wir im Leben sind.*
> *Nun freut euch lieben Christen.*

Incarnation, The, 347.
Index Prohibitorum, 12 sq.
Independents (Congregationalists), 347.
Indulgences, 130.
Innspruck, Battle of (1552), 203.
"Institution of a Christian Man," 105, 314.
Interim of 1548, 97 sq., 125, 166, 201-3, 208 sq., 214, 343.
Introits, 249 sq., 276, 291-4.
Invocation of Saints, 164, 182, 185.

Jane Seymour, Queen (d. 1537), 96.
Jena, University of, 200, 347.
Jenkyns, Rev. Henry, 112, 136, 215.
Jennings, 101.
Jewel, John, Bishop of Salisbury (b. 1522, d. 1571), 210.
John Frederick, Elector of Saxony (b. 1503, d. 1554, Elector from 1532), 67, 128, 159, 166, 194, 199, 200-05.
Jonas, Dr. Justus (b. 1493, d. 1555), 76, 123, 153, 167, 216, 224, 315, 352.
   Jr., 315.
Joye, George (d. 1553), 34.
Juda, Leo (b. 1482, d. 1542), 117.
Justification, Definition of, 95, 138.
   Condition of, 96, 162.
Justin Martyr (b. 103, martyr 165), 299.

Keys, Power of, 182.
Kite, John, Bishop of Carlisle (d. 1537), 83.
Kliefoth, Dr. Theodore (b. 1810), 247 sq., 285, 291, 312.
Knight, Charles (b. 1791, d. 1873), 150.
Knox, Dr. John (b. 1505, d. 1572), 11, 340, 342, 344.
Köstlin, Dr. Heinrich A. (now Prof. at Friedberg), 285.
Kymæus, John (b. 1498, d. 1552), 224.
Kyrie, 294 sq.

Lambert, Francis (b. 1486, martyr 1530), 7, 13, 18, 183.
Language of Public Service, 222, 260.
Lasco a, John (b. 1499, d. 1560), 208, 217, 275 sq., 344.
Lathbury, Thomas (b. 1798, d. 1865), 100.
Latimer, Hugh, Bishop of Worcester (b. 1491, martyr 1555), 6 sq., 11 sq., 77, 81-3, 97, 100, 104 sq., 150 sq., 153, 216.
Latin Versions of the Bible, 117.
Laurence, Richard, Archbishop of Cashel (b. 1760, d. 1839), 56, 89, 94 sq., 99, 253, 278.
"League, The Christian," 197.
Learning the Old and the New, 3, 77, 192.
Lee, Edward, Archbishop of York (b. 1482, d. 1544), 20, 21, 35, 83.
Leo I. (Pope 440, d. 461), 219, 297.
Leonine Sacramentary, 297.
Lesse, Nicholas (Translator), 352.
Lessons, 299.
Lewis, Duke of Bavaria and Count Palatine (d. 1534), 7.
Lingard, John (b. 1771, d. 1851), 99.

Index. 369

Link, Wenceslaus (b. 1483, d. 1547), 46.
Litany, 84, 230-41, 303 sq., 344.
Liturgies, Gallican, 219, 256.
    Gothic, 256.
    Mozarabic, 219.
    Roman, 219.
Löhe, William (b. 1808, d. 1872), 106, 246, 290 sq., 297.
Lollards, 2, 3, 84.
Longfellow, H. W. (b. 1807, d. 1882), his poem on Nürnberg, 45.
Lonicerus (b. 1557, d. 1590), 13.
Lübeck, 147.
Luft, Hans (b. 1495, d. 1584), 19, 126.
Luther, Dr. Martin (b. 1484, d. 1546), 4-7, 9-13, 17-32, 34-38, 40. 43, 45, 50,
    51, 57, 58, 62, 69-71, 74, 94, 98, 104, 106 sq., 110, 117-122, 124, 126,
    130-32, 135, 151-3, 159-67, 178, 181 sq., 187-9, 210, 220-26, 233-40,
    251-3, 256-60, 272, 284, 290, 296, 300-5, 309 sq., 316-325, 330, 344.
Lutheran, 35-38, 68, 211, 213.
    Baptism, Is it valid? 345.
    Orders Classified, 223.
Lutherans, 4, 6, 10, 21, 36, 52.

Mabillon, John (b. 1632, d. 1707), 256.
Magdeburg, 200.
Mamertus of Vienna (d. 475), 231.
Mammon, Luther and Tyndale on, 30 sq.
Mantua, Council at, 111, 351.
Marbach, John (b. 1521, d. 1581), 208.
Margaret of Navarre (b. 1492, d. 1577), 53.
Mark-Brandenburg Order (1540), 223, 256, 260, 268, 271.
Marlborow, 19.
Marriage, with brother of deceased husband, 40 sqq., 49 sqq.
    of priests, 153, 157, 165, 182.
    Order, 269-72.
Marshall's Primer (1535), 234, 237.
Martyr Peter (b. 1500, d. 1562), 207, 209-11, 216, 275, 344.
Mary, Queen (b. 1516, d. 1558, reigned from 1553), 41, 43, 49, 62, 79, 126,
    191, 194, 198, 205, 210, 343.
Masone, John (d. 1566), 196, 201.
Maskell, William (b. 1814),
Mass, Luther's Formula of, 220, 249.
    Sermon on (1520), 220.

Mass, Roman, 182.
Masses, Private, 156.
Mathesius, John (b. 1504, d. 1564), 250.
Matins, 246 sq., 249.
Matthews, Thomas (Pseudonym), 126, 145 sq., 191.
Maurice, Duke of Saxony (b. 1521, d. 1553), 194, 199 sq., 203.
May, William (d. 1560), 245.
Mecklenburg Order (1552), 288 sq.
Mekins, Richard (martyr, 1540), 192.
Melanchthon, Dr. Philip (b. 1497, d. 1560), 13, 49-51, 53, 55-59, 61-63, 67-72, 76 sq., 81, 86, 89-96, 125-131, 139, 141, 148-67, 199 sq., 206, 224, 337, 341 sq., 344.
Methodists, 8.
Missals, Bamberg, 219.
    Gallican, 219.
    Gothic, 251.
    Nürnberg, 219.
    Roman, 219, 249, 252.
Mitchell, Prof., 124.
Moebanus, Ambrose. (b. 1494, d. 1554), 124.
Mogner, Leonard (Pastor at Siegrau), 142.
Mombert, Dr. J. I. (b. 1829), 19 sq., 24, 117, 126.
Monasticism, 165, 174 sq., 182.
Monmouth, Humphrey (London Alderman, d. 1537), 16, 181, 183.
More, Sir Thomas (b. 1480, d. 1534), 17, 35, 78.
Morning Service, 245-252.
Morris, Dr. John G. (b. 1803), 339.
Morysinne (Morrison), Sir Richard (d. 1556), 201, 204.
Mount (Mont), Dr. Christopher, (d. 1572), 129, 148, 152, 194, 196, 201, 214.
Mozarabic Liturgy, 219, 310.
Mühlberg, Battle of (1547), 199.
Mullins, John (d. 1591), 346.
Muratori, Ludovico Antonio (b. 1672, d. 1750), 298.
Musculus, Wolfgang (b. 1497, d. 1563), 353.
Myconius, Frederick (b. 1491, d. 1546), 129-134, 141, 148, 167, 177, 196, 205, 224.

Nassau, Reformation in, 141.
    Church Order, 142 sq., 254 sq.
Naumburg, 128 sq.
Navarre, King of (1561), 210.

Index. 371

New Learning, The, 3, 77, 192, 352.
Nicholas, John, 7.
Nicholson, Sygar, 10.
Nordhausen, 199.
Norton, Thomas, (b. 1532, d. 1584), 332.
Noth-Taufe, 255, 262 sq.
Nowell, Alexander (b. 1507, d. 1601), 332.
Novatus, Heresy of, 163.
Nürnberg, 45 sqq., 104, 123, 196, 223, 244, 250, 274, 289, 307, 315.
    Kinder-Predigten, 216.
    Order of Service, 46, 240-2, 257, 282.
    Peace of, 51
Nunc Dimittis, 310.
Nyx, Richard, Bishop of Norwich (d. 1536), 83.

"Obedience of a Christian Man," 32 sqq., 37, 105.
Occasional Offices, 274.
Œcolampadius, John (b. 1482, d. 1531), 49, 354.
Offertory, 303.
Order, Common, of Service, 48, 285.
Orders, Sacrament of, 111.
Original Sin, 91, 137 sq.
Osiander, Andrew (b. 1498, d. 1552), 46 sqq., 104, 129, 148, 206, 223, 240, 260, 270-2, 289, 315, 335 sq., 352.
Ott-Heinrich Order (1543), 256, 260, 268, 271.
Overall, John, Bishop of Lichfield (b. 1559, d. 1619), 332.
Oxford, University of, 2, 4, 8, 10, 14 sq., 44, 48, 62, 192, 209, 275.

Paissy, Colloquy of (1561), 210.
Palmer, William (b. 1803), 256 sq., 259, 268, 272 sq.
Papacy, 161, 182.
Parker, Matthew, Archbishop of Canterbury (b. 1504, d. 1575), 8.
Passau, Peace of (1552), 203.
Paul III. (b. 1466, Pope 1534, d. 1549), 194.
Pax, The, in the Communion Service, 309.
Paynell, Thomas (d. 1563), 9, 148.
Pellicanus, Conrad (b. 1478, d. 1566), 117.
Penance, Sacrament of, 91.
Perry, George S., 101.
Peter, Dr. William, 82.
Philip, Landgrave of Hesse (b. 1504, d. 1567), 67, 152, 194, 197.
Pirkheimer, Willibald (b. 1470, d. 1531), 45.

Pole, Reginald, Cardinal (b. 1500, d. 1558), 44, 75.
Pollanus (Poullain), Valerandus (d. 1558), 343.
Polydore, Vergil (b. 1470, d. 1550), 4.
Polygamy, Melanchthon on, 50.
Pomeranian Order of 1542, 304.
Ponet (Poinet), John (d. 1556), 331.
Potter, Thomas, 355.
Prayer, Tyndale on, 31.
    Confessional, 278, 281 sq.
    General, 303.
Preface, The, in the Service, 306.
Preparatory Service, 278, 287.
Prologues, Tyndale's, 25 sq.
Private Baptism, 262.
    Confession, 267.
    Mass, 68.
Procter, Frances, 243, 257, 273, 330.
Prussian Order, 223, 255.
Psalter of "Common Prayer," 124.
Public Baptism, 263 sq.
Puffendorf, Samuel, Baron (b. 1632, d. 1694), 348.
Purgatory, 165.
Puritanism, 11, 346.

Ranke, Leopold von (b. 1795, d. 1886), 96, 101.
Ratisbon (Regensburg), Diet of (1532), 45, 196, 351.
Reformation, English, Theories of, 1.
Regius, Urban (b. 1490, d. 1541), 13, 52 sq., 352 sq., 356 sq.
Repentance, 93, 96.
Repetitio of 1536, 89.
Repetition of Augsburg Confession, 71.
Rice, Richard, 353.
Ridley, Nicholas, Bishop of London (b. 1500, d. 1555), 9 sq., 207, 215, 245.
Ring, The, in the Marriage Ceremony, 271.
Robinson, Richard, 357 sq.
Rogers, Daniel (b. 1538, d. 1591), 126.
    John (b. 1500 or 1509, martyr 1555), 125 sq., 145 sq., 181.
Roman Liturgies and Missals, 219.
Romish Leaven in the X Articles, 96.
Rostock, 141.
Roy, William (martyr, 1531), 17.
Rupertus (d. 911), 297, 299.

Index.

Sachs, Hans (b. 1494, d. 1576), 46, 123 sq.
Sacrament, Definition of, 86, 112.
Sacramental and Sacrificial Elements of Worship, 285 sqq.
Sacramentarians, 94, 180, 297.
Salig, Christian August (b. 1692, d. 1738), 125, 203.
Salutation, The, 296, 365.
Sampson, Thomas (b. 1517, d. 1589), 354.
Sanctus, The, 221, 307. [351.
Sarcerius, Erasmus (b. 1501, d. 1559), 140, 146, 148, 153, 167, 179, 180, 224,
Sarum, Use of, 220, 239, 242, 251 sqq., 260, 269, 271.
Sastrow, Barth. John (b. 1520), 179.
Saxon Order of 1539, 256, 273, see Herzog-Heinrich.
    Visitation Articles, 255.
    Articles of 1551, 341.
    Lower, Order of (1585), 273.
Schaff, Dr. Philip (b. 1819), 101, 339.
Schmucker, Dr. Beale Melanchthon (b. 1827, d. 1888), 80.
Schnepff, Erhard (b. 1495, d. 1558), 52, 72, 347.
Schœberlein, Dr. Ludwig Frederick (b. 1813, d. 1881), 294.
Schœffer, P. (b. 1430, d. 1503), 20.
Schwabach Articles (1529), 91, 335.
Schwabach-Hall Order (1543), 242, 249, 254-6, 270 sq., 327.
"Schwarmerians," 180.
Scotland, Reformation in, 2. [196.
Seckendorf, Veit Ludwig von (b. 1626, d. 1692), 71 sq., 136, 139, 159, 166,
Selnecker, Nicholas (b. 1530, d. 1592), 358.
Sermon, The, 302.
Service, The Lutheran Chief, 283-313.
Seymour, Edward, Duke of Somerset (b. 1500, d. 1552), 198, 214.
Shakespeare, 193.
Shaxton, Nicholas, Bishop of Salisbury (d. 1556), 10, 83, 150, 156.
Sherborne, Robert, Bishop of Chichester (d. 1536), 83.
Shirrye, Richard (martyr, 1556), 354.
Sick, Visitation of the, 273.
Six Articles, The, 145 sq., 150-9, 167 sqq., 191 sqq., 201.
Sixty-seven Points, The, 83.
Skip, John, Bishop of Hereford (d. 1552), 10.
Smalcald Articles, 110 sq., 160 sq., 164, 166, 203, 341.
    League, 51-62, 142, 168, 194, 196, 199.
    War, 197, 214.
Smithfield, 183.

Smythe, Richard (d. 1563), 209 sq.
Solm, Count (d. 1545), 72.
Somerset, Duke of, see Seymour, Edward.
Spalatin, Dr. George (b. 1484, d. 1545), 62, 148.
Spengler, Lazarus (b. 1479, d. 1534), 46, 122, 124.
Speratus, Paul (b. 1484, d. 1551), 122, 124.
Sponsors, Address to, 260.
St. Andrew's, University of, 2.
St. Lawrence's, Nürnberg, 45 sq.
St. Paul's, London, 2, 5, 12, 230.
St. Sebald's, Nürnberg, 45 sq., 250.
Stafford, George (d. 1529), 9.
Standish, Dr. Henry (d. 1535), 39.
      Dr. John (b. 1509, d. 1570), 186.
Staupitz, Dr. John (d. 1524), 45.
Stokesley, John, Bishop of London (d. 1539), 83, 104.
Strassburg, 152, 208-10, 333, 346 sq.
      Mass (1524), 227-9, 276-9, 303.
Strigel, Victor (b. 1514, d. 1569), 347.
Strype, John (b. 1643, d. 1737), 74, 99, 150, 160, 166, 315.
Sturm, Jacob (b. 1489, d. 1553), 72.
Sumner (d. 1528), 11.
Surplice, 344.
Sursum Corda, 306.
Syngylton, Robert (Translator of Augsburg Confession, hanged March 7th, 1544), 354.
Synods in Nassau, 147.

Taverner, Richard (b. 1505, d. 1575), 11, 44, 80 sq., 140, 143, 146 sq., 179, 192, 337, 351.
Taylor, John, Bishop of Lincoln (d. 1554), 245.
Te Deum, 183, 302 sqq.
Telesphorus (Bishop of Rome 128-139), 296.
Ten Articles of 1536, 80, 88-104, 128, 138 sq.
Testament, Erasmus' New, 3, 7.
Tetzel, Dr. John (b. between 1450 and '60, d. 1519), 130, 142.
Thirteen Articles of 1535, 63.
      1538, 136-9.
Thirty-Nine Articles, 136, 339-42.
Thixtell, 9.
Toledo, 219.

Tonstall, Cuthbert, Bishop of London (b. 1475, d. 1559), 16, 21, 83, 146, 150.
Tracts for the Times (1833-41), 100.
Traheron, Bartholomew (Dean of Chichester, 1550), 216 sq.
Transubstantiation, 164.
Trent, Council of (1545-63), 194, 200, 219, 264, 267, 342, 357.
Trinity, 137, 184.
Trollope, William, 330.
Turner, Wyllyam (d. 1568), 9, 352.
Turrecremata (Torquemada) Juan de (b. 1388, d. 1468), 297.
Twelve Apostles, Teaching of, 306.
Tyndale, Wiliiam (b. 1484, martyr 1536), 11, 14-39, 74, 105, 116-8, 126, 181, 183, 207.

Ulmis ab, John, 216.
Ulrich, Duke of Würtemberg (b. 1487, duke from 1503, d. 1550),

Vergerius, Peter Paul (b. 1498, d. 1565), 64.
Vespers, 221, 247 sqq., 281.
Vestments, Episcopal, 207.
Votum, The, 303.

Walch, Dr. J. G. (b. 1693, d. 1775), 159, 209.
Walpole, Thomas, 191.
Walter, Henry, 17 sq., 30.
Warham, William, Archbishop of Canterbury (b. 1450, d. 1532), 4, 22, 43.
Wartburg, 220.
Weimar Archives, 160.
Welsh, Sir John, 15.
Wesleys, The, 8, 348.
Wessel, John (b. 1420, d. 1489), 13.
Wescott, Dr. Brooke Foss, Bishop of Durham, (b. 1825), 23, 25, 29, 116 sq.
Wheatly, Charles (b. 1686, d. 1742), 250.
Whitsunday, a time for Baptism, 254.
Whittingham, Dr. William (b. 1524, d. 1579), 344.
Wiclif, John (b. 1324, d. 1384), 2, 10, 13.
William, Count of Nassau, 141 sq., 144.
William, Prince of Orange (b. 1533, assassinated 1584), 141, 143.
Winkworth, Catherine (b. 1825), 119.
Wittenberg, Barnes at, 181 sq.
      Beyer at, 343.
      Captured, 200.
      Concord, 210 sq.

Wittenberg, Faculty, 74-7, 80, 101, 129, 145, 169, 177, 223.
        Negotiations at (1536), 55, 62, 68, 74, 144, 152.
        Rogers at, 125 sq.
        Sarcerius at, 141.
Wolsey, Cardinal Thomas (b. 1471, d. 1530), 4, 10, 12, 32, 41-3, 61, 78.
Worms, Luther at, (1521), 192.
Würtemberg Confession (1552), 339, 341, 346.
        Order (1553), 254 sq., 260-3.

York, Use of, 220, 260, 271.

Zürich, 210, 214 sq., 276, 346.
    Bible, 116 sq.
Zwingli, Ulrich (b. 1484, d. 1531), 38, 49, 117, 166, 207, 209, 276, 287, 354.

www.ingramcontent.com/pod-product-compliance
Lightning Source LLC
Chambersburg PA
CBHW032029220426
43664CB00006B/411